COURTESY LOST

Dante, Boccaccio, and the Literature of History

In *Courtesy Lost*, Kristina M. Olson analyses the literary impact of the social, political, and economic transformations of the fourteenth century through an exploration of Dante's literary and political influence on Boccaccio. The book reveals how Boccaccio rewrote the past through the lens of the *Commedia*, torn between nostalgia for elite families in decline and the need to promote morality and magnanimity within the Florentine Republic.

By examining the passages in Boccaccio's *Decameron*, *De casibus*, and *Esposizioni* in which the author rewrites moments in Florentine and Italian history that had also appeared in Dante's *Commedia*, Olson illuminates the ways in which Boccaccio expressed his deep ambivalence towards the political and social changes of his era. She illustrates this through an analysis of Dante's and Boccaccio's treatments of the idea of courtesy, or *cortesia*, in an era when the chivalry of the declining aristocracy was being supplanted by the civility of the rising merchant classes.

(Toronto Italian Studies)

KRISTINA M. OLSON is an assistant professor of Italian in the Department of Modern and Classical Languages at George Mason University.

Courtesy Lost

Dante, Boccaccio, and the Literature of History

KRISTINA M. OLSON

UNIVERSITY OF TORONTO PRESS
Toronto Buffalo London

© University of Toronto Press 2014
Toronto Buffalo London
www.utppublishing.com

Reprinted in paperback 2015

ISBN 978-1-4426-4707-7 (cloth)
ISBN 978-1-4426-2926-4 (paper)

Toronto Italian Studies

Library and Archives Canada Cataloguing in Publication

Olson, Kristina M., 1976–, author
    Courtesy lost : Dante, Boccaccio, and the literature of history/Kristina M. Olson.

(Toronto Italian studies)
Includes bibliographical references and index.
ISBN 978-1-4426-4707-7 (bound) . – ISBN 978-1-4426-2926-4 (pbk.)

1. Boccaccio, Giovanni, 1313–1375 – Criticism and interpretation.   2. Dante Alighieri, 1265–1321 – Influence.   3. Courtesy in literature.   4. Chivalry in literature.   5. Florence (Italy) – History – To 1421.   I. Title.   II. Series: Toronto Italian studies

PQ4293.H5047 2014   858'.109   C2014-905017-8

University of Toronto Press acknowledges the financial assistance to its publishing program of the Canada Council for the Arts and the Ontario Arts Council, an agency of the Government of Ontario.

Contents

Acknowledgments vii

Note on Editions and Translations ix

Introduction. "Fateci dipignere la Cortesia": Historicizing *cortesia* 3

1 Boccaccio's History of *cortesia*: The Incivility and Greed of the Elite 29
    Cortesia and the Florentine Elite from the Early Commune to the Age of Dante 30
    The Dantean *cornice* of *Inferno* 16 and *cortesia* Lost: *Decameron* 1.8, 6.9, and *Esposizioni* 16 34
    The Greed of the Genoese (Not Florentine) Elite: *Decameron* 1.8, Guiglielmo Borsiere, and Ermino Grimaldi 40
    The Incivility of *cortesia*: *Decameron* 6.9, Betto Brunelleschi, and Guido Cavalcanti 44
    Conclusion 53

2 Boccaccio's Politics of *cortesia*: Narrating the Elite and the *gente nuova* 56
    Florentine Politics and Economics from Dante to Boccaccio: The Older Elite Families and the *gente nuova* 59
    From Dantean Prophecy to Boccaccian Enactment: Florence from 1300 to 1302 65
    Figuring Florentine Conflict: Corso Donati (*cortesia*) versus Vieri de' Cerchi (*avarizia*) 71
    The Elite and the *popolo*: The Case of Cisti and Geri Spini 86
    The Arno Runs Red: Narrating Florentine Violence 94
    Conclusion 97

3 The Ethical (and Dantean) Framework of the *Decameron*:
   The Avarice of Clerics and Merchants   99
      Cangrande della Scala: Dante's Generous Host Experiences
         an Unusual, and Momentary, Affliction of Avarice   101
      Pope Boniface VIII: Figuring Avarice at the Beginning
         and End of the *Decameron*   110
      A Tempered "epopea dei mercatanti": Musciatto Franzesi
         and the Avarice of the Merchant Class   120
      The Dantean *cornice* of Avarice: *Esposizioni* 1 and
         Decameron 10.3   127
      From Finance to Fowling: The Case of the Gianfigliazzi
         Family   134
      Conclusion   137

4 Constructing a Future for *cortesia* in the Past: Virility, Nobility,
   and the History of the Guelphs and the Ghibellines   139
      The Familial Court of *cortesia*: The Civil Acts of the
         Malaspina Family   143
      Cortesia Was Chaste: The Virility of the Guelphs and the
         Ghibellines   157
      Virility as Nobility: *Cortesia* in Romagna   168
      Nobility's Inheritance: The Case of Federigo degli
         Alberighi   176
      Conclusion   182

Notes   185

Bibliography   221

Index   237

Acknowledgments

This book could not have been written without the guidance of Teodolinda Barolini and Joan Ferrante. Teodolinda, the primary reader of this book from start to finish, nurtured its writing with support and enthusiasm. I feel immense gratitude for having had her as my *more-than* mentor through this journey. Joan's influence is evident in the questions addressed by this book. I hope to have answered them here to her satisfaction.

Numerous colleagues in medieval and Italian studies have provided support over the course of writing this book. I would like to thank in particular John Ahern, Albert Russell Ascoli, Susanna Barsella, Christopher Celenza, Francesco Ciabattoni, George Dameron, Martin Eisner, Elsa Filosa, Pier Massimo Forni, Tobias Foster Gittes, Millicent Marcus, Giuseppe Mazzotta, Jason Houston, Simone Marchesi, Michael Papio, and Wayne Storey for fruitful conversations about this project and, in some cases, invitations to present excerpts from it. Special thanks are due to William Caferro for generously reading and commenting on an earlier draft of the second chapter. Many thanks are due as well to Carolin Hahnemann for providing translations of selected passages from Petrarch's *Rerum memorandarum libri*.

I am grateful to my colleagues at George Mason University for their magnanimity. Behind these pages stands, in particular, the memory of Jeffrey Chamberlain's *courtosie*. I wish to thank Julie Christensen and my colleagues in the Department of Modern and Classical Languages, and especially Lisa Rabin and Martin Winkler for offering feedback on this project during its first stages. Thanks are due to the Office of the Provost for a one-semester junior faculty leave, and the College of Humanities and Social Sciences for a second semester's leave in the form of the Mathy Junior Faculty Award in the Arts and Humanities. The staff of the Interlibrary Loan Office at Fenwick Library has been stalwart in furnishing me with precious tomes that were necessary for this research.

I would like to thank the two anonymous readers of this manuscript, whose insights have been essential in helping me realize its final form. Ronald Schoeffel, the book's first editor, was the true embodiment of courtesy in his gracious and generous support from the very start. I thank Suzanne Rancourt for seeing this project through to its final stages, and Terry Teskey for her diligent work as copyeditor.

My deepest thanks are reserved for my family: my husband, Michael, my sons, Liam and Alex, and my daughter, Isabelle. This book began when we were two; it sees its final, published form now when we are five. Liam, who was born at the beginning of this project, will challenge Boccaccio as a storyteller in days not long to come. Isabelle, who arrived mid-course in the middle of her own journey, has taught me the importance of separating history from fiction, and the equal value in revising the past for the present. Born during the book's final revisions, Alex has brought the promise of continued joy. I dedicate this book to Michael, my *consorte* in our endless golden age.

Note on Editions and Translations

All citations of Dante's *Commedia* are from Giorgio Petrocchi's edition, *La commedia secondo l'antica volgata* (Milan: Mondadori, 1966–67). All translations of the *Commedia* are by Jean and Robert Hollander (New York: Doubleday, 2000–7), which is also available online as part of the Princeton Dante Project (http://etcweb.princeton.edu/dante/index.html, last accessed 12 March 2014). Citations from Dante's lyric production are from the edition by Teodolinda Barolini, *Rime giovanili e della Vita nuova* (Milan: BUR Rizzoli, 2009). Citations from the *Convivio* are from the edition by Cesare Vasoli and Domenico de Robertis in the critical edition series of Dante's minor works (Milan: Ricciardi, 1995). Translations from the *Convivio* are taken from Richard Lansing's edition, *Dante's* Il convivio: *The Banquet* (New York: Garland, 1990). Citations from the *De vulgari eloquentia* are from Pier Vincenzo Mengaldo's edition in the critical edition series of Dante's minor works (Milan: Ricciardi, 1996). If publication information is not provided in a note, commentaries of the *Commedia* can be found on the website of the Dartmouth Dante Project (http://dante.dartmouth.edu/, last accessed 12 March 2014).

Citations of Giovanni Boccaccio's works, unless otherwise indicated, are from Vittore Branca's ten-volume critical edition (*Tutte le opere di Giovanni Boccaccio* [Milan: Mondadori, 1964–68]). Two exceptions are the frequently-cited *Esposizioni sopra la Comedia*, in which case I have cited Giorgio Padoan's two-volume critical edition (Milan: Mondadori, 1965), and Pier Giorgio Ricci's edition of the *Trattatello in laude di Dante* found in his *Vite di Dante* (Milan: Mondadori, 2002). Unless otherwise indicated, all translations of Boccaccio's *Decameron* are taken from the second edition of G.H. McWilliam's translation of that work (New York:

Penguin, 1995). Translations of the *Esposizioni* are from Michael Papio's edition, *Boccaccio's Expositions on Dante's* Comedy (Toronto: University of Toronto Press, 2009). Translations of the *Trattatello in laude in Dante* are from Vincenzo Zin Bollettino's *The Life of Dante (Trattatello in laude di Dante)* (New York: Garland, 1990).

All citations from Giovanni Villani's *Nuova cronica* are from the edition by Giuseppe Porta (Parma: Guanda, 1990–91). Translations from Villani's *Nuova cronica*, unless otherwise noted, are from the translation by Rose Selfe, published as *Villani's Chronicle: Being Selections from the First Nine Books of the* Croniche Fiorentine *of Giovanni Villani* (London: Archibald, Constable & Co., 1906). Citations from Dino Compagni's *Cronica* are from the edition by Gino Luzzatto (Turin: Einaudi, 1968). Translations from Compagni's *Cronica*, unless otherwise indicated, are from Daniel Bornstein's edition, *Dino Compagni's Chronicle of Florence* (Philadelphia: University of Pennsylvania Press, 1986).

Translations that are not attributed to any of these sources are my own.

COURTESY LOST

Dante, Boccaccio, and the Literature of History

Introduction
"Fateci dipignere la Cortesia":
Historicizing *cortesia*

When Guiglielmo Borsiere exhorts Ermino Grimaldi (Ermizio Avarizia), in *Decameron* 1.8, to have *cortesia* depicted on the walls of the Genoese merchant's luxurious abode ("Fateci dipignere la Cortesia"), he poses a mimetic challenge that speaks explicitly and implicitly to the questions of influence and interpretation to which this book responds. What did *cortesia* look like to Dante and Boccaccio – and specifically to Boccaccio writing under the influence of Dante's poem, as, for instance, he gives new narrative life to a Dantean character such as Guiglielmo Borsiere?[1] *Cortesia*, as Borsiere notes, is more deeply appreciated once it has been noticed as lacking. To lament its absence, and dream of its future return, is to narrate the progress and failures of civilization, to critique political figures and parties, and to consider social conduct writ both large and small, from the level of political and religious institutions to the spheres of smaller social and economic groups such as the family and the neighbourhood. How Boccaccio participates in this sociological, political, and historical mode of thought in the shadow of Dante and other medieval chroniclers is the focus of this book.

In the *Decameron* and the *Esposizioni sopra la Comedia*, Boccaccio rewrites several moments of Florentine and Italian history that can be found in Dante's *Commedia* through the lens of the political and social contexts of the middle to late fourteenth century. In the chapters that follow, I attend to the concept of *cortesia* as a heuristic by which to survey Boccaccio's revisions of this mediated history. I read *cortesia* in these contexts primarily as a sociological term that describes the cultivation of a "chivalric mentality" among Italian elites,[2] a phenomenon that Ronald Witt and others locate after the Peace of Constance in 1183.[3] By "chivalric mentality" I mainly refer to the ways in which members of the socio-political elite, acting on their understanding of courtly life and literature from France, fashioned themselves as feudal barons and took matters of justice and honour into their own hands, most clearly manifested in *vendette*.

Boccaccio often conflates this definition of *cortesia* with a different, and seemingly contradictory, one that can be placed within the classical tradition, as a relative of Aristotle's articulation of liberality in Book Four of the *Nicomachean Ethics* and Cicero's parsing of *honestas* and temperance (*De officiis*, 1.27.93–4). This other definition of *cortesia*, as a social ethic related to liberality, generosity, and hospitality, informs the structure of the *Decameron* itself, as the tales that foreground both *cortesia* or liberality and the vice of avarice appear in Days One and Ten. One such example can be seen in the quote above when Guiglielmo Borsiere exhorts Ermino Grimaldi to have *cortesia* figured. Boccaccio interprets Dante's historical vision along the lines of both these definitions of *cortesia*, with a sense of nostalgia for an aristocracy that can also practice liberality, especially those patrons and hosts of Dante in exile. This historiography encompasses moments of larger peninsular or continental history, and it reflects Boccaccio's nuanced notions of social groupings and political affiliation.

Boccaccio's "re-chronicling" of this period is mediated through Dante but also through the volatile and changing political and social climate of the middle to late fourteenth century. Boccaccio views this other *buon tempo antico* in the aftermath of the Black Death, the bankruptcy of the Florentine banking companies, the austerity measures of Walter of Brienne's *signoria* (1343), and the rise of a third popular government (1343–48). These watershed events serve to explain Boccaccio's distaste for the rising power of the *gente nuova* of his own times and his affection for magnates who were banned from political office by the popular government. At the same time, he witnesses such historical trends as the rise of accusations of Ghibelline ancestry levelled by the Parte Guelfa against its political adversaries. Boccaccio writes about posterity in the shadow of his present, locating the place of *cortesia* in both worlds as one measure of civilization.

Courtesy, courtliness, and chivalry, understood broadly, were ethical and social values widespread over the continent from the Carolingian period onwards, with discernible origins in Roman thought. They were concepts that guided lives at court and within the warrior class, as well as of those who dwelled in both worlds, forming a crucial and inherent part of articulations of civilization throughout the medieval and early modern period.[4] To study courtesy, courtliness, and chivalry in their various permutations in courtly literature, troubadour poetry, Arthurian romance, and conduct literature from the time after the Carolingian era up to the sixteenth century (*Il libro del Cortegiano* by Baldassar Castiglione) is nothing less than to survey the history of thought on civilization, not just a literary trope. Scholars such as Norbert Elias, Stephen Jaeger, and Aldo Scaglione believe that courtliness first developed in the life at court, as a sociological reality that then becomes a staple of literary production. The practice of courtly ethics and the literature meant to serve a didactic role (as in courtesy books and conduct literature) enter into a symbiotic relationship that is difficult to tease apart.

"Courtesy" is a term that is often employed in the same way as "courtliness" (as a sociological practice), though more often it signifies the bivalence of courtliness as a literary phenomenon and a sociological practice. In contrast to what Elias and Jaeger maintain, Scaglione and Giuseppe Sansone do not trace a strict genealogy from courtesy as a practice of the courts to its literary life. Sansone in particular writes that any endeavour to establish which came first, the refinement of feudal customs after 1000 or the emergence of Provençal lyric – courtesy as an expression of daily life and as a cultural manifestation – is destined to fail.[5] If the genealogy of courtesy is difficult to parse, a standard definition of the term is likewise difficult, as authors across the European continent discuss or describe courtesy variously depending upon local political and economic realities as well as the narrative traditions (vernacular, lyric, etc.) in which they envisioned themselves. Courtesy claims a literary and a historical genealogy and legacy that bear the textual accretion of vast geographical and chronological breadth.

Dante and Boccaccio participate in the "figuring" of *cortesia* when they comment upon the disappearance of courtly ways or envision the future outside the court of those practices and behaviours that comprise courtesy, such as honesty, liberality, eloquence, and refinement in appearance. Before the age of Dante, courtesy had already undergone transformations in Germany, France, and England in troubadour lyric, Minnesang, epic, romance, and courtly literature. By the time of the mid-thirteenth century, as Jaeger writes, there is a general awareness in this literature that a "great age had passed."[6] The nostalgia for a lost golden age of civic comportment, otherwise known as the *laudatio temporis acti*, has a historical correlative in economic and political realities, from the rise of a new monetary economy to the weakening of the emperor.

More generally, addressing the status of courtesy in society becomes an important mode of talking about the present day in the shadow of posterity. Dante and Boccaccio, among others, also lament the absence of a time marked by the ways of courtesy, though with different conclusions. Figuring courtesy as "lost" becomes, for Dante and Boccaccio as for many who precede them, the lens through which the chivalric mentality of an aristocratic culture is nostalgically evoked, corruption and greed are condemned, exemplary individuals are exalted, and generosity (*liberalità*) is lauded. It signals a way for these authors of the thirteenth and fourteenth centuries to understand the transitions taking place in their societies among dominant social groups, from the decline of the old aristocracy to the advent of a new elite.

By analysing this dimension to Boccaccio's activity as *dantista*, the chapters that follow speak to the transformation of the spirit of political invective that the Certaldese author inherits from his greatest Florentine predecessor, as he draws inspiration from Dante's poetry of ethics and moralism to script the prose of social moralism, and, in certain moments, the prose of a new republic. *Cortesia* would not be figured as lost if it were not meant to be regained in some way, for Boccaccio. For this to happen, Dante's identification of *cortesia* as an aspect of courtly life from the past must become the cosmopolitan practice of *cortesia*, as "atti civili" outside of the courts, as Boccaccio describes. *Cortesia* must become an ethical value for an age that witnessed vast economic and political upheavals, the demographic changes that ensued from the outbreaks of the plague, and the revision of social orders in Italy during the middle to late fourteenth century. If for Dante *cortesia* was a practice of the courts, as the *Convivio* conveys, then for Boccaccio *cortesia* becomes a staple of civil life, the "atti civili" that exist both inside and outside of the court. *Cortesia*, as a social ethic, had to be envisioned – or figured, to evoke Guigliemo Borsiere's words in *Decameron* 1.8 – alongside the decline of an aristocratic culture that claimed it for its namesake.[7] It had to be developed as a new civic ethic for a society in transition.

Before we can address how *cortesia* becomes a mode by which the influence of Dante upon Boccaccio can be examined within the context of their lives and works, it is necessary to discuss the theoretical origins of courtesy and courtliness, and to survey, if briefly, the literary and historical pedigree that *cortesia* carries into the Italian Trecento. Courtesy has been argued by many (including Elias and Jaeger) to be sociological in origin, but then to have existed in symbiosis with the literature that meant to reflect it: epic tales, lyric and romance, and conduct treatises/ courtesy books.[8] It existed alongside a related but different ideal of chivalry interpreted as a modification of the ideals of courtesy that could be identified in the warrior class. Many view it as a product of the feudal system (though the idea of feudalism in itself is debated by some), a later form of the interdependence of vassalage and knighthood inherited from the Carolingian period that can be found particularly within the Germanic past.[9]

Courtesy (or courtliness) has been said to emerge around the eleventh century,[10] but as Burnley notes, that claim may reflect a lack of sources more than it does reality; he argues that courtly values did not replace but joined the exaltation of military heroism after the Carolingian period.[11] Elias, in *The Civilizing Effect*, proposes that courtesy – which he defines as an aristocratic self-consciousness and socially acceptable behaviour – was nurtured in the conditions of court life, and that moderation and restraint were, in essence, the mechanics of civilizing, or, more importantly, of the formation of the "super ego" (*Über-Ich-Bildung*).[12] He locates this process as the result of power struggles between the nobility, the church, the princes, and the emerging bougeoisie over the control of land.[13] *Courtois* codes of behaviour, according to Elias, originated within the court elite and radiated out to other social orders: "They say: that is how people behave at court. By these terms certain leading groups in the secular upper stratum, which does not mean the knightly class as a whole, but primarily the courtly circles around the great feudal lords, designated what distinguished them in their own eyes, namely the specific code of behavior that first formed at the great feudal courts, then spread to rather broader strata."[14] As the knightly-feudal warrior nobility went slowly into decline over the centuries, and with the rise of the bourgeoisie, *courtoisie* was gradually replaced by the concept of *civilité*.[15]

While Elias believes courtesy to be the result of these power struggles, in addition to the growth of wealth and rise of a new monetary economy, Jaeger claims that courtliness was an "instrument," not an end but a means that encouraged the process of civilizing, which can be found in the system of education and its curriculum.[16] For Jaeger, the birthplace of courtesy can be located in the court of Brun, brother of Otto the Great, in 939, which was renowned for its cultivation of philosophy and the liberal arts.[17] Jaeger believes that the forces that produced courtly ethics were present in Carolingian court culture, and then were articulated from the eleventh century onwards with the ideals of courtesy, urbanity, and statesmanship inherited from ancient Rome. The emergence of these values, Jaeger argues, comes with the emergence of the educator and the statesman from the imperial bishoprics, social orders that become superior to the warrior class.[18]

In terms of its etymological origins, courtesy can be linked to both the word-form *curt*, which comes from the Latin *cohortem*, and the medieval Latin *curtis*, both of which mean "company" and "enclosure."[19] *Curt* has also been interpreted as stemming from the Latin *curia*, which referred to the meeting place of the Roman Senate and then the Imperial Court, the place of the *curiales*.[20] The *curiae*, or royal courts, in Germany and France between 950 and 1150 saw the emergence of teachers, future imperial bishops who had first been *magistri scholarum*, who instructed their students in the ways of *curialitas*, which can be described as a combination of morality and social conduct (curiality).[21] *Curialitas* resembles, as Scaglione argues, a mixture of Christian virtues with Ciceronian/Stoic virtues, such as *formositas* (beauty), *eruditio* (education, learning), *virtus* (virtue), *mansuetudo* (gentleness), *discretio* (discretion), *amabilitas* (affability), and *mensura* (moderation).[22] *Curialis* in Anglo-Latin means "courtier" by 1065, and *curialiter* means "in the ways of the court; in courtly style" before 1140. In Anglo-Norman texts, *curialiter* is associated with related virtues such as *facetia* (wit), *eloquentia* (eloquence), *urbanitas* (urbanity), and *benignitas* (affability, benevolence, kindness), and is constrasted with *rusticitas* (lack of sophistication), which is in keeping with the Ciceronian qualities of *urbanitas* (sophistication, polish), *verecundia* (modesty), *temperantia* (moderation), *decorum* (propriety), *affabilitas* (affability), *jocunditas* (charm), and *hilaritas* (cheerfulness), among others listed in the *De officiis*.[23] The courtier was thus seen as an urbane man who possessed the eloquence and refinement that assisted him in his business affairs and that contrasted with a man from the country, a distinction that can be seen in Boccaccio's comparison, for instance, of Corso Donati with Vieri de' Cerchi. The courtier's *elegantia morum* also included self-restraint (*disciplina*) and the harmony between a beautiful appearance and inner nobility (*kalokagathia*).[24]

Courtliness, courtesy, and chivalry constitute the principal themes of much vernacular production that begins in the mid-twelfth century, from Provençal (troubadours and trobairitz), Anglo-Norman (Wace's *Brut*), French (trouvères, *chansons de geste*; the *romans d'Alexandre, d'Énéas, de Troie,* and *de Thèbes*; Chrétien de Troyes's works), and Middle

High German (the Minnesang, Gottfried's *Tristan*, Wolfram's *Parzival*, Hartmann's *Iweinn*, for example) to Middle English traditions (*Sir Gawain and the Green Knight*). Though not written in the vernacular, Andreas de Capellanus's *De amore libri* naturally enters into this production as well, and its precepts of courtly love, largely understood as a parody, will be the source of future critiques of courtly love, as Giuseppe Mazzotta has seen in *Decameron* 5.8, for example.[25]

In lyric, epic, and romance traditions in Anglo-Norman texts and old French, *cortois* changes in meaning over the centuries as the economic and social landscapes of the thirteenth and fourteenth centuries evolve. *Cortois* and *vilain* in French and Provençal texts, from as early as the first third of the thirteenth century, first signified socially distinct classes but came to signify personal qualities until the middle of the fourteenth century; if the *cortois*, an aristocrat or a noble, is a successful lover, for example, then the *vilain*, a peasant, lacks in his ability to love.[26] A life in court enabled one to become *cortois*.[27] Being *cortois* involved the possession of eloquence in speech, good manners, a sense of measure, hospitality, humility, consideration, loyalty, a handsome appearance, high intelligence, a religious sensibility, admiration by the opposite sex, and esteem from one's friends.[28] These qualities all appear in a range of texts, from Wace's *Brut* (1136) and Geoffrey Gaimar's *L'Estorie des Engles* (1136) to the personification of Courtoisie in the *Roman de la Rose* (circa 1230).

Because it is the birthplace of *fin'amors*, Provençal lyric poetry is often credited with the origins of courtly literature and also of the idea of *cortezia*. Courtly life and literature are seen to first form their symbiotic relationship in the works of troubadour poets, particularly insofar as the complex construction of *fin'amors* – an eroticized interpretation of the chivalric component of *cortezia* – finds its origins here.[29] At the same time, the socio-economic realities that formed the ideas of courtesy, courtliness, and chivalry for the late-twelfth century were also changing vastly. According to the traditional feudal model, knights sought protection and maintenance in return for their loyalty, but also the *auxilium* (financial assistance) and *consilium* (advice) pledged to their lord.[30] The *proz* of a knight combined this multifaceted loyalty and integrity that distinguished him from the *vilain*;[31] military prowess had to be matched by intelligence. Courtliness was seen to emerge not only by means of an education afforded by clerics within the court,[32] but also from the skills of *consilium* and the social experiences of life in the feudal hall.[33] But in the post-Carolingian landscape in which the knight faced competition for scant resources in land and positions of authority, certain aspects of courtesy were intended to foster survival, such as *mezura*, arguably the recognition of financial and social limits. As well, his humility (*umildat*) and obedience (*obediensa*) as demonstrated to the *midon* (lord) were necessary in order to qualify as faithful (*fis*).[34] The knight's quest for survival and ascendance becomes reflected in troubadour lyric.

Troubadour lyric and Arthurian romance arguably form the greatest influence upon Dante and Boccaccio in how they theorized *cortesia*, most specifically in terms of their invectives against those vices that banish courtesy, such as envy and avarice. As Scaglione argues, a "striking closeness" exists between these invectives of such poets as Marcabru, Guiraut de Bornelh, and Peire Cardenal and Dante's own invectives against the corrupting influence of these vices, such as can be found in *Inferno* 16.65–75 (see chapter 1). Dante would inherit not just the notion of *cortesia*, but more precisely the rhetoric of nostalgia for *cortesia* from the Provençal tradition. Poets such as Giraut de Bornelh, Marcabru, Peire Cardenal, Bertran de Born, and Sordello (among others) lamented the decadence of the courts in the forms of *cansos* (songs; the antecedent to the *canzone*), *planhs* (laments), and *sirventes* (satirical *cansos*), claiming that courtly virtues have abandoned them. Cited as the vernacular poet of mortal rectitude by Dante (*De vulgari eloquentia* 2.2.8), Giraut de Bornelh (c. 1138–1215) claimed that "solatz," or courtly pleasure, has been exiled from this world in his *canso* "Per solatz revelhar" ("Per solatz revelhar,/que s'es trop endormitz,/e per pretz, qu'es faiditz, acolhir e tornar,/me cudei trebalhar," vv. 1–5; "To reawaken courtly pleasure,/which had too long slept,/and to welcome glory, to bring it back from exile,/I thought to give myself some pains").[35] This particular *canso* must have influenced Dante in his vision of *cortesia* as an irretrievable custom; for example, Giraut writes that he thought that he would bring back "solatz," but that such a task cannot be done ("car non es d'achabar," v. 8). Wooden horses and low-born knights, together with robbers of sheep, now populate these times, and the poet himself is grateful that his own house has not yet been robbed. Peire Cardenal (c. 1180–c. 1278) rallied against moral corruption, specifically that of the clergy and the nobility. For the troubadours, moral corruption was the main symptom of the disappearance of *solatz*, the Occitanian precursor to *cortesia*.

However, a fundamental difference arises between the place of wealth and liberality in troubadour lyric and Dante's *Convivio*, as Scaglione notes.[36] Troubadours criticized the wealth of their lords in the hope of gaining financial reward, particularly in their condemnation of the "rics malvatz," as can be seen, for example, in the verse of Folquet de Romans ("Ben volgr'aguessem un senhor"), Peire Cardenhal ("A totas partz vei mescl' ab avaresa"), and Giraut de Bornelh ("Cardaillac, per un sirventes").[37] This topos reflects the situation of poor knights who went without remuneration for their services; because of the theologized view of the courtly lord, the liberality of lords was experienced as the reward for a life pleasing to God.[38] *Larguesa*, as Ivos Margoni writes, became the "virtù cortese per eccellenza," while the avarice, or *escarsetatz*, of lords tested their true adherence to *cortesia* understood as courtly love; the miserly lord was seen as incapable of love.[39] It became common practice to lament the momentary lapses in liberality of lords, such as Folquet de Roman's poem about Frederick II,[40] something that can be found as well in Boccaccio's letters about Nicola Acciaiuoli, as I will treat ahead. Later troubadours did not view excessive liberality favourably, but instead advocated a middle way, or *mesura*, in order to avoid the dissipation of one's patrimony.[41] Practices of hospitality and generosity as defining characteristics of *cortois* behaviour stem from French and German epic and romance traditions as well. Knights had to possess the financial means necessary to be liberal, as can be seen in Chrétien's *Yvain*, in which Arthur's liberality is foregrounded, as well as in Hartmann's *Erec*, *Gregorius*, *Iwein*, and, in the German tradition, Gottfried's *Tristan*.[42]

It is a common understanding that Italy claimed a weak feudal nobility in the eleventh century, so it is not historically correct to speak of a strict "feudal" past in Italy. Scaglione proposes the possibility of the influence of German bishops upon Italian episcopal courts and cathedral schools during the Carolingian revival up to the late twelfth century, as a part of Jaeger's thesis that courtesy developed out of an educational model.[43] Yet, as Scaglione indicates, even if feudalism did not adhere in central and northern Italy as it did in southern Italy and France, the ideology of the nobility, most notably a chivalric mentality,[44] and many of its practical powers thrived, transmitted as well through the literary traditions examined.

Italians, nonetheless, were among the first authors of courtesy books. Tommasino dei Cerchiari, a priest in the court of Wolfger von Ellebrechstkirchen in Aquileia (also known as Thomasin von Zirklaria in German courts), authored a poem on court matters in German, *Der Wälsche Gast* (1215–16).[45] The poem offers instruction on table manners and other matters of courtly behaviour, emphasizing *mâze* (moderation), *milte* (generosity), and *reht* (respect for law). The work of the grammarian Bonvesin de la Riva (c. 1250–1315), author of *De quinquaginta curialitatibus ad mensam*, also belongs to the genre of conduct literature, instructing its readers, as the title indicates, in fifty rules of moderation and measure at the table.[46] In these texts, as in others to follow, the cultivation of *cortesia* becomes the means by which nobility is acquired; one no longer needed to belong to the aristocracy in order to be noble, as later texts of the second half of the thirteenth century would suggest.[47]

Emperor Frederick II's sonnet "Misura, providenzia e meritanza" marks the arrival of this term within the literary production of the Sicilian court in the thirteenth century. In these verses, nobility is described not as inherited but as gained through the practice of *cortesia*, which he defines in this poem as an "ordinata costumanza" (measured practice), thereby dismissing, as Kleinhenz notes, "the Aristotelian association of nobility with wealth."[48] Other members of the *scuola siciliana* such as Re Enzo (1220–1272, son of Frederick II) and, later, the Tuscan poet Folgore da San Gimignano would compose verse about *cortesia* that either identify Tuscany as the kingdom of *cortesia* or that lament the autumn of a bygone chivalric age. While, by and large, other poets of the Sicilian School would discuss analogous notions of *cortesia* in the erotic sphere of feminine *bontà*, Re Enzo composed a canzone that locates *cortesia* geographically in Tuscany. He writes: "Va' canzonetta mia,/.../Salutami Toscana,/quella ched à sovrana/in cui regna tutta cortesia" ("Go, my dear *canzone*, [...]/Greet Tuscany for me,/She who is sovereign/and where courtesy reigns throughout").[49]

If *cortesia* was still figured as present in Tuscany during the times of Re Enzo, by the time that Folgore da San Gimignano (1270–1332) composed his *canzone* "Cortesia cortesia cortesia chiamo" it would be lost.[50] In these verses, Folgore claims that *cortesia* is "hidden by the one who should reveal it," and, as a consequence, he who is in need of it must live in poverty. Avarice has captured the populace and has destroyed any noble sentiment, for which the poet laments to God. *Cortesia*, the poet's "madre," has been trodden underfoot to the extent that she cannot rise again. While riches remain on this earth ("l'aver ci sta"), the powerful ("possenti") do not remain on earth forever. We are all mortals, born of Adam and of Eve; even though the powerful have the means, they do not give or spend as they should. *Cortesia*, for Folgore, is synonymous with liberality; neither courtly life nor the life of the *brigata* that this poet would describe in his sonnet sequence can exist without the generosity of others. The disappearance of *cortesia* for Folgore can be attributed in part to the changing social and political landscape of the end of the thirteenth century. As Kleinhenz notes, "the commune replaced the court as the cultural and literary locus of society, and the notion of *cortesia* was, on the one hand, enriched with greatly elaborated ethical and spiritual meanings and charged, on the other hand, with a vibrant sensuality and worldly quality."[51] *Cortesia* enters into the rhetorical realm of nostalgia, the *laudatio temporis acti*, as the original courtly structures that saw it flourish in France and Germany give way to a chivalric mentality in the Italian commune.

The *Tesoretto*, one of the first treatises on social manners in Italy, would also influence Dante's interpretation of *cortesia*. Written by Brunetto Latini (c. 1220–1294), chancellor of the first popular government (1250–60), the *Tesoretto* (c. 1260) stages the education of a knight by the personified virtues Temperanza, Fortezza, Virtù, Cortesia, Larghezza, Leanza, and Prodezza.[52] Taught to avoid the excesses and violence of elite culture, the knight of the *Tesoretto* could be seen to undergo the kind of education that the *popolo* wished for its elite families, engaged in vendettas and profligate in spending.[53] Latini implies that Cortesia functions as a subcategory of Larghezza when Cortesia says that she is "il capo e la grandezza/di tutto mio mistero" (vv. 1587).[54] It is this point with which Dante would disagree in the *Convivio*. Indeed, in the text attributed to Dante, *Il Fiore* (influenced, clearly, by the personification of Courtoisie in the *Roman de la Rose*),[55] he often links Cortesia and Larghezza but never favours one over the other. Yet Latini's favourable view of a measured Larghezza as intrinsic to the practical functions of the courtly world is not one with which Dante would disagree later on in the writing of the *Commedia*.[56]

Brunetto Latini is not the only Florentine writer to highlight the dimension of *cortesia* as *larghezza*. In yet another Florentine text, that of the anonymous *Novellino* (compiled between 1280 and 1300), *cortesia* stands as a social value intrinsic to moral instruction in a good urban life: "Fiore di parlare di belle cortesie e di belli risposi e di belle valentie, di belli donari e di belli amari." Upon closer examination, though, *cortesia* appears in the text carrying the valence of liberality. For example, chapter rubrics link it repeatedly with *liberalità* (i.e., in Novelle XIX and XX: "Della grande liberalità e cortesia del Re Giovane," "Della grande liberalità e cortesia del Re d'Inghilterra").[57] The valence of *cortesia* as financial largesse, as presented in these texts, would appear as one important dimension to Dante's (and Boccaccio's) adoption of this term.

But the *Novellino*'s uncritical exaltation of the chivalric world, which the Florentine elite certainly read in forming their own collective identity under the rubric of *cortesia*, is quite different from the ethic of the *popolo* that one could discern in the *Tesoretto*, for instance.[58] Dante, and more so Boccaccio, both influenced by these works, would internalize the discrepancy between this nostalgic, dream world of *cortesia* and the critical voice of the *popolo*, who thought that the lifestyle of the elite was detrimental to the vitality of the republic.

At the beginning of the fourteenth century, Dante inherits *cortesia* in all of its historical and literary breadth, from its presentation in Troubadour lyric, to its associations with *fin'amors*, to its elaborations within the courtly literature tradition of French prose romances,[59] and finally to its function as a sociological term that describes the courtly behaviour in imperial courts.[60] Dante exploits the wide range of significance for *cortesia* in numerous works: in his lyric production (the *Rime*), the prose and lyric poems of the *Vita nuova*, the *De vulgari eloquentia*, the *Convivio*, and the *Commedia*. One could argue, along with Erminia Dispenza Crimi, that the exploitation of *cortesia* in its full range of significance reaches its apex in Dante's treatment of this term. Similar, as well, to the multiple meanings of the term within specific areas of production (e.g., Provençal writers, the Sicilian School), *cortesia* can be glossed differently in each of the works cited above. As Joan Ferrante notes, in the *De vulgari eloquentia* (1.28.4), *curialis* is a political term, as it signifies "a balanced rule for action; although Italy has no single unified court, the parts of its body exist, unified by the light of reason, which we have by divine grace."[61] In this moment as well as in others in the *De vulgari*, Dante is most likely thinking of the ideal of the unrealized court of the Hohenstaufen dynasty, whose end was marked during his lifetime.[62] For Dante, the end of the imperial court is defined by the death of Henry VII, the "alto Arrigo" of *Paradiso* 30.137, in Buonconvento (1313, the same year in which Boccaccio is born).

One can also witness the multiple dimensions to Dante's understanding and interpretation of *cortesia* in the *Convivio*, in the light of *fin'amors* and for its function as a sociological and political term. In commenting upon the verses "Mira anche quanto è/saggia e cortese nella sua grandezza" in the *Convivio*, Dante notes how *cortesia* befits the beloved lady: "nulla cosa sta più in donna bene che cortesia" (2.10.7–8), thus locating *cortesia* in an erotic sphere that is more reminiscent of its usage in the Sicilian School and in the *dolce stil novo*. But then Dante departs from this context to discuss *cortesia* as a social practice. In doing so, he takes issue, apparently, with Brunetto Latini's definition of *cortesia* as "larghezza" in the *Tesoretto* ("E non siano li miseri volgari anche di questo vocabulo ingannati, che credono che cortesia non sia altro che larghezza; e larghezza è una speziale, e non generale, cortesia!" 2.10.7; "And the wretches of the common herd should not be deceived as well by this word, thinking courtesy nothing other than liberality; for liberality is a special, not a general, kind of courtesy," Lansing, 64). *Cortesia*, he claims, is much more than "larghezza," but is one and the same as "onestade":

> cortesia e onestade è tutt'uno: e però che nelle corti anticamente le vertudi e li belli costumi s'usavano, sì come oggi s'usa lo contrario, si tolse quello vocabulo dalle corti, e fu tanto a dire cortesia quanto uso di corte. Lo qual vocabulo se oggi si togliesse dalle corti, massimamente d'Italia, non sarebbe altro a dire che turpezza.
>
> Courtesy and dignity are one and the same; and because in the courts in times past virtue and fine manners were practiced, just as the contrary is now the case, this word was derived from courts and "courtesy" was as much as to say "the custom of the court." If this word were derived from the courts of the present day, especially those of Italy, it would mean nothing but rudeness. (Lansing, 64)

Here his interest lies in *cortesia* as "onestade," which one might identify as Dante's Ciceronian pedigree of *honestas*, an upright, "outward disposition which is a sign of inner qualities."[63] But it should be noted that Dante does not discard *larghezza* as a kind ("speziale") of *cortesia*.[64] Later, for Boccaccio, *larghezza*, the financial dimension to *cortesia*, comprises a crucial element of his nostalgia for the former days of *cortesia*.

In his lyric production, *cortesia* for Dante carries its association with courtly love, as it refers to the generous acts of the beloved lady (as in Beatrice or the lyric beloved in his *Rime* and in the *Vita nuova*), combining, as it were, the significance of "gallanteria" from its Provençal origins with its Sicilian pedigree of "bontà." *Cortesia* is a quality of the lady in such poems as "Madonna, quel signor che voi portate," "Deh ragioniamo insieme un poco, Amore," "Due donne in cima de la mente mia." *Cortesia* and knowledge ("savere") are among the first virtues fitting to a loving woman and to a lover in "Savere e cortesia, ingegno e arte"

(47). Beatrice is the "donna de la cortesia" (12.2) and God is the "sire de la cortesia" (42.3) in the *Vita nuova*.[65]

For Dante *cortesia* finds its origins in Provençal lyric production, and is reminiscent of the culture of the courts of southern France, but also remains the shade of the unfulfilled imperial court. Dante figures *cortesia* as having been banished from the present. The most vivid example of this can be found in his poem "Morte villana, di pietà nemica," where the poet claims that Death has sent *cortesia* out of this *secolo*: "dal secolo hai partita cortesia" (v. 13). The term "secolo" refers to much more than its temporal definition, "century," but more broadly to "world" or "milieu." In a related example from the *Vita nuova*, Beatrice herself earns a place in heaven, the "grande secolo," due to her unspeakable *cortesia* ("per la sua ineffabile cortesia, la quale è oggi meritata nel grande secolo," 3.2). That *cortesia* is a value that comes from an inherited lyric tradition is clear, but Dante implies here and elsewhere that *cortesia* is a cultural quality that belongs to a specific *milieu*. *Cortesia*, in other words, is historical and sociological, finding its place in the *secoli* of this world and of the otherworld.

Courtesy became, for Dante, a value existing in feudal and imperial courts, as well as one that could carry a valence to an imagined heavenly court, as in the "corte del ciel" of *Paradiso*, as Ferrante explored for the text of the *Vita nuova* and the early *Rime*.[66] But while *cortesia* could be attributed to the acts of God in *Paradiso* (7.91: "che Dio solo per sua cortesia"), it is impossible to sustain that courtliness only signifies, for Dante, the "proprietà di Dio," as one finds in the *Fioretti* ("La cortesia è una delle proprietà di Dio, il quale dà il sole suo e la sua piova a' giusti e agli ingiusti, per cortesia, ed è la cortesia sirocchia della carità, la quale spegne l'odio e conserva l'amore").[67] For example, in the text of the *Convivio*, *cortesia* belongs to both the erotic and the political sphere; it describes the beloved lady and also the social practices of the courts. In "Doglia mi reca," as Teodolinda Barolini observes, Dante revises the traditional view of the beloved lady as promoted by conventions of courtly literature. He reverses courtly literary conventions by linking the trope of erotic desire to that of an insatiable and governing desire for wealth with the figure of the "avaro," the one who "desires always to desire," as Barolini has noted: "Corre l'avaro, ma più fugge pace" (v. 65).[68]

The intersection of *cortesia* with financial, erotic, and socio-historical discourses within the works of Dante is sometimes neglected by critics who choose to see only a theological end for this discourse in the canticle of *Paradiso*.⁶⁹ While not denying this element as one of the meanings of courtliness for Dante, I wish to emphasize Dante's equally secular vision of *cortesia* and Florentine history in the *Commedia*. One reason for doing so comes from the text itself: *cortesia* appears more frequently in the *Commedia* with a secular valence (four times) than a spiritual one (twice). In *Inferno* 16, it refers to a prelapsarian Florence; in *Purgatorio* 14 and 16, it belongs to a memory of the chivalrous age of the Romagna; and finally, in *Paradiso* 17, the *cortesia* described is that of the Gran Lombardo.⁷⁰ *Cortesia* may find its narrative climax in the *Commedia* in the heavenly court, but the social practices of this world also determine its meaning in the afterlife of the poem. The confluence of social, political, and economic terms in his discourse of *cortesia* within Florentine history is most strongly articulated in *Inferno* 16, as I will examine in chapter 1. In this canto, Dante bitterly reflects upon the change in Florentine mores, a change that is seen as the result of pride as well as the mishandling of money, or the economic form of "dismisura," a characteristic and a practice far from true "cortesia."

Though one can no longer talk of a feudal court during the age of Dante, the poet did experience the liberality, or *cortesia* in action, so to speak, of the various princely courts of Ravenna, Verona, and elsewhere that hosted him in exile, a fact of Dante's biography that was of course not lost upon Boccaccio, who himself passed many years in the royal court of Naples, though not at the expense of his lords in the same way as Dante. This experience of *cortesia* will inform the *Commedia* and, in turn, Boccaccio's reading of these moments in the *Decameron* (such as 1.7, the *novella* of Cangrande). The opposition of avarice and *cortesia* – what I suggest we call Boccaccio's ethical historiography – originates in a meditation on the events that immediately precede and follow Dante's exile. The clash between the Cerchi and the Donati, the generosity of Cangrande, and the avarice of Pope Boniface VIII participate in this history.

Boccaccio's experience and articulation of the multifaceted concept of *cortesia* – one that he inherits from Dante and the Provençal and French traditions, not to speak of the education of the statesman in Cicero's *De officiis*⁷¹ – reveal the panorama of significance that the term carries from these various sources. A preoccupation with *cortesia* as a code of comportment, an education in manners, eloquence, refinement in speech and in appearance, and financial *largesse* spans his literary output. Arguably a kind of symbiosis exists between his life and his *oeuvre* in this regard. Boccaccio's fictions of courtly life are multiple, from his descriptions of the court of Venus and its female courtiers (who are all members of the Neapolitan aristocracy) in the *Caccia di Diana* (c.1333?) to the allusions to courtly comportment in the French courts and to the Neapolitan aristocracy in a variety of works – the *Filocolo* (1335–6?), the transformation of Troy into thirteenth-century Naples in the *Filostrato* (1335?), the chivalry and generosity of Arcita and Palemone in the *Teseida* (1339–41), the allusions to Arthurian romance in the *Amorosa visione* (1342), the *Elegia di Madonna Fiammetta* (1343–4), and the *De casibus virorum illustrium* (1355–62). These fictions find a counterpart in Boccaccio's experiences in the Angevin court of King Robert (1327–40), as well as his time spent in the court of Polenta in Ravenna (1345) and in Forlì in the court of Francesco Ordelaffi (as described in *Epistola* VI). Even Boccaccio's imaginative autobiographical account of a noble Parisian mother has been interpreted as a pretense to nobility in order to secure a more lasting place in the Neapolitan court.[72] The desire for a career as a court poet would never be satisfied.

In addition to depictions of courtly life in the early vernacular works cited above, the concept of *cortesia* reappears in Boccaccio's *oeuvre* often within the register of nostalgia or regret for a bygone golden age. *Cortesia* and its opposing vice, in the form of avarice and lack of generosity, become the lens through which Boccaccio sculpts his historical vision of Florence and Italy vis-à-vis that of Dante, referring constantly to the loss of a world marked by *cortesia*, as the chapters ahead explore. But when he writes about the vicissitudes of his own life, as for example in his letters, he expresses nostalgia for the remote period of *cortesia* he experienced in his youth. Boccaccio's experience of the Angevin court of King Robert was made possible by his father's association with the Bardi company and also perhaps through the figure of Nicola Acciaiuoli, who became the Grand Seneschal (Gran Siniscalco) under Giovanna of Naples, and was once perhaps the childhood friend of Boccaccio under the tutelage of Giovanni da Strada.[73] His experiences in the court in Naples were coloured by the generosity of King Robert.[74] Though he calls Robert the "secondo Salomone" in the *Genealogia deorum gentilium* (XIV.9), Boccaccio, like Giovanni Villani, was not loathe to criticize Robert's periodic avarice.[75] Despite (and, one could argue, perhaps also because of) these periodic shortcomings, King Robert stands in Boccaccio's life among those royal hosts who embodied the spirit of *cortesia*, presiding over Boccaccio's veritable paradise on earth that was Naples, where he likewise gained an education in literature and specifically Provençal poetry, the literary tradition most credited with the development of *fin'amors*.[76]

The Angevin court was not Boccaccio's only experience of courtly life. After a brief sojourn in Naples following the tumultuous banishment of the Duke of Athens (1345–6?), he was hosted by the Ostagio da Polenta (the cousin of Dante's host in exile), to whom he dedicated his translation of Livy, and perhaps also by da Polenta's son Bernardino. In 1347, Boccaccio was in Forlì in the court of Francesco Ordelaffi, of whom he writes that he was a "hospes gratissimus" in *Epistola* VI, dedicated to Zanobi da Strada. It was in these courts that Boccaccio began to cultivate his memories of Dante, as reflected, perhaps, in the two eclogues and songs with Giovanni del Virgilio, as well as the letter from Frate Ilaro.[77] He would spend time in Padua, in the court of Louis of Bavaria, and would return as well to Ravenna in 1357, after his first disappointment in Naples in 1355.

The generosity and hospitality that he received in the Angevin court of King Robert are often contrasted with the faulty patronage of the Great Seneschal, Nicola Acciaiuoli, who, as Branca defined him, was for Boccaccio "l'uomo che lungo tutta la vita fu per il Boccaccio segno delle più aspre contraddizioni, di amori e di rancor, di entusiasmi e di rampogne" (the man who was the symbol of the most bitter contradictions – love and hatred, passion and rebuke – for all of Boccaccio's life).[78] One of Boccaccio's letters from his late years, *Epistola* XIII, forms an essential part of this interpretive lens. In 1363, precisely the year in which the intended recipient of his letter, Francesco Nelli, was to succumb to the plague, Boccaccio describes the reasons from his departure from Naples. Nelli had invited Boccaccio back to Naples to be court *literatus* under Nicola Acciaiuoli, but instead of an experience such as that of Dante at the court of Can Grande or Petrarch in the court of the Visconti, Boccaccio found the conditions not suitable, calling the room that he had to share with his brother Jacopo a "sewer." Mainardo Cavalcanti took pity on Boccaccio in those conditions and received him as a guest in his own home ("sono costretto a tornare alla liberalità del nobile giovane cittadino nostro Mainardo Cavalcanti," §42; I am forced to return to the generosity of our young, noble compatriot, Mainardo Cavalcanti), but fortune turned unkind yet another time when he had to follow Acciaiuoli's court from Nocera to Baia, where once again the lodging was unfit. After receiving a letter from Acciaiuoli in which the poet is accused of being an intolerant "man of glass," Boccaccio inveighs against the conditions of his stay under the seneschal, sarcastically calling Acciaiuoli the "egregio albergo delle Muse" (§6; honorable host of the Muses) and "del mio oste cortese" (§68; my generous host), and moreover referring to his generosity as "questa sua abominevole magnificienzia" (§67; his abominable generosity). Having already journeyed back to Naples in anticipation of Acciaiuoli's hospitality in 1355 but been ultimately disappointed, Boccaccio has no kind words left for the seneschal, for whom he was supposed to write a panegyric but has come up short. As a result of the failed trip of 1355, he writes to Nelli that he feared not the "larghe promesse" (empty promises) or the "disusata liberalità" (unusual generosity) of Acciaiuoli during this stay. Providing excruciating detail of the squalors of life for Acciaiuoli's entourage at Nocera, Boccaccio asserts to Nelli that he had gained experience of courtly life when he grew up in Naples ("Conobbi dalla mia puerizia i costumi de' cortigiani e la vita loro," §33; I experienced the customs and life of a courtier beginning in my youth). Boccaccio's own experiences of the *cortesia* of his hosts, and the *avarizia* of Acciauoli, have predisposed him to viewing the traditions of thought on *cortesia* with a particular interest. Boccaccio's ethical historiography thus forms a provocative counterpoint to his own autobiography.

His attention to the *cortesia* and avarice of his patrons resonates with his contrasting views of Florence and Naples, the former city full of "miserly and avaricious people" (*Elegia di Madonna Fiammetta* II.6) and the latter, in the same work, exalted for its courtly life. This characterization of Florence reflects Boccaccio's treatment of Dante's Florence in the *Trattatello in laude di Dante*. In a text written slightly after the *Decameron*, and thus before the *Esposizioni*, Boccaccio composed the first redaction of the *Trattatello in laude di Dante*. The *Trattatello* strives to monumentalize Dante's life in poor letters ("lettere povere") by crafting a new biography of his life that focuses on the terms of his exile. A sharp, bitter tone of rebuke of Florence's misdeeds against Dante marks the first redaction, as opposed to the subsequent editions of this text (known as the *Compendio*). Florence has neglected to honour one of its greatest citizens, Boccaccio writes, and the *Trattatello* attempts to correct this injustice. For as a citizen of Florence, he believes himself to share in the city's obligation to Dante. Thus Boccaccio attempts to do what the city of Florence has not done ("quello che essa dovea verso lui magnificamente fare, non avendolo fatto, m'ingegnerò di far io," §8; Since she did not do that which she should have generously done for him, I will now undertake it myself).

Like Boccaccio, Dante's vicissitudes before and during exile as recounted in the *Trattatello* were subject to the whims of Fortune, to be tempered only by the generosity of his hosts and cities in exile. First Dante enjoys Fortune's favours and is elevated to great civic stature within the Priorate of the city; then, after exerting great effort to mend the division between the Black and White Guelphs, he is unjustly sent into exile. Following Verona and Lunigiana, Ravenna, in the form of Guido Novello da Polenta (the nephew of Francesca da Rimini), takes in Dante with open arms. Boccaccio emphasizes the "liberalità" of Guido; with his generous spirit ("liberale animo") he invited Dante, unsolicited, to stay in his home. The generosity of Guido greatly pleased Dante ("piacendo sommamente a Dante la liberalità del nobile cavaliere," §80–1; "the generosity of the noble knight having pleased Dante most of all").

The *cortesia* of Guido Novello da Polenta – whose familial *cortesia* Boccaccio himself would experience – and of Dante's other hosts in exile stands in counterpoint to the avarice and ingratitude of Dante's native city. At the approximate midpoint of the first redaction, Boccaccio inveighs against Florence for having exiled Dante, in a tone that mimics that of the pilgrim in *Inferno* 16 or the poet at the beginning of *Inferno* 26 ("Godi, Fiorenza, poi che se' sì grande"; "Take joy, O Florence, for you are so great"). Florence cannot pardon itself, Boccaccio claims, for having abandoned Dante during an era of political turmoil, since it never welcomed its poet back (though Dante did have the chance to accept terms proposed by Florence in 1315). Here Boccaccio asks, rhetorically, whether Florence will aspire foolishly for glory in its merchants or artists, who are now also corrupted by greed:

> Deh! Gloriera'ti tu de' tuoi mercatanti e de' molti artisti, donde tu se' piena? Sciocamente farai: l'uno fu, continuamente l'avarizia operandolo, mestiere servile; l'arte, la quale un tempo nobilitata fu dagl'ingegni, intanto che una seconda natura la fecero dall'avarizia medesima è oggi corrotta e niente vale. (§94)

> Alas! Will you glory in your merchants and craftsmen, of whom you have plenty? You will do so foolishly. Commerce, continually goading one with avarice, is a menial trade; craftsmanship was at one time engaged in nobly by men of genius until a second mercenary nature made it corrupt and worthless. (Bollettino, 26)[79]

Where Florence has lacked in generosity, or *cortesia*, now avarice fosters a desire for transitory wealth among its merchants and even among its artists, who were once inspired by talent and reason. The merchant class and the artistic one do not belong to separate social classes, but are both susceptible to the forces of avarice. In the *Trattatello*, avarice becomes a civic, and not a class-specific, vice. It is no longer characteristic of the merchant class only, but becomes the dominant vice of all of Florence. When located outside of the court and within the parameters of the city, *cortesia* now dwells with artists in exile from Florence. The temporary glories sought in the name of greed spell the end of Florence's greatness. More than the death of an idea of courtly behaviour, the lament for *cortesia* now reads as the lament for the city of Dante.

Reading Boccaccio's biography and his biography of Dante in terms of his reception of Dante's *Commedia* and the vision of Florentine and Italian history described therein reveals these convergences. Boccaccio's nostalgic accounts of his life in the Angevin court of King Robert of Naples resonate with his reception of the topos of *cortesia* from Dante's poem. A nostalgia for *cortesia* informs Boccaccio's interpretation of Dante's historical world, from the adaptation of such figures as Ciacco, Guiglielmo Borsiere, and the noble families of Ravenna, the Onesti and Anastagi families, in his *novelle*, to discussions of the political history of the Guelphs and the Ghibellines and the changing papacy.

Methodology

This book began as a study concerned primarily with the combination of the following approaches: an analysis of realism (Ascoli, Auerbach, Barolini, White) in the *Decameron* and the *Commedia*, considered vis-à-vis their intertextual relationship with the *Esposizioni*; a study of the influence of Dante upon Boccaccio (Bloom); and a version of the practice of *logomimesis*, the rhetorical enactment of ideas and realization of figures from the *Commedia* in the *Decameron* (Forni). After drawing from these different perspectives, it then developed into a historicized study of how the concept of *cortesia* intersected with Boccaccio's interpretation of Dante's sense of the political and social past, one that is informed by the work of many historians in the period (Becker, Brucker, Cardini, Dameron, Jones, Lansing, Najemy, Witt).

I began with the study of analogous passages in the *Decameron* and the *Esposizioni*, the text of what we take to be Boccaccio's public lectures on the *Commedia* from 1373 to 1374. These passages all deal with crucial moments and issues in Florentine social and political history that are marked by the cultures of *cortesia*: the clash between the Black and White Guelphs, the role of the rising merchant class in the disappearance of *cortesia* as liberality, and the vice of avarice within the rising merchant class. In these pages, I examine the differences between

Boccaccio's prose realization of these moments in the *Decameron* and then approximately twenty years later in the *Esposizioni*, in light of Boccaccio's negotiation of Dante's influence and considering thirteenth- and fourteenth-century political, social, and economic realities. Whereas Dante articulates history as culminating on the stage of church and state politics, Boccaccio foregrounds these historical vicissitudes within the individual contours of biography, of the personal. Boccaccio imagines quotidian exchanges between singular artistic and political figures who represent the literary and social communities that populated Dante's world. *Courtesy Lost* attends to how Boccaccio transforms related historical narratives linked with these figures of *cortesia*, such as in the chronicles of Dino Compagni and Giovanni Villani.

Reading the *Commedia* as a "historical text," one that contributes to our understanding of the political history of Dante's life and times, has rarely been absent from the commentary tradition, nor from the scholarship of historians focusing on Florentine and papal history, though similarly historicized readings by literary scholars have been less frequent.[80] More rare, though with several notable exceptions,[81] have been critical readings of Boccaccio's *Decameron* as an interpretation of various political and social realities pertaining both to his lifetime and to Dante's life and work. In this way, *Courtesy Lost* aims to address the remaining lacuna in analysing the influence of Dante's history amidst the earliest reception of the *Commedia* – indeed, at the origins of Dante studies itself, in the work of Giovanni Boccaccio and his activity as *dantista*. Boccaccio forges Dante's histories of political and social events first within the versatile narrative of the *Decameron*, which he variously defines in the Proem as "novelle, o favole, o parabole o istorie" ("novelle, fables, parables or (his) stories") and then within the commentary form of the *Esposizioni*.

The field of Boccaccio studies is generally less inclined to view the "istorie" of the *Decameron* as rewritings of history. While the analogous nature of several of the textual moments I discuss in the pages ahead is noted by Giorgio Padoan in his edition of the *Esposizioni*, and certain critics, including Vittorio Russo and Francesco Bruni, have also noted some of these parallels, criticism has not yet framed their significance in larger terms.[82] Russo notes these passages for the purpose of documenting the material evidence of "continuità" between the *Decameron* and the *Esposizioni*.[83] Likewise, Bruni highlights these similarities but states that Boccaccio "neutralizza le opposizioni politiche" (neutralizes political tension) and asserts that "al massimo politica e cronica forniscono uno sfondo piuttosto generico" (at the most, politics and chronicles provide a rather generic backdrop).[84] Bruni's statement reveals a similar critical limitation that has continued to affect Boccaccio scholarship despite the work of scholars such as Vittore Branca, one that wholeheartedly denies the penetration of political and historical issues (and thus of "serious" material) into the *hortus conclusus* of the *fabulae*, as well as scholarship that only considers the *Decameron* as diametrically opposed to Dante's poem.

Franco Fido, on the other hand, has endorsed a view of Boccaccio as being a much more perceptive reader of Dante at the time of the *Decameron*. In his chapter "Dante personaggio mancato del *Decameron*," Fido concludes by observing, "un'ammirazione e un'indipendenza di giudizio, in altre parole, che paradossalmente potrebbero farci riconoscere nell'irriverente autore del *Decameron* un lettore della *Commedia* più acuto e felice del devoto scoliasta delle *Esposizioni*" (an admiration and independence of thought, in other words, that paradoxically could lead us to perceive, in the irreverent author of the *Decameron*, a more keen and happy reader of the *Decameron* than the devout scholar of the *Esposizioni*).[85] Fido's essay, which also addresses the *Commedia* as a "serbatoio di situazioni narrative e di personaggi" (a reserve of narrative situations and characters), strongly influenced my perception of Boccaccio's *ars narrandi* in interpreting Dante's poem.

It is my ambition in the pages ahead to think of how Boccaccio's activity as a *dantista* necessitates a view of the author as a historian in a different sense, sometimes as a writer with a particular political agenda, but also as an author who wrote history along ethical lines. It is specifically what he perceived in Dante's writings as the loss of *cortesia* that inflected his sense of realism, both in the mid-fourteenth century when composing the *Decameron* and towards the end of his life when writing the *Esposizioni*. I am thus reluctant to believe that Boccaccio entered into a "moral" phase of literary production only in the second half of his life, after the writing of the *Decameron*. The ethics of the *Decameron* might be hidden by the "corteccia" of our own preconceptions regarding the content of these stories, but upon closer investigation of his interpretation of Dante's historical worlds, they come through strong and clear. Boccaccio's social moralism might originate in his reading of Dante, but that does not disinherit them as Boccaccio's own ideologies.

Boccaccio *dantista*

That Boccaccio was deeply familiar with the *Commedia* along with other works of Dante is an indisputable fact. Two of Boccaccio's works, the

Trattatello in laude di Dante (1351–55) and the incomplete collection of his public lectures on *Inferno* 1 to 17, commonly called the *Comento* but more precisely referred to by Giorgio Padoan as the *Esposizioni sopra la Comedia di Dante* (October 1373–January 1374), each testify, albeit in different ways, to this truth.[86] The *Esposizioni*, the first *lectura Dantis* offered to the people of Florence, held in the church of Santo Stefano in Badia, most explicitly demonstrate Boccaccio's close reading of Dante's text, and though it is an unfinished work (and is most likely not the exact content of the public lectures), it remains an invaluable resource in the study of the early commentary tradition and serves as a portal through which one can witness the late Boccaccio actively engaging with his most influential predecessor.[87]

The field of Boccaccio *dantista* has experienced a resurgence in interest over the twentieth century, and a qualified renaissance (forgive the pun) over the past few decades. While echoes of Dante's verse have also been discerned in several other of Boccaccio's works (such as the *Elegia di madonna Fiammetta*, the *Caccia di Diana*, the *Amorosa visione*, and the *Corbaccio*), studies of Dante's presence in the *Decameron* emerged only in the late twentieth century.[88] I refer specifically to two special editions of *Studi sul Boccaccio* (volumes 13 and 14) published between 1981 and 1984 that include articles by Attilo Bettinzoli, Robert Hollander, and Victoria Kirkham that explore the influence of Dante's *capolavoro* upon Boccaccio's.[89] The longest treatment of the intertextual relationship between the *Commedia* and the *Decameron* is still Robert Hollander's *Boccaccio's Dante and the Shaping Force of Satire* (1997), which addresses thematic similarities (such as Ser Cepparello and Brunetto Latini) in support of his argument that Boccaccio ultimately reverts to Latin models of satire when coming to terms with the power of the *Commedia*'s realism.[90] Most recently, Jason Houston's book *Building a Monument to Dante: Boccaccio as* dantista (2010) examines Boccaccio's activity as *dantista* from the multiple perspectives of editor, apologist, commentator, and biographer.[91]

Overview

When portraying the Florentine aristocracy from Dante's times, Boccaccio attends (often unlike Dante) to the ways in which members of the Florentine elite manifest a chivalric mentality, exhibiting a clear preference for the Black Guelphs (Corso Donati, most of all). On the other hand, he attends to the idea of *cortesia* as a civic ethos, which he finds lacking among merchants (chapters 1–3) and clerics (chapter 3) in general, in the spirit of Dante. Yet his definition of *cortesia* differs from that offered by Dante in the *Convivio*, as a long-lost custom of the courts. Articulated in *Esposizioni* 16 as the practice of "atti civili" (civil acts), *cortesia* appears to be infused with Boccaccio's republican spirit, an ethos that is not limited to the courts but belongs to the world beyond them:

> Cortesia e valor: cortesia par che consista negli *atti civili, cioè nel vivere insieme liberalmente e lietamente*, e fare onore a tutti secondo la possibilità. (16.53, emphasis added)

> "Courtesy and valour." "Courtesy" pertains to civil comportment, that is, to living both generously and contentedly, doing honour to everyone according to one's means. (Papio, 581)

Boccaccio does not give *cortesia* the framework of the court as Dante does in the second book of the *Convivio*.[92] He instead claims that *cortesia* consists of civil acts ("atti civili") characteristic of a condition of living together generously and happily. A civil existence that exists outside of the court in the spirit of financial generosity (but not prodigality) and mutual respect evokes the many customs of the court alluded to by Dante. Whereas Dante evokes *cortesia* as a practice of the past, one that cannot exist in the absence of the court, Boccaccio uses the present tense to indicate the practice of *cortesia* in the present.

In the case of the Florentine poet, the social practice of *cortesia* had been lost along with the dream of an imperial future; for Boccaccio, writing in the wake of the many changes within the Florentine political, social, and economic landscape (chapter 2), *cortesia* might exist in the future, though this hope for the future also depends upon an act of historical revisionism (chapter 4). In treating Dante's history of Florence and the disappearance of *cortesia* lamented in *Inferno* 16, Boccaccio highlights the aristocratic culture of factionalism among those elite Florentine families who claimed the namesake of *cortesia* (*Dec*. 6.9). Thus, though it apparently contrasts with the civic ethic of *cortesia* as he defines it in *Esposizioni* 16, Boccaccio's nostalgia for this world accompanies his interest in a code of conduct that benefits society at large and the world outside of the court, a social ethic that would anticipate, arguably, the idea of civic humanism.

Boccaccio's interpretation of the history of the Florentine aristocracy thus serves as an interesting counterpoint to the conclusion of Marvin

Becker, who has viewed the discriminatory efforts to rein in magnate disorder and violence as a precursor to the fostering of Florentine civic humanism.[93] *A modo suo*, Boccaccio locates the need for the cultivation of *cortesia* as a civic ethic for a troubled Florence of the middle and late fourteenth century, yet at the same time he evokes those very same elite protagonists who were seen by the *popolo* as the enemies of social order and progress. Boccaccio's voice, in the variety of the texts under examination here, does not align itself with the voice of the *popolo*, as did Dante in a certain measure, but most notably with others such as Compagni and the unknown author of the *Cronica fiorentina*.[94]

In the texts I will examine, Boccaccio shows that the elite culture and rhetoric of a chivalric *cortesia*, especially among the Florentine magnate families, is inextricable from the practice of "incivility." If incivility occurs in the form of violence or *vendette*, as hinted at within the tale of *Decameron* 6.9 but enacted in 9.8 (addressed in chapter 3), Boccaccio will not figure the magnate protagonists of those well-documented eruptions of conflict in acts of violence. These individuals include Guido Cavalcanti, Betto Brunelleschi, Vieri de' Cerchi, Corso Donati, and Geri Spini, who were targeted for their violent deeds by the popular government, as in the Ordinances of Justice in 1293. Instead, these narratives hint at aggression or violent deeds, or figure instead their lackeys (Ciacco or Biondello) in *zuffe*, minor altercations, on their behalf, showing as well the ways in which they were public performances, as Najemy notes.[95] Yet these moments of discord are few, perhaps as a parallel to the historical reality, as described by Dameron, that bloodshed, or "bloody vendettas," were rare.[96] Only when Boccaccio attempts to enact a future for the past generations of the Dantean (and Romagnole) families of *cortesia*, namely in the *novella* of Nastagio degli Onesti (5.8), will *vendette* be vividly depicted as violence directed at women (chapter 4).[97] The hostility and violence that is prominent in Boccaccio's history of *cortesia* is thus directed against those who pose an obstacle to the flourishing of aristocratic culture, namely the *popolani* and, in the case of 5.8, women unwilling to marry into elite families.

Boccaccio's reworking of Dante's history of *cortesia* does not only treat the elite families of thirteenth-century Florence, such as the Cavalcanti and the Brunelleschi, but also includes an elite Genoese family, the Grimaldi. It is here, in this related tale, that Boccaccio expands upon the civic ethic of *cortesia*, an ethic useful for the mercantile elite. In the tale of Guiglielmo Borsiere (*Dec.* 1.8), he identifies the disproportionate greed of a fictional member of one of the largest elite families in Genoa, Ermino Grimaldi (also known as Ermino Avarizia in 1.8) as antithetical to the ways of *cortesia*. Borsiere, fashioned as a courtier in Boccaccio's hands, belongs to Dante's historical past of the thirteenth century. The juxtaposition of a Florentine courtier and a Genoese merchant, a fictional member of one of the most powerful magnate families in Genoa, allows Boccaccio to revise Dante's lament for the lost years of Florentine *cortesia* within the peninsular context of the merchant class. If Boccaccio identifies the Cerchi as the *gente nuova* of *Inferno* 16 in the *Esposizioni*, in the *Decameron* he extends this critique of a vice of the mercantile elite by looking to Genoa as well, a city to which not only Boccaccio but also Betto Brunelleschi and Corso Donati would carry out embassies in their political careers on behalf of Florence.[98] I will begin with an examination of these tales in order to evince the nuances of Boccaccio's view of *cortesia* and the elite as influenced by Dante's vision of Florence's past, a historical vision coloured by those years that elapsed between the two authors.

In the pages ahead, I aim to answer the other question that Guiglielmo Borsiere's exhortation prompts: how does one figure the bivalent concept of *cortesia*? Moreover, how does one conceive of an ethic of generosity that is also associated with the practice of violence? By attempting to answer these questions, I believe, one can arrive at an appreciation of yet another contradiction in Boccaccio's works: his nostalgia for an aristocratic past on the eve of civic humanism.

1 Boccaccio's History of *cortesia*: The Incivility and Greed of the Elite

The standard bearers of *cortesia* among the well-established thirteenth-century Italian elite did not follow the ethic concept of *cortesia* as a code of conduct, such as in the spirit of Ciceronian *urbanitas* and the study and cultivation of *curialitas* in the French and German *curiae* and cathedral schools.[1] Instead, northern and central Italian elite families largely espoused a life of factionalism and warfare, a form of *cortesia* that more resembled a version of chivalry based on feudal power and violence than a social ethos meant to promote civic harmony. This version of *cortesia* began to be cultivated in the era after the Peace of Constance (1183), when the *milites*, a social group composed of families with true claims to nobility and those with noble pretensions, lost power of their consular regimes. In the thirteenth century, as the Italian elite gradually grew more distant from its origins as a warrior aristocracy, this new courtly culture in Italy fed upon chivalric epic and romance, which inspired a rhetoric of knighthood that legitimized violence. In Florence, the acts of violence committed both within and between elite families, as well as against the *popolo*, the non-elite guildsmen and merchants, marked the mid-thirteenth-century history of Guelph and Ghibelline struggle and the period of civil war between the Black and White Guelph factions at the turn of the fourteenth century. This history of internecine conflict and social upheaval forms an integral part of the civic history of Dante's Florence throughout the *Commedia* in moments such as *Inferno* 6, 10, 16, and 28.[2]

Boccaccio's works capture the apparent incongruity between a feudal, chivalric sense of *cortesia* and an interest in *cortesia* as a civic ethic that would evoke the idea of *urbanitas* and *curialitas* (among other qualities), perhaps as a sign of the author's nostalgia for the Florentine aristocracy of Dante's era fused with his republican spirit, his passion for the well-being of the commune. Thus he would depict the "incivility" of elite families (what are referred to in the original sources as the "*grandi, possenti, casastici, nobili,* or *magnati*," according to Dameron)[3] and also display an interest in the concept of *cortesia* as a civic ethic that would restore Florentine society after the trials and tribulations of the Black Death and other economic disasters that occurred in the mid-fourteenth century. This is a form of historiography that shows that the writing of the *Decameron*, and arguably his latter works, as David Wallace asserts, "complement rather than compete with Boccaccio's dedication to the Florentine body politic."[4] In those moments marked by his activity as *dantista* in the *Decameron*, the *Trattatello*, and the *Esposizioni*, Boccaccio interprets this fraught period of history (mid-thirteenth to turn-of-fourteenth-century Italy, and mainly Florence) through the lens of *cortesia*, in a double sense: both as an aristocratic culture in decline and as an ethic that suited a republican ideology.

Cortesia and the Florentine Elite from the Early Commune to the Age of Dante

Given the extent to which early theories of courtesy and courtliness were seen to have been inspired by the Ciceronian ideal of *urbanitas* and its associated qualities (Scaglione and Jaeger), it is paradoxical, as Witt notes, that a "chivalric morality ... fed urban warfare" in northern and central Italian cities during the late twelfth century. This chivalric morality was countered by the earliest seeds of humanism in the early thirteenth century by authors such as Albertano da Brescia and Lovato dei Lovati, who wrote of the Roman civic heritage of Italy.[5] Spread by the diffusion of French literature, chivalry was thus seen as antithetical to a civil society, as theorized by the Romans, during a period of time in which internecine strife between ruling families resulted in open warfare in the streets. Witt locates the emergence of this social upheaval in the times following the Peace of Constance (1183), which was formed after the conclusion of the wars between Frederick Barbarossa and the Lombard communes. One result of the Peace was the search for a new courtly identity on the behalf of the lords of Monferrato, Biandrate, Malaspina, and Este (in Piedmont, Liguria, and Lombardy), suddenly free of imperial control. They chose to foster a courtly culture in the style of the French, where they acted as patrons of literature and the arts, receiving poets from Provence, thus allowing for their language and style to influence Italian poets.[6]

Alongside the rise of Italian court culture and the infusion of Provençal and French literature and poetry in the principalities, the cities that had been ruled by consular regimes led by the *milites* (a mixture of agnatic families and families of the *gente nuova* who lived like nobles), once empowered by the empire, experienced a loss of legitimacy. This led to an increase in violence both from within ruling groups and from the *populares* underneath them.[7] At the same time, Italian elites, who had developed a great appreciation for the chivalric literature of the West and its code of "courage, honor, strength, liberality and elegance in manners,"[8] brought together the images of the Carolingian epic hero and the knight in love in their attempt to fashion an image of knighthood in a time when the legitimacy of noble claims was in question. Their recourse to chivalric epic, romance, and troubadour lyric was supported as well by their interest in the acquisition of noble status vis-à-vis the aristocratic self-fashioning as the chivalric knight.[9] Because the thirteenth-century Florentine elite, in particular, was not neatly divided between merchants and non-merchants, the culture of knighthood, Najemy suggests, allowed specific elite families to distinguish themselves by referencing a distant feudal past. In emulating knighthood, they were aligning themselves with the upper classes in Lombard principalities and the Neapolitan kingdom.[10] As Lansing writes, "For prosperous Florentines, knighthood was not so much a vocation as a social model."[11]

The *popolo*, and authors who could be seen to align themselves with the voice of the *popolo* (such as Brunetto Latini, Dino Compagni, and others), identified the chivalric ethic, with its propensity to warfare and personal *vendette*, as antithetical to a peaceful urban existence.[12] This criticism can be detected in the anonymous *Cronica fiorentina compilata nel secolo XIII*, which contains the first extant account of the murder of Buondelmonte dei Buondelmonti in 1216, often cited as the original event that precipitated the elite violence that fed the Florentine civil strife, or, as Najemy writes, the "original sin that required the *popolo*'s punishment of the elite."[13] In the description of this event, as Najemy indicates, the elite protagonists of the original incident – during a celebration of the ordination to knighthood by Mazzingo Tegrimi dei Mazzinghi, a hired jester ("uno giuocolare di corte") grabbed the plate of Uberto degli Infangati – react with nothing less than exaggerated offence, expressed in a rude way (the author modifies the actions of both Buondelmonte and Oddo Arrighi with the term "villanamente").[14] An uproar occurs in this "corte," and Buondelmonte wounds Oddo Arrighi with a knife ("villanamente il fedio"), which, of course, exacerbates the conflict. The marriage of Buondelmonte to Arrighi's niece comprises the plan for a reconciliation, but this plan too falls apart as Madonna Gualdrada, the wife of Forese Donati, convinces Buondelmonte not to follow through with the marriage, but instead to marry her own daughter. She exhorts him to change his course of action by referencing his "shamed" knighthood: "Cavaliere vitiperato, ch'ài tolto moglie per paura dell'Uberti e di Fifanti; lascia quella ch'ài presa e prendi questa, e sarai sempre onorato cavaliere" (Shamed knight, you who have taken a wife out of fear of the Uberti and the Fifanti, leave the wife you have taken and take this one, and you will always be an honoured knight).[15] Dante, as well, would locate the cause of much of Florence's suffering in the Buondelmonti murder, precisely in the words of Cacciaguida in *Paradiso* 16.136–44. Compagni's *Cronica* (1.2) identifies this moment as the beginning of the conflict between the Florentine Guelphs and Ghibellines at the very beginning of his chronicle; however, his account of Gualdrada Donati's words differs. In all of these moments, elite families are shown as prone to outbursts of violence over small offences[16] (which are parodied by Boccaccio in *Dec.* 9.8).

This elite ideology was countered by the *popolo* with specific legislation to curb magnate power (such as the Ordinances of Justice from 1293, as I will discuss at the end of this chapter), and also in literature, with an ideology of civic responsibility that was based on Roman thought. In line with the voice of the *popolo*, early humanists such as Albertano da Brescia, as in his *Liber consolationis et consilii* (1246), aimed to foster what Witt calls an "urban morality" that would promote the ideal of a peaceful urban existence as an ultimate individual goal, standing in sharp contrast with the chivalric ethic that bred rivalries and violence.[17] This ideological battle, in which chivalry was pitted against civility, lasted for many centuries.[18]

Chivalric epic and romance were not the only source of inspiration in the self-fashioning of the thirteenth-century Italian elite. Another way in which to read the aspirations to knighthood of these families, such as the Donati, is as reclamation of the culture of twelfth-century Italian *milites*, when knights formed a greater percentage of the Florentine population. This recollection of the warrior aristocracy might have informed the aspirations of thirteenth-century elite families, during which time the number of knights in Florence had decreased (from 250 knights in Florence in the 1280s, according to Giovanni Villani, to 65 in the 1330s).[19] Dante's history of *cortesia* begins with this golden age, the era of his great-great-grandfather, the crusading knight Cacciaguida (c.1091–1148), at a time when the Florentine elite was a warrior aristocracy.[20]

Though Cacciaguida's Florence is, as Charles Davis writes, the "necessary counterpart of the degenerate city" described in *Inferno* 16, it is not this era in which Dante locates a lost *cortesia*.[21] The times of Cacciaguida, according to Dante's vision, are infused with Roman virtues, austerity and simplicity, restraint and the absence of greed and excess. That Romanized "buon tempo antico" differs from another lost golden age, that of the times of *cortesia*, which can be located for Dante in Florence before the times of Guiglielmo Borsiere (*Inf.* 16), and in Lombardy, before Frederick II's death in 1250 (*Purg.* 16.115–20). Dante will also benefit from "la cortesia del gran Lombardo," Bartolomeo della Scala (*Par.* 17.71) in the future, so though Dante might lament the absence of *cortesia in Inferno* 16 and *Purgatorio* 16, as well as in the *Convivio*, the pilgrim will have direct experience of *cortesia*, as hospitality, in the future.

Like Cacciaguida's Florence, the era during which *cortesia* was reputed to have thrived in the Tuscan commune, the times before the Guelph and Ghibelline conflicts of the mid-thirteenth century come to signify an irretrievable, utopian moment in society against which the new social upheavals created by political conflict, a booming population, and large mercantile gains can be criticized. In *Inferno* 16, Dante bitterly reflects upon changes in Florentine *mores*, the result of pride as well as the mishandling of money, or the economic form of "dismisura." After Brunetto Latini's characterization of the Florentine people as "avara, invidiosa e superba" (68) in *Inferno* 15, the pilgrim in *Inferno* 16 bemoans the "gente nuova" of Florence and their quick gains as the source of pride and intemperance that have afflicted the city:

> "Se lungamente l'anima conduca
> le membra tue," rispuose quelli ancora,
> "e se la fama tua dopo te luca,
>   cortesia e valor dì se dimora
> ne la nostra città sì come suole,
> o se del tutto se n'è gita fora;
>   ché Guiglielmo Borsiere, il qual si duole
> con noi per poco e va là coi compagni,
> assai ne cruccia con le sue parole."
>   "La gente nuova e i sùbiti guadagni
> orgoglio e dismisura han generata,
> Fiorenza, in te, sì che tu già ten piagni." (64–75)

("That your spirit long may guide/your limbs," he now added/"and your renown shine after you,/tell us if valor and courtesy still live/there in our city, as once they used to do,/or have they utterly forsaken her?/Guiglielmo Borsiere, grieving with us here/so short a time, goes yonder with our company/and makes us worry with his words."/"The new crowd with their sudden profits/have begot in you, Florence, such excess/and arrogance that you already weep.")

Inferno 16 marks a development in the rhetorical tradition of *cortesia* (as surveyed in the Introduction). Similar to some of its Provençal precedents, the former age of *cortesia* becomes a historicizing trope with which an author can inveigh against the corruption of a particular socio-economic class, the *gente nuova*. Whereas once *cortesia* was linked with *larghezza*, now it is the proliferation of new wealth, such as that accumulated by the Cerchi family (he does not name them directly here, though he does in *Paradiso* 16), that has banished courtesy. This invective against the *gente nuova* laments the changes inherent in the social upheavals of the mid-thirteenth century, favouring, both here and in *Paradiso* 16, the earlier ways of an aristocracy that followed the principal of *cortesia*, when a chivalric mentality was not at odds with social harmony. Boccaccio's interest in the chivalric culture of a Florentine aristocracy and *cortesia* as a civic *ethos* thus evokes this moment from Dante's historical vision.

The Dantean *cornice* of *Inferno* 16 and *cortesia* Lost: *Decameron* 1.8, 6.9, and *Esposizioni* 16

Boccaccio translates Dante's moral indignation into narratives that participate in the same nostalgic lament present in the *Commedia*. But just as he changes the pilgrim's invective of *Inferno* 16 into the *pronta risposta*, for example, of Guiglielmo Borsiere, Boccaccio refines this lament into a specific vision of history in social and economic terms. For Boccaccio, the nostalgia for *cortesia* in *Inferno* 16 becomes a depiction of the chivalric culture of the Florentine elite in *Decameron* 6.9 and of the mercantile elite in *Decameron* 1.8. The loss of *cortesia*, for Dante, might have been a casualty of the changing political landscape, in the rising power of the Cerchi family, but for Boccaccio the Florentine elite (as exemplified by Guido Cavalcanti and Betto Brunelleschi) are nostalgically evoked, despite their propensity for factionalism and incivility.

Before elaborating upon the political implications of these tales, I will present the details of the intertextual relationship of *Inferno* 16,

Decameron 1.8 and 6.9, and *Esposizioni* 16. An analysis of the presence of Dante's *Commedia*, and more specifically *Inferno* 16, in these narratives explains further the concepts of *inventio* and *dispositio* in the *Decameron* as discussed by Pier Massimo Forni: "the task of determining how one particular Boccaccian *novella* was born or put together often cannot be separated from the investigation of how and why it was put together with other *novelle*."[22] Such a task for these *novelle* requires situating them within their Dantean cornice of *Inferno* 16.

The widely studied *novella* that features Guido Cavalcanti, *Decameron* 6.9, contains one of the few passages that Boccaccio appropriates almost verbatim within the text of the *Esposizioni*. While its latter half is often studied for the puzzling *pronta risposta* uttered by Cavalcanti when hemmed in by Betto Brunelleschi and his *brigata*, the less-studied exordium of 6.9 involves Elissa's lament for the hospitable traditions of Florentine *brigate*, which have been banished from the city because of the avarice that has fomented alongside new-found wealth:

> Dovete adunque sapere che ne' tempi passati furono nella nostra città assai belle e laudevoli usanze, delle quali oggi niuna ve n'è rimasa, mercè della avarizia che in quella con le ricchezze è cresciuta, la quale tutte l'ha discacciate. Tralle quali n'era una cotale, che in diversi luoghi per Firenze si ragunavano insieme i gentili uomini delle contrade e facevano lor brigate di certo numero, guardando di mettervi tali che comportare potessono acconciamente le spese, e oggi l'uno, domani l'altro, e così per ordine tutti mettevan tavola, ciascuno il suo dì, a tutta la brigata; e in quella spesse volte onoravano e gentili uomini forestieri, quando ve ne capitavano, e ancora de' cittadini: e similmente si vestivano insieme almeno una volta l'anno, e insieme i dì più notabili cavalcavano per la città e talora armeggiavano, e massimamente per le feste principali o quando alcuna lieta novella di vittoria e d'altro fosse venuta nella città. (6.9.4–6)

> I must first of all remind you that in days gone by, our city was noted for certain excellent and commendable customs, all of which have now disappeared, thanks to the avarice which, increasing as it does with the growing prosperity of the city, has driven them all away. One of these customs was that in various parts of Florence a limited number of the gentlemen in each quarter of the city would meet regularly together in one another's houses for their common amusement. Only those people who could afford to entertain on a suitably lavish scale were admitted to these coteries, and they took it in turn to play the host to their companions, each of them being allotted his own special day for the purpose. Distinguished visitors

to Florence were frequently invited to these gatherings, and so too were a number of the citizens. At least once every year they all wore the same kind of dress, whilst on all the more important anniversaries they rode together through the city, and sometimes they tilted together, especially on the principal feasts or when the news of some happy event had reached the city, such as a victory in the field. (McWilliam, 466–7)

A select number of gentlemen from the different quarters of Florence would gather together, forming *brigate* of their own, to share the financial burden of hosting large meals so that each could comfortably afford the cost. These gatherings served a diplomatic function of welcoming distinguished visitors to the city and honouring citizens of distinction at home. The nostalgic lament continues with an account of how these gentlemen, on select days of the year, would dress alike and ride through the city, sometimes even jousting together, in celebration of a holiday or some great military victory.

An allusion to this custom of the *brigata* at the beginning of *Decameron* 6.9 can be located in *Esposizioni* 16, Boccaccio's commentary on *Inferno* 16:

> Soleva essere in Firenze questo costume, che quasi per ogni contrada solevano insieme adunarsi quegli vicini, li quali per costumi e per ricchezza poteano, e fare una lor brigata, vestirsi insieme una volta o due l'anno, cavalcare per la terra insieme, desinare e cenare insieme, non trasandando né nel modo del convitare né nelle spese: e così ancora invitavan talvolta de' lor vicini e degli onorevoli cittadini; e se avveniva che alcun gentile uomo venisse nella città, quella brigata si riputava da più che prima il poteva trarre dell'albergo e più onorevolmente ricevere. (16.56)

> It used to be customary in Florence, in nearly every neighbourhood, for neighbours (according to their traditions and means) to meet together to form their own groups, to dress alike once or twice a year, to ride through the city together, and to lunch or dine together (though never going to excess either in the preparation of meals or in the expenses they incurred), at times inviting their other neighbours or other honourable citizens. If it happened that some gentleman came to the city, the group who was swiftest to take him out of the inn and most honourably receive him was regarded as the best. (Papio, 582)

Similarly to that which he had put forth in *Decameron* 6.9, here Boccaccio describes how participants would gather together to form their own *brigate*, dress in the same manner once or twice a year, ride through town, and dine and invite visitors or distinguished fellow citizens to their homes. He thus elaborates a ritual that was banished as a result of the social and moral upheaval in Florence, the same ritual that was described earlier in the *novella* of 6.9. Thus that Boccaccio rehearses the same material in his commentary on Dante's poem approximately twenty years after the composition of the *Decameron*, indicates that *Inferno* 16 and its discussion of the lost *cortesia* of Florentine society recalls the same social, political, and moral issues raised in the *novella* of Guido Cavalcanti.[23]

Decameron 1.8, which explicitly addresses the effects of mercantile and elite avarice, belongs to the intertextual genealogy of *Inferno* 16, *Esposizioni* 16, and *Decameron* 6.9. The protagonist of 1.8, Guiglielmo Borsiere, is first named in the *Commedia* in *Inferno* 16, after the cited invective from that canto ("La gente nuova e i subiti guadagni," 73–5). Iacopo Rusticucci asks Dante if "cortesia e valor" still exist in Florence, as their fellow Florentine, Guiglielmo Borsiere, has reported disturbing news about the state of contemporary Florentine society to his fellow citizens located among the sodomites in the Seventh Circle:

> ché Guiglielmo Borsiere, il quale si duole
> con noi per poco e va là coi compagni,
> assai ne cruccia con le sue parole.   (*Inferno* 16.70–2)

> (Guglielmo Borsiere, grieving with us here/so short a time, goes yonder with our company/and makes us worry with his words.)

Boccaccio's gloss in *Esposizioni* 16 of Rusticucci's words is followed by the analogous passage to *Decameron* 6.9 ("Soleva essere in Firenze ..."):

> Assai ne cruccia con le sue parole, dicendone che del tutto partita se n'è. *Soleva essere in Firenze questo costume, che quasi per ogni contrada ...* (16.55–6, emphasis added)[24]

> "*Has greatly aggrieved us with his words*" (72) telling us that they (courtesy and valor) have wholly vanished. It used to be customary in Florence, in nearly every neighbourhood ... (Papio, 582)

The end of this paragraph once again mentions Borsiere:

> E tra loro sempre si ragionava di cortesia e d'opere leggiadre e laudevoli: e questo è quello di che costui domanda se più in Firenze s'usa, con ciò

fosse cosa che alli lor tempi s'usasse, disiderando di saperlo dall'autore, come che *Guiglielmo Borsiere*, il quale visse sì lungamente che mostra che a' suoi tempi quella usanza vedesse, e così ancora la vedesse intralasciata. (16.57, emphasis added)

Within these groups, the members always spoke of courtesy and of magnificent, praiseworthy deeds. It is whether this custom is still observed in Florence, as it was during their times, that this shade asks, and he wishes to know this from the author, because Guglielmo Borsiere, who lived so long that he could tell of having seen this custom practised, has now seen this tradition forsaken. (Papio, 582)

It is here that Boccaccio elaborates on his invention of the *brigata* of Florence's yesteryear; while *Inferno* 16 indicates that Borsiere's words cause pain ("assai ne cruccia con le sue parole," *Inf.* 16.72), it does not contain a description of the custom of the *brigata*, as Boccaccio claims in *Esposizioni* 16. As Boccaccio begins the narrative of *Decameron* 6.9 with an *exordium* written in the vein of Dantean nostalgia, so in *Esposizioni* 16 he fabricates Borsiere's words to other damned souls as well as his biography, using Dante's text as the point of departure.[25]

Commentators before Boccaccio (such as the Ottimo and Guido da Pisa, which on other occasions were sources for the *Esposizioni*) offer little new information regarding Guiglielmo Borsiere's life other than what can be deduced from Dante's text.[26] It is not until Boccaccio's *Esposizioni*, in his gloss on *Inferno* 16.70 – "ché Guiglielmo Borsiere, il quale si duole" – that a full characterization of Borsiere can be found:

Questi fu cavalier di corte, uomo costumato molto e di laudevol maniera; ed era il suo essercizio, e degli altri suoi pari, il trattar paci tra grandi e gentili uomini, trattar matrimoni e parentadi e talora con piacevoli e oneste novelle recreare gli animi de' faticati e confortargli alle cose onorevoli. (16.54)

This man was a courtly knight as well as a gentleman of great sophistication and laudable behaviour. He (and his peers) performed tasks such as negotiating peace between grand, genteel men and mediating the unions of spouses and families. He also sometimes distracted the minds of those who were distressed with pleasant and decent stories and encouraged them to behave honourably. (Papio, 582)

Boccaccio, whose elaborate prose could be said to outshine the brief mention of Borsiere in *Inferno* 16, fashions Borsiere as a noble man, peacemaker, diplomat, and counsellor – an exemplary person who did not have many contemporary equivalents.

The profile of Guiglielmo Borsiere in the *Esposizioni* also existed in Boccaccio's imagination at the time of composing *Decameron* 1.8, where Borsiere is the protagonist. This is evidence again of the extent of *Inferno* 16's sustained influence upon Boccaccio when writing both the *Decameron* and drafting the *Esposizioni*. The similarities between the two descriptions of Borsiere are as striking as those that exist between *Esposizioni* 16 and *Decameron* 6.9:

> Avvenne che in questi tempi … arrivò a Genova *un valente uomo di corte e costumato e ben parlante,* il qual fu chiamato Guiglielmo Borsiere, non miga simile a quegli li quali sono oggi, li quali, non senza gran vergogna de' corrotti e vituperevoli costumi di colouro li quali al presente vogliono essere gentili uomini e signor chiamati e reputati, son più tosto da dire asini nella bruttura di tutta la cattività de' vilissimi uomini allevati che nelle corti. *E là dove a que' tempi soleva essere il lor mestiere e consumarsi la lor fatica in trattar paci, dove guerre o sdegni tra gentili uomini fosser nati, o trattar matrimonii, parentadi e amistà, e con belli motti e leggiadri ricreare gli animi degli affaticati e sollazzar le corti e con agre riprensioni, sì come padri, mordere i difetti de' cattivi, e questo con premii assai leggieri.* (1.8.7–9, emphasis added)

> Now … there arrived in Genoa a worthy courtier, Guiglielmo Borsiere by name, who was refined of manner and eloquent of tongue, altogether different from the courtiers of today. For to the eternal shame of those who nowadays lay claim, despite their corrupt and disgraceful habits, to the title and distinction of lords and gentlemen, our modern courtiers are better described as asses, brought up, not in any court, but on the dungheap of all the scum of the earth's iniquities. In former times, their function usually consisted, and all their efforts were expended, in making peace whenever disputes or conflicts arose between two nobles, negotiating treaties of marriage, friendship or alliance, restoring tired minds and amusing the courts with fine and graceful witticisms, and censuring the failings of miscreants with pungent, fatherly strictures, all of which they would do for the slenderest of rewards. (McWilliam, 59–60)

Adopting the nostalgic tone of *Decameron* 6.9, the narrator recounts the function in society of courtiers, executed without great reward: making peace between noblemen; negotiating marriages, friendships, or alliances; and rejuvenating the fatigued and entertaining the courts with graceful witticisms as well as censuring mistakes with biting comments. The latter two items bear a particular significance for the narrative of *Decameron* 1.8 and the function of the *pronta risposta*, as a closer reading of these *novelle* shows. What is most striking about this passage is how Boccaccio elaborates upon Borsiere as the figure of the model courtier in the attempt to fashion the realism of the *Decameron* in response to the nostalgia of the *Commedia*. It enacts Dante's historical past in ways in which the brevity of Borsiere's appearance in *1Inf.* 16 does not allow. In essence, Boccaccio's portrait of Borsiere fulfils what he himself recommends to Ermino Grimaldi ("Fateci dipignere la Cortesia"): a depiction of *cortesia*, one that shows it to be a civic *ethos*.

The Greed of the Genoese (Not Florentine) Elite: *Decameron* 1.8, Guiglielmo Borsiere, and Ermino Grimaldi

Inspired by Filostrato's multilayered narrative in which Bergamino, a courtier, cures Cangrande of an unusual moment of avarice by means of a story (*Dec*. 1.7), Lauretta tells the tale of how another noble courtier cured the greed of a rich merchant ("La precedente novella, care compagne, m'induce a voler dire come un valente uomo di corte similmente, e non senza frutto, pugnesse d'un ricchissimo mercatante la cupidigia," 1.8.3; "The previous story, dear friends, implants in me a desire to tell you how, in similar fashion and not without fruitful effects, a worthy courtier derided the covetous habits of a very rich merchant," McWilliam, 59). The merchant of whom she speaks, Ermino de' Grimaldi from Genova, is not only rich but, as far as was known, wealthier than anyone else in Italy ("trapassava la ricchezza d'ogni altro ricchissimo cittadino che allora si sapesse in Italia," 1.8.4; his wealth surpassed that of every rich man in Italy [translation mine]). Just as Ermino surpasses all others in his wealth, so he exceeds all as a miser. Ermino will not lavish wealth upon his guests ("in onorare altrui teneva la borsa stretta," 1.8.5; "he would entertain on a shoestring," McWilliam, 59) nor upon himself, and contrary to the usual habits of the Genoese people, who dressed themselves fashionably, he deprived himself of fine clothing as well as of fine food and drink. Because of his serious affliction of avarice, Lauretta recounts, Ermino lost his last name of Grimaldi and became known as Ermino Avarizia.

The hyperbolic nature of Ermino's portrait, as Kirkham notes, renders him less a historical personage and more an "archetype of greed."[27] Ermino is not simply rich, he is richer than any other person in Italy; he is not only a miser, he outdoes every other miser in the country. His habits of dress and eating differ from those of every other Genoese, making him seem less an inhabitant of that city than a rare individual who stands out on a national scale. Such are the dimensions of Ermino's avarice and miserliness that he is called Ermino Avarizia. In this way, Boccaccio, while not completely stripping Ermino of his national, local, or personal identity (and the narrator compares him once again to the Genoese at the end of the *novella*), makes him in part a personification of avarice.

Though Boccaccio seems to draw attention away from Ermino Grimaldi's geographical provenance by renaming him Ermino Avarizia, Ermino is presented as a native of Genoa at the beginning of the *novella* ("Fu adunque in Genova ...") and, after his transformation at the end of the tale, is reinserted into the community of the Genoese; he becomes "il più liberale e 'l più grazioso gentile uomo e quello che più e' forestieri e i cittadini onorò che altro in Genova fosse a' tempi suoi" (1.8.18; "the most courteous and generous gentleman in the Genoa of his time, and was respected above all others, not only by his fellow-citizens, but by visitors to the city," McWilliam, 61). While Boccaccio himself is not necessarily friendly in his treatment of the Genoese people (one need only look to the story of Landolfo Rufolo in *Dec.* 2.4 where Lauretta, again the narrator, claims they are "uomini naturalmente vaghi di pecunia e rapaci a doverlo aver" (2.4.14; "being by nature a rapacious, money-grubbing set of people," McWilliam, 93), Dante's famous invective against the Genoese people in *Inferno* 33 is equally, if not more, damning:

> Ahi Genovesi, uomini diversi
>   d'ogne costume e pien d'ogne magagna,
>   perché non siete voi del mondo spersi?
> Ché col peggiore spirto di Romagna
>   trovai di voi un tal, che per sua opra
>   in anima in Cocito già si bagna,
> e in corpo par vivo ancor di sopra.   (*Inferno* 33.151–7)

(O men of Genoa, race estranged/from every virtue, crammed with every vice,/why have you not been driven from the earth?/With the most heinous spirit of Romagna/I found a son of yours who, for his evil deeds,/even now in Cocytus bathes his soul/while yet his body moves along the living.)

In the third zone of the ninth circle (Tolomea), the pilgrim has just learned that though the physical body of the Genoese Branca Doria still wanders on earth inhabited by a demon, his soul can be found next to Frate Alberigo. Branca Doria's sin was to have murdered, together with another relative, his father-in-law, Michele Zanche, himself guilty of barratry.

Immediately before the invective against the Genoese we find the pilgrim's refusal to clear Frate Alberigo of the frozen tears that seal his eyes: "E io non gliel' apersi;/e cortesia fu lui esser villano" (149–50). This is the only other appearance of the word "cortesia" in the *Inferno*, and it is one of the few times in the *Commedia* where it means "kindness" or "generosity."[28] Its significance here lies in the seeming paradox of the pilgrim's actions; in other words, here among the sinners (to revise the aphorism slightly), it is kind to be cruel. Likewise, in *Decameron* 1.8 Guiglielmo Borsiere's biting remark "Fateci dipignere la Cortesia" momentarily discomfits Ermino Avarizia and leads him to recognize the fault of his miserly ways. As Borsiere metaphorically opens the eyes of his host, in the case of *Inferno* 33, by literally not opening the eyes of one who betrayed his guests, the pilgrim who had promised to help Frate Alberigo not only conforms to God's will but also betrays a traitor. The pilgrim performs *cortesia* to a soul who did not follow the ways of *cortesia*.

If the sins of Branca Doria, who belonged to a long-standing Ghibelline family in Genoa, earned him eternal punishment in Dante's Hell, one could imagine him being featured in the *Decameron* for having not acted in the ways that nobility should, namely for having not followed the ways of *cortesia* with one's guests. The Genoese characters that appear in the *Decameron* – Ermino Grimaldi, the Genoese crew of Landolfo Rufolo's ship (2.4), the two merchants in the tale of Alatiel (2.7), Bernabo and Ginevra (2.9), and Paganino (2.10) – all convey a view of the Genoese as rapacious, libidinous, calculating, and violent. Steven Epstein comments that Boccaccio would not have had access to Genoese authors, but that these stories "give a sense of what Genoa's reputation was like outside the city on the eve of the Black Death."[29]

While an Ermino Grimaldi does not appear in the family genealogies, the Grimaldi of the thirteenth and fourteenth centuries indeed belonged, as Boccaccio conveys, to the merchant class, having established their wealth through maritime commerce, as Kirkham notes.[30] Boccaccio himself was familiar with the Grimaldi family; there is record of a mission he made in 1365, sent by the Signoria of Florence, to appeal on behalf of the Grimaldi, who were being mistreated by the Doge of Genova.[31] Florence was interested in the welfare of the Grimaldi because of their support during the conflicts with Pisa (which date to before Dante) that finally ended in the early 1360s.[32] While Boccaccio's mission to Genoa postdates the composition of the *Decameron* by several years, *Decameron* 1.8 suggests that Boccaccio was aware beforehand of the Grimaldi family and of their allegiance with Guelph Florence against Ghibelline Pisa. Although the initial nature of Ermino is exceptionally negative, the positive result of 1.8, that Ermino becomes "cortese," suggests that, like the other characters of the First and Sixth Days of the *Decameron* who stand "corrected" in an exemplary *novella* (such as Cangrande della Scala in 1.7, Salah-din in 1.3), such a transformation is possible. Any possible affinity or appreciation that Boccaccio felt for the Grimaldi family in their efforts to support Florence might underlie the necessity and good will inherent in Borsiere's transformation of Ermino; in other words, Boccaccio wanted the Grimaldi to be known as exceptionally generous to the same extent as the general reputation of the Genoese was negative.

For that transformation to occur, Boccaccio suggests in essence that the historical lesson of *Inferno* 16 must be reversed: the *gente nuova* must learn the ways of *cortesia*, not lead to its extinction, which Boccaccio locates in his own times, not just those of the pilgrim living alongside the Cerchi family (as I will discuss in chapter 2). By not overtly stating Guiglielmo Borsiere's Florentine origins or making specific reference to Florentine customs and traditions as can be found in the *Esposizioni*, Boccaccio departs from a Dantean context to address the general state of *cortesia* in his times.[33] After introducing Borsiere, Lauretta launches into her invective against the disintegration of the court and the disappearance of truly noble courtiers, evoking the moral and political language of *Inferno* 16, with its focus on Florence, and thus recalls the continued indebtedness of this *novella* to Dante's influence: "gran vergogna e biasimevole *del mondo presente*, e argomento assai evidente che le virtù, di qua giù dipartitesi, hanno nella feccia de' vizii i miseri viventi abbandonati" (1.8.10, emphasis added; "All of which is greatly and culpably to the shame of the modern world, and proves very clearly that the present generation has been stripped of all the virtues, and left to wallow abjectly in a cesspit of vices," McWilliam, 60). Boccaccio features Guiglielmo Borsiere, it would appear, in order to claim Dante's historical past as his own, so that, as Mario Baratto writes, the absolute past becomes the recent past ("il passato remoto tende a diventare, nel *Decameron*, passato prossimo, dal Duecento agli inizi del Trecento").[34]

The stylistic and interpretive differences between the articulations of Dante and Boccaccio's historical visions of this past speak to the nature of the *Decameron* as an exemplary work. In other words, the difference between these two texts can be seen by the way in which the invective in 1.8 "fails" and its *pronta risposta* "succeeds." After conveying her own anger against the alleged courtiers of today (with the moral indignation of the pilgrim in *Inferno* 16), Lauretta claims that she did not intend to indulge in such a digression ("Ma tornando a ciò che io cominciato avea, da che giusto sdegno un poco m'ha trasviata più che io non credetti ...," 1.8.11; "But to return to what I had begun to say before my righteous anger carried me somewhat further astray than I had intended ...," McWilliam, 60). While Boccaccio includes this invective, and thus intends that it form part of the *novella*, it is an aberration from the storyline, one that serves to highlight Borsiere's exemplary nature but that has no discernible effect upon Lauretta's listeners (Boccaccio does not note how the *brigata* reacts to her tale as a whole). Such an invective can be called a digression, for while it occurs in the middle of the *novella*, Lauretta promptly puts it aside to finish (or, actually, start!) the story, only to have the narrative negotiate the implications of her invective at the very end of the novella when the *pronta risposta*, "Fateci dipignere la Cortesia," (Have Courtesy painted there) is delivered.

Boccaccio transforms the invective of the pilgrim in *Inferno* 16 into the *pronta risposta*. In both contexts, the hortatory nature of words is emphasized: words can change social behaviour.[35] Notably, it is by engaging with *Inferno* 16 that Boccaccio asserts the superiority of the narrative of the *novella* and its series of causes and effects to fulfil and supersede the reality represented in the *Commedia*.[36] The words of Borsiere noticeably change the behaviour of Ermino Grimaldi. But the chivalric mentality (to adopt Witt's phrasing) displayed by the Florentine elite is not pliable and receptive to correction. *Decameron* 6.9 conveys that, even in this city, the *pronta risposta* highlights the aggression and conflict between members of the elite.

The Incivility of *cortesia*: *Decameron* 6.9, Betto Brunelleschi, and Guido Cavalcanti

If Dante walks among the dead and speaks of them in his poem, Boccaccio will resurrect those same characters and have them perform in his historical fiction of Florence's past, giving new life to the *figurae* of the *Commedia* that makes them appear closer chronologically to the time of the *Decameron*. Boccaccio repopulates his plague-stricken Florence by turning to the recently departed, so to speak, of Dante's afterlife. If the "passato prossimo" of the *Commedia* should be the "passato remoto" of the *Decameron*, then it is also true that these characters seem closer to the narrative time of the cornice, as if they were to exist in a "passato prossimo" accessible to Boccaccio's readership.[37] The shared temporal context of the *Commedia* – from the afterlife of the poem to its literary afterlife in Boccaccio's works – translates into this sense of what Baratto calls the "passato prossimo" of the *Decameron*. This chronological condensation also achieves what Hayden White termed the "fulfillment of a prefiguration of a piece of historical reality."[38]

It is also from Dante's Florence, though not from Dante's characters, that Boccaccio draws inspiration in the writing of *Decameron* 6.9.[39] This is attested by the fact that the opening paragraph of this *novella* is paraphrased in Boccaccio's commentary on *Inferno* 16, a canto concerned with the effects of the *gente nuova* upon the practice of *cortesia* in the city. The *brigate* portrayed by Boccaccio, both in his commentary on this canto and at the beginning of *Decameron* 6.9, belong to the chivalric world that comprises the other side of *cortesia*. In this section, I address how Boccaccio identifies the origins of the disappearance of the former elite, magnate families who were leaders within the Black and White factions. Boccaccio's investment in the Florentine Republic would have predisposed him to promote the civic values that ensured the safety of the commune. But the factionalism of the former elite – and especially of the Black Guelphs – was by Boccaccio's lights a necessary component of the chivalric culture of past *cortesia*. Here in the character of Betto Brunelleschi, he alludes to the violence and aggression of the Black Guelphs, the faction that most styled itself within the new ideologies of *cortesia* discussed earlier. He likewise alludes to the greed of the White Guelphs, the faction that was led by a prominent merchant class, the Cerchi, and in this story is represented by a seemingly "aloof" intellectual and poet, Guido Cavalcanti. The elite of the late-thirteenth century, though, has most to fear from the greed of the *popolo* that has led to its disenfranchisement and decline.

In order to appreciate the political and social critique inherent in this *novella*, one must look to the similarities and differences between the "historical" traditions of the *brigate* mentioned in both *Decameron* 6.9 and *Esposizioni* 16, and how they differ from this *novella*'s *brigata* led by Betto Brunelleschi. The Florentine *brigate* in these two texts were populated by a certain number of gentlemen who would meet in each other's homes (6.9), or were neighbours (*Esp.* 16), and would entertain each other always within their financial means ("guardando di mettervi tali che comportare potessono acconciamente le spese, e oggi l'uno, domani l'altro," *Dec.* 6.9; "li quali per costume e per ricchezza poteano," *Esp.* 16). Boccaccio does not present these *brigate* as running the risk of prodigality, an extravagance that Dante warns against, for example, in his depiction of the Sienese *brigata spendereccia* in *Inferno* 29, or which Folgore da San Gimignano describes in his cycle "Sonneti per l'armamento di un cavaliere."[40] The *brigate* described as having been lost to the advent of avarice are thus an ideal social group that differ from the historical accounts of the *brigate* found in such sources as Compagni's *Cronica*, as Lansing notes. She writes that male youths, some of them with military training, were the source of civic violence in the social group of the *brigata*.[41] In addition to the *brigate* not dominated by youths (those of Corso Donati in 1.10, and Rossellini della Tosa in 3.8), the principal *brigate* (where the word occurs the most in any section of the *Cronica*) include the band of violent youths who provoke the Cerchi youths, the first agents in the pivotal conflict between the two leading families that will end in bloodshed in May 1300, and then the *brigate* of the Cerchi and the Donati (1.22):

> Perché i giovani è più agevole a ingannare che i vecchi, il diavolo, accrescitore de' mali, si fece da una brigata di giovani che cavalcavano insieme: i quali, ritrovandosi insieme a cena una sera di calendi maggio, montarono in tanta superbia, che pensarono scontrarsi nella brigata de' Cerchi e contro a loro usare le mani e i ferri. In tal sera, che è il rinovamento della primavera, le donne usano molto per le vicinanze i balli. I giovani de' Cerchi si riscontrorono con la brigata de' Donati, tra' quali era uno nipote di messer Corso, e Bardellino de' Bardi, e Piero Spini, e altri loro compagni e seguaci, i quali assalirono la brigata de' Cerchi con armata mano. (1.22)

> Because the young are easier to deceive than the old, the devil – that sower of evils – made use of a band of youths who used to ride around together. These youths gathered for dinner one evening, on the first of May, and they grew so arrogant that they decided to confront the Cerchi band and use their fists and swords against them. On that evening, which marks the return of spring, the ladies were accustomed to hold dances in the neighborhoods. The Cerchi youths encountered the Donati band, which included a nephew of messer Corso, Bardellino de' Bardi, Piero Spini, and

other companions and followers, who attacked the Cerchi band with arms in hand. (Bornstein, 25)

Similar to this passage in Compagni, the "real" *brigata* in *Decameron* 6.9 plays a political or at least an aggressive function, as Franco Cardini states: "svolge un'evidente attività politica a carattere se non altro intimidatorio."[42]

Boccaccio's political understandings become evident in this *novella* when Elissa claims that among such *brigate* was one led by Betto Brunelleschi (6.9.7).[43] The irony of this selection is evident, for two reasons: first, the noteworthy exclusion of Guiglielmo Borsiere, a figure whom Boccaccio has already linked to *cortesia* and diplomacy in 1.8, and second, the seeming inappropriateness of Betto Brunelleschi as an example of *cortesia* as a civic ethic. It is difficult to read Elissa's lament for the lost graces of a civil society as sincere because of the inclusion of Betto Brunelleschi, the other protagonist of the *novella* alongside Guido Cavalcanti, whose biography sheds light upon what is at stake in the plot of this story. Instead, the lament indicates the extent to which *cortesia* has become a perversion of its Ciceronian pedigree, *urbanitas*.

Betto Brunelleschi was a leading figure in Florentine politics at the turn of the thirteenth century, during the period of civil war between the White and Black Guelph factions. Though his family was traditionally aligned with the Ghibellines, Brunelleschi changed parties after the events of 1301 (Charles of Valois's arrival in Florence and the subsequent rise of the Black Guelphs) and became one of the most powerful rulers among the Black Guelphs. He eventually conspired with others to bring about the death of their leader, Corso Donati, and in 1311 was himself murdered by two of Corso's relatives.[44] Compagni's portrait of Brunelleschi towards the end of the *Cronica* conveys his critical view of this political figure, known for his wealth and grain-hoarding, as well as for his embassies:

> Messer Betto Brunelleschi, e la sua casa erano di progenie ghibellina. Fu ricco di molte possessioni e d'avere; fu in grande infamia del popolo, però che ne' tempi delle carestie serrava il suo grano, dicendo: "O aronne tal pregio, o non si venderà mai." [...] *Molto era aoperato in ambascerie, perché era buono oratore.* E famigliare fu assai con Papa Bonifazio; e con messer Napoleone Orsino Cardinale, quando fu legato in Toscana, fu molto dimestico, e tennelo a parole, togliendoli ogni speranza di mettere pace tra i Bianchi e i Neri di Firenze. Questo cavaliere fu in gran parte cagione della

morte di messer Corso Donati; e a tanto male s'era dato, che non curava né Dio né 'l Mondo, trattando accordo co' Donati, scusando sè e accusando altri. […] dopo alquanti dì, arrabbiato sanza penitenzia o soddifazione a Dio e al Mondo, e con gran disgrazia di molti cittadini, miseramente morì: della cui morte molti se ne rallegrarono, perché fu pessimo cittadino. (3.39, emphasis added)

Messer Betto Brunelleschi and his house were of Ghibelline stock. He was rich in land and goods. He was infamous among the *popolo*, for in times of famine he locked up his grain and declared: "Either I get this price for it or it will never be sold." […] He was often employed on embassies since he was a good orator. He was on familiar terms with Pope Boniface. When messer Napoleone Orsini was cardinal legate in Tuscany, he was thoroughly at home with him and held him in conversation, removing any hope of making peace between the Whites and Blacks of Florence. This knight was largely responsible for the death of messer Corso Donati. Yet he was so thoroughly dedicated to evil that he did not care for God or the world; he discussed an agreement with the Donati, excusing himself and accusing others. […] But some days later he died miserably, in a rage, without penitence or satisfaction to God or the world, and with the great ill will of many citizens. Many rejoiced at his death, for he was a terrible citizen. (Bornstein, 99–101)

While Compagni's position as a member of the *popolo* would have certainly biased him against Brunelleschi, throughout his *Cronica* he repeatedly refers to Brunelleschi's corrupt political manoeuvres. His evil-doing, according to Compagni, extended to his function as ambassador; perhaps the most explicit example of Brunelleschi's calculating "ambascerie" (embassies) can be found in his treatment of Cardinal Orsini, who was sent to bring peace to Florence but was thwarted by the Black Guelphs. Compagni writes, "I Neri, beffando il Cardinale, cercarono per più vie di vituperarlo, mostrando volerli ubbidire. E ritornati in Firenze, vi mandorono ambasciadori messer Betto Brunelleschi e messer Geri Spini; i quali il faceano volgere e girare a lor modo, traendo da lui grazie, e pareano i signori della sua corte" (3.18; "The Blacks mocked the cardinal and sought to heap scorn on him in many ways, while acting as if they wished to obey him. After they returned to Florence, they sent him as ambassadors messer Betto Brunelleschi and messer Geri Spini, who made him turn and spin to their tune, extracting favors from him and acting like the lords of his court," Bornstein, 81). Villani, in his *Nuova cronica*, similarly recounts the "parole superbe e disoneste" (proud and dishonest words) of Brunelleschi on another occasion in which he represented Florence (3.199). Other than what can be found in Compagni and Villani, it seems that the historical record for Brunelleschi has also characterized his other diplomatic missions less as attempts to keep the peace than as efforts to intimidate or thwart others.[45] Accordingly, Cardini notes that the portrait of Brunelleschi that emerges from the chronicles differs greatly from his depiction as a "sottile e intendente cavaliere" (subtle and perspicacious knight).[46] I would argue that the difference Cardini notes between the historical record for Brunelleschi and his depiction in *Decameron* 6.9 speaks to Boccaccio's noteworthy affection for former elite culture, and especially for those who were aligned with the Black Guelphs, as will be the case for Boccaccio's characterization of Corso Donati (which I discuss in chapter 2).

One of Brunelleschi's diplomatic missions is of great importance to the intertextual relationship of *Decameron* 1.8 and 6.9. As Nicola Ottokar writes, Brunelleschi was sent with Corso Donati to Genoa in order to mediate a dispute between Genoese and Florentine merchants in the city of Nîmes in 1291, before he became a leader of the Black Guelphs.[47] Boccaccio, himself an ambassador on behalf of the commune of Florence on different occasions, might have been familiar with this fact about Brunelleschi. If so, then his decision to feature Brunelleschi in 6.9 and not in the related tale of 1.8 is even more significant. If courtiers should be peacemakers, Boccaccio draws attention to Brunelleschi as an unsuitable choice for an ambassador by his absence in 1.8, the tale concerning a Florentine courtier and a Genoese merchant.[48] Indeed, it is Ermino Avarizia who recalls Brunelleschi's greed, especially according to Compagni's account of how Brunelleschi hoarded grain during times of famine, selling only to the highest bidder. Borsiere, on the other hand, is lauded by Boccaccio as someone who occupied himself with making peace accords and creating harmony out of conflict. Given all of these factors, the tongue-in-cheek phrase of "savio e intendente cavaliere" used to describe Brunelleschi means to draw attention again to the brutality and infamy of those who, in those times, called themselves knights.

Not only was Brunelleschi infamous in his own right, Guido Cavalcanti's own biography and family reputation, considered separately from the fundamental contribution of his literary production, were likewise notorious. Though highly esteemed by Boccaccio for his intellect and artistic talents (one only need consider, for example, Boccaccio's editorial inclusion of "Donna me prega" into the L.V. Chigiano 176),[49] Cavalcanti was also one of the protagonists in the factional discord afflicting Florence at that time, viewed by the *popolo* as a rabble-rouser who possessed an aristocratic disdain (which resonates with the "disdegno" of *Inferno* 10). Compagni, who wrote that Guido was "courtly and bold, but disdainful and solitary and fixed on his studies" in his *Cronica* (1.10), also wrote a *sonetto rinterzato* that has been interpreted as addressing Guido Cavalcanti, mocking his "cortesia."[50]

Adept in prowess ("pro' e valente,/E come sai di varchi e di schermagli"), Cavalcanti is here portrayed as the nimble and valorous knight capable of bounds ("varchi") and clashes ("schermagli") redolent of his barbed retort and leap over the tomb in *Decameron* 6.9. Despite these qualities as a knight, he is not in need of nobility ("E grande nobilità non t'ha mestiere"), nor of a *brigata* ("Né gran masnada avere"), because he possesses "cortesia" ("Che cortesia mantien leggera corte"), the author notes with sarcasm. If God were to set fortune straight for everyone, then he would give "cortesia" to he who needs it ("Daria cortesia cui è mestiere"), a verse that plays on the double meaning of "mestiere" both as "need" and as "profession." This verse can be read as a condemnation of Cavalcanti's lack of true *cortesia*, insofar as Compagni believes Cavalcanti needs "cortesia," or even that his occupation, as a "knight," should follow the ways of "cortesia." If this were to happen, God would make Cavalcanti a member of the working class (the guild-based *popolo*), so that he might earn and give back abundantly ("E te faria ovriere/Pur guadagnando e ridonando forte"). The criticism of Cavalcanti's superficial sense of *cortesia*, coupled with his intelligence ("come sei saggio, dico, intra la gente," "E come assai scrittura sai a mente/sofisticosamente"), resonates with a view of his negative portrayal in 6.9, even though Boccaccio's esteem of Cavalcanti was by nature different from that of Compagni.

In addition to this critical portrait in Compagni's work, Cavalcanti's familial line, according to sources such as Villani's *Nuova cronica*, was plagued with conflicts with the Black Guelphs and particularly with Betto Brunelleschi. Members of the old Guelf elite, the Cavalcanti family was designated as a magnate family by the Ordinances of Justice in 1293, and their primary roles in vendettas were recorded by Compagni and Villani. Villani (9.1) notes that Guido Cavalcanti and Corso Donati despised each other, and each had made attempts on the other's life. It is more than a coincidence as well that Cavalcanti was sent into exile in Sarzana in 1300, and that this date coincides with the rise of Brunelleschi's political power – something figured, perhaps, in Cavalcanti's fleeing the cemetery of Santa Reparata in the face of Brunelleschi's mob. Thus, Cavalcanti's *pronta risposta*, "Signori, voi mi potete dire a casa vostra ciò che vi piace" ("Gentlemen, in your own house you may say whatever you like to me," McWilliam, 468) can also be read as a farewell to his native city, "casa sua," that he had been forced to leave, but that Betto Brunelleschi and other Black Guelphs had been fortunate enough to see again.[51] From Cavalcanti's perspective Florence in effect became "casa vostra."

The hostility between the Brunelleschi and Cavalcanti families culminated in 1303, when Brunelleschi and his men decapitated Masino Cavalcanti, one of Guido's relatives.[52] With these considerations in mind, it is more than likely that, as Robert Durling has argued, the *brigata*'s attraction to Cavalcanti is suspect.[53] The confrontation in *Decameron* 6.9 between Brunelleschi and his *brigata* and Cavalcanti evokes this history of antagonism, enacting the culture of *vendette* that was cultivated by the members of the Florentine thirteenth-century elite. The historical context implies that their desire to corner Guido and make him a member of their *brigata* might be for vengeance as well as for financial gain. When Boccaccio writes that Cavalcanti was "un de' miglior loici che avesse il mondo e ottimo filosofo naturale (*delle quali cose poco la brigata curava*)" (6.9.8, emphasis added; "he was one of the finest logicians in the world and an expert natural philosopher (to none of which Betto and his friends attributed very much importance)," McWilliam, 467), this invites a different interpretation of the *brigata*'s interest. Much more valuable than Cavalcanti's knowledge, even more than his adeptness at conversation, was his wealth. Naturally Brunelleschi and his *brigata* would be interested in attracting someone with the means to sponsor their dinners, as Elissa herself contends, when she states that the *brigata* had to include a certain number of people in order to have enough money (6.9.5).

Boccaccio's choice of Betto Brunelleschi's *brigata* as an example of one of the virtuous *brigate* of times past essentially throws into question the opening paragraph of this *novella* and thus the *Inferno* 16 context of "cortesia e valor." What emerges is the contradiction in the conduct of those who adopt the cultural trappings of knighthood, members of the elite such as Brunelleschi and Cavalcanti, while espousing a life of brutality and incivility. Of these elite protagonists here, Boccaccio would later identify the avarice of the Cerchi family in the *Esposizioni*, the *gente nuova* of Dante's times, as those principal in the disappearance of "buoni costumi":

> Dice adunque [che] la "nuova gente," intendendo per questa coloro li quali, oltre agli antichi, divennero abitatori di Firenze: e sì, come io estimo, esso dice questo per molti nuovi cittadini, e massimamente per la famiglia de' Cerchi, li quali poco davanti a' tempi dell'autore erano venuti del Piviere d'Acone ad abitare in Firenze, e subitamente, per l'esser bene avventurati in mercatantie, erano divenuti ricchissimi, e da questo orgogliosi e fuor di misura; e per ciò che, come altra volta è stato detto,[54] erano salvatichetti, poco con gli altri cittadini comunicavano e *in questo aveano in parte ritratto indietro il buon costume delle brigate*. E, oltre a ciò, *per la loro alterigia aveano Firenze divisa*, come davanti è stato mostrato, e aveanla in sì fatta guisa divisa che la città già se ne dolea, in quanto molti scandoli e molti mali e uccisioni e ferite e zuffe n'eran seguite. (16.58–9, emphasis added)

> He says, then "parvenus," by which he means those who came to live in Florence alongside the established families. I believe that he says this in reference to the many new citizens (especially the Cerchi family) who not long before the author's day had come from the parish of Acone to live in Florence. Because they were immediately successful in the merchant trade, they became rich, which in turn made them prideful and immoderate. Therefore, as mentioned earlier, they were somewhat uncouth and seldom socialized with other citizens. On account of this behaviour, they rather contributed to the decay of the customs associated with these groups of private citizens. What is more, they divided Florence out of arrogance, as explained above, and they did so in such a way that the city suffered greatly, for many scandals and numerous ills, murders, injuries and rows were caused by their actions. (Papio, 582–3)

The fault lies with the new denizens of Florence and especially the reclusive[55] Cerchi, who were allegedly not integrated into the social life of Florence. By opting instead for a Black Guelph, Betto Brunelleschi, to lead the *brigata*, Boccaccio seems to follow the logic he later put forth in this passage from the *Esposizioni*, in which the Cerchi, and thus by association the White Guelphs, did not keep the custom of the *brigate* alive.

Conclusion

Dante laments the disappearance of the aristocratic world of *cortesia* with the arrival of the *gente nuova*, the category of new-found elite merchant families that often claimed origins in the *contado*, such as the Cerchi. Boccaccio, additionally, bears witness to the social and political histories of *cortesia* as part of an elite culture – ironically, perhaps, the standard bearers of *cortesia* – that was notorious for its factionalism and violence. Alongside this historical vision, an ethic of *cortesia* can continue to be practiced outside of the court, but his interpretation of Dante's history of this topic is equally optimistic (as in *Dec.* 1.8 and *Esp.* 16) and pessimistic (*Dec.* 6.9 and, in other moments, *Esp.* 16 as well). Genoese merchants, such as the Grimaldi, can be shown to practice the generosity and hospitality, the *larghezza*, that partly comprises *cortesia* for Boccaccio. If for Dante the disappearance of *cortesia* can be ascribed to the pride, excesses, and avarice of the *gente nuova*, then the subtext of *Esposizioni* 16 to *Decameron* 6.9, influenced undoubtedly by the social and economic changes that took place in the 1350s and 1360s (as I will discuss in the next chapter), suggests that the "avarizia" that has banished the culture of *cortesia* can be located in the greed of the White Guelphs, namely that of Vieri de' Cerchi.

The allusion to magnate violence in *Decameron* 6.9 resonates with the chronicles of the time, as I have discussed here and will continue to examine in the next chapter. Such pivotal events as the Buondelmonti murder, seen as the origins of the Guelph-Ghibelline divide,[56] as well as the brawl between the Donati and Cerchi factions in May 1300[57] or their clash at the funeral of a woman from the Frescobaldi family at Santa Trinita,[58] events at which members of different familial clans participated in the form of *brigate*, were instances of intra-class violence. These events comprised the majority of elite violence, as opposed to acts of violence perpetrated against others, such as the *popolo*.[59] Vendettas for the elite were considered, as Najemy writes, to belong to a "codified private justice: a system for handling and sometimes resolving disputes without the intervention of law or courts," that speaks to an interpretation of how a "chivalric" society should manage its conflicts, via such rituals as feuds. Najemy theorizes that some occasions of elite violence were a form of competition for followers, a way to thwart the *popolo* by recruiting followers from their midst.[60] Seen in this light, these brawls were instrumental in exacting revenge and maintaining class conflict to the advantage of the elites. Boccaccio will allude again to these dynamics of *vendette* and violence in *Decameron* 9.8, a story of the petty nature of *vendette* and elite factionalism that was inspired by the "rigida" *vendetta* of 8.7, the tale of the scholar and the widow: "così me muove la rigida vendetta, ieri raccontata da Pampinea, che fé lo scolare, a dover dire d'una assai grave a colui che la sostenne, quantunque non fosse per ciò tanto fiera" (9.8.3; "I too am prompted, by the account Pampinea gave us yesterday of the scholar's bitter vendetta, to tell you of another vendetta, which, whilst it was no laughing matter for its victim, was at the same time rather less brutal"; McWilliam, 684).

Just as Boccaccio depicts the elite as insulated within their world of petty revenge, in both *Decameron* 6.9 and 9.8, the popular government was able to disenfranchise the elites through legislation precisely because of their propensity to violence. This legislation officially began in 1281, though the most notable body of legislation was the issuance of the Ordinances of Justice (1293), which designated magnate families by name (both the new mercantile elite and the existing elite), excluded all knights from serving in the Priorate, codified penalties for magnate acts of violence against non-magnates, and established the federation of the guilds.[61] As Lansing writes, there were three criteria that defined magnate status in the anti-magnate laws during the 1280s and 1290s: (1) those whom popular opinion held to be magnates, (2) those who had posted a security against the possibility of committing a future act of violence against a non-magnate, and (3) those houses that could count a knight among its number at that point in time or over the past twenty years.[62] The irony, as she indicates, is that knights were supposed to defend a given society. Yet, as she writes, "knighthood instead identified the group which posed a military threat to the state. Their status was shaped not by their positive social function but by their violent challenge to public order."[63] The anti-magnate legislation made this clear, and defined the role of the *popolo* in rising to the defence of social order and peace.

For Boccaccio, elite factionalism and violence would continue to prevail even in post-1348 Florence, though the period 1300–1302, the culmination of the conflict between the White and Black Guelphs, marked its peak.[64] As Brucker writes of the later elite families, "In this congenitally unruly society, still impregnated with feudal *mores*, the resort to violence was a conventional solution to a dispute or conflict."[65] Boccaccio turns to Dante's times in his reconstruction of Florentine history to show how such petty brawls, *zuffe*, during his own times were the legacy of this generation of Florentine magnates. Yet his preference for the old, consular aristocracy, such as the family of the Donati, over the then *gente nuova*, such as the Cerchi, speaks to Boccaccio's mitigation of the realities of violent magnates. Even Corso Donati, with his strong reputation for violence and conspiracy, would not elicit as much consternation from Boccaccio as the greed and wealth of the Cerchi family, the "ancestors," so to speak, of the mid-fourteenth-century *gente nuova* he loathed. This could be due to the fact that despite the lack of practice of *cortesia* as a civic ethic on behalf of the magnates (the Parte Guelfa by Boccaccio's times and the families connected to the Angevin court in Naples), the practice of certain feudal rites and rituals – what Cardini calls "fantasie equestri" – remained the cultural trappings of their lineages and not of the *gente nuova*. As Cardini writes, there was a decline in this activity in the period after the exile of Walter of Brienne, concomitant with the rise of the *gente nuova*, the group that did not share this sensibility.[66]

In the next chapter, I survey the changing political and economic landscape from the mid-thirteenth to the late fourteenth century in terms of the changing elite, when Boccaccio was completing these works. While Boccaccio's condemnation of the White Guelphs may sound like a rehearsal of Dante's own political agenda, it also reflects the economic realities of the fourteenth-century rise to power of a "new" *gente nuova*. Boccaccio's identification of the Cerchi family as the "gente nuova" in *Inferno* 16, which he first introduces in his gloss of *Inferno* 6's "parte selvaggia," indicates the extent to which he wished to criticize his contemporary *gente nuova* and contrast their realities with the disenfranchised nobles. The Cerchi, protagonists in Florence's turbulent period of civil war at the turn of the thirteenth century, were an ideal family to figure as the protagonists for commercial greed and elite factionalism and violence, as they belonged to a vivid historical memory that was fostered in the chronicles. Despite Corso Donati's reputation for violence, Boccaccio favours him over Vieri de' Cerchi, leader of the Black Guelphs and a member of one of the last Florentine families that could claim to be knights. This revision of history speaks to the complexity of Boccaccio's historical thought, as well as to his own sympathies for the last generation of families with true claims to knighthood, those aligned with the Black Guelphs, whose lack of wealth mirrored, perhaps, his own personal frustrations with insufficient patronage.

2 Boccaccio's Politics of *cortesia*: Narrating the Elite and the *gente nuova*

> The history of Florence, even at its most democratic, remains in large measure the history of its principal families.
> – P.J. Jones, "Florentine Families and Florentine Diaries in the Fourteenth Century," 184

Dante's indictment of the *gente nuova*, as readers of the *Commedia* are well aware, does not only appear in *Inferno* 16. In a canto analogous for its nostalgia for a golden age of Florence, *Paradiso* 16, the poet's ancestor Cacciaguida identifies the mixture of different populations as the cause of Florence's ills ("la confusion delle persone/principio fu del mal della cittade," 67–8). If only, he cries, the Church had not been a stepmother to Caesar ("Cesare noverca," 59), then Montemurlo would still belong to the counts Guidi and not been sold to Florence (64);[1] the Cerchi would still dwell in the province of Acone (65); and the Buondelmonti family, protagonists of Florentine factionalism from the thirteenth century, would likewise still reside in the Valdigrieve 66. Boccaccio, despite the span of years that separates him from Dante, designates the Cerchi family as the main representatives of the *gente nuova*, as seen in *Esposizioni* 16. Decades later, new realities inform Boccaccio's interest in this moment of political history, and particularly the *gente nuova*, before and during the composition of the *Decameron* (ca. 1348–53) and of the *Esposizioni* (1373–74). The Cerchi family, an elite family designated as magnates by the Ordinances of Justice issued in 1293, would no longer classify as the *gente nuova* in the mid-fourteenth century, of course. The "new" *gente nuova*, in the aftermath of the demographic changes that marked the post-plague era, would increase considerably and ascend to political power rapidly, much to the distaste of Boccaccio, whose own family had been members of the *gente nuova* at the turn of the thirteenth century, one of those cited by Cacciaguida in *Paradiso* 16 as hailing from Certaldo: "Ma la cittadinanza, ch'è or mista/di Campi, di Certaldo, e di Figghine" (49–50).[2]

How Boccaccio viewed the changed (and changing) composition of the *gente nuova* around the time of the Black Death and afterwards – the political circumstances that led to their rise to power, the *popolo*, and other elite families in terms of their propensity for *vendette* and greed – informs his reading of the Florentine political history surrounding Dante's exile. This was seen in the first chapter, in his treatment of Betto Brunelleschi and Guido Cavalcanti (*Dec.* 6.9). For Boccaccio, the Cerchi family – immigrants from the Valdarno, bankers, and protagonists in the shift of power to the Guelphs after the defeat of Manfred at Benevento (1266) – would embody the avarice and greed that clashed with the pride and generosity (*cortesia*) of the landed aristocracy of the Donati family. Hence the conflict between the leader of this *parvenu* family, Vieri de' Cerchi, and his political opponent Corso Donati would figure as the tension between the new financial upstarts and a titular aristocracy with true claims to knighthood, something that Boccaccio would perceive, arguably, as a watershed moment before the shifts in social groups after the Black Death.

Because of Boccaccio's nearly exclusive focus on Corso Donati and Vieri de' Cerchi, his history of Florence reads as the history of interfamilial division spurred by the opposition of avarice and *cortesia*: the former ascribed to the newer elite, the latter an inherited custom kept vibrant by the standard-bearers of a longstanding, and impoverished, nobility. For Dante, history is written with these protagonists on the stage of papal and state politics, but for Boccaccio, history is performed by these figures more within domestic and civic spheres – wherever the "homes of the dead" might be found (as in the "case de' morti" of *Dec.* 6.9) – inventing and rehearsing the personal motivations that are re-enacted in his biographical mode, in what could be called a kind of "personalization" of history. In this chapter, I explore how political history manifests itself as biography in another constellation of related passages, *Decameron* 9.8 and 6.2 and *Esposizioni* 6 and 8. Here Boccaccio comes to terms with the implications of the political message of Dante's poem regarding the Florentine internecine conflict around the turn of the fourteenth century. *Inferno* 6, the first political prophecy in the *Commedia*, accuses Pope Boniface VIII of being instrumental in fortune's rise and fall for the opposing Guelph factions. As mentioned in the previous chapter, Boccaccio criticizes the Cerchi family more strongly in the *Esposizioni* than in the *Decameron*, where a Black Guelph, Messer Geri Spini, is depicted as a flawed leader, inexpert in the ways of *cortesia* as an ethos of hospitality and generosity. Yet Boccaccio favours Corso Donati in both texts, in a unique departure not only from Dante's own opinion of this Black Guelph leader but also from characterizations of this controversial figure, known for his violence, found in the chronicles of Compagni and Villani, the latter one of Boccaccio's sources in writing the *Esposizioni*.[3]

The variations in their versions of the political events in Florentine history between 1300 and 1302 reveal the differences in how Dante and Boccaccio theorize history. In the *Commedia* Dante incorporates political protagonists both actual (Pope Boniface VIII, Mosca dei Lamberti, etc.) and historically uncertain (Ciacco, Filippo Argenti, etc.) from this period, as he attends to individual and institutional agency in the unfolding of events. Boccaccio also does not foreground the role of the papacy or the commune in his history of Florence; instead he elaborates on the role of the individual character as first portrayed by Dante, thus expanding the place of biography within history. Florence is in decline because those political figures whose familial lines partake in the lineage of *cortesia*, such as Corso Donati, belong to families who have suffered a tyrannical government (in the form of Walter of Brienne, also known as the Duke of Athens) and attacks from the *popolo*, and who have diminished in size and political power after the plague. Viewed from this historical perspective, political history unfolds along the lines of those families who have inherited and maintained *cortesia* and those families whose commercial practices and ambitions marked the commercial elite in the mid-fourteenth century. For Boccaccio, the most important biographies that comprise Florentine history are of those individuals who embody *cortesia* and avarice, and, as I discuss in chapter 3, they are related to defining historical moments surrounding Dante's exile.[4]

This chapter begins by considering broadly the changes in the political and economic landscape between the different times of Dante and Boccaccio. It establishes the source of *Decameron* 9.8 in *Inferno* 6 by way of its intertextual connection with *Esposizioni* 6, moving then to consider Boccaccio's interpretation of the events that Ciacco prophesizes for 1300–1302. I next contrast Boccaccio's account of the conflict between the Black and White Guelphs with what can be found in the *croniche* of Compagni, a White Guelph but more considered a voice of the *popolo*, and Villani, a Black Guelph.[5] Boccaccio's emphasis on lost *cortesia* is then interpreted through his preference for Corso Donati in light of the tale of Cisti *fornaio* and the Black Guelph leader Geri Spini in *Decameron* 6.2, a *novella* that shares the historical context of *Decameron* 9.8. How all of this relates to the tension between the figure of Filippo Argenti and Ciacco's prophecy of Dante's exile in *Esposizioni* 8 forms the conclusion as we read the ways in which Boccaccio personalizes history.

Florentine Politics and Economics from Dante to Boccaccio: The Older Elite Families and the *gente nuova*

Before Boccaccio sets himself to the task of composing the first pages of the *Decameron* between 1348 and 1353, and then, later on, before the start of the lectures of the *Esposizioni* in 1373, numerous events, natural and man-made, will mark Florence as a changed city from the times of Dante. Many of the pivotal events in the 1330s and 1340s – a flood,[6] a famine,[7] the plague of 1340 and of 1348 – were natural disasters from which Florence was variously able to recover, as recounted by Villani. Villani identifies the flood of 1333, from which Florence recovered with relative strength, as a divine message to the Florentines to cease their avaricious ways. Villani also viewed man-made disasters, such as the crisis and eventual bankruptcy of the Bardi and Peruzzi banking companies in 1345, as punishment of the vices of the Florentines by divine intervention, which the chronicler could interpret with the benefit of hindsight.[8] The fall of the Bardi company would affect Boccaccio directly, as his father Boccaccino was their associate in Naples until 1338, and Giovanni himself would help his father manage commercial transactions in the region of Portanuova (perhaps also working as an apprentice at the "banco" of the Frescobaldi or the Acciaiuoli).[9] Yet, as Branca indicates, Boccaccino's appointment with the Bardi family was more than a simple apprenticeship, for his duties were interpreted within the context of the Angevin court's dependence upon these Florentine bankers; Boccaccio's association with the Angevin court was made possible by his father's appointment as a counsellor and chamberlain by King Robert.[10] Thus his association with mercantile activity went hand in hand with the young Boccaccio's experience of the Angevin court, not to mention his own prosperity (such as he recounts in *Epistola* XII, "Vedevano me ... assai dilicatamente vivere"). The crisis of the banking companies during the late 1330s would be the preamble to the end of the golden age of Boccaccio's Neapolitan years, as both father and son would leave the Angevin city in 1340 or 1341, the former reportedly having come into financial hardship.[11]

The end of the association with the Bardi company thus could be seen to coincide with the end of the bourgeois and Angevin dream for Giovanni Boccaccio (though not for the Boccaccio family as a whole). Many of his relatives were members of that earlier wave of *gente nuova* whom Cacciaguida himself identifies in *Paradiso* 16. Vanni, the son of Boccaccio's grandfather, Chelo, left Certaldo to set up residence in San Frediano, Florence, in 1297, in order to begin, as Branca writes, "la grande avventura mercantile."[12] Vanni and his brother, Boccaccino, are believed to have practiced their trade in San Pier Maggiore in 1313–14 as well as in 1318. But their ambitions were not limited locally. Branca describes their commercial activity in Paris in 1313,[13] which speaks to the wider, European dimensions of their business. That the family chose to extend their practice outside of Florence aligns them with the more cosmopolitan scope of the burgeoning merchant class of the time. Yet it is an ambition that finds its end in the middle of the fourteenth century with the collapse of the banking companies. As Branca writes, "La famiglia di Boccaccio vive attivamente e pugnacemente questa grandiosa vicenda, ne goda la vitalità e lo splendore, ne soffre i drammi, ne sente con angoscia la crisi nel cuore del Trecento."[14]

The precipitating factors that caused the downfall of the banking companies are multiple, though Walter of Brienne, Duke of Athens, was credited popularly with its collapse, a sentiment that serves to explain Boccaccio's antipathy towards Walter and those responsible for bringing him in as *signore*, through the mouthpiece of Dante's spirit in the *De casibus* (Book IX).[15] Commercial activity in Florence was in a "slump," as Brucker writes;[16] the financing given by the Bardi and Peruzzi families to England placed Florentine bankers in poor stead with France. King Robert of Naples, who largely supported these Florentine companies, began to lose faith in the ability of companies like the Bardi and Peruzzi to pay back their depositors.[17] Once Naples demanded its deposits in return from the companies, bankruptcy was inevitable.[18] It was in this moment, in 1342, that Walter of Brienne was brought in as *signore*, a position that involved military and political leadership, by bankers (who thought he would bail out their failing companies), magnates (who hoped to regain control of the government), and members of the *popolo* – each group with different hopes that would ultimately be unsatisfied. Yet his austerity measures and policies, which included, among many things, ending the war against Pisa, a harsh tax policy (the revival of the *estimo*), and the abolishment of the Ordinances of Justice, did not reverse the downward trends in the Florentine economy; instead they alienated elite supporters while simultaneously reaching out to guildsmen.[19] The effect of his policies was to exacerbate existing social unrest. After his expulsion in July 1343, street fighting between the *popolo* and the magnates ensued, and many of the properties of several magnate families, including the Bardi, were burned to the ground.[20] Seen as the protagonist of this period of social and economic upheaval, Walter of Brienne acquired legendary status as a despotic figure, which he is depicted as not only in the passage from *De casibus* cited earlier but also in *Decameron* 2.7 and, as some scholars such as Ginsberg and Houston believe, in the guise of another Gualtieri, the tyrannical protagonist of 10.10, which I analyse at the end of chapter 4.[21]

Shortly after the rule of Walter of Brienne and the collapse of the banking companies, the plague of 1348, the Black Death, would drastically affect the political and social orders of Florence. Because of the high death toll, electoral lists became obsolete, which resulted in a different balance of guild and elite power within the government.[22] On the whole, the Black Death would reduce the elite families in size and power and allow for the "new" *gente nuova* to rise to power. These new *gente nuova* are those whose families, Brucker writes, were not represented in the Signoria before 1343.[23] These *parvenus*, involved in mercantile, industrial, and financial businesses, competed with the older mercantile patriciate, such as the Cerchi, and managed even to enter the Calimala guild, which was the "exclusive" guild, as Brucker writes, of the old mercantile patriciate, now listing the Cerchi, Bardi, Spini, and Peruzzi families among their number.[24] At the same time as this *gente nuova* became a new land-owning class in the mid-fourteenth century, there is also documentation that a large portion of the older mercantile class – specifically the magnate families such as the Bardi and Cerchi families – retreated from large business endeavours.[25] Brucker vividly describes the climate of social tension from both perspectives after 1348: "Once wealthy and prominent families had become impoverished, sustained by memories of past glory and by rancor against the *nouveaux riches*. Men whose ancestors had been leaders in communal politics were jostled from power, replaced by newcomers. Conversely, the *parvenus* were apprehensive, fearful of losing the social and economic advantages they had gained."[26] Brucker emphasizes that the the aristocracy's distaste for the *gente nuova* during the second half of the fourteenth century was very pronounced among writers from Franco Sacchetti to Donato Velluti, including Boccaccio in his letter to Pino de' Rossi,[27] as I will discuss below.

Boccaccio, I would argue, projects his own distaste for the *gente nuova* of his times upon the Cerchi family of Dante's age. The antagonism between the Cerchi and Donati families is the legendary conflict in the chronicles between a member family of the thirteenth-century *gente nuova* and an elite magnate family; the Donati were, in fact, consular aristocracy, one of the oldest elite families of the city. Boccaccio turns his attention to the clash between these two families because their conflict is prominent within the series of internecine strife that leads to Dante's exile; not only do the Cerchi remain the original family of the *gente nuova*, they are participants (though not the protagonists, necessarily) of the events that led to the Florentine poet's exile. He also turns to them in the *Decameron* and the *Esposizioni* in order to express his own distaste for the *gente nuova*, despite the fact that the Cerchi had long since ceased to be counted as *parvenus*. Dante's text would be useful to him in writing that moral invective against the vices of the *gente nuova*. Thus Boccaccio interprets their conflict from an era when the *gente nuova* were largely despised by aristocracy (and vice versa), at the same time as his own family history overlaps with the first generation of the *gente nuova* in Florence.

The Donati and Cerchi families were still prominent on the Florentine political stage, despite the fact that magnate power was diminished by the government of Walter of Brienne and the *gente nuova* in the communal government. These families were seen to belong to the opposing political factions of the White and Black Guelphs respectively (notwithstanding some political divisions within several magnate families, such as the "Cerchi Neri") and both were designated as magnate families by the Ordinances of Justice (1293) for their propensity to violence. Though we will examine below their characterizations and appearances in the chronicles for the events before and between 1300 and 1302 specifically, in the mid-fourteenth century the Donati house, with origins that hark back to Cacciaguida's Florence,[28] still retained its power as one of the most ancient patrician families in Florence. It became the target of the *popolani* in their assault on magnate families in 1343 after Walter of Brienne's *signoria*, but recovered following this assault.[29] Though the Corso Donati of Dante's times had passed away in 1308, during the social upheavals after the government of Walter of Brienne, a new Corso Donati – Corso di messer Amerigo di messer Corso Donati – was implicated in numerous plots with the Visconti family in Milan, attempts to foment a revolution in Florence, for which he was condemned to death in 1344.[30] Thus the Donati family maintained its reputation as the family of a traditional, ancient Florence, standing with other magnates against the popular government, as later generations were implicated in acts of conspiracy and revenge against non-elite and magnate classes – much in the spirit of Corso Donati, a figure admired by Boccaccio for his conservative spirit as well as for his symbolic function as a long-standing member of the elite, the bulwark of *cortesia*.

The Cerchi family experienced a fall from fortune and then a relative recovery over the course of the fourteenth century. As P.J. Jones notes, one branch of the family, the "Cerchi Neri" – the Cerchi members who aligned themselves with the Blacks – were exiled in 1302, while the "Cerchi Bianchi," the White Cerchi (or the Cerchi "del Garbo"), went through bankruptcy between 1310 and 1311. Their various business undertakings through this century, from their *fondaco* to their more minor sources of financial revenue such as their roles as *rentiers*, are documented by a few letters and accounts. From the *ricordanze* of Michele de' Cerchi in the 1360s we know that the family recovered somewhat from its collapse at the beginning of the century, and by 1363 they were declared *popolani*, a transition in status that was sought after by several magnates so as to enter into popular government.[31] Between 1372 and 1375, a member of the Cerchi family was proscribed, along with some members of the *gente nuova*, a Peruzzi and an Admiari. Thus, viewed in terms of this longer history, it is the Cerchi family that dispensed with its magnate status to become members of the *popolo*, not the Donati family. Boccaccio's sympathies for the Donati family can be interpreted as his affiliation with those patrician families that were the direct victims of the upheaval around Walter of Brienne's *signoria*, an upheaval in which the *popolo* were seen as active participants (one need only think of the destruction of the twenty-two Bardi residences by the *popolo*),[32] not to those individuals who would align themselves with the popular government.

That Boccaccio aligned himself with the standard bearers of *cortesia*, the old nobility to which the Donati family belonged, and not with the new elites or the *popolo*, who viewed themselves as the victims of the violence of the elite, can be detected in his letter to Pino de' Rossi, a member of the long-standing Florentine magnate family.[33] Pino de'

Rossi, whose property was seized by the government in 1345, played a decisive role in the conspiracies against a new popular government that took shape after the downfall of Walter of Brienne, something for which he and others such as Niccolò di Bartolo del Buono, a friend of Boccaccio, were sent into exile in 1360.[34] In the epistle widely known as the *Consolatoria*, Boccaccio offers comfort to his banished friend, reminding him of the stupidity and wickedness of those in power – the *gente nuova* of their Florence, who had risen to power within government:

> [...] [P]er la sciocchezza o malvagità di coloro che l'anno avuto a fare, le redini del governo date sono. Io non biasimerò l'essere a ciò venuti chi da Capalle, quale da Cilicciavole, e quale da Sugame, o da Vimiriccio, tolti dalla cazzuola o dall'aratro, e sublimati al nostro magistrato maggiore [...][35]

> [...] Because of the stupidity or wickedness of those involved, the reins of the government have been handed over. I will not blame those who have come into this situation from Capalle, Cilicciavole, Sugame, or Vimiriccio, taken from the trowel or the plough and risen to our greatest magistrate [...]

The avarice, pride, and envy of those from the towns of Capalle, Cilicciavole, Sugame, and Viminiccio, taken from their modest, rural occupations (the trowel and the plough) and now risen into political power, have dragged Florence into a state of poverty, Boccaccio continues. Avarice, pride, anger, and envy, vices also assigned to the *gente nuova* by Dante in *Inferno* 16 and *Paradiso* 16, are the vices that have continued to cause the downfall of Boccaccio's Florence. Like Dante, Boccaccio does not hesitate to point to the *popolo* as one of the agents of its moral deterioration and structural collapse, citing, as he does at the end of this letter, verses from the political invective at the end of *Purgatorio* 6: "ch'a mezzo novembre/non giugno quel che tu d'ottobre fili" (143–4). If we, like Najemy, interpret this as a condemnation of the zeal and imprudence of the popular governments (as in the earlier verses, 132 and 134, that could refer sarcastically to the integrity of the "popolo"),[36] then it is noteworthy that Boccaccio includes these verses at the end of his letter to Rossi. The Boccaccio that emerges from this letter, as well as from the texts analysed in these pages, is disdainful of the *gente nuova*, those that constituted the *popolo*, and not of the magnate elite families. His empathy for Pino de' Rossi will echo his compassionate treatment of Corso Donati, another magnate whom he perceived, arguably, as the victim of the rise of the *gente nuova*. The affections of the Certaldese author defied his family's suburban origins, finding their place instead in the oligarchy, where the idea of *cortesia*, replete with its code of violence and *vendette*, had been taken up by the magnates of Oltrarno, Por San Pietro, and other neighbourhoods of Florence, by all those who acted like feudal barons.

From Dantean Prophecy to Boccaccian Enactment: Florence from 1300 to 1302

Boccaccio recreates the climate of elite factionalism and violence from those times most explicitly described in *Decameron* 9.8, narrated by Lauretta, yet another tale of the intimidation, aggression, and greed of the elites. The Eighth Tale of the Ninth Day brings us back to the Florentine "houses of the dead" before the plague, as Filomena states at the beginning of the first *novella* in the Ninth Day: "a entrare nelle case de' morti" (9.1.4). So Lauretta guides the *brigata* in her storytelling back to Dante's Florence in 9.8, a city populated by characters from the *Commedia*, such as Ciacco and Filippo Argenti, and also by the protagonists of its dramatic political climate at the turn of the fourteenth century: Vieri de' Cerchi, head of the White Guelphs, and Corso Donati, the prominent leader of the Black Guelphs. Lauretta's tale of "beffa e controbeffa" displays Boccaccio as the historian who weaves the alternative *storie* of Dante's *storia*, bringing the real and fictive personages that inhabit Dante's world into direct and indirect conflict with each other and re-enacting scenes of quotidian life filled with petty revenge, which Boccaccio envisioned, one might even say nostalgically, in the Florence of those times.[37] Boccaccio's history of the political conflict between the Whites and the Blacks fulfils the realism of Dante's world while identifying the moral stakes – the opposing forces of avarice and *cortesia* – at play within the political battlefield of the city.

Lauretta begins her tale by introducing Ciacco, a gluttonous man whose financial means are not sufficient to sustain his vice but whose skills in jesting and banter make him a frequent dinner guest (sometimes invited, other times not) in the homes of wealthy Florentines. One day at the fish market Ciacco encounters Biondello – who like Ciacco lives on the good graces of the rich – buying two lampreys for Vieri de' Cerchi. When Ciacco asks for whom the lampreys are being purchased, Biondello deceives him by responding that he is buying them for Corso Donati, who is preparing to have guests over for dinner. Biondello asks whether or not Ciacco will be attending the meal at the Donati residence, and Ciacco, oblivious to Biondello's *beffa*, enthusiastically responds that he will. Ciacco presents himself at the Donati residence at the appropriate hour, where Corso Donati graciously welcomes this uninvited guest. Dinner, consisting of chickpeas, tuna, and fried fish from the Arno, is served, and Ciacco immediately realizes Biondello's deception – though the nature of the deception is not articulated by the narrator – and swears to avenge himself. Ciacco next encounters Biondello, who asks him how Corso Donati's lampreys tasted. He responds by saying that within eight days Biondello will know how to answer that question.

Ciacco realizes that Corso is not as wealthy as the Cerchi, despite his generosity – his *cortesia* – in hosting Ciacco unannounced. Insulted, Ciacco proceeds with his plan for revenge by enlisting the help of an intermediary, to whom he gives a glass flask and sends him to the Cavicciuli residence, where Filippo Argenti degli Adimari lives. He instructs the *mezzano* to present himself to Filippo Argenti on behalf of Biondello, who asks Filippo to "arubinargli" ("rubify") the flask with his excellent red wine, with which he could "sollazzar con suoi zanzeri" (9.8.14), an expression that means that Biondello would with this wine "amuse himself with his buddies." The intermediary duly incites the wrath of Filippo Argenti, who, confused by the obscure terms of the request, immediately believes himself to be the victim of one of Biondello's *beffe*. Filippo cannot contain his wrath, and attempts to harm the *mezzano*, but luckily the *mezzano*, forewarned by Ciacco, manages to escape.

To bring his scheme to fruition, Ciacco seeks out Biondello, and reports that Filippo Argenti is looking for him. As soon as Filippo Argenti, who is consumed with rage over the words of Biondello's supposed intermediary ("in se medesimo si rodea," 9.8.23), sees Biondello approaching, he punches him in the face.[38] He then reduces Biondello to a pulp with his iron-like fists, asking him what he meant by "arrubinatemi" and "zanzeri," and whether Biondello takes him for a fool ("paioti io fanciullo da dovere essere uccellato?" 9.8.25). Some bystanders finally succeed at tearing Filippo away, and Biondello, who understands that this is the work of Ciacco, goes home. After Biondello's bruises have somewhat faded, he ventures outside to find Ciacco, who asks Biondello if he enjoyed Filippo's wine. Biondello responds by saying that he found it as Ciacco found the lampreys of Corso Donati. Ciacco, triumphant, exclaims that if Biondello should ever try again to provide him with a meal in that fashion, he would likewise present him with more wine. Biondello, defeated and aware of having more desire than strength to hurt Ciacco, goes on his way and never tricks Ciacco again.

Reminiscent of his appropriation of Dante's Guiglielmo Borsiere as the protagonist of *Decameron* 1.8, Boccaccio incorporates two other figures from the *Inferno*, Ciacco and Filippo Argenti. In this way he brings to new fruition the imagination of the *Commedia*, elaborating on the few details provided by the poem and enacting the characteristics of their Dantean fate. Ciacco, a glutton, appears in *Inferno* 6 in the third circle among the gluttonous who lie in the mud created by the constant falling of dirty, cold rain, harassed by Cerberus. Filippo Argenti, a wrathful soul, appears in *Inferno* 8 in the muddy Styx. As in the case of Guiglielmo Borsiere, no biography can be recuperated for Ciacco, and it is not certain whether "Ciacco" was simply a nickname used by his fellow Florentines (which would mean "pig," as Guido da Pisa notes in his commentary) or his proper name. *Inferno* 6 seems to imply the former: Ciacco claims that his fellow Florentines called him "Ciacco" ("Voi cittadini mi chiamaste Ciacco," 52), not that such was his *name* (in other words, he does not say "Mi chiamai Ciacco").[39] From Dante's poem we also learn that Ciacco died after the pilgrim was born ("tu fosti, prima ch'io disfatto, fatto," 42), but nothing more.

Ciacco's political prophecy in *Inferno* 6 concerning the vicissitudes of the Blacks and the Whites, and of the poet himself, dominates the nature of his characterization in Dante's poem. His political discourse determines his poetic biography; Ciacco's nature is the prophecy of civic upheaval. The first Florentine to appear in the *Commedia*, Ciacco characterizes Florence as overflowing with envy: "La tua città, ch'è piena/d'invidia sì che già trabocca il sacco,/seco mi tenne in la vita serena" ("Your city, so fully of envy/that now the sack spills over,/held me in its confines in the sunlit life," 49–51). If his discourse determines his character in the *Commedia*, it will subsequently become the plot of *Decameron* 9.8: the squabble between Ciacco and Biondello performs the civic envy mentioned in *Inferno* 6.

In Dante's poem, Ciacco responds with a chronology of the events between 1300 and 1302 when posed with the pilgrim's tripartite question on the fate of Florence: how far the citizens of the divided city will go in their extreme actions, whether therein resides a citizen free of guilt, and what was the cause of this discord (60–3):

> E quelli a me: "Dopo lunga tencione
> verranno al sangue, e la parte selvaggia
> caccerà l'altra con molta offensione.
> Poi appresso convien che questa caggia
> infra tre soli, e che l'altra sormonti
> con la forza di tal che testé piaggia.
> Alte terrà lungo tempo le fronti,
> tenendo l'altra sotto gravi pesi,
> come che di ciò pianga o che n'aonti.
> Giusti son due, e non vi sono intesi;
> superbia, invidia e avarizia sono
> le tre faville c'hanno i cuori accesi." (64–75)

(And he to me: "After long feuding/they shall come to blood. The rustic faction,/having done great harm, shall drive the others out./But it in turn must fall to them,/within three years, by power of him/who now just bides his time./These in their arrogance will long subject/the other faction to their heavy yoke,/despite its weeping and its shame./Two men are just and are not heeded there./Pride, envy and avarice are the sparks/that have set the hearts of all on fire.")

"Foreseeing" events that had already occurred by the time of the composition of the *Inferno*, Ciacco claims that the two parties will come to blows. Then the "parte selvaggia," the White Guelphs (called "selvaggia" because they came from the "contado"), will expel the Blacks. The "parte selvaggia" must fall within three years, Ciacco continues. The other party, the Blacks, would then rise with the power, most likely, of Pope Boniface VIII. The Black Guelphs, Ciacco says, will keep power in the city for a long time, oppressing the Whites despite their cries and protests. There are only two just men there, and they are not heeded by the city, Ciacco states ambiguously. In response to the pilgrim's third question, Ciacco unambiguously answers that the three causes of the discord in Florence are pride, envy, and avarice (74–5), an answer that is repeated by Brunetto Latini in *Inferno* 15.68 ("gent'è avara, invidiosa e superba").

Before Boccaccio interpreted this text within the *Decameron* and then the *Esposizioni*, early commentators, such as Guido da Pisa and the Ottimo, explicated these verses in very similar terms.[40] Generally speaking, they did not venture to provide precise historical analogues to the events prophesied by Ciacco, nor did they discuss the leading figures of the two Guelph parties. After the Selmiano commentary, it is Boccaccio who brings Ciacco to narrative life, first within the text of *Decameron* 9.8, as discussed here, and then in *Esposizioni* 6, where he also defines the political events referenced by *Inferno* 6. As in the case of the analogous representations of Guiglielmo Borsiere in *Decameron* 1.8 and *Esposizioni* 16, the content of this description is repeated in a very similar fashion:[41]

> Fu costui uomo non del tutto di corte; ma per ciò che poco avea da spendere ed erasi, come egli stesso dice, dato del tutto al vizio della gola, era morditore e le sue usanze erano sempre co' gentili uomini e ricchi, e massimamente con quelli che splendidamente e dilicatamente mangiavano e beveano, da' quali se chiamato era a mangiare, v'andava, e similmente, se invitato non era, esso medesimo s'invitava; ed era per questo vizio notissimo uomo a tutti i Fiorentini. Senza che, fuor di questo, egli era costumato uomo, secondo la sua condizione, ed eloquente e affabile e di buon sentimento; per le quali cose era assai volentieri da qualunque gentile uomo ricevuto. (6.25, esp. litt.)

> This Ciacco was not exactly a habitué of the courts of the great families; rather, because he had very little to spend and was, as he himself says, completely given over to the vice of gluttony, he performed the role of a jokester and in this way regularly passed his time in the company of noblemen and the rich, especially with those who ate and drank sumptuously and extravagantly. When he was summoned by noblemen to supper, he gladly obliged. Similarly, when they did not invite him, he invited himself and became, on account of this vice, very well known among all the Florentines. In addition, he was acutely well-mannered (considering his station), eloquent, affable, and respectable, all characteristics that made him quite welcome in the homes of fine gentlemen. (Papio, 307)

Ciacco was a "uomo non del tutto di corte" ("not exactly a habitué of the courts") but his jesting capacities made him a welcome guest (again, invited or not) in the homes of the rich, and especially those who ate and drank well. Boccaccio testifies to Ciacco's good manners and other positive traits that the author also notes in 9.8 ("essendo per altro assai costumato e tutto pieno di belli e di piacevoli motti"; "he was also a highly cultivated person, never at a loss for something clever and amusing to say," McWilliam, 686).

Boccaccio's gloss of "Voi cittadini mi chiamaste Ciacco" in the *Esposizioni* exactly recalls the description of Ciacco in 9.8. Lacking information about Ciacco, most commentators of the *Commedia* refer to Boccaccio's characterization of the Florentine in 9.8 as the earliest existing biographical material; even before the *Esposizioni*, Ciacco's "biography" could be found in the *Decameron*. Lauretta's presentation of Ciacco in 9.8 provides a fleshed-out portrait, so to speak, of the glutton from Dante's text:

> E per ciò dico che essendo in Firenze *uno da tutti chiamato Ciacco*, uomo ghiottissimo quanto alcuno altro fosse giammai, e non potendo la sua possibilità sostener le spese che la sua ghiottornia richiedea, essendo per altro assai costumato e tutto pieno di belli e di piacevoli motti, si diede a essere *non del tutto uom di corte, ma morditore* e a usare con coloro che ricchi erano e di mangiar delle buone cose si dilettavano; e con questi a desinare e a cena, ancor che chiamato non fosse ogni volta, andava assai sovente. (9.8.4, emphasis added)

> I would have you know, then, that in Florence there was once a man known to everyone as Ciacco, who was the greatest glutton that ever lived. Since his purse was unequal to the demands made upon it by his gluttony, and since he was also a highly cultivated person, never at a loss for something clever and amusing to say, he built a reputation for himself, not exactly as a jester but rather as a wit, and took to mixing with wealthy people possessing a taste for good food, with whom he regularly supped and breakfasted even when not invited. (McWilliam, 685–6)

Consistent with *Inferno* 6, Lauretta gives the name of the protagonist as if it were a nickname ("uno da tutti chiamato Ciacco"). The most gluttonous man ever to have lived, Ciacco's financial means were not sufficient to pay for all the food he wished to consume. Ciacco was not, like Guiglielmo Borsiere, "un valente uomo del corte," but more of a jester: "non del tutto uom di corte, ma morditore." Because of this trait, Ciacco was able to get by as a parasite of the rich, even visiting their homes uninvited (as in the case of 9.8) and partaking of their meals.[42]

The importance of Ciacco over the course of Boccaccio's engagement with *Inferno* 6 is apparent from his appearance in these texts. From serving as the agent of political prophecy to a satirical enactment of the acts foreseen in *Inferno* 6, Ciacco's transformation from Dante to Boccaccio speaks to his utility for the latter in constructing a historical discourse that would critique partisan politics as a matter of personal conflict and the absence of *cortesia*. *Decameron* 9.8, furthermore, shows that certain noble families that carried the feudal traditions of *cortesia*, such as the Donati, did not have the financial means to support the ways of *cortesia* (as we saw in the case of Betto Brunelleschi in *Dec.* 6.9). In addition to a manifestation of Boccaccio's lack of sympathy for the rich families, such as the Cerchi, of the *gente nuova*, it also could demonstrate his own sympathy with those who suffered from poverty, which he laments in his letters (see chapter 1), and which he discusses in his letter to Pino de' Rossi. It is noteworthy, in this regard, that the only character portrayed in an arguably benevolent light within this story is Corso Donati; not only Dante, but also Villani and Compagni, criticize the historical Corso Donati for his conspiracies and violence. Boccaccio's preference for this leader of the Black Guelphs reveals the author's vision of history in personal and moral, rather than institutional, terms – as the battle between avarice and *cortesia*.[43]

Figuring Florentine Conflict: Corso Donati (*cortesia*) versus Vieri de' Cerchi (*avarizia*)

Ciacco's prophecy in *Inferno* 6 of the events to occur in Florence between 1300 and 1302 reads like a condensed history of the rise to and fall from power of both the Whites and the Blacks that concludes with a general condemnation of the vices that have befallen Florence: pride, envy, and avarice. Boccaccio's realism enacts these events in the *Decameron* while exposing the personal, petty nature of these political events; he incarnates the vices that Ciacco enumerates. This style suits the narrative of the *Decameron* in its spirit as a text in the tradition of the *fabliaux* and moral *exempla*.[44] The *Esposizioni*, however, as a gloss, explicate the allegorical significance of Ciacco's political history, which does not name any of the major political protagonists whose actions are recorded by Villani or Compagni. In fact, that is precisely what Boccaccio does: he creates a political history for these events that depends upon the personal conflict between what he views as the two leaders of the opposing parties: Vieri de' Cerchi and Corso Donati. Thus, in the same way that Boccaccio interprets these events in *Decameron* 9.8, he enacts a battle of vices between these two figures, putting faces and names to the parties to which they were associated.

The storyteller relishes the opportunity in the "esposizione litterale" to formulate characterizations of the Cerchi and Donati families that cannot be found in *Inferno* 6. According to the *Esposizioni*, Florence had "many envies," but the most significant and influential one was the envy felt by the Donati family towards the Cerchi. Compared to the relative silence with which the other early commentators pass over the "invidia" of *Inferno* 6.50, Boccaccio's gloss of that same verse comprises a *novella* in itself. Not only did Florence overflow with envy – many different "envies," manifested in different situations ("per ciò che tra l'altre invidie, che in Firenze erano") – but, as Boccaccio implies, the most harmful envy was harboured by the impoverished Donati aristocrats when confronted with the rich Cerchi merchants ("la famiglia de' Cerchi, li quali in quei tempi erano mercatanti grandissimi"; the Cerchi family, who in those times were great merchants). The Donati, Boccaccio explains, were constantly exposed to the outward signs of Cerchi wealth ("tutti ricchi e morbidi e vezosi"; "rich and lax and sophisticated," Papio, 307) and power ("nel reggimento della città e nello stato potentissimi"; "extremely powerful in the government of the city and in social circles," Papio, 307). Envious of both the money and power in civic affairs that the Cerchi possessed, the Donati finally could no longer contain their envy. Boccaccio recounts these disastrous results in an almost empathetic tone – as if the poverty of the Donati family excused their jealousy ("non potendola dentro più tenere, non molto poi con dolorosi effetti la versaron fuori"; "unable to contain it any longer, they soon spilled it all out to woeful effect," Papio, 307).

The empathy that Boccaccio communicates in this passage from *Esposizioni* 6 can also be detected in the portrait of Corso Donati's poverty in *Decameron* 9.8. When a deceived Ciacco arrives at the Donati home, unannounced, for what he anticipates to be a luxurious meal of lampreys, Corso Donati, despite the poverty of the meal he has to offer, welcomes him ("Tu sie 'l ben venuto: e per ciò che egli è tempo, andianne," 9.8.10; "'You are most welcome,' said Messer Corso. 'And since the meal is now ready, let us go and eat,'" McWilliam, 686). On the other hand, as the Cerchi never speak in this *novella*, it could be said that Biondello, as their lackey, represents the Cerchi family and thus an implied lack of generosity and willingness to be socially integrated. Boccaccio addresses the lack of social grace of the Cerchi family in *Esposizioni* 6, in his gloss of "la parte selvaggia" (6.34, esp. litt). Here Boccaccio interprets "selvaggia" not as an indication of their country origins, as do other early commentators, but as a description of the social roughness of the Cerchi. Their pride and unfamiliarity with the ways of social life in the city, which they moreover did not care about,

Boccaccio argues ("né gli careggiavano"; "they cared little for urban niceties," Papio, 309), were all the alleged result of their wealth and power. The wealth and power of the Cerchi family – indeed, the result of their status as prominent merchants – are at the origins of the conflict between the Cerchi and the Donati; despite being poor, the latter family embodied the ways of *cortesia*.

Boccaccio elaborates on this compassionate portrait of "povero Corso Donati" when he later addresses the second appearance of "invidia" in Ciacco's concluding verses ("superbia, invidia e avarizia sono/le tre faville c'hanno i cuori accesi"). Again, without any explicit indication in Dante's poem that the "invidia" Ciacco refers to belongs to Corso Donati, Boccaccio identifies this envy as Corso's own. Whereas Boccaccio first attributes the "invidia" of *Inferno* 6.50 to the entire Donati clan, here he focuses on Corso and his envy (*Esp.* 6.47–8, esp. litt.). Corso Donati's envy, Boccaccio argues, is an understandable reaction to witnessing the difference between his financial state and that of Vieri de' Cerchi ("come suole avvenire, che sempre alle cose, le quali più felici sono stimate, è portata invidia"; "messer Corso was envious of him, as often happens, for envy is always inspired by those things that are deemed to be better in others," Papio, 311). Vieri's higher position in state affairs exacerbated Corso's "invidia," which commonly results for all those who find themselves in that condition ("al quale generalmente tutti color, che in istato non si vedevano, portavano invidia;" "the preeminence of his station was also a source of envy, as rank is generally coveted by all those who are of lower status," Papio, 311). This envy, Boccaccio concludes, naturally led to "discordia," for which it seems that Boccaccio did not hold Corso Donati morally responsible.[45]

This compassionate representation of Corso Donati stands in sharp contrast to what we find in Dante's own poem as well as in the chronicles of Dino Compagni and Giovanni Villani, which is notable given the different political leanings of these authors, the former considered by many to be the voice of the *popolo*, the latter a merchant and a Guelph.[46] In *Purgatorio* 24 (not coincidentally, perhaps, the terrace of the gluttonous), Forese Donati identifies his brother Corso as the source of Florence's ruin, the place, as the pilgrim states, that loses its virtue day by day (80–1):

"Or va," diss' el; "che quei che più n'ha colpa,
vegg'io a coda d'una bestia tratto
inver' la valle ove mai non si scolpa.

> La bestia ad ogne passo va più ratto,
>   crescendo sempre, fin ch'ella il percuote,
>   e lascia il corpo vilmente disfatto." (*Purg.* 24.82–7)

("How true," he said, "and I see him who bears/the greatest blame dragged behind a beast/toward the valley where there is no absolution./ The beast goes faster with each step,/and faster, until it hurls him to the ground/and leaves his body horribly disfigured.")

Corso, Forese states, is the individual responsible for Florence's bleak future. Moreover, Forese prophesies, the city itself is destined for ruin, so he foretells that Corso will be dragged to his death by a horse (and possibly to hell or Florence – "la valle ove mai non si scolpa"). Villani, in his *Nuova cronica*, recounts that Corso had fallen from a horse while being driven back into Florence by Catalan soldiers (8.96). Regardless of its historical veracity, what is striking about this passage from *Purgatorio* 24 is that Dante, through Corso's brother Forese, squarely blames Corso for Florence's ruin without the pity or compassion that Boccaccio, in his commentary to Dante's poem, conveys. Though Corso is passively being dragged to his death (and thus is presented as the victim of a cruel fate, much in the way that Boccaccio interprets Corso's jealousy as being beyond his control), Dante looks to Corso's actions in life as meriting a cruel fate. This is reiterated when his sister, Piccarda, recalls her violent abduction at Corso's hands from the "dolce chiostra" (*Par.* 3.107) of Santa Chiara in Monticelli, with the purpose of marrying her to Rossellino della Tosa for political gain. Corso here is remembered for being "more disposed towards evil than towards good" ("a mal più ch'a bene usi," *Par.* 3.106).

Chronicler and politician Compagni, whose advocacy for the *popolo* would have naturally biased him against Corso Donati, manages however to convey the varied aspects of Corso Donati's personality and reputation, providing a composite of Corso that neither exclusively condemns this leader of the Black Guelphs, as Dante does, nor empathizes with his circumstances, as Boccaccio does. Compagni seems to have regarded Corso with a mixture of admiration and contempt as a ruthless yet brave knight. In his account of the 1289 battle at Campaldino (in which Dante also participated), he notes Corso Donati's readiness for warfare (as well as that of Vieri de' Cerchi) in leading the Pistoiese squadron against the Aretines in contrast to the cowardliness of other individuals such as Guido Novello, who left before the end of the battle

(1.10). Later in the *Cronica*, in the midst of the pages that describe the upheaval that Charles of Valois brought to the city, Compagni indulges in a digression on the cruel yet charming Corso, who had recently returned from exile:

> Uno cavaliere della somiglianza di Catellina romano, ma più crudele di lui, gentile di sangue, bello del corpo, piacevole parlatore, addorno di belli costumi, sottile d'ingegno, con l'animo sempre intento a malfare, col quale molti masnadieri si raunavano e gran seguito avea, molte arsioni e molte ruberie fece fare, e gran dannaggio a' Cerchi e a' loro amici; molto avere guadagnò, e in grande alteza salì. Costui fu messer Corso Donato che per sua superbia fu chiamato il Barone; che quando passava per la terra molti gridavano, "Viva il Barone"; e parea la terra sua. La vanagloria il guidava, e molti servigi facea. (2.20)

> A knight in the mold of Catiline the Roman, but more cruel; noble of blood, handsome of body, a charming speaker, adorned with good breeding, subtle of intellect, with his mind always set on evil-doing; one who gathered many armed men and kept a great entourage, who ordered many arsons and robberies and did great damage to the Cerchi and their friends, who gained many possessions and rose to great heights: such was messer Corso Donati, who because of his pride was called the Baron. When he passed through the city many cried "long live the Baron," and the city seemed to belong to him. He was led by vanity, and bestowed many favours. (Bornstein, 48–9)

Compagni mixes the positive and negative attributes of Corso, who is described as being handsome, noble, shrewd, and a good speaker but always bent on evil-doing, having committed arson and theft, and moreover damaged the Cerchi and their friends. The chronicler does not hide his ambivalence, yet seems to admire the reputation that proud Corso enjoyed as a baron of Florence. The comparison with Catiline, a Roman aristocrat from one of the oldest patrician families, leader of the Fiesolan rebellion and enemy of the most notable *novus homines*, Cicero, is provocative for several reasons.[47] Catiline's efforts to thwart Rome by rallying the people of Fiesole, and his legacy as an enemy not only of Rome but of Florence as well, recall Corso Donati's own attempt in 1308 to attack the Palazzo dei Signori (*Cronica* 3.9). Compagni's portrait, both here and in the passage ahead, borrows conceptually as well as stylistically from Sallust's description of Catiline's arrogance and violence.[48] But Boccaccio himself, like Dante,[49] speaks of Catiline as a figure of danger to Rome (*Esp.* 4.329, esp. litt.), having conspired against its civic health (*Esp.* 15.41). If Compagni is influenced by Sallust's "ritratto paradossale" of Catiline in the *Bellum Catalinae*,[50] Boccaccio would thus not have been influenced in the same way, holding Catiline in contempt in the *Esposizioni*. For Boccaccio, Corso Donati was not a threat to the Florentine Republic.

Compagni conveys a similar ambivalence about Corso Donati when he tells of the knight's death in 1308. The Black Guelphs, at that time, enjoyed control over Florence but were divided among themselves, with certain members of their party vying for control, such as Rosso della Tosa, Pazzino de' Pazzi, Betto Brunelleschi, and Geri Spini. Compagni, in fact, believed that Betto Brunelleschi was specifically responsible for Corso's death (3.39). According to Compagni, Corso did not die while being dragged by a horse, as Forese prophesies in *Purgatorio* 24, but after being caught by Catalan soldiers (believed to be sent at the behest of Rosso della Tosa, Pazzino de' Pazzi, and Betto Brunelleschi) and defending himself verbally ("si difendeva con belle parole, sì come savio cavaliere," 3.21). He was struck by one of the soldiers in the throat and in the side, and was knocked to the ground. He was then carried by monks to the abbey of San Salvi, where he later died. Though Compagni's account of Corso's death conveys its brutality, it is not the humiliating death we find in *Purgatorio* 24. Compagni seems to have wanted to attribute integrity to Corso and viewed him as being larger than life. The chronicler considered Corso's death to have been reprehensible ("la morte reprensibile"), as shown in Compagni's final words dedicated to the dead leader:

> [M]olto si parlò della sua mala morte in varii modi, secondo l'amicizia e inimicizia: ma parlando il vero, la sua vita fu pericolosa, e la morte reprensibile. Fu cavaliere di grande animo e nome, gentile di sangue e di costumi, di corpo bellissimo fino alla sua vecchiezza, di bella forma con dilicate fatteze, di pelo bianco; piacevole, savio e ornato parlatore, e a gran cose sempre attendea; pratico e dimestico di gran signori e di nobili uomini, e di grande amistà, e famoso per tutta Italia. Nimico fu de' popoli e de' popolani, amato da' masnadieri, pieno di maliziosi pensieri, reo e astuto. (3.21)
>
> Messer Corso's bad death was talked about in various ways, according to whether the speaker was his friend or enemy. But to tell the truth, he lived dangerously and died reprehensibly. He was a knight of great spirit and

renown, noble in blood and behavior, and very handsome in appearance even in his old age, of fine form with delicate features and white skin. He was a charming, wise, and elegant speaker, and always undertook great things. He was accustomed to dealing familiarly with great lords and noble men, and had many friends, and was famous throughout all Italy. He was the enemy of the *popolo* and of *popolani*, and was loved by his soldiers; he was full of malicious thoughts, cruel and astute. (Bornstein, 84)

Whereas Boccaccio expresses empathy with Corso's poverty – upon which Compagni does not focus with the same intensity – Compagni, throughout the *Cronica*, manages to balance the *grandeur* of this figure with the poor reputation of his actions.

Though Compagni might be expected to hold a bias against Corso Donati, since he witnessed the actions that endangered the welfare of his party, the White Guelphs, he offers a relatively balanced portrait of Corso, arguably due to the influence of Sallust. Boccaccio, on the other hand, is not tempered in his description of Corso and his family. This can be seen in a comparison of Boccaccio's text in *Esposizioni* 6 with Compagni's chronicle. Even Villani,[51] a merchant who aligned himself with the Blacks when the Guelph party divided into two factions, and whose chronicle is claimed by Boccaccio in *Esposizioni* 6 to be a source of historical information,[52] does not hesitate to expose Corso Donati's weaknesses. After recounting Corso's death at the hands of Catalan soliders, Villani reflects on the legacy he left behind:

Questo messer Corso Donati fu de' più savi, e valente cavaliere, e il più bello parlatore, e il meglio pratico, e di maggiore nominanza, e di grande ardire e imprese ch'al suo tempo fosse in Italia, e bello cavaliere di sua persona e grazioso, ma molto fu mondano, e di suo tempo fatte in Firenze molte congiurazioni e scandali per avere stato e signoria. (3.182)

This Messer Corso Donati was among the most sage, and was a valiant cavalier, and the finest speaker, and most skilled, and of the greatest renown and of the greatest courage and enterprise of any one of his time in Italy, and a handsome and gracious cavalier in his person; but he was very worldly, and in his time caused many conspiracies and scandals in Florence to gain state and lordship. (Selfe, 385)

Villani, like Compagni, notes Corso's prowess, eloquence, and passion as well as his impressive physical presence, but he also acknowledges

Corso's malice and the scandals he instigated in Florence in order to gain power. Villani's description of Corso's shortcomings as an individual and a political figure makes Boccaccio's overly compassionate characterization of Corso seem even more radical.

Boccaccio's bias towards Corso Donati can be detected throughout the section of *Esposizioni* 6 that glosses Ciacco's discussion of Florence, and is especially apparent when Boccaccio's description is compared with Villani's chronicle, which was a definite source for the composition of the *Esposizioni*.[53] In the thirty-ninth chapter of the eighth book of his *Nuova cronica*, entitled "Come la città di Firenze si partì e si sconciò per le dette parti bianca e nera," Villani first describes the golden age of Florence and then observes the series of evils that caused its division:

> Nel detto tempo essendo la nostra città di Firenze nel maggiore stato e più felice, che mai fosse stata dappoi ch'ella fu redificata, o prima, sì di grandezza e potenza, e sì di numero di genti [...] e di nobiltà di nuova cavalleria e di franco popolo e di ricchezze grandi, signoreggiando quasi tutta Toscana; il peccato della *ingratitudine*, col sussidio del nimico dell'umana generazione, *della detta grassezza fece partorire superbia e corruzione*, per la quale furono finite le feste e l'allegrezze de' Fiorentini, che infino a que' tempi stavano in molte delizie, e morbidezze, e tranquillo, e sempre in conviti, e ogni anno quasi per tutta la città per lo calen di Maggio, si faceano le brigate e le compagnie d'uomini e di donne, di sollazzi e balli. (8.39, emphasis added)

> In the said time, our city of Florence was in the greatest and happiest state which had ever been since it was rebuilt, or before, alike in greatness and power and in number of people [...] and she was great in nobility of good knights, and in free populace, and in riches, ruling over the greater part of Tuscany; whereupon the sin of ingratitude, with the instigation of the enemy of the human race, brought forth from the said prosperity pride and corruption, which put an end to the feasts and joyaunce of the Florentines. For hitherto they had been living in many delights and dainties, and in tranquillity and with continual banquets; and every year throughout almost all the city on the first day of May, there were bands and companies of men and of women, with sports and dances. (Selfe, 324)

As Boccaccio describes a jovial, pre-lapsarian Florence from both *Decameron* 6.9 and *Esposizioni* 16 (as examined in the preceding chapter), Villani attributes the root of the city's discord to ingratitude and the workings of the devil, the enemy of humanity ("nimico dell'umana generazione"). These, together with pride and corruption ("superbia e corruzione"), put an end to the good old times of Florence ("furono finite le feste e l'allegrezze de' Fiorentini").

In the city's changed social climate, Villani points specifically to "invidie" as the cause of Florence's factions:

> Avvenne che per *le invidie* si cominciarono tra' cittadini le sette; e una principale e maggiore s'incominciò nel sesto dello scandalo di porte san Piero, tra quegli della casa de' Cerchi e quegli de' Donati, l'una parte per *invidia*, e l'altra per *salvatica ingratitudine*. (8.39, emphasis added)

> But now it came to pass that through envy there arose factions among the citizens; and one of the chief and greatest began in the sesto of offence, to wit of Porte San Piero, between the house of the Cerchi, and the Donati; on the one side through envy, and on the other through rude ungraciousness. (Selfe, 324)

Villani blames both "invidia" and "salvatica ingratitudine" for the conflict between the Cerchi and the Donati, and views both families as being at fault. Boccaccio (in the description of Corso Donati in *Esposizioni* 6) claims that the most harmful form of "invidia" was the one harboured by the Donati towards the Cerchi family (6.23–4, esp. litt.), thus identifying one principal cause for the city's evils: the Donati jealousy of Cerchi wealth. As explained earlier, in this passage Boccaccio shows a degree of compassion when explaining the origin of Corso Donati's "invidia" as the state of being constantly exposed to signs of Cerchi wealth.

Villani, however, presents the strengths and faults of both the Cerchi and Donati families:

> Della casa de' Cerchi era capo messer Vieri de' Cerchi, e egli e quegli di sua casa erano di grande affare, e possenti, e di grandi parentadi, e ricchissimi mercatanti, che la loro compagnia era delle maggiori del mondo; uomini erano morbidi e innocenti, salvatichi e ingrati, siccome genti venuti di piccolo tempo in grande stato e podere. Della casa de' Donati era capo messer Corso Donati, e egli e quegli di sua casa erano gentili uomini e guerrieri, e di non soperchia ricchezza, ma per motto erano chiamati *Malefami*. Vicini erano in Firenze e in contado, e per la conversazione della loro invidia colla bizzarra salvatichezza, nacque il superbio isdegno tra loro […] (8.39)

> The head of the family of the Cerchi was one Messer Vieri dei Cerchi, and he and those of his house were of great affairs, and powerful, and with great kinsfolk, and were very rich merchants, so that their company was among the largest in the world; these were luxurious, inoffensive, uncultured and ungracious, like folk come in a short time to great estate and power. The head of the family of the Donati was Messer Corso Donati, and he and those of his house were gentlemen and warriors, and of no superabundant riches, but were called by a gibe the Malefami. Neighbours they were in Florence and in the country, and while the one set was envious the other stood on their boorish dignity, so that there arose from the clash a fierce scorn between them [...] (Selfe, 324)

Villani mentions the wealth and power of the Cerchi family, but also their social roughness and ingratitude ("salvatichi e ingrati"), characteristics, the chronicler claims, of people who have recently come into a higher social status. The Donati, on the other hand, were noble men and warriors who did not have much wealth, but were also known for their bad reputation ("Malefami" could perhaps signify "male fama"). These two families were neighbours both in the city and in the countryside, and the coupling ("la conversazione") of Donati jealousy with Cerchi roughness resulted in hatred between the two families.

The equal attention Villani pays to the strengths and flaws of both the Donati and the Cerchi stands in sharp contrast to Boccaccio's obsession with the wealth and lack of social grace of the Cerchi family and his belief that the Black Guelphs suffered more than the Whites or were passive participants in the conflicts that took place during 1300–1301. Boccaccio's gloss of Ciacco's words from *Inferno* 6, "e la parte selvaggia/caccerà l'altra con molta offensione" (65–6), is one example. Instead of giving the reasons that certain Black Guelphs had to pay high fines, Boccaccio portrays them as victims of evil-doing and oppression exerted by the Blacks ("male e oppressioni ricevute da' Neri," 6.36, esp. litt.; "the oppression and misdeeds endured by the Blacks," Papio, 309). He views them as victims because of their poverty in relation to the Whites ("perché poveri erano per rispetto de' Bianchi," 6.36, esp. litt.; "given that they had fewer resources with which to pay them, since they were not as wealthy," Papio, 309). Boccaccio omits information here that would point to the violent actions of both the Blacks and the Whites in order to give the impression that the Blacks never instigated such conflicts.

It is surprising that such information can instead be found in Villani, whose text Boccaccio used in his writing of the *Esposizioni*. Villani describes the readiness of both Whites and Blacks to fight at the funeral for a woman in the piazza of the Frescobaldi, an event that led to both parties being penalized by the city:

> Avvenne, che del mese di Dicembre seguente, andando messer Corso Donati e suoi seguaci, e que' della casa de' Cerchi e loro seguaci armati a una morta di casa i Frescobaldi, sguardandosi insieme *l'una parte e l'altra*, si vollono assalire, onde tutta la gente ch'era alla morta si levarono a romore [...] messer Gentile de' Cerchi [and other Whites] corsono a san Piero maggiore, ov'era messer Corso co' suoi consorti e raunata, da' quali furono riparati, e rincacciati e fediti con onta e vergogna de' Cerchi e de' loro seguaci; *e di ciò furono condannati l'una parte e l'altra dal comune*. (8.41, emphasis added)

> It came to pass in the month of December following that Messer Corso Donati went with his followers, and they of the house of the Cerchi with their followers, to the burial of a lady of the house of Frescobaldi; and when the two parties came face to face, they were minded to assault one another, wherefore all the folk which were at the burial rose in uproar [...] Messer Gentile dei Cerchi [and other Whites] went in haste to Porte San Piero to the house of the Donati, and not finding them at Porte San Piero, hastened to San Piero Maggiore, where was Messer Corso with his companions and assembly, and by them they were stoutly resisted and driven back and wounded, to the shame and dishonour of the Cerchi and of their followers; and for this they were condemned, both the one party and the other, by the commonwealth. (Selfe, 329)

Following a separate event in the countryside at Nepozzano and Pugliano, where a clash between the Donati and Cerchi took place, both parties suffered penalties, but, Villani notes, the Donati suffered more because they were not able to pay their fines and consequently were placed in prison:

> per la qual cosa l'una parte e l'altra furono accusati e condannati della raunata e assalti; *e quegli di casa i Donati la maggior parte per non potere pagare andarono dinanzi*, e furono messi in pregione. (8.41, emphasis added)

> for the which cause both one side and the other were accused and condemned for the assemblage and assaults; and the greater part of those of the house of the Donati, not being able to pay their fine, chose imprisonment, and were put under confinement. (Selfe, 329)

Though Villani, like Boccaccio, does state that the Donati suffered more as a result of these fines, he offers this opinion in a longer account of the violent deeds of both parties, and thus in a much more balanced context than Boccaccio does in *Esposizioni* 6.

Boccaccio's assertion of the relative innocence of the Blacks in the dramatic events that occurred in Florence around the turn of the fourteenth century is most obvious in his account of papal intervention in the city's divisions. When he speaks of the visit of Cardinal Matteo d'Acquasparta to Florence on the behest of Pope Boniface VIII in June 1300, he only claims that the White Guelphs did not obey the cardinal's efforts to restore peace to the city ("poichè per messer Matteo d'Acquasparta, cardinale e legato di papa, non s'era potuta raconciare, non volendo i Bianchi ubidire al detto legato," *Esp.* 6.38; "especially given that messer Matteo d'Acquasparta, cardinal and papal legate, had previously been unable to do so, since the Whites refused to obey him," Papio, 309). Boccaccio does not acknowledge that the cardinal was sent to Florence at the request of the Black Guelphs to regain their power in the city, nor that the pope himself would consequently benefit from the rise to power of the Blacks.[54] Villani, in his more lengthy account of the events in Florence from 1300 to 1301, describes these hidden motives of the Blacks in inviting the cardinal to Florence ("per ricoverare loro stato si mandarano ambasciadori a corte a papa Bonifazio a pregarlo che per bene della cittade e di parte di Chiesa vi mettesse consiglio," *Nuova cronica* 8.40; "and moreover those which held with the Black party, to recover their estate, sent ambassadors to the court to Pope Boniface to pray him, for the good of the city and for the party of the Church, to take some action," Selfe, 328). Villani also justifies the Whites' refusal to obey the cardinal's recommendations because of their suspicions of the pope ("Quegli della parte bianca che guidavano la signoria della terra, per tema di non perdere loro stato, e d'essere ingannati dal papa e dal legato per la detta riformazione, presono il peggiore consiglio e non vollono ubbidire," 8.40; "They of the White party which were at the head of the government of the city, through fear of losing their estate, and of being deceived by the Pope and the legate by means of the said reformation, took the worse counsel, and would not yield obedience; for the which thing the said legate was offended, and returned to court, and left the city of Florence excommunicate and under interdict," Selfe, 328). In Villani, the reaction of the Whites to Cardinal Acquasparta is understandable given the circumstances of the Blacks' and the pope's ulterior motives; in Boccaccio's *Esposizioni* 6, the reaction of the Whites does not seem justifiable but instead appears to be fueled by pride and the "salvatichezza" of the Cerchi family.

Boccaccio identifies the pride of Vieri de' Cerchi as the reason why peace could not be restored to Florence by Pope Boniface. He asserts that Charles of Valois, brother of the king of France, was sent to Florence as a peacemaker ("sotto nome di paciaro") by the pope, and that the Whites fled the city rather than heed Charles's order to present themselves to him. Villani, on the other hand, names two motives behind Charles's visit to Florence that clash with his alleged mission as peacemaker (8.43): he was sent to Florence, Villani claims, to help the Angevins and the Church against Frederick of Aragon in Sicily in reacquiring that territory, and also to take back Florence by force. Villani writes that though Charles was given the title of peacemaker, this was a deception construed by multiple parties, including the Blacks. Boccaccio does not allude to multiple motives at play in the events he describes in *Esposizioni* 6, despite the fact that his acknowledged source for this history is the more complex account given by Villani in his *Nuova cronica* (which he names in a paragraph following the mention of Charles de Valois).

Boccaccio similarly simplifies the support of Pope Boniface for the Blacks as a matter of favouritism. In his explication of *Inferno* 6.67–9 ("Poi appresso convien che questa caggia/infra tre soli, e che l'altra sormonti/con la forza di tal che testé piaggia"), where Ciacco prophesies the fall of the White Guelphs and the rise of the Blacks with the assistance of Pope Boniface, Boccaccio is constrained to offer a judgment of Pope Boniface. He asserts that Pope Boniface was indeed biased towards the Blacks, that he did not "piaggiare," or show equal regard for both parties at the same time ("l'animo tutto gli pendeva alla parte Nera," 6.42, esp. litt.; "his position was completely in favor of the Blacks," Papio, 310). While this implication of papal corruption in collaborating with the Blacks may seem to contradict the tone of Boccaccio's pro-Black account in *Esposizioni* 6, the commentator quickly blames Vieri de' Cerchi for Pope Boniface's loyalty to the Blacks. Corso Donati, Boccaccio claims, earned the loyalty of Pope Boniface through his obedience, and Vieri de' Cerchi lost such a privilege as a result of his coarse social comportment ("messer Vieri era stato salvatico e duro," 6.43, esp. litt.; "Messer Vieri was uncouth and unyielding," Papio, 310). Boccaccio does not claim that Pope Boniface could have been inspired to support Donati and his followers for his personal gain or that the church. This version of the political rise and fall of both Blacks and Whites reduces this period of Florentine history – which is really the story of the conflicting ambitions of numerous political parties and individuals – to a tale of favouritism.

That Boccaccio viewed the pivotal events in Florence during the turn of the fourteenth century as motivated by the desires of a few protagonists strongly recalls his earlier treatment of this subject matter in *Decameron* 9.8. Though the actions of Corso Donati and Vieri de' Cerchi were much more serious in their ramifications than the "beffa e controbeffa" of Biondello and Ciacco, nonetheless Boccaccio distills the causes of Florentine strife down to the harbouring of "superbia, invidia e avarizia" by the protagonists of this *novella*. Besides revealing his own interest in the anecdotes, or *novelle*, so to speak, which lie at the heart of history, the author of the *Decameron* and the *Esposizioni* attempts in these two texts to convey that larger historical events are spurred by the ambitions and desires of a small circle of individuals. For what stands out both in Boccaccio's *novella* of Ciacco and Biondello and in his version of Florentine history in *Esposizioni* 6 is the attention he pays to the emotional texture of society: how loyalty ensues from being obeyed, how envy breeds in the face of ostentatious wealth, and how offence is taken at the lack of grace in others. Boccaccio, it seems, is not as interested in taking the correct side in the story of partisan politics that marked Dante's times as he is in unravelling the personal motivations at the heart of its fabric. This accords with Giuseppe Mazzotta's observation that Boccaccio attends to "the power of private passions to endanger the stability of the political frame of order."[55]

Thus it would be more correct to say that Boccaccio openly favours the Blacks over the Whites in *Esposizioni* 6 not because he agreed with their political agenda but because he favoured the Donati family over the Cerchi family. As observed in his portrait of the generosity of Corso Donati in *Decameron* 9.8 and his sympathetic treatment of the Black Guelph leader in *Esposizioni* 6, Boccaccio seems to have been moved by the poverty of the Donati family and by their social grace. Conversely, he was offended by the avarice and lack of social grace of the Cerchi family, as we saw previously in *Esposizioni* 16 (examined in the previous chapter) and now here in *Esposizioni* 6.

Those individuals whose conflicts and desires instigated historical events interested Boccaccio perhaps because he viewed them as the singular powerful protagonists in Florentine politics of that time. While Pope Boniface VIII, Cardinal Matteo d'Acquasparta, and Charles of Valois were greater figures of international power, the local conflicts between the relatively small but mighty families of the Cerchi and the Donati, in Boccaccio's narrative in the *Esposizioni*, spawned the sequence of events that determined the viscissitudes of Florence. This can also be seen in *Decameron* 9.8, where the *invidia* and *avarizia* of the two families are passed down to other Florentines, such as Ciacco and Biondello, who come into contact with them, similar to the spreading of a contagious disease (or plague, if you will) among the "houses of the dead." Boccaccio himself shares this view of the Cerchi and Donati families and their arbitrary control over Florence in *Esposizioni* 7 in his gloss on the verses from *Inferno* 7 that describe Fortune's agency in the rise and fall of different peoples ("ordinò general ministra e duce/che permutasse a tempo li ben vani/di gente in gente e d'uno in altro sangue,/ oltre la difension di senni umani," 79–81; "who shifts those worthless goods, from time to time,/from race to race, from one blood to another/beyond the intervention of human wit"). Not only does Boccaccio note the ephemeral nature of the power of these two families, which is decided by Fortune, but he likens their power to the arbitrary nature of Fortune herself:

> Furon de' nostri dì i Cerchi, i Donati, i Tosinghi e altri in tanto stato nella nostra città, che essi *come volevano* guidavano le piccole cose e le grandi *secondo il piacer loro*, ove oggi appena è ricordo di loro. (7.63, esp. litt., emphasis added)

> In our own time, the Cerchi, the Donati, the Tosinghi, and others were once in such pre-eminence in our city that they controlled small and great affairs alike according to their whims. (Papio, 342)

The Cerchi and Donati families directed large and small affairs as they wished, or according to their pleasure, just as Fortune, seen as an arbitrary force without her divine mandate, seems to control the rise and fall of peoples on this earth. If the fortune of Florence is decided by certain families, Boccaccio seems to say, then the biographies of those families are the main narratives of Florentine history (as P.J. Jones has written), though the Cerchi, Donati, and Tosinghi families no longer held that same power in his own era. On the other hand, in Boccaccio's times the elite families had been challenged by Fortune, in the shape of flood, famine, and plague, by the bankruptcies of the banking companies, by the tyranny of Walter of Brienne, and, last but not least, by the *popolo* and the *popolo minuto*, the voice of the *gente nuova*, the "upwardly mobile, nonnoble families" (to adopt Dameron's language),[56] and of the guilds.

The Elite and the *popolo*:
The Case of Cisti and Geri Spini

I previously suggested, vis-á-vis Boccaccio's unflattering characterization in *Decameron* 6.9 of Betto Brunelleschi, the other Black Guelph leader whose greed and propensity towards violence were antithetical to the traditions of *cortesia*, that Boccaccio's politics run along familial and not partisan lines. Boccaccio's sympathy for Corso Donati, a symbol of pride but also of the tradition of *cortesia*, is thus not necessarily an indication of the author's partisanship on the side of the Black Guelphs. This is suggested by the characterization of another Black Guelph, Geri Spini, who appears in the chronicles as among those responsible for Corso Donati's downfall. Boccaccio figures him in *Decameron* 6.2, where Spini – by means of his servant – must be reminded of the idea of moderation, and thus of the principle of *cortesia* as a code of conduct, in the *novella* of Cisti the Baker. This *novella* relates to *Decameron* 9.8 both in its historical setting and by means of the motif of requesting wine from others, a matter in itself of historical interest, insofar as wine production and consumption increased in the era after the Black Death.[57] Furthermore, the *novella* illustrates the lack of knowledge of the ways of *cortesia* among the mercantile elite (Spini), and the tension between Spini's social group – the elite *popolani* who sought knighthood as a marker of status, like the Cerchi (the Spini were labelled as magnates in the Ordinances of Justice) – and the non-elite *popolani*, including the *popolo minuto*, who consolidated themselves in guilds. *Decameron* 6.2 dramatizes the rising voice of the *popolo minuto* – the guildsmen, bakers (such as Cisti), and merchants of smaller enterprises and profits – in the face of magnate power (such as the Spini family).[58] Given this context, the *novella* of Geri Spini, one of the members of the banking family of Pope Boniface VIII, casts him as a magnate experiencing the constraints of the *popolo*, for example those imposed by the Ordinances of Justice.

The *novella* of Cisti *fornaio* shares the same time frame as the events discussed in *Esposizioni* 6, though Boccaccio does not specify the time as such. Pampinea opens the *novella* by giving a general sense that the story takes place at the time when Pope Boniface VIII sent Cardinal Matteo d'Acquasparta to Florence, though she conveys this indirectly:

Dico adunque che, avendo Bonifazio papa, appo il quale messer Geri Spina fu in grandissimo stato, mandati in Firenze *certi* suoi nobili ambasciadori per *certe* sue gran bisogne, essendo essi in casa messer Geri smontati, e egli con loro insieme *i fatti* del Papa trattando, avvenne che, *che se ne fosse cagione*, messer Geri con questi ambasciadori del Papa tutti a piè quasi ogni mattina davanti a Santa Maria Ughi passavano, dove Cisti fornaio il suo forno aveva e personalmente la sua arte esserceva. (6.2.8, emphasis added)

I say, then, that when Pope Boniface, who held Messer Geri in the highest esteem, sent a delegation of his courtiers to Florence on urgent papal affairs, they took lodging under Messer Geri's roof; and almost every morning, for one reason or another, it so happened that Meser Geri and the Pope's emissaries were obliged by the nature of their business to walk past the Church of Santa Maria Ughi, beside which Cisti had his bakery, where he practised his calling in person. (McWilliam, 448–9)

Despite the ambiguity of Pampinea's language ("certo," "fatti," and the phrase "che se ne fosse cagione"), she provides just enough information to allow us to speculate that this mission was the visit of Cardinal Matteo d'Acquasparta in June 1300 to establish peace in Florence. This can be assumed for two reasons: first, the Spini (and particularly Nero Cambi), according to Compagni, were the Pope's principal creditors and were instrumental in getting Pope Boniface to send his legates to Florence:[59]

Sedea in quel tempo nella sedia di San Piero papa Bonifazio VIII [...] Erano con lui sua mercatanti gli Spini, famiglia di Firenze ricca e potente [...] Nero Cambi [...] tanto aoperò col Papa per abassare lo stato de' Cerchi e de' loro sequaci, che mandò a Firenze messer frate Matteo d'Acquasparta, cardinale Portuense, per pacificare i Fiorentini. Ma niente fece, perché dalle parti non ebbe la commessione volea, e però sdegnato si partì di Firenze. (1.21)

At that time the throne of St. Peter was occupied by Pope Boniface VIII [...] He was supported by his bankers, the Spini, a rich and powerful Florentine family [...] Nero Cambi [...] worked so hard to convince the pope to lower the prestige of the Cerchi and their followers that the pope sent to Florence the friar messer Matteo di Acquasparta, cardinal of Porto, to pacify the Florentines. But the cardinal accomplished nothing because the factions would not grant him the powers he wanted, and so he left Florence in anger. (Bornstein, 24)

Second, as the Spini lived near Santa Trinità, the papal legates would have naturally passed in front of the church Santa Maria Ughi on the way to the houses of the Cerchi and the Donati, who were consulted in an effort to establish peace in the city.[60]

Boccaccio not only omits this information (which can be found in Compagni but not in Villani), but also the deeper story of the conflict between the Spini and the Cerchi briefly alluded to in the passage concerning Nero Cambi. Compagni, at different points in his *Cronica*, gives reason to believe that the Spini family had a particular desire to lower the prestige of the Cerchi family. Whether or not this was due to competition between rival banking families is undecided among historians.[61] In a moment from Book 2 in which the narrative takes on the tone of political invective, Compagni exclaims, "O messer Geri Spini, empi l'animo tuo: diradica i Cerchi, acciò che possi delle fellonie tue viver sicuro" (2.22; "O messer Geri Spini, fulfill your desire: uproot the Cerchi, so that you can live securely in your felonies," Bornstein, 51). Compagni here refers to the offence given to the Cerchi family during the famous "zuffa" in May 1300, when Ricoverino de' Cerchi's nose was reportedly slashed by Piero Spini ("Nel quale assalto fu tagliato il naso a Ricoverino de' Cerchi da uno masnadiere de' Donati, il quale si disse fu Piero Spini, e in casa sua rifuggirono," 1.22; "In the assault Ricoverino de' Cerchi's nose was slashed by one of the Donati followers (it was said to be Piero Spini, in whose home they took refuge)," Bornstein, 25). Boccaccio himself, in *Esposizioni* 6, discusses the injury suffered by Ricoverino but does not mention Piero Spini ("e tra gli altri fu fedito Ricovero di messer Ricovero de' Cerchi e fugli tagliato il naso, di che tutta la città fu sommossa ad arme," 6.33, litt.; "a number of men were wounded, including Ricovero di messer Ricovero de' Cerchi whose nose was sliced off, an act that brought the entire city to a state of arms," Papio, 308). It is unclear whether this omission is intentional or due simply to Boccaccio's not finding it in Villani's chronicle.

Geri Spini's switch of allegiance in regard to Corso Donati also forms a crucial element in considering Boccaccio's various affinities for the political figures of this period. According to Compagni, the Black Guelfs split into factions around 1308 when Corso Donati began to view himself as benefitting the least politically from his efforts, in comparison to

Rosso della Tosa, Pazzino de' Pazzi, Betto Brunelleschi, and Geri Spini: "Il qual fu, che messer Corso Donati, parendoli avere fatta più opera nel racquistare la terra, gli parea degli onori e degli utili avere piccola parte o quasi nulla: però che messer Rosso dalla Tosa, messer Pazino de' Pazzi, messer Betto Brunelleschi e messer Geri Spini, con loro seguaci, di popolo, prendevano gli onori, servivano gli amici, e davano i risponsi, e faceano le grazie: e lui abbassarono. E così vennono in grande sdegno negli animi: e tanto crebbe, che venne in palese odio" (3.19; "It seemed to messer Corso Donati that he had worked hardest to regain the city but won little or no part of the offices and profits, whereas messer Rosso della Tosa, messer Pazzino de' Pazzi, messer Betto Brunelleschi, and messer Geri Spini, with their followers among the *popolo*, took the offices, served their friends, made the decisions, and did the favours – and brought him low. And so their dislike for one another began to increase, and it grew so much that it came to open hatred," Bornstein, 82). The reference here is to the *popolani grassi*, not the *popolo minuto*, to which Cisti and other members of the minor guilds would belong, as Compagni clarifies in the following passage ("costoro ànno i falsi popolani").[62]

Given Boccaccio's favouring of Corso Donati, it is clear that he wished to cast Spini in a more negative light as regards the ways of *cortesia*. This most likely reflects the difference in social groupings between the Donati and the Spini; whereas both were elite families, the former were a member of the knighted consular aristocracy, the latter members of the *popolani*, the upwardly mobile, non-noble banking and mercantile families, as Dameron calls them.[63] Thus, the Spini were not, like the Donati, one of the original families who were the standard-bearers of *cortesia*, nor were they members of the *popolo minuto*. Geri Spini is, despite being a Black Guelph, a member of the *gente nuova* just like the Cerchi family. Boccaccio thus will portray him as inexpert in the ways of *cortesia*.

In this story, Boccaccio draws attention to the difference in social groupings between Geri Spini and the *popolo minuto*, and Geri's lack of social awareness in contrast with that of Cisti *fornaio*, despite the former's higher social standing.[64] Cisti proves his sensibilities in this arena from the beginning of the *novella*. Moved by the desire to be courteous to Messer Geri and the Pope's emissaries by sharing some of his precious white wine with them as relief from the heat, Cisti searches for a way to offer them some without making the *faux pas* of inviting them to his house: "s'avisò che gran *cortesia* sarebbe il dar lor bere del suo buon vin bianco; ma avendo riguardo alla sua condizione e a quella di messer Geri, non gli pareva onesta cosa il presummere d'invitarlo" (6.2.10; "it occurred to Cisti that [...] he might as well do them the kindness of offering them some of his delicious white wine. But being sensible of the difference in rank between himself and Messer Geri, he considered it would be presumptuous of him to issue an invitation," McWilliam, 449). The difference in rank between Geri and Cisti is that between a member of an elite banking family and an upcoming member of the *popolo*, perhaps not the *popolo grasso*, but a possible ally to the elite factions.

Najemy suggests that the public acts of violence on behalf of elite families were sometimes intended to recruit from the ranks of the *popolani*;[65] this *novella*, which instead features Cisti's staged performance outside of his shop in order to attract the attention of Geri Spini, is an interesting reversal of this class-based dynamic, one that depicts the power of the *popolani*. Cisti stages a daily charade outside his home, in which he drinks some of his own wine with gusto, so that Messer Geri and the emissaries would observe him and eventually request some wine themselves. When Spini does make such a request, Cisti prepares a table for them but advises their servants that this wine was not intended for them. Geri and the pope's emissaries enjoy Cisti's wine so much that they place orders daily with Cisti. Cisti, though he claims not to be presumptuous in his treatment of Geri, instead orchestrates their relationship so that he has the upper hand.

Cisti's warning to the servants sets the stage for the *pronta risposta* at the end of the *novella*. Messer Geri arranges to hold a banquet with some of the most distinguished citizens in Florence as his guests, and sends a servant to Cisti (who refused an invitation to attend, "il quale per niuna condizione andar vi volle") to bring back some of his wonderful wine. The servant brings a large flask to Cisti. Cisti responds in a few words, but refuses the servant's request, stating that Messer Geri has not sent him to his wine stores, but instead to the Arno ("A Arno"). The servant returns to Messer Geri, reports Cisti's words, and shows him the size of the flask. Messer Geri immediately comprehends the error of his servant, furnishes his servant with a more modestly sized flask, and sends him back to Cisti, who happily fills it with wine. Perhaps more than coincidentally, Compagni noted that the only guild in Florence, that of the bakers, protested the arrival of Charles of Valois in 1301, which would lead to certain bloodshed (*Cronica* 2.5–7). Whether or not Boccaccio was aware of this particular detail (which appears in only a brief sentence in the *Cronica*), Cisti's wisdom and desire to teach Geri Spini serves as an interesting fictional representation of Compagni's claim.[66] Cisti's *pronta risposta* conveys the discontent and growing political power of the *popolo minuto*.

That same day Cisti makes a point of clarifying the error committed with Messer Geri in person. It was not the size of the flask, Cisti claims, but rather that it seemed to him that Messer Geri had forgotten that this wine was not intended for servants ("parendomi che vi fosse uscito di mente ciò che io a questi dì co' miei piccoli orcioletti v'ho dimostrato, cioè che questo non sia vin da famiglia, vel volli staman raccordare," 6.2.28; "But since you appeared to have forgotten what I have shown you with the aid of my small flagons during these past few days, namely, that this is not a wine for servants, I thought I would refresh your memory," McWilliam, 451). Cisti then informs Messer Geri that he has sent him the rest of this wine to do with as he pleases. Messer Geri is grateful to Cisti for his gift and from that day on regarded him as a friend ("e sempre poi per da molto l'ebbe per amico," 6.2.30; "regarded him as a friend of his for life," McWilliam, 451), implying that the differences in social rank between them had been erased by Cisti's generosity and lesson in etiquette.

Cisti's wisdom and respect for the rules of social etiquette, repeatedly demonstrated in the plot of this *novella*, show Messer Geri to be relatively crude in these matters, as befitting a member of the *gente nuova*. Insofar as Boccaccio would express interest in the code of conduct that Cisti communicates here, Cisti's words could reveal the author's own sentiments. In the allegorical exposition of *Esposizioni* 6, Boccaccio rages against the gluttony on display during large banquets, claiming that the quantity and extravagance of food and wine consumed causes individuals to act contrary to their social identity:

> In queste così oneste e sobrie comessazioni, o conviti che vogliam dire, come i ventri s'empiano, come tumultuino gli stomachi, come fummino i cerebri, come i cuori infiammino, assai leggier cosa è da comprendere a chi vi vuole riguardare. In queste *insuperbiscono i poveri, i ricchi divengono intollerabili, i savi bestiali*. (6.26, all., emphasis added)

> Anyone who cares to have a look at these very respectable and subdued dinners, or banquets we might say, will have no difficulty whatsoever in understanding how their bellies are filled, what turmoil takes place in their stomachs, how the vapours cloud their brains, and how their hearts

are set afire. At these feasts, the poor get uppity, the rich become intolerable, and the wise turn stupid. (Papio, 323–4)

Not only do these dangerous shifts in social identity occur during these banquets (with the poor becoming proud, the rich intolerable, and the wise like animals), but in the midst of these meals matters of state are discussed and resolved:

> E in queste medesime così laudevoli cene s'ordina e solida lo stato della republica, diffinisconsi le quistioni, compongonsi l'oportunità cittadine e i fatti delle singulari persone; ma il come nel giudicio de' savi rimanga. In queste si condanna e assolve cui il vino conforta o cui l'ampiezza delle vivande aiuta o disaiuta: e coloro, a' quali i prieghi unti e spumanti di vino sono intercessori, procuratori o avvocati, le più volte ottengono nelle lor bisogne. (6.27)

> At these very same praiseworthy meals, the republic itself is managed and organized, issues are debated, the needs of the citizenry are decided, and the affairs of individual men are judged. Let us hope that there is still some bit of discernment left in these sages. At these feasts, they condemn and absolve men whom wine consoles or whom the variety of dishes may help or hurt. Those whose entreaties to jurists and procurators are fattened or frothed with wine succeed more often than not in obtaining what they want. (Papio, 324)

While Boccaccio here refers to a "male costume" that afflicted Tuscany during the time he wrote the *Esposizioni* (and therefore almost half a century after the days of Geri Spini, who was dead by 1332),[67] the harmful effects of inordinate consumption of food and wine during meals (especially those banquets that involved matters of state, as Messer Geri's banquet in *Dec.* 6.2 presumably must have done), are foregrounded in *Decameron* 6.2. As Guiglielmo Borsiere is the emblem of lost *cortesia* in Florence in *Decameron* 1.8, so Cisti, whose awareness of *cortesia* as a social code of conduct in this *novella*, unifies a narrative on moderation in matters of consumption with one that treats the self-awareness necessary to preserve the categories of social hierarchy.

The superficial nature of *cortesia* as embodied by the non-noble elites also comes through in Boccaccio's depiction of Geri Spini as an ambassador. If Betto Brunelleschi's diplomatic abilities stand in contrast with those of Guiglielmo Borsiere, then Geri Spini appears as an imperfect mediator, though he hosts Pope Boniface's emissaries in Florence. Spini and Brunelleschi are noted by Compagni as sharing several "diplomatic" missions to Rome, likewise without the intention of establishing peace but rather to persuade religious figures to support the Blacks. Compagni writes of their visit to Cardinal Orsini that they got him to sing to their tune ("vi mandarono ambasciadori messer Betto Brunelleschi e messer Geri Spini; i quali faceano volgere e girare a lor modo, traendo da lui grazie, e pareano i signori della sua corte," 3.18; "they sent him as ambassadors messer Betto Brunelleschi and messer Geri Spini, who made him turn and spin to their tune, extracting favors from him and acting like the lords of his court," Bornstein, 81). While Brunelleschi and Spini served as the spin doctors for a corrupt political party, and thus can be viewed as sowers of discord for Florence as a whole, they also caused the division of their own party around 1306, when different Black Guelph leaders sided against Corso Donati (3.19). In Compagni's chronicle, both individuals appear divisive to the commune and their own party.

While the flaws of these Black Guelph leaders are rewritten into Boccaccio's own histories of this era, Corso Donati's poverty redeems his shared role as a violent and divisive leader. This preference, I would argue, was inspired by what Boccaccio viewed as Corso Donati's alleged interest in maintaining customs of *cortesia*, as shown in 9.8, despite his relative poverty – in comparison not only with the Whites but as well with other wealthier, non-noble Blacks, such as Brunelleschi and Spini. The motif of the Arno in both 6.2 and 9.8 as a free source of food and wine reinforces the never-ending abundance of Corso's generosity; his dish of chickpeas, tuna, and "pesce d'Arno fritto" contrast with the lampreys bought by Biondello at the market for the Cerchi family. In the same way, Cisti's *pronta risposta* to Messer Geri's servant, "A Arno," indicates that the Arno can cheaply and abundantly satisfy the thirst of all people, but that resources should be consumed in moderation (one might think, here, of Brunetto Latini's lessons on moderation in the *Tesoretto*; see the Introduction) and, moreover, be meted out differently in accord with civic status. Legislation, such as the Ordinances of Justice, reflected this concern with moderation and class differentiation. Cisti's sentiment to the servant is not in the spirit of wasteful consumption or prodigality; it is, instead, the sentiment of the non-elite *popolo*.

The Arno Runs Red: Narrating Florentine Violence

Boccaccio, most likely, would not have viewed favourably the *popolo*'s historical constraints on the elite, especially the constraints on the true knighted consular aristocracy, such as the Donati family. The compromise that is reached between Cisti and Geri Spini embodies a utopian vision of the harmony between the elite and the *popolo minuto*. Or it portrays the rise to power of even someone like Cisti, his movement from the *popolo minuto* to the *popolo grasso*. Like the lamented "avarizia" at the beginning of *Decameron* 6.9, it could also signal the rising power of non-elite guildsmen, whose disenfranchisement of the elite could be categorized under the rubric of greed. Boccaccio's characterization of the violent "spirito fiorentino," Filippo Argenti, exacts a kind of authorial *vendetta*, if you will, upon those antagonists of *cortesia*. Argenti participates in the tale of Ciacco and Biondello (*Dec.* 9.8), Boccaccio's dramatization of the "superbia, avarizia e invidia" that ignited the hearts of Blacks and Whites, and the resulting "zuffe" that took place in Florence during the turn of the century. The figure of Filippo Argenti thus represents yet another dimension in Boccaccio's writing of Dante's version of Florentine history, one that participates in the recording of violence that was rampant in Florence during the time but, I would argue, is inspired by the author's own resentment towards the greed of the Cerchi family, as representatives of the *gente nuova*.

As in the tale of Cisti and Messer Geri Spini, here the proper consumption of food and wine as well as the interaction between members of the elite and non-elite classes are twin aspects of Boccaccio's preoccupation with *cortesia*: on the one hand, as a code of conduct (as in *Esp.* 6, all.), and on the other hand as the marker of a dangerous change in social groupings (*Esp.* 6, litt.). While in *Decameron* 6.2 Cisti thwarts the attempt of Messer Geri's servant to overreach the boundaries ("trapassar il segno") of social identity, the request of Ciacco's servant in 9.8 is meant to incite the anger of Filippo Argenti and consequently to dramatize the results of petty *vendette* and the destructive forces of anger, with the Cerchi lackey, Biondello, suffering as a result. Instead of "rubifying" the flask of Ciacco's servant, as requested, Filippo in anger becomes red in the face, or "rubified" in his countenance ("tutto tinto nel viso"). Filippo's anger can be explained in one way as the result of this breach in the observation of social rank, or as an expression of anger against the "selvatichezza" of the Cerchi clan in the presence of Filippo Argenti, who is described as a "cavaliere."

The figure of Filippo Argenti in and of itself embodies conflict and strife, as his Dantean pedigree suggests. In fact, Filippo Argenti's irascibility is the only information we can glean from Dante's text, as his appearance in *Inferno* 8 is limited to a series of *botta/risposta* with the pilgrim, whose righteous anger with Filippo is applauded by Vergil. It is only from Boccaccio and other early commentators (such as the *Chiose Cassinesi*) that we learn that Filippo Argenti (Filippo de' Cavicciuli degli Admari) was a rather wealthy Black Guelph. As in the case of Ciacco and Guiglielmo Borsiere, Boccaccio's characterization of Filippo in *Esposizioni* 8 is analogous to the description of him in *Decameron* 9.8:

> Fu questo Filippo Argenti, secondo che ragionar solea Coppo di Borghese Domenichi, de' Cavicciuli, cavaliere ricchissimo, tanto che esso alcuna volta fece il cavallo, il quale usava di cavalcare, ferrare d'ariento e da questo trasse il sopranome. Fu uomo di persona grande, bruno e nerboruto e di maravigliosa forza e, più che alcuno altro, iracundo, eziandio per qualunque menoma cagione. (8.68, esp. litt.)

> This Filippo Argenti, according to what Coppo di Borghese Domenichi used to say, was an extremely wealthy knight, so wealthy that he once had a horse he used to ride shod with silver, an act from which derived his nickname. He was a man of large stature, dark and muscular, and of great physical strength. More irascible than anyone else, he used to get angry for the least little reason. (Papio, 395)

In *Decameron* 9.8, Boccaccio portrays Filippo with the same words, though he does not give the same amount of information ("un cavaliere chiamato messer Filippo Argenti, uom grande e nerboruto e forte, sdegnoso, iracundo e bizzarro più che altro," 13–14; "Messer Filippo Argenti – a huge, powerful, muscular-looking fellow, who was as haughty, hot-tempered, and quarrelsome a man as ever drew breath," McWilliam, 687). The choice of Dante's term "bizzarro" in describing Filippo reveals Boccaccio's meditation upon *Inferno* 8: "'l fiorentino spirito bizzarro" (*Inf.* 8.62). Boccaccio himself notes the specifically Florentine origin of this term in *Esposizioni* 8: "e credo questo vocabolo 'bizarro' sia solo de' Fiorentini, e suona sempre in mala parte, per ciò che noi tegnamo bizarri coloro che subitamente e per ogni piccola cagione corrono in ira, ne' mai da quella per alcuna dimostrazione rimuovere si possono" (8.69, esp. litt.; "I believe that the term 'bizarre' is used in this way only by Florentines, and that it always has negative connotations, for we consider bizarre those people who fly into a rage for any little reason and who cannot be dissuaded from their anger no matter what is done," Papio, 395). In rehearsing the figure of Filippo Argenti, Boccaccio sought to incorporate the figure of Florentine conflict whose lexical individuality signified violence.

Filippo Argenti's position in a discourse on Florentine violence locates him as well in an account of the violent actions that transpired around Dante's exile. The text of *Esposizioni* 8 opens with a long rendition of certain circumstances around Dante's exile (such as the theft of his belongings), for Boccaccio a subject relevant to this canto because he believed that only the first seven cantos were written in Florence. His perception that Dante composed *Inferno* 1–7 in Florence and the remaining cantos of the *Commedia* in exile seemingly affected Boccaccio's reception of the historical content of these cantos. Boccaccio's particular concern with the theft of Dante's belongings evokes Filippo Argenti once again, since Filippo's brother Boccaccino allegedly obtained Dante's property from the city of Florence.[68] The fact that Ciacco and Filippo Argenti are united in Boccaccio's discourse on Dante's exile in *Esposizioni* 8 gives reason to believe that these two figures, the first Florentines to appear in the *Commedia*, were associated in Boccaccio's mind with the poet's exile as well as with the political circumstances that caused it.

Hence I suggest reading Boccaccio's rewriting of internecine strife in Florence in these texts as a performance of the events surrounding Dante's exile, much in the way I would suggest one read *Decameron* 6.9 as a dramatization of the civic conflict that led to Cavalcanti's forced departure. It is possible to read *Decameron* 9.8 as Boccaccio's dramatization of Ciacco's political prophecy; as Ciacco orders his servant to incite the wrath of a Black Guelph, Filippo Argenti, against Biondello, a servant of the White Guelph Vieri de' Cerchi, the terms of his prophecy in *Inferno* 6 are literally enacted. Though Biondello, representing the White Guelphs, initially tricks Ciacco (just as the Whites first rose to power), Ciacco is vindicated through the violence of Filippo Argenti, a Black Guelph, who triumphs in the end (*Inferno* 6.71). The unspoken character of this *novella*, Dante, suffers exile as the result of these conflicts, just as Cavalcanti is forced to leap over the *arche* of Santa Reparata in the direction of the city walls, presumably to flee Florence. If they were the two just men who were not understood by their people ("Giusti son due, ma non vi sono intesi," *Inferno* 6.73), as Boccaccio writes in *Esposizioni* 6, then in both *Decameron* 6.9 and 9.8 Boccaccio conveys the circumstances that led to their exile. Boccaccio's revision of the political history of Florence, in this way, participates in the biographical narrative of Dante's life, once the poet was deprived of the *cortesia* – the generosity and hospitality – of his native city.

Conclusion

These moments of history in Boccaccio's *novelle* and in his commentary indicate two aspects of his mode of historical narrative. First, they imply that the history written under the influence of a literary text will and will not be informed by that previous author's biography. In the first two chapters, I have largely treated the ways in which Boccaccio's interpretation of the Florentine history from Dante's times is influenced by his own historical vantage point(s) at the second half of the fourteenth century. Yet, as I have just mentioned, the history of Florentine – and Italian – politics and society can also be interpreted vis-à-vis the exile of Dante.[69] The tension between these two perspectives, one internal and another external to Dante's historical vision, will be highlighted over the next two chapters as the scope of the material extends outside of Florence and further back in time, to the origins of the Guelph and Ghibelline conflict.

Boccaccio's particular interpretation of institutional responsibility for this moment in Dante's biography and his preference for Corso over Vieri de' Cerchi indicate the other aspect to writing history while under the influence of a literary predecessor: the desire to distinguish oneself by rewriting that history to suit one's purposes. Boccaccio refashions Corso Donati's life to silence Dante's occasional and erratic favouring of the *popolo*, in order to exalt and commemorate the old aristocracy in decline. He attends to the difference within the elite families, siding with those who belonged to the knighted consular aristocracy instead of others who were of non-noble families, the *gente nuova* of the *popolo*, as well as the *popolo minuto*, in this history. For Boccaccio, the downfall of Dante's Florence was due not to the clash between the Blacks and the Whites, but to the clash between the vice of the *gente nuova* (*avarizia*) and aristocratic values (*cortesia*), as that clash is performed between individual representatives of those social groups. History, for Boccaccio, can be better understood as the result of the intermingling of the desires and ambitions of few individuals, such as in what Villani calls the "conversazione" of the Cerchi and Donati families. In this way, Boccaccio writes history along the contours of the *novella* genre, recounting *storia* as personal *storie*.⁷⁰ This explains why the texture of his account of Florentine politics in his commentary on Dante's poem is so similar to that of the *novella* of Florentine civic strife in *Decameron* 9.8.

Boccaccio does not neglect the vices of individual religious and political figures who operated in both local and broader political events that relate to Dante's life, such as Pope Boniface VIII. Such criticisms, combined with Boccaccio's sustained condemnation of the merchant class in the *Decameron* and the *Esposizioni*, need to be contextualized in their relationship to Boccaccio's historical vision of Dante's world. In the following chapter, I examine how these "ethical" biographies formed by his histories of Dante's life and works inform the ethical structure of the *Decameron*, a structure that finds its voice in dialogue with Dante's moral invectives and political alignments, but that forms its own purpose amidst a changed social and economic landscape.

3 The Ethical (and Dantean) Framework of the *Decameron*: The Avarice of Clerics and Merchants

Boccaccio's inclination to script the civic events of Florentine history around the turn of the thirteenth century as the battle of avarice, as embodied by Vieri de' Cerchi, and *cortesia*, as personified by Corso Donati, does not limit itself to this particular interfamilial conflict – nor does it limit itself to the histories of the Florentine elite. His ethical figuration of social and political vicissitudes extends to other, often non-Florentine, protagonists that appear in the biography of Dante's exile. This historical interpretation bears the influence of the *Commedia*'s anti-clerical strain and its pro-imperial stance, an influence that the *Decameron* and the *Esposizioni*, in particular, variously embrace and reject. The juxtaposition of avarice and *cortesia* enters into the imperial and papal arena with Boccaccio's treatment of Cangrande della Scala and Pope Boniface VIII, who come to embody this social ethic and vice in a similar contrast. His depiction of these two figures in terms of avarice and *cortesia* – in this chapter, understood as an ethic based upon the idea of hospitality and the virtue of liberality, and not as a chivalric mentality – conveys the Dantean belief that the imperial court was the natural sphere of *cortesia*, while the Church witnessed the avarice of corrupt leaders. Secular figures, such as Cangrande and, in another *novella*, Ghino di Tacco, there a figure of church reform, locate *cortesia* outside of clerical spheres and, in the case of Dante's host in exile, within the aristocracy of the imperial cause.

Though Boccaccio does not directly criticize Pope Boniface VIII, he nonetheless elaborates upon Dante's frequent rebuke of church leaders as possessed more by greed than by liberality (one need only think of the recurring criticism of the Donation of Constantine, such as in *Inf.* 19, or the invectives of St Peter against a corrupt papacy in *Par.* 27).[1] His presentation of Pope Boniface VIII, the only pope named in the *Decameron*, as Cormac Ó Cuilleanáin writes, is "bland."[2] Yet, as Ó Cuilleanáin also implies, there is an oblique criticism of Boniface in the pages of the *Decameron*, one that is achieved by a parody of the generosity of Cangrande della Scala in 1.7 and a correction of the Abbot of Cluny's avarice in 10.6. When Cangrande experiences a momentary affliction of avarice that must be cured by a tale of the unlikely *cortesia* of the Abbot of Cluny (1.7), the author depends upon Cangrande's reputation for liberality from the *Commedia*. When reading a subsequent *novella* that also features the Abbot of Cluny (10.6), one finds that Boccaccio consistently characterized this abbot in terms of his greed and gluttony. The abbot's *cupiditas* must be cured by the Sienese Ghino di Tacco, a figure of church reform. References in both *novelle* reveal, I argue, that the Abbot of Cluny represents Pope Boniface VIII, who is referenced in both narratives, to a certain degree. The figure of Pope Boniface looms in the background of these tales of avarice corrected, but his muted presence does not function as an absence. Instead, it is Boccaccio's way of responding to this figure of corruption from Dante's world in a way that mirrors Boniface's own "non"-appearance in the *Commedia*; it is the indirect criticism of a man whom Boccaccio portrays as ambitious and shrewd in the *Esposizioni*.

If Boccaccio's portrayal of these church figures does not convey the same indignation as Dante's, the Certaldese author's scorn is discernible nonetheless – a scorn, one might argue, born in solidarity with Dante's spirit. Conceivably, Boccaccio would not have directly criticized Pope Boniface VIII, as any such criticism would have aligned him with the papacy's greatest critics during that time – the *popolo*. Brucker writes that the Florentine church of the mid-fourteenth century was "largely the creature of the city's aristocracy," noting the "ties of material interest" that bound the aristocracy to the church and to the papacy.[3] Relations between Avignon and Florentine bankers largely determined the economic prosperity of Florence, primarily in terms of the health of its lending industry.[4] Hence Boccaccio's indignation at avarice aligns itself with the network of relations between the papacy and Florence, the area of mercantile activity patronized by the church, as in the case of the Spini family.[5] Merchant bankers, such as Musciatto Franzesi, at the helm of one of the most important merchant-banking companies with ties to the papacy,[6] are the focus of criticism not only in the *Decameron* but also in the *Esposizioni*, for their commercial activity, some of which can be categorized as usury. The relation between Musciatto Franzesi and the events linked to Dante's exile speak to the

Dantean origins of this ethical historiography, one that here reflects the concerns of a larger mercantile, and non-noble, population of Boccaccio's times.

The ethical thrust of this historiography culminates in the ethical framework itself of the *Decameron*, integrating the Aristotelian concept that avarice is remedied by liberality (*Nichomachean Ethics* IV) with the Dantean rubric of avarice as the particular vice of clerical and merchant spheres.[7] Musciatto Franzesi is the historical figure that comprises the point of departure for a thematic of avarice versus liberality from the First to the Tenth Day. As in this *novella* (*Decameron* 1.1), which implicates Pope Boniface VIII, in the *Esposizioni* Boccaccio relates the vice of avarice both to clerics and to merchants. His commentary on the first canto integrates a lengthy treatment of avarice (as represented by the *lupa*) and the definition of the *veltro* as a figure of liberality while using the language of commerce and merchant activity. The textual connections between this commentary and a *novella* from the Tenth Day, that of Nathan and Mitridanes (10.3), speak directly to the ethical *cornice* of the *Decameron*, which is Dantean and not just Aristotelian in its origins.

Coming closer to the writings of Thomas Aquinas, though, Boccaccio does nuance the concept of vice for a monetary economy that has since become even more dependent upon mercantile activity.[8] Just as Aquinas writes that mercantile gain for the welfare of the family and the community is not a sin, so Boccaccio endorses trade for the greater public good. His panoramic treatment in *Esposizioni* 7 of these shades of difference, along with a condemnation of the evils of avarice, such as usury – while focusing on corrupt church members – reveal a new way of thinking about social realities outside of an extremist Franciscan belief in poverty.[9] Paralleling Dante's use of the language of commerce in his poem (such as the image of the merchant in "E qual è quei che volontieri acquista,/e giugne 'l tempo che perder lo face," *Inf.* 1.55–6) to warn his merchant readers of the abuses of commerce, as Ferrante argues, Boccaccio (with personal ties to the world of commerce) warns his merchant audience of the perils of usury.[10]

Cangrande della Scala: Dante's Generous Host Experiences an Unusual, and Momentary, Affliction of Avarice

Boccaccio features Cangrande della Scala (1291–1329), imperial vicar of Verona and Vicenza under Henry VII and Ludwig of Bavaria, captain of the Ghibelline league, and Dante's host in exile in Verona, in a *novella* in which the Lombard prince has to be cured of an "unusual and momentary affliction of avarice" ("d'una subita e disusata avarizia"). In doing so, the Certaldese author fashions a conspicuous subversion of Dante's depiction of a magnanimous host offered in *Paradiso* 17, embellishing upon popular legends about Cangrande recorded by other contemporary writers, such as Petrarch.[11] When Filostrato states that Cangrande's reputation for courtesy rings loud and clear throughout the world ("Sì come chiarissima fama quasi per tutto il mondo suona, messer Can della Scala, al quale in assai cose fu favorevole la fortuna, fu uno de' più notabili e de' più magnifichi signori che dallo imperadore Federigo secondo in qua si sapesse in Italia," 1.7.5; "It is a matter of very common knowledge throughout the greater part of the world that Can Grande della Scala, upon whom Fortune smiled in so many of his deeds, was one of the most outstanding and munificent princes that Italy has known since the Emperor Frederick the Second," McWilliam, 55), he explicitly refers to Cacciaguida's "prediction" in *Paradiso* 17 with respect to the reputation of the young Lombard prince. *Decameron* 1.7 depends upon a readerly knowledge of Dante's poem and his world; in the same way that Boccaccio depicts Cangrande as a skilled reader of the *Commedia*, so is the ideal reader of *Decameron* 1.7 able to identify the literary and historical contexts essential to understanding the terms of Boccaccio's parody in this *novella*.

The *cortesia* of Cangrande represents the exemplary case mentioned in the *Commedia* of Dante's experience of generosity in exile. In *Paradiso* 17 Cacciaguida delves into specific details of Dante's exile, prophesies of which the pilgrim heard from such figures as Farinata (*Inf.* 10) and Brunetto Latini (*Inf.* 15). During his stay with Bartolommeo della Scala (the most plausible candidate for the "gran Lombardo" referenced in *Par.* 17.71),[12] Cacciaguida claims that Dante will meet the young Cangrande, Bartolommeo's brother (the "colui" of the first verse here cited):

> Con lui vedrai colui che 'mpresso fue,
>   nascendo, sì da questa stella forte,
>   che notabili fier l'opere sue.
> Non se ne son le genti ancora accorte
>   per la novella età, chè pur nove anni
>   son queste rote intorno di lui torte;
> ma pria che 'l Guasco l'alto Arrigo inganni,
>   parran faville de la sua virtute

>   in non curar d'argento né d'affanni.
> Le sue magnificenze conosciute
>   saranno ancora, sì che' suoi nemici
>   non ne potran tener le lingue mute.
> A lui t'aspetta e a' suoi benefici;
>   per lui fia trasmutata molta gente,
>   cambiando condizion ricchi e mendici.   (*Par.* 17.76–90)

(In his company you shall find one who, at birth,/so took the imprint of this mighty star/that his deeds will truly be renowned./As yet the people, because of his youth,/take small note of him, since these wheels/have revolved above him only for nine years./But, before the Gascon can deceive the noble Henry,/sparks of his virtue shall at first shine forth/in his indifference to wealth or toil,/and his munificence shall one day be so widely known/even his enemies will not contrive/to keep their tongues from praising it./Look to him and trust his gracious deeds./On his account many will find alteration,/rich men changing states with beggars.)

Though Cangrande is only nine years old in 1300 (the time of the poem), by the writing of the *Paradiso* he had become imperial vicar of Verona and Vicenza under Henry VII and had established a name for himself as a prince who upheld the claims of the empire against those of the papacy.[13] Cacciaguida describes Cangrande as one who will not be lured by promises of honour from military conquests or by riches, and is therefore neither proud nor miserly but generous and magnanimous, qualities from which Dante would directly profit during his time in exile. The exact dates of Dante's residence in Verona, thought to be circa 1317–1318 to 1320, are unknown.[14]

Filostrato's tale of Cangrande and Bergamino in *Decameron* 1.7 takes the form of a dual narrative. In the dominant narrative, Cangrande arranges for a large festival to take place at Verona, to be attended by court entertainers, but at the last minute decides to cancel the event and send everyone home with a gift. He arbitrarily decides not to give a gift to a certain Bergamino, one of the entertainers in attendance, believing that anything given to Bergamino would be wasted. Cangrande does not share these thoughts with anyone, but Bergamino stays on in Verona with the hope of receiving something. Bergamino entertains such hopes in vain, as days pass and he has to pay his lodging costs by means of bartering three rich robes in his possession. When Cangrande notices Bergamino's melancholy state and asks him to speak, Bergamino immediately launches into a *novella* of his own, one that recounts the story of the grammarian Primas and his stay in the rich Benedectine monastery at Cluny. In this tale, Bergamino projects his disappointment with Cangrande onto Primas's similar experience with the wealthy Abbot of Cluny. By recounting the abbot's realization of his own miserliness to Primas, he succeeds in making Cangrande aware of his momentary affliction of avarice.

Bergamino's tale likens its teller to Primas and Cangrande della Scala to the Abbot of Cluny, thus succeeding in a process of "figuration" that is comprehensible to Cangrande ("in altrui *figurando* quello che di sè e di lui intendeva di dire," 1.7.4, emphasis added; "by telling a charming tale in which he represented, through others, what he wanted to say about himself," McWilliam, 54–5). This process of figuration renders explicit the analogous relationship between the two narratives, which mirror each other in their symbols and structure; it also foreshadows the depiction of Cortesia that will be exhorted in the subsequent *novella*, *Decameron* 1.8. As Primas sought to enjoy the reputed hospitality of the Abbot of Cluny, setting out with three loaves of bread for sustenance that he consumed while awaiting the abbot's invitation to join the dinner table, so does Bergamino have to support himself by selling his three precious robes while waiting for Cangrande's gifts. The abbot is similarly seized by an unusual desire not to be generous with Primas (1.7.18); however, he recognizes his miserliness without any assistance (1.7.23). Upon hearing the tale of the abbot, Cangrande, an intelligent man (1.7.27), recognizes his own avarice: "Bergamino, assai acconciamente hai mostrati i danni tuoi, la tua virtù e la mia avarizia e quel che da me disideri: e veramente mai più che ora per te da avarizia assalito non fui, ma io la caccerò con quel bastone che tu medesimo hai divisato" (1.7.27; "Bergamino, you have given an apt demonstration of the wrongs you have suffered. You have shown us your worth, my meanness, and what it is that you want from me. To tell you the truth, I was never seized before with the meanness I have lately felt on your account. But I shall drive it away with the stock that you yourself have furnished," McWilliam, 58). Cangrande then rewards Bergamino in exactly the same manner as the abbot rewarded Primas, with a robe, money, and a horse, along with an invitation to stay and go as he pleases.

While Boccaccio's allusion to Cangrande's reputation for magnificence in *Paradiso* 17 can be quickly perceived, the method by which Cangrande recognizes his uncharacteristic lack of hospitality, by means of the tale of Primas and the Abbot of Cluny, constitutes a tongue-in-cheek criticism of the avarice of the clergy. Bergamino does not just compare Cangrande with an allegedly generous person, he likens him to a prelate of the church whose wealth was second only to that of the Pope ("il più ricco prelato di sue entrate che abbia la Chiesa di Dio dal Papa in fuori," 1.7.12; "who was believed to have a higher revenue from his estates than any other prelate in God's Church, with the exception of the Pope," McWilliam, 56). The wealth of this Benedictine monastery seems to be viewed positively in this *novella*, as it benefits both Primas and, the abbot states, others in need ("Io ho dato mangiare il mio, già è molt'anni, a chiunque mangiar n'ha voluto," 1.7.23; "For years I have provided food for any man who cared to eat it," McWilliam, 58). But the wealth and charitable inclinations of the Cluniac monastery contrast too sharply with the hypocrisy of the religious in the preceding *novella*, 1.6, where the inquisitors and friars at Santa Croce would give the poor their leftover soup (not a substantial meal), leading Filostrato at the beginning of 1.7 to speak of the "ipocrita carità dei frati" (1.7.4, "the hypocritical charity of friars"). Their "brodaiuola ipocrisia" (1.6.20; "guzzling hypocrisy," McWilliam, 54) reveals instead their avaricious inclinations, or in Emilia's words in this *novella*, the "pistilenziose avarizie de' cherici" (1.6.9; "the disease of galloping greed amongst the clergy," McWilliam, 52).

If the attack on the clergy in 1.6 were not sufficient to cause the reader to doubt that Boccaccio viewed the Abbot of Cluny as a figure of integrity, then the *novella*'s reference to Dante's description of the Cluniac monks from *Inferno* 23 should give reason to reflect on Boccaccio's narratives in both 1.6 and 1.7:

> La giù trovammo una gente dipinta
>   che giva intorno assai con lenti passi,
>   piangendo e nel sembiante stanca e vinta.
> Elli avean cappe con cappucci bassi
>   dinanzi alli occhi, fatte della taglia
>   che in Clugnì per li monaci fassi.
> Di fuor dorate son, sì ch'elli abbaglia;
>   ma dentro tutte piombo, e gravi tanto,
>   che Federigo le mettea di paglia. (*Inf.* 23.58–66)

(Down there we came upon a lacquered people/who made their round, in tears, with listless steps./They seemed both weary and defeated./The cloaks they wore, cut like the capes/sewn for the monks at Cluny,/had cowls that hung down past their eyes./Gilded and dazzling on the outside,/within they are of lead, so ponderous/that those imposed by Frederick would seem but straw.)

These painted people are monks wearing heavy mantles in the style of those at Cluny, cloaks that are dazzling and golden in appearance but heavy with lead. In addition to Boccaccio's own tale of the hypocrisy of the religious in 1.6, Dante's only mention of the monks at Cluny among the hypocrites in *Inferno* 23 bestows upon the Abbot of Cluny a negative pedigree that can be perceived in Boccaccio's text – most especially in the reference to Bergamino's own rich robes.

That Cangrande would read this subtext in Bergamino's *novella*, and the possibility that he would take issue with the Abbot of Cluny, is suggested as well by the reference to Frederick II in *Inferno* 23, in addition to the information in the *Trattatello* that Cangrande received copies of the *Commedia*. In the last *terzina* quoted above, Dante alludes to a popular legend concerning one of Frederick II's methods of punishment, placing leaden mantles on the accused and throwing them into a fire. This legend can be found in several of the early commentaries, and undoubtedly reached Boccaccio as well.[15] The desire of Emperor Frederick II (1199–1250) to strip the church of its wealth led, ultimately, to one of his four excommunications.[16] Thus, Dante discusses the hypocritical wealth of the religious (according to Dante, the church should be poor, as seen in the parade in the Earthly Paradise) with a figure who had criticized papal greed in these *terzine*.

Boccaccio as well juxtaposes the excessive wealth of the religious with imperial figures, such as Cangrande, here in 1.7. Frederick II himself appears in the narrative of 1.7 when Boccaccio identifies Cangrande as one of the most magnificent lords to have existed in Italy since Frederick (1.7.5). Boccaccio thus evokes Frederick's court for its reputation of "valore e cortesia" (which can be found in *Purg.* 16: "In sul paese ch'Adice e Po riga,/solea valore e cortesia trovarsi,/prima che Federigo avesse briga," 115–17; "In the land watered by both the Adige and the Po/valour and courtesy once could be found/before Frederick encountered opposition"). Yet these two political figures also belong to another context in that, as Ghibelline leaders of one kind or another, they shared an interest in contesting the papacy's attempt to exert its power against the empire – something that Boccaccio does not foreground, but a context that is nonetheless present.[17] Cangrande's role as imperial vicar and status as captain of the

Ghibelline league all speak to his desire to revive the Holy Roman Empire, whose last ruler was Frederick II.[18] In this way the author subtly brings figures linked to the imperial cause into a narrative that belongs to the general category of *novelle* about *avarizia* and *cortesia*. With this background in mind, it can be understood why Cangrande would so suddenly reform his ways upon hearing Bergamino's tale: not only would he not wish to seem lacking as a host, but most certainly would not want to be unfavourably compared to an exceedingly rich church prelate.

Cangrande's quick interpretation of the *novella* told by Bergamino may attest to his reputed role as an astute reader of Dante's *Commedia*. As Boccaccio himself recounts in the *Trattatello in laude di Dante*, in the midst of his description of the composition of the *Commedia*,[19] Dante used to send between six to eight *canti* at a time to his esteemed Cangrande for his examination:

> Egli era suo costume, quale ora sei o otto o più o meno canti fatti n'avea, quegli, prima che alcuno altro gli vedesse, donde che egli fosse, mandare a messer Cane della Scala, il quale egli oltre ad ogni altro uomo avea in reverenza; e poi, che da lui eran veduti, ne facea copia a chi la ne volea. (1.183–4)[20]

> It was his custom, wherever he was, before anyone else had seen them, to send six or eight or a similar number of cantos to Messer Cane della Scala, whom Dante respected more than any other man. After Messer Cane had read them, Dante would make copies and give them to all who requested them. (Bollettino, 49–50)

Boccaccio reiterates his belief that Cangrande read early drafts of the *Commedia* a few paragraphs later in the *Trattatello*, in his account of how Iacopo Alighieri and Piero Giardino found the "missing" last thirteen *canti* of *Paradiso*:

> Per la qual cosa lietissimi, quegli riscritti, secondo l'usanza dell'autore prima gli mandarono a messer Cane, e poi alla imperfetta opera ricongiunsono come si convenia. (1.189)

> And so, overjoyed, they copied them, and following the author's custom, they sent them first to Messer Cane della Scala, and then added them, as was fitting, to the unfinished text. (Bollettino, 51)

Though Boccaccio believed that Dante sent Cangrande these preliminary drafts of *canti*, he was not convinced regarding the dedication of the work to anyone in particular. According to some, Boccaccio states, Dante dedicated the three canticles respectively to Uguiccione della Faggiuola, Moroello Malespina, and Frederick III, King of Sicily. Others still believed that the entire work was dedicated to Cangrande:

> Alcuni vogliono dire lui averlo intitolato tutto a messer Cane della Scala; ma, quale si sia di queste due la verità, niuna cosa altra n'abbiamo che solamente il volontario ragionare di diversi; nè egli è sì gran fatto che solenne investigazione ne bisogni. (1.193–4)

> There are some who like to say that he dedicated the whole poem to Messer Cangrande della Scala. It is impossible to decide which of these two statements is true, since we have nothing to go on except the freely bandied words of various men; but this matter is not of such importance as to demand further investigation here. (Bollettino, 52)

Though Boccaccio makes use of the dedicatory letter to Cangrande in the *accessus* to the *Esposizioni*, he does not seem to have had much invested in establishing the authenticity of this document, perhaps because he simply accepted it as genuine.[21]

The implications of Boccaccio's belief in this readerly relationship between Dante and Cangrande bestow yet another valence on the text of 1.7.[22] If Cangrande can aptly "read" Bergamino's *novella*, then Bergamino, a wandering *conteur* who projects his disappointment with Cangrande onto Primas (who in his exiled state must know the bitter taste of his last three loaves of bread, so to speak), could be said to represent Dante in this *novella*. In the same way that Bergamino succeeds "in altrui figurando quello che di sè e di lui intendeva di dire" (1.7.4; "in which he represented, through others, what he wanted to say about himself," McWilliam, 54–5), as Filostrato states, Boccaccio uses the anonymous figure of Bergamino to "figure" what he had to say about Dante's life.

A precedent for a fabled conversation in Cangrande's court between Cangrande and Dante himself already exists, in Petrarch's *Rerum memorandarum libri*, also a source for an analogue to Guido Cavalcanti's barbed retort in 6.9.[23] Even more interesting is the fact that Petrarch's anecdote of "Dantes Allegherius" and "Canis Magnus" immediately follows Petrarch's second account regarding Dino del Garbo in the second book of the *RML* (a text related to *Dec.* 6.9). In Petrarch's version of an encounter between Dante and Cangrande, which must have enjoyed an oral tradition that brought it to Boccaccio, Dante points to Cangrande's flaws in character:

> Dantes Allegherius, et ipse concivis nuper meus, vir vulgari eloquio clarissimus fuit, sed moribus parumper contumacior et oratione liberior quam delicatis ac fastidiosis etatis nostre principum auribus atque oculis acceptum foret. Is igitur exul patria cum apud Canem Magnum veronensem, comune tunc afflictorum solamen ac profugium, versaretur, primo quidem in honore habitus deinde pedetentim retrocedere ceperat minusque in dies domino placere. Erant in eodem convictu histriones ac nebulones omnis generis, ut mos est; quorum unus procacissimus obscenis verbis ac gestibus multum apud omnes loci ac gratie tenebat. Quod moleste ferre Dantem suspicatus Canis, producto illo in medium ac magnis laudibus concelebrato, versus in Dantem: "Miror" inquit, "quid cause subsit, cur hic cum sit demens nobis tamen omnibus placere novit et ab omnibus diligitur, quod tu qui sapiens diceris non potes." Ille autem: "Minime" inquit, "mirareris, si nosses quod morum paritas et similitudo animorum amicitie causa est." (Petrarch, *RML*, 98–9)

> Dante Alighieri, he too a recent fellow-citizen of mine, was a man greatly renowned for his facility with the vernacular, but in character was more defiant and in speech more frank than would be appreciated by the pampered and disdainful ears and eyes of the rulers of our age. He, then, lived in exile from his native city with the Can Grande of Verona, the common source of consolation and refuge for victims of misfortune at the time. Whereas at first he held his host in honour, later Dante began to withdraw step by step and to find less favour with his lord every day. As was the custom, there were actors and scoundrels of every kind staying there too, of whom one, being most impudent in his use of obscene words and gestures, occupied a position of high regard and popularity with all. Sensing that this situation irked Dante, Can Grande, having led that man into the middle of the room and showered him with praises, turned to Dante and asked him, "I wonder what could be the reason why this man is here. Although he is deranged, nonetheless he knows how to find favour with us and is liked by all, a thing which you, who are reputed to be wise, are not able to manage." "You would not wonder at this," replied Dante, "if you were aware that the basis for any friendship is similarity of character and likeness of disposition."[24]

Though it is impossible to prove that Dante's barbed retort to Cangrande, as Petrarch recalls it here in the *RML*, was a popular legend that Boccaccio meant to embellish upon in *Decameron* 1.7 (or that, on the other hand, Petrarch's is a fictive account that repeats yet another story), in both texts we can find a portrait of an imperfect Cangrande, a far cry from his idealized reputation in *Paradiso* 17. In addition to illustrating the conflict between an imperial church and empire in Cangrande's times, Boccaccio (and Petrarch in the *RML* as well) embellishes upon a flawed – and more human – Cangrande. When the two are read together, *Decameron* 1.7 challenges the tale of Dante's exile in Verona as alluded to in *Paradiso* 17, offering a "realistic" look at the frustrations Dante must have felt with Cangrande and his hospitality – which in Petrarch's tale seems excessive to a fault. In that measurement of realism, the *cortesia* of Cangrande, which fades only for a moment but then returns, reveals its value for Boccaccio's history of this social ethic – an ethic for secular and clerical leaders.

Pope Boniface VIII: Figuring Avarice at the Beginning and End of the *Decameron*

Beyond evoking the *cortesia* that Dante experienced in the court of Cangrande, Boccaccio weaves into *Decameron* 1.7 a host of issues related to Dante's exile, namely the Florentine poet's view of the avarice of the church and its imperial pretensions. The appearance of Cangrande, Dante's host in exile, together with the discussion of the corruption of the church, brings to mind the ultimate figure of papal corruption for Dante, whose collaboration with Charles of Valois and the Black Guelphs led to the poet's banishment: Pope Boniface VIII.[25] When Bergamino introduces the Abbot of Cluny as among the wealthiest prelates of the church, second only to an unspecified pope (1.7.12), it is natural to think of Pope Boniface VIII, whom Dante accused of simony in *Inferno* 19 for, together with Pope Nicholas III and Clement V, making gold and silver their god ("Fatto v'avete Dio d'oro e d'argento," 112). Filostrato's discussion of the "viziosa e lorda vita de' cherici" ("the foul and corrupt way of life of clerics") and how their hypocrisy is "di cattività fermo segno" ("a sitting target of evil," McWilliam, 54) also relates to the Dantean context of 1.7 by means of Pope Boniface VIII, whose imperial pretensions cast him as one of the most outstanding examples of avarice and hypocrisy of the poet's times.[26]

Boccaccio encourages such an association between clerical avarice, hypocrisy, and Pope Boniface by implicitly featuring the latter in 10.2

together with none other than the Abbot of Cluny, whose role in 1.7 has just been examined. Building on the opening of 1.7, where the hypocrisy of the clergy is referred to as a "fermo segno," here Elissa remarks on the rare generosity of priests. While the munificence of a secular leader (a king) is a virtue, the munificence of a prelate is nothing less than a miracle, given their extreme avarice:

> Dilicate donne, l'essere stato un re magnifico e l'avere la sua magnificenzia usata verso colui che servito l'avea non si può dire che laudevole e gran cosa non sia: ma che direm noi se si racconterà un cherico aver *mirabil magnificenzia* usata verso persona che, se inimicato l'avesse, non ne sarebbe stato biasimato da persona? Certo non altro se non che *quella del re fosse virtù e quella del cherico miracolo*, con ciò sia cosa che essi tutti avarissimi troppo più che le femine sieno, e d'ogni liberalità nimici a spada tratta. (10.2.3–4, emphasis added)

> Tender ladies, there is no denying that for a king to have acted munificently, and bestowed his munificence upon one who had served him well, is all very fine and commendable. But what are we to think when we are told about a member of the clergy whose munificence was all the more remarkable in that he bestowed it on a person whom no one would have blamed him for treating as his enemy? Surely we can only conclude that whereas the munificence of the King was a virtue, that of the priest was a miracle; for these latter are so incredibly mean that women are positively generous by comparison, and they fight tooth and nail against every charitable instinct. (McWilliam, 706)

As the munificence of Cangrande della Scala is to be expected not only because of his personal reputation but because of his role as a secular leader, the initial miserly reaction of the Abbot of Cluny to Primas is consistent with the expectation that the clergy is avaricious. Here, however, we expect to hear a tale of how the same Abbot of Cluny ("il quale si crede essere un de' più ricchi prelati del mondo," 10.2.6; "who was reputed to be one of the richest prelates in the world," McWilliam, 707) experienced a momentary "affliction" of liberality. That the Abbot of Cluny's so-called liberality in 10.2 would be presented as uncharacteristic underscores the likewise unexpected nature of his conversion *in bono* in Bergamino's tale in 1.7, thus highlighting the severity of Bergamino's veiled rebuke of Cangrande's momentary miserliness.

The liberality shown by Cangrande to Bergamino and by the Abbot of Cluny to Primas is materially quantifiable (as in the gift of robes), and therefore can more easily be interpreted as *cortesia*. But while Elissa claims that this *novella* sets out to illustrate how a prelate can be generous ("come un cherico magnifico fosse, nella mia seguente novella potrete conoscere aperto," 10.2.4; "in the story you are about to hear, you will plainly discover how one of their number revealed his munificence," McWilliam, 707), I believe that it can also be read as Boccaccio's condemnation of the avarice of the church, as well as a moment in which the Abbot of Cluny and, by association, Pope Boniface are subtly scrutinized for their corruption, much within the anti-clerical vein of the *Commedia*. Boccaccio features Ghino di Tacco, a Sienese Robin Hood, so to speak, who was banished by the counts of Santafiore from his native city after leading a rebellion against the church; he was remembered by Dante in *Purgatorio* 6 for his assassination of the Aretine Benincasa da Laterina ("Quiv'era l'Aretin che dalle braccia/fiere di Ghin di Tacco ebbe la morte," 13–4; "The Aretine was there who met his death/at the fierce hands of Ghino di Tacco"), a judge who had allegedly condemned Ghino's brother to death.[27] Ghino di Tacco opposed Boniface's papacy in both words and deeds, as in his assassination of Benincasa in Boniface's court in Rome. Boccaccio, whose characterization of Ghino in 10.2 was taken by later commentators as historical fact,[28] states that Ghino occupied the castle of Radicofani, a town located strategically along the via Cassia, on the frontier between Siena and the territory of the church. I would argue that Boccaccio selects this particular historical figure and his stronghold at Radicofani in order to create a narrative in which the Abbot of Cluny's avarice is purged and Pope Boniface, by means of association, is implicitly taught a similar lesson.

The *novella* of 10.2 begins in the court of Pope Boniface VIII, not a place of hospitality for those seeking refuge but one described as a site of gluttony and greed of prelates. After Elissa's brief introduction in 10.2 of Ghino di Tacco, she clarifies the historical background of the *novella* as the period during which Boniface VIII was the ruling pope in Rome ("Ora, essendo Bonifazio papa ottavo in Roma," 10.2.6). In contrast with Cangrande's court in 1.7, where Bergamino and others with scarce financial means feasted and enjoyed the generosity of this secular leader, in 10.2 the location is Boniface's court of plenty where the Abbot of Cluny, one of the richest prelates in the world, has ruined his stomach, presumably by eating too much ("e quivi guastatoglisi lo stomaco," 10.2.6). The abbot is advised to go to the baths at Siena in order to cure himself. In addition to his apparent gluttonous tendencies, he also suffers from greed, as revealed by the description of his entourage ("con gran pompa d'arnesi e di some e di cavalli e di famiglia entrò in camino," 10.2.6; "accompanied by a huge and splendid train of goods, baggage, horses and servants," McWilliam, 707).

Seemingly oblivious to Ghino's reputation as a highway robber, the abbot ventures into an area close to the former's territory of Radicofani.[29] Ghino has laid nets ("tese le reti") across the abbot's path; when the abbot and his retinue are blocked off, Ghino sends a lieutenant to request that the abbot go to his castle. Indignant, the abbot refuses, but Ghino's lieutenant opens the abbot's eyes to the nature of the circumstances in which he finds himself: "Messere, voi siete in parte venuto dove, dalla forza di Dio in fuori, di niente ci si teme per noi, e dove le scomunicazioni e gl'interdetti sono scomunicati tutti" (10.2.9; "My lord, you have come to a place where except for the power of God we fear nothing, and where excommunications and interdicts are entirely ineffectual," McWilliam, 707). The abbot has found himself in a "no-prelates land," so to speak, where even excommunications are "excommunicated," where the church and its mandates have no consequence – a fictional dramatization, perhaps, of the realities of the church's limited power of legal enforcement, as Ó Cuilleanáin notes.[30] The abbot realizes that he is surrounded and heads to Ghino's fortress, where he is lodged in a small dark room, his *brigata* is lodged comfortably, and his horses and belongings are stored away.

The abbot has arrived in Ghino di Tacco's court, a far cry from the material comforts of Pope Boniface's court in Rome. He reveals to Ghino's lieutenant that he had intended to visit the baths in order to cure his "stomaco guastato" ("ruined stomach"), and the lieutenant, claiming that Ghino had studied medicine, introduces the abbot to a diet of "due fette di pane arrostito e un gran bicchiere di vernaccia da Corniglia, di quella dello abate medesimo" (10.2.12–3; "two slices of toasted bread wrapped in a spotless white cloth, together with a large glass of Corniglia wine from the Abbot's own stores," McWilliam, 708). By moderating the amount of food the abbot is allowed to eat, Ghino succeeds in bringing back the abbot's appetite and, thus, "cures" him – indeed, Ghino cures him by means of the abbot's own stores of wine. Ghino releases the abbot from his "infermeria" and has a lavish banquet prepared for him and his company, during which the abbot learns that his retinue was treated much more hospitably than he had been. This is yet another parallel with Bergamino's *novella* in 1.7, in which Primas had to survive in the same abbot's court by means of eating his own bread (1.7.20). In Ghino's fortress, the abbot pays the price for the miserliness he showed to Primas by literally getting a taste of his own medicine.

A disposition to share one's wealth with guests – the material practices of *cortesia*, along the lines of a measured *larghezza* – bring to mind as well the *novella* of Ciacco and Filippo Argenti in 9.8. The correction of the abbot's gluttony by means of the sparse meals offered him by Ghino di Tacco resembles the trick played by Biondello on the glutton Ciacco, who is misled into attending Corso Donati's home for a simple meal of chickpeas, tuna, and fried fish from the Arno. In much the same way that Boccaccio emphasizes the poverty and nobility of Corso Donati, conditions he deems favourable in 9.8 and *Esposizioni* 6, he here characterizes Ghino as a poor nobleman, bereft of money and his native city – similar to Corso Donati, who suffered time in exile at the hands of the Whites. When Ghino discloses his identity to the abbot, he states:

> Messer l'abate, voi dovete sapere che l'esser gentile uomo e cacciato di casa sua e povero e avere molti e possenti nimici hanno, per potere la sua vita difendere e la sua nobiltà, e non malvagità d'animo, condotto Ghino di Tacco, il quale io sono, a essere rubatore delle strade e nimico della corte di Roma. (10.2.21)

> My lord Abbot, you must realize that gentle birth, exile, poverty, and the desire to defend his life and his nobility against numerous powerful enemies, rather than any instinctive love of evil, have driven Ghino di Tacco, whom you see before you, to become a highway robber and an enemy of the court of Rome. (McWilliam, 710)

Corso Donati, a member of the old Florentine aristocracy who, according to Boccaccio, was led by circumstance to become an accomplice to the court of Rome, is kindred spirit to Ghino di Tacco– though the events of Donati's life led him to become a friend, not an enemy, of the court of Rome. The similarities between Ghino and Corso lead me to believe that Boccaccio would also have viewed Ghino di Tacco favourably.

As Boccaccio casts the characters of Corso Donati and Ghino di Tacco in a positive light, so does he characterize the figures of the Abbot of Cluny and Pope Boniface VIII as "proud" leaders unflinching in their ambitions for material possessions and power. From Elissa's critique of clerics at the beginning of 10.2, which casts them as "avarissimi" (much the same way as the Cerchi family are stamped as miserly in the *Esposizioni*), this *novella* consistently refers to the pride ("superbia") of the Abbot of Cluny. When Ghino first invites him to his castle, the abbot responds that he is not interested in dealing with Ghino at all, betraying a sense of arrogant superiority. The abbot alternately reacts with disdain and resignation to being in Ghino's clutches; he first puts aside his pride to talk with Ghino's lieutenant ("aveva *l'altierezza* giù posta," 10.2.12, emphasis added), but once he is given some food he reveals his disdain ("L'abate [...] ancora che con *isdegno* il facesse, sì mangiò il pane e bevve la vernaccia e poi molte *cose altiere* disse," 10.2.14, emphasis added; "the Abbot ate the bread and drank the wine, at the same time displaying his indignation. He then became very truculuent," McWilliam, 708). Ghino, in comparison, does not acknowledge the Abbot's "altierezza" but responds with magnanimity ("assai *cortesemente* rispose," 10.2.15, emphasis added). Exposure to Ghino's generosity cures the abbot not only of his ill stomach, along with his avarice and gluttony, but also of his pride ("Maravigliossi l'abate che in un rubator di strada fosser parole sì *libere*: e piacendogli molto, subitamente *la sua ira e lo sdegno caduti*, anzi in *benivolenzia* mutatisi, col cuore amico di Ghino divenuto," 10.2.24, emphasis added; "The Abbot was astonished and delighted to hear such generous sentiments from the lips of a highway robber, and promptly shed his anger and disdain, being filled instead with a feeling of goodwill towards Ghino, whom he was now disposed to look upon as a bosom friend," McWilliam, 710). The medicine Ghino prescribes for the abbot is intended to cure this cleric in many different ways, both literally and spiritually. Like the dish of chickpeas and fried fish from the Arno in *Decameron* 9.8, this is the nobleman's remedy for the unchecked avarice of the *gente nuova* – yet here the avarice of religious figures whom Dante himself deemed corrupt.

Boccaccio's critique of the abbot's pride is not unique in his treatment of the church and its representatives, especially in moments defined by his activity as a *dantista*. In *Esposizioni* 1, Boccaccio accuses the "sede apostolica" ("Apostolic See") of keeping alive the Roman pride of that "umile Italia/Per cui morì la vergine Camilla" ("Humble Italy,/for which the virgin Camilla died," *Inf.* 1.106–7). He specifically accuses Pope Boniface of pride, but claims that Dante's view of Boniface accentuated the pope's alleged pride because of Boniface's stance against the White Guelphs:

Nè per la ruina del romano imperio cessò però la romana superbia, perseverando in essa la sede apostolica: nella quale, al tempo che l'autore di prima pose mano alla presente opera, sedeva Bonifazio papa ottavo, il quale, *quantunque altiero signor fosse molto, parve per avventura ancor molto più all'autore*, in quanto piegare non fu potuto a' piaceri nè alle domande fatte da quegli della setta della quale fu l'autore. (1.148, esp. litt.)

Nor did this area's pride wane after the fall of the Roman Empire, for it became the location of the Apostolic See. There, around the time that the author began work on this book, ruled Pope Boniface VIII. Although he was in fact a very arrogant man, he perhaps seemed even more so to the author on account of his unwillingness to bend to the desires and the requests of the faction to which the author belonged. (Papio, 76)

The above paragraph illustrates the nature of Boccaccio's historiography as a narrative of national or international events triggered by human emotions: Roman pride has persevered in the church (international), and particularly in the figure of Pope Boniface (individual). Boccaccio's judgment of Pope Boniface is based on the impact of Boniface's pride – his collaborating with the Blacks rather than the Whites – had on Dante's life.

This passage from *Esposizioni* 1 sheds light on 10.2, allowing for an interpretation of the abbot and the pope in similar terms of pride and corruption. I would speculate, moreover, that the abbot's tale of his captivity at the hands of Ghino di Tacco is comprehensible to Pope Boniface because they contain an implicit rebuke of his own pride and stealthy actions in securing the papacy. In other words, just as we can read 1.7 as consisting of two narratives, one being the tale of Bergamino and Cangrande and the second that of Primas and the Abbot of Cluny, 10.2 comprises two narratives as well: the first is the tale of the abbot and his stay in Boniface's court in Rome, and the second consists of the abbot's adventures with Ghino di Tacco. Bergamino's tale serves to check Cangrande's avarice, and by the abbot's tale of being held hostage by Ghino di Tacco Boccaccio intends to reform the pride and avarice of Boniface, though indirectly, much in the style of the *Commedia*'s criticisms of Pope Boniface, who is only named in Dante's poem.

Boccaccio's oblique criticism of Boniface is as complex as it is subtle. This pope is exposed to another clerical figure of pride in the person of the abbot, and is also implicitly criticized for his actions in seizing the papacy from Celestine V by the figure of Ghino di Tacco. For though Ghino di Tacco is labelled as a highway robber in this *novella*, his actions are ultimately for the good of the abbot and the church. This is not true with respect to Pope Boniface's own career, according to Dante and also Boccaccio, as Boniface was seen to have coerced Celestine V into abdicating the papacy and afterwards had him sequestered, according to a popular legend that can be found in Boccaccio's own words in *Esposizioni* 3 (in his gloss of "colui/che fece per viltade il gran rifiuto," *Inf.* 3.59–60; "him/who made, through cowardice, the great refusal"). Desirious of seizing the papacy, Benedetto Gaetano, soon to become Pope Boniface VIII, cleverly devised a way to exacerbate Celestine's feelings of incompetency:

> La cui semplicità considerando, messer Benedetto Gatano cardinale, uomo avvedutissimo e di grande animo e disideroso del papato, astutamente operando, gli incominciò a mostrare che esso in pregiudicio dell'anima sua tenea tanto officio, poichè a ciò sofficiente non si sentia. (3.43, esp. litt.)

> In light of his simplicity, Cardinal Benedetto Caetani, a brilliant and bold aspirant to the papal throne, astutely worked to convince him that being pope was detrimental to the well-being of his soul until Celestine himself believed he was unfit for the task. (Papio, 152)

Boccaccio portrays Boniface in terms that highlight his sharp intelligence as well as his ambition and manipulation ("uomo avvedutissimo e di grande animo" and "astutamente operando"), phrases that recall Ghino di Tacco's flawless tactics in capturing the abbot (10.2.7).[31]

Strikingly, Boniface's astute operations as depicted in *Esposizioni* 3 could be read as sharing a similar spirit with Ghino's deeds in 10.2. In these pages from the *Esposizioni*, Boccaccio reiterates a legend diffuse among early commentators of Dante that Boniface had servants sent to Celestine to whisper the words, "Renounce, Celestine!" in his sleep:[32]

> Alcuni vogliono dire che esso usò con alcuni suoi segreti servidori che la notte voci s'udivano nella camera del predetto papa, le quali, quasi d'angeli mandati da Dio fossero, dicevano: – Renunzia, Cilestrino! Renunzia, Cilestrino! – Dalle quali mosso, ed essendo uomo idiota, ebbe consiglio col predetto messer Benedetto del modo del poter renunziare. Il quale gli disse: – Il modo sarà questo, che voi farete una decretale, nella

quale si contenga che il papa possa nelle mani de' suoi cardinali renunziare il papato. (3.44, esp. litt.)

> Some say that Caetani and some of his servants arranged to have Celestine hear voices at night in his bedroom that, as if spoken by angels sent from God, said: "Renounce, Celestine! Renounce, Celestine!" Moved by these words, and being dim-witted, he consulted with Caetani regarding how to give up his office. Caetani told him, "Here's how you do it: just pronounce a decree stating that the pope may turn over the papacy to his cardinals." (Papio, 152)

Boniface's astute measures coupled with what Boccaccio calls Celestine's "simplicity" made it possible for Boniface to secure the papacy by means of a new decree stating that the pope could renounce his seat with the support of his cardinals. Boniface garnered the support of twelve cardinals in Naples in exchange for helping King Charles II in his fight to keep Sicily, and thus secured the papacy by means of their decree, as Boccaccio recounts in these pages. Pointedly similar to Ghino's seizure of the abbot in his stronghold at Radicofani is the forced isolation of the former Celestine V, Piero del Morrone, in Fummone by Boniface, who feared the lingering devotion shown to Piero by his followers:

> Il quale [Boniface] ivi a poco tempo, per ciò che vedeva gli animi di molto inchinarsi ad avere nel detto frate Piero, quantunque rinunziato avesse, divozione come in vero papa, fece il predetto frate Piero chiamare dal monte santo Agnolo in Puglia dove per divozione andato n'era e quindi, secondo che alcuni affermano, era disposto di passarsene in Ischiavonia e quivi in montagne altissime e salvatiche finire in penitenzia i dì suoi; *il fece chiamare e fecenelo andare alla rocca di Fummone, e quivi tenerlo mentre visse;* ed essendo morto, il fece in una piccola chiesicciuola fuori della rocca senza alcuno onore funebre sepellire in una fossa profondissima, acciò che alcuno non curasse di trarne giammai il corpo suo. (3.47–8, esp. litt., emphasis added)

> Not long afterwards, however, Boniface realized that there were many who still revered Pietro as a genuine pope, despite his renunciation. He ordered Pietro to return from Mount St Angelo in Apulia where, some say, he had gone in pilgrimage with the intention of travelling on to Slavonia to end his days in penitence atop some tall unpopulated mountains. Boniface sent him then to the fortress of Fumone, where he was held until his death. After Pietro died, Boniface had him buried without a funeral service in a

quite deep pit within a tiny little church outside the fortress in order than no one should ever be tempted to disinter his corpse. (Papio, 153)

By having Piero del Morrone live out his days in the isolation of Fummone and depriving him of any kind of recognition at the moment of his death, Boniface metes out for Piero, who would later be canonized under Clement V, a fate opposite to that of the *Decameron*'s Cepparello, a blackguard revered as a saint.[33]

Boniface's history of stealth tactics, which Boccaccio himself records in *Esposizioni* 3, brings a different valence to the conclusion of 10.2, and affects how we interpret Boccaccio's views on this pope. Even if he was mainly influenced by Dante's version of papal history, Boccaccio's own take on Boniface, while certainly not as explicitly negative, is by no means positive. When the abbot returns to the court of Rome and requests that Pope Boniface reconcile with Ghino, Elissa's statement that the pope was a good person always well disposed to virtuous men (10.2.30) seems sarcastic given *Esposizioni* 3's reference to the "grande animo" of Pope Boniface (his "ambition").[34] It is possible that Boccaccio did not intend for the conclusion to 10.2 to be read in a straightforward manner. Aside from the fact that a true reconciliation between the historical Ghino di Tacco and Boniface would have been unlikely at best,[35] Boniface's "grande animo" might not have endeared him to a figure of papal reform such as Ghino, thus highlighting the ambiguous nature of this *novella*'s conclusion.

Furthermore, Elissa's statement that Boniface was well disposed to virtuous men evokes Pope Boniface's reputation as accumulated from two other *novelle*. Who, in fact, were these "valenti uomini" within the world of the *Decameron*? They include no less than Geri Spini, leader of the Black Guelphs, who appears in 6.2 with Cisti the baker (6.2.8), and Musciatto Franzesi, the corrupt merchant-banker of Boniface and Charles de Valois who begins the first *novella* of the *Decameron*.[36] Boccaccio's tale of the social roughness of Geri Spini, a non-noble magnate whose family had recently become knights, is discussed in chapter 2. Musciatto Franzesi remains a crucial historical figure who highlights Pope Boniface's corrupt machinations at the turn of the fourteenth century, actions that associate clerical avarice with the category of merchants most "at risk" of the vice of avarice: those who lent money internationally, such as the Ricciardi family, who financed Pope Boniface VIII, or those who financed Edward III's campaigns in France in the 1330s, or, later on, those who financed Avignon.[37]

A Tempered "epopea dei mercatanti": Musciatto Franzesi and the Avarice of the Merchant Class

Boccaccio's meditations on the vices of the merchant class are closely associated with his historicization of the circumstances that led to Dante's exile. The opposition of avarice/*cortesia*, Boccaccio's ethical historiography, originates in a meditation on the events that immediately precede and follow Dante's exile. The clash between the Cerchi and the Donati, the generosity of Cangrande, and the avarice of Pope Boniface VIII participate in this history. What arises from an analysis of Musciatto Franzesi and the merchant class at large within the *Decameron* and the *Esposizioni* is that a discussion of avarice, for Boccaccio, originates with Dante's criticisms of the church but ends with an admonition for merchants.

This is the moment in which his Dantean historiography reveals its new temporal coordinates in his own world. It is where the fixed denizens of Dante's world speak to the navigating merchants of Boccaccio's milieu, populating the ethical *cornice* within which Boccaccio's interpretation of current affairs is produced. The navigating merchants under examination here resemble those international banking companies, such as the Bardi, Peruzzi, and the Gianfigliazzi families, who practised both at home and abroad, distinguishing themselves from other "long-distance merchants" by the size of their assets.[38] These banking families, who (except for the smaller, elite families, such as the Bardi) belonged to the Mercanzia (the *universitas mercatorum*) – which, perhaps not coincidentally, was formed in 1308, the year of Corso Donati's death – gained protection from the commercial legislation passed by this association. Just as the year of its formation marked the gradual end of the era of a knighted and consular aristocracy for Boccaccio, the Mercanzia offered, as Najemy writes, "a new image of a changing elite," one that included a new, powerful economic elite.[39] Though the Peruzzi would suffer a financial collapse in 1343 and then bankruptcy in 1345, similar to other families in the Mercanzia, it would continue throughout Boccaccio's lifetime as an association mainly intended for Florentine bankers who operated on an international scale.

The Franzesi family in particular – of which Musciatto Franzesi, whose reference in *Dec.* 1.1 inaugurates, I would argue, this ethical *cornice* in the *Decameron* – was, as Goldthwaite notes, "the most notorious of this early generation of bankers abroad."[40] The first *novella* of the

Decameron opens with a reference to the particular case of the Franzesi, which experienced a dramatic rise and fall (Dante himself would have witnessed both events, as the Franzesi house collapsed in 1304),[41] and to an event that directly resulted in Dante's exile: the visit of Musciatto Franzesi and Charles of Valois to Tuscany in 1301.[42] Boccaccio does, in fact, have Panfilo commence storytelling under a specific temporal rubric, that of the corruption of the papacy and the civic conflict that led to the exile of the Florentine poet – combined with a reference to mercantile avarice, in the figure of Musciatto Franzesi:

> Ragionasi adunque che essendo Musciatto Franzesi di ricchissimo e gran mercatante in Francia cavalier divenuto e dovendone in Toscana venire con messer Carlo Senzaterra, fratello del re di Francia, da papa Bonifazio addomandato e al venire promosso. (1.1.7)

> It is said, then, that Musciatto Franzesi, having become a fine gentleman after acquiring enormous wealth and fame as a merchant in France, was obliged to come to Tuscany with the brother of the French king, the Lord Charles Lackland, who had been urged and encouraged to come by Pope Boniface. (McWilliam, 25)

What Panfilo unambiguously alludes to in this opening sentence is the trip Musciatto Franzesi and Charles of Valois made to Italy at the request of Pope Boniface VIII, which Boniface claimed was a peacemaking mission (as Boccaccio writes in *Esposizioni* 6, "sotto nome di paciario") but was in fact an attempt to thwart the White Guelphs and support the Black Guelphs in taking control of Florence. Dante condemns Charles of Valois ("Carlo Senzaterra") through the words of Hugh Capet on the terrace of the avaricious and the prodigal in Purgatory:

> Tempo vegg'io, non molto dopo ancoi,
>   che tragge un altro Carlo fuor di Francia,
>   per far conoscer meglio e sè e' suoi.
> Sanz'arme n'esce e solo con la lancia
>   con la qual giostrò Giuda, e quella ponta
>   sì, ch'a Fiorenza fa scoppiar la pancia.
> Quindi non terra, ma peccato e onta
>   guadagnerà, per sè tanto più grave
>   quanto più lieve simil danno conta   (*Purg.* 20.70-78)

(I see a time, not very long from now,/that brings another Charles away from France/to make himself and then his kin more known./He comes alone, armed only with the lance/that Judas used to joust. And with one thrust/he bursts the swollen paunch of Florence./From this he shall acquire, not land,/but sin and shame, so much the heavier for him/the lighter he considers such disgrace.)

Thus Charles of Valois also carries a Dantean pedigree for avarice that complements Boccaccio's theme of the avarice of the merchant class in this *novella*.

Boccaccio most certainly relied upon Musciatto Franzesi's legendary evil-doing, confirmed in the chronicles of both Dino Compagni and Giovanni Villani, as a prelude to the figure of Ser Cepparello. Compagni, using language that is reminiscent of *Decameron* 10.2 and *Esposizioni* 3, writes in his *Cronica* that Franzesi was a "cavaliere di *grande animo*, picciolo della persona, ma di grande malizia" (2.4, emphasis added; "a very wicked knight, small in stature but great in spirit," Bornstein, 34). Villani specifically recounts how Musciatto made his wealth in France through counterfeiting money and by exploiting the wealth of Italian merchants abroad.[43] Musciatto Franzesi is an emblem of what Branca termed the "ragion de mercatura" of the *Decameron*, though he truly represents a mercantile ethos of ruthless, self-serving ambition.[44]

Rather than offer Andreuccio or Landolfo Rufolo as an introduction to the Italian merchant class,[45] Boccaccio presents us with two representatives guilty of the sins and crimes native to commerce, such as avarice and usury.[46] Branca's crucial reading of this *novella* as a depiction of the life of hostility and deceit led by merchants abroad (as evinced by the tactics of the two Florentines who host Cepparello and the protagonist's sacrilegious confession) offers support for reading the *Decameron* as a mercantile "epic": by beginning with this story, does Boccaccio attempt to warn us immediately of the inhuman extremes of this rising class in 1.1 (as Branca writes, "gli aspetti disumani di questa potente e prepotente civiltà")?[47] Though Boccaccio celebrates the protagonists of the rise of European capitalism throughout the *Decameron*, on the threshold of the hundred *novelle* he portrays the vices (or "inhuman aspects," to paraphrase Branca) to which this powerful class must not (but often does) succumb.

Boccaccio nuances this merchant class, highlighting its vices and virtues and differentiating its means of making profits. In *Esposizioni* 7, he delves into a complex definition of avarice based on Aristotle's *Ethics*, which he applies first to representatives of the church in the literal exposition, and then to the merchant class in the allegorical exposition. A consideration of the corrupt merchant Musciatto Franzesi in the *Decameron* leads the reader to the figure of Pope Boniface in the same work. Similarly, Boccaccio first glosses avarice as the plague of the church (as Dante explicitly addresses it in *Inferno* 7), and then expands on such a definition in terms of the merchant class for his Florentine audience. Again, a discussion of avarice, for Boccaccio, originates with the church but ends with an admonition to the merchant class. In the literal exposition, Boccaccio uses Aristotle's definition of avarice from the *Nicomachean Ethics* IV to gloss *Inferno* 7.48 ("in cui usa avarizia il suo soperchio," "in whom avarice achieves its excess"): "È avarizia, secondo Aristotile nel IIII della sua *Etica*, la 'nferiore estremità di liberalità, per la quale oltre ad ogni dovere iniuriosamente si disidera l'altrui, o si tiene quello che l'uom possiede" (7.42, esp. litt.; "According to the fourth book of Aristotle's *Ethics*, avarice occupies the lowest grade of liberality, for which, beyond all moral obligations, a man injuriously desires that which belongs to others or retains for himself what he possesses," Papio, 339).[48] That the excess ("soperchio") associated with this vice can be found in clerics is classified by Boccaccio as an empirical fact, which we can witness every day with our own eyes: "Questo vizio dice l'autore usare 'il suo soperchio,' cioè il disiderare più che non bisogna e tenere dove non si dee tenere, ne' cherici, li quali tutti intende per queste due maggiori qualità nominate: la qual cosa se vera è o no, è tutto il dì negli occhi di ciascuno, e perciò non bisogna che io qui ne faccia molte parole" (7.42, esp. litt.; "The author says that this vice effects 'its excess,' its inordinate desire to have what one should not have, in clerics, whom he comprehensively represents with regard to these two main qualities mentioned. The answer as to whether such an accusation is true or not is before everyone's eyes day in and day out; thus, there is no need for me to spend many words on it," Papio, 339).

Boccaccio does not dwell on the literal exposition of this sin in the church; instead he goes on to discuss the "superiore estremo di liberalità, cioè la prodigalità" (7.42, esp. litt.; "the highest grade of liberality," Papio, 339) and the remaining subjects ("Fortuna," "gl'iracundi," and "gli accidiosi") treated in *Inferno* 7. When he returns to the subject of avarice in the allegorical exposition, Boccaccio relates it to commercial activity, as would be fitting for his post-plague, mercantile audience. This shift from a discussion of the church to one of the merchant class occurs as early as his unique gloss on Pluto. There were two Plutos,

Boccaccio claims, one of whom was the son of Jason, a merchant, and Ceres, goddess of the harvest ("al tempo del diluvio il quale fu in Tesaglia a' tempi del re Ogigio, si trovò in Creti un mercatante, il quale ebbe nome Iasonio," 7.5, esp. all.; "At the time of the flood that took place in Thessaly during the reign of King Ogyges, a merchant called Iasion [Jason] happened to find himself in Crete," Papio, 355). Jason, who possessed a large amount of grain, decided to sell to a flood-ridden Thessaly some of his bounty, thereby amassing much money. Boccaccio interprets this allegorically: an inordinate amount of wealth (Pluto) was born out of the marriage of a merchant (Jason) and grain (Ceres). This myth of the origin of avarice is Boccaccio's own invention, and underscores, near the beginning of the allegorical exposition, how Boccaccio viewed the merchant class as fundamentally avaricious.

He reiterates this view in yet another tale of origins in the allegorical exposition, his rendition of the Golden Age.[49] During the reign of Saturn, the desire for worldly riches never consumed his people since all temporal goods were shared. Coins and, most importantly, those symbols and means of merchant activity such as ships, did not exist:

> nè mercatante nè navilio o alcuna altra cosa, per la quale aparer potesse alcuno in singularità avere appetito di possedere quello che agli altri non fosse commune, si conoscea. (7.46, esp. all.)

> They knew neither merchant nor ship nor anything else that could have made them think that someone could have a special desire to possess more than what they all shared in common. (Papio, 362)

Because merchants and their ships did not enter into Saturn's Golden Age, no one desired more than what was available to them as a people. Then, unfortunately, the devil introduced the two pronouns "mine" and "yours" (7.49, esp. all.) and spread the poisonous desire of wanting more than what one needed beyond a "natural bisogno" ("a natural need"), which in turn spelled the end of the Golden Age.

Even worse than those who simply want more than they need are those who, driven by the desire to acquire, navigate to the ends of the earth but are never sated with what they find. This is the second category of the avaricious, to which the merchant class belongs:[50]

> Sono adunque alcuni, li quali, non essendo, in tanto disiderio s'accendono di divenir ricchi, che il trapassar l'Alpi e le montagne o' fiumi, e navicando

divenire alle nazioni strane, tirati dalla speranza e sospinti dal disiderio, par loro leggierissima cosa. (7.58, esp. all.)[51]

There are some people who, not being pulled by hope and spurred on by desire, think it is the easiest thing in the world to cross the Alps and mountains or rivers and go by ship to foreign nations, for they are enflamed with an enormous desire to become rich. (Papio, 364)

This "navigar" ("navigation") of merchants would be fine, Boccaccio states, if it led them to a "convenevole termine" ("fitting goal," Papio, 365) with which they could be happy, after hard, honest labour, with their gains (7.60, esp. all.). While Boccaccio does not explicitly name the merchant class in this passage, it is quite clear, from the discussion of navigations, that they are the party carrying out these endeavours.[52] We could, he implies, excuse their natural desire to possess if, having achieved their goal, they were content.

Even worse, Boccaccio writes, is when the desire to acquire more than necessary goads people into committing usury, theft, and violence (7.61, esp. all.).[53] Boccaccio's condemnation of the merchant class climaxes with the conclusion that the "appetito concupiscibile" ("covetous desire," Papio, 365) leads to further vices, most of which find illustration in the *Decameron*, and are best exemplified by Musciatto Franzesi, a usurer. Boccaccio calls these sinners the "pessima spezie d'avari" (7.63, esp. all.; "the worst type of greedy men," Papio, 365).

Yet the merchant class, and usurers in particular, are not altogether evil, Boccaccio will sustain in the *Esposizioni*, in contrast with the characterization of Musciatto Franzesi in the *Decameron*. While up to this point in the allegorical exposition his condemnation of this class has been clear, he is quick to distinguish respectable mercantile activity from the vices described above:

> Alcuni altri, per non stare oziosi, con ogni lealtà faranno una loro arte, *alcuna mercatantia*, li quali, quantunque più che lor non bisogna avanzin di questa, *non sono perciò da reputare avari*. Altri s'ingegnano di riscuotere e di racquistare quello o che hanno creduto o cha hanno prestato del loro ad altrui: nè questo è da dire avarizia, quantunque sia più che quel che bisogna a chi il radomanda. (7.64, esp. all., emphasis added)

Still others will carry out their art or business with great dedication in order to avoid idleness and, though they may generate more than what is necessary from it, should not be considered greedy. Others strive to redeem guarantees or to regain what they have lent to others. This too is not to be considered avarice although the one who gains receives more than what is necessary. (Papio, 365–6)

Honest, hard-working merchants who engage in commerce in order to meet their needs – and perhaps produce beyond need – are not avaricious. Neither are those who work to regain loans lent to others, a possible reference to those banking companies who lent money to Edward III, or other international political figures who sought funding from Florentine banking homes. Thus Boccaccio, twenty years earlier, could find it possible to celebrate the protagonists of the merchant class in the *Decameron* for their ingenuity, as Branca has shown.

In his conclusion of his treatment of the types of avarice, Boccaccio returns to those other protagonists of the *Decameron*, the clerics, whose avarice is most grave:

> E di questi medesimi si posson dire essere i cherici, ne' quali è questo peccato tanto più vituperevole quanto con men difficultà l'ampissime entrate posseggono, non di loro patrimonio, non di loro acquisto pervenute loro; e oltre a ciò, con men ragione le ritengono, per ciò che i loro essercizi deono essere intorno alle cose divine, all'opere della misericordia e di ciascuna altra pietosa cosa: deono stare in orazione, digiunare, sobriamente vivere, e dar di sè buono essempio agli altri in disprezare le cose temporali e 'l mondo, e seguire con povertà le vestige di Cristo, acciò che, bene adoperando, apaiano le loro opere esser conformi alla dottrina. Le quali cose come essi le fanno, Idio il vede. (7.70, esp. all.)

> Members of this group, we may say, are the clerics, in whom this sin is as deplorable as it is easy for them to take possession of enormous profits, which derive neither from their own patrimonies nor from their own gains. What is more, it is even less rational for them to keep their money, insofar as they are bound to carry out works related to divine things and to perform acts of charity and other compassionate tasks. They should pray, fast, live a sober life, and set a good example for others as models of disdain for temporal goods and for the world, and they should follow Christ's footsteps in poverty so that, by doing good works, their actions may seem to be in conformity with doctrine. Whether they do this, only God Who sees them knows. (Papio, 366–7)

By shifting back to the clerics, whom Dante accuses of avarice, at the end of the allegorical exposition, Boccaccio signals the salience of this criticism for the church as well as for the world of commerce. Clerics, who should spend their time in prayer and live a sober life of poverty, while holding worldly things in disdain and following Christ as an example, here are the object of a sharp rebuke that recalls Boccaccio's general disapproval of the church examined earlier. In fact, the language of this passage from *Esposizioni* 7 vividly recalls the lengthy diatribe of Tedaldo degli Elisei in *Decameron* 3.7, which accuses friars of the sins of lust and avarice, an accusation that is repeated in the *novella* of Friar Rinaldo in 7.3.[54] Because friars do not follow the example of Christ they themselves cannot serve as an example, as Tedaldo states (3.7.42–3). Perhaps because he viewed the corruption of the church as a lost cause – or perhaps, as Timothy Kircher has argued, Boccaccio's response to clerical hypocrisy went "beyond feelings of detachment"[55] – such invectives as the one in *Esposizioni* 7 remain precisely that, invectives. Boccaccio's anatomy of avarice as it applies to merchants is much more detailed; the definition of this vice in the allegorical exposition seems intended to admonish its listeners in the church of Santo Stefano to follow the right path. It is maybe no coincidence, then, that avarice is also the extended focus of Boccaccio's attention in *Esposizioni* 1, at the beginning of his commentary (much in the way that Musciatto Franzesi inaugurates this vice in *Decameron* 1.1), where Boccaccio again and necessarily adopts the language of commerce.

The Dantean *cornice* of Avarice: *Esposizioni* 1 and *Decameron* 10.3

With a few words in his gloss on the "lupa" in *Inferno* 1, Boccaccio's commentary immediately distinguishes itself from other early commentaries and shows itself to be an explicit reflection of the merchant society of his times. In his explication of "E quale è quei che volentieri acquista," Boccaccio writes:

> Per questa comparazione ne dimostra l'autore qual divenisse per lo impedimento pòrtogli da questa bestia, dicendo: *E qual è que'*, o *mercatante o altro, che volentieri acquista,* cioè *guadagna.* (1.42, esp. litt., emphasis added)
>
> In this comparison the author shows us how he became on account of the obstacle presented by the beast, saying: *And like one*, whether a merchant or other man, *who gladly acquires,* earns. (Papio, 59)

While Boccaccio's interpretation of the *lupa* as avarice is harmonious with other early commentaries that also view the *lupa* in economic terms,[56] the words "o mercatante o altro" that he inserts into an almost verbatim transcription of Dante's verse are Boccaccio's true hallmark; the insertion of these words shows what is at stake for Boccaccio in a discussion of avarice/*cupiditas*, and how Boccaccio configures these vices in discussing contemporary merchant society. References to the merchant class appear rarely in the *Esposizioni*, but when Boccaccio finds it necessary to integrate a discussion of this social class into his explication of the poem it is nearly always within the context of a treatment of avarice, as here in *Esposizioni* 1 and 7 (as would be expected for a canto that explicitly concerns avarice). In the remaining part of this chapter, I highlight the importance of avarice for Boccaccio at the beginning of the *Esposizioni* and show how this moment is integrated with his own commentary on the vices and virtues of the merchant class.

An association of avarice with the figure of the merchant, as well as a constant reflection on material possessions, continues in *Esposizioni* 1 in the text of the allegorical exposition. When Boccaccio anticipates the question of why poets need to write allegorically, he describes how individuals naturally guard their material possessions (and do not "tenerle in piazza," 1.4, esp. all.; "keep them in the *piazza*") in order that these objects do not lose value by being copied or by becoming commonplace. The second reason for which a poet would not wish to expose the "mellifluo e celestial sapore" locked within verse is the same reason for which one is inclined to more attentively guard those objects that were hard earned:

> Suole quello, che con difficultà *s'acquista*, piacer più e guardarsi meglio che quello che senza alcuna fatica o poca si truova: e questo le grandi eredità rimase a' nostri giovani cittadini hanno mostrato. (1.10, esp. all., emphasis added)

> It is normal for something acquired with difficulty to be more pleasing and better protected than what is found through little or no effort. The great inheritances left to our young citizens have shown this to be true. (Papio, 81)

As in the case of the large inheritances left to Florentine youth of today, Boccaccio claims, which are instead squandered (one only need think of the profligate *brigate* that populated Florence; see chapter 1), so should this other level of significance for poetic verse be guarded. The presence of "s'acquista" recalls what Boccaccio describes as the activity of the merchant in his gloss of *Inferno* 1.55–60: "E quale è quegli che volentieri acquista." It should be emphasized that Boccaccio found it appropriate to explain even something as abstract as the concept of allegory to his audience in Santo Stefano in Badia in such material terms, which they (and especially the merchants among them) would readily understand.

Boccaccio dedicates several pages in the allegorical exposition to glossing the *lonza* (lust) and the *leone* (pride), but the most vivid passages describe the vice of avarice as represented by the *lupa*. In one such passage Boccaccio magisterially depicts the figure of an avaricious man by deploying the storytelling style that evokes the *Decameron* (such words could describe Ermino Avarizia himself):[57]

> Metterassi l'avaro in una piccola casetta, e in quella, in continua dieta, per non spendere, dimorando senza muoversi, *diece o venti anni presterrà ad usura*, vestirà male e calzerà peggio, rifiuterà gli onori per non onorare, e, dove egli dovrebbe de' suoi acquisti esser signore, esso diventa de' suoi tesori vilissimo servo; e, quanto maggiore strettezza fa del suo, tanto tien gli occhi più diritti all'altrui. Sempre è pieno di ramarichii, sempre dice sè esser povero e mostrasi; e, brievemente, faccendosi de' beni della fortuna tristissima parte, quanto l'animo suo sia piccolo e misero manifestamente dimostra. Nelle quali cose si può comprendere l'avarizia acompagnarsi con la più misera condizione de'uomini che si truova, come la lupa col più tristo de' lupi si congiugne. (1.129–30, esp. all., emphasis added)

> The greedy man will set himself up in a little shack and will live there on a meagre diet (to avoid spending money), without going anywhere else. He will make ten- and twenty-year loans, his clothes will be terrible and his shoes even worse, he will refuse honours so as not to reciprocate, and, whereas he should be the lord of his earnings, he will become a vile slave to his fortune. The tighter he holds on to his own money, the more intense is his gaze upon that of others. He is always full of complaints and always says (and acts like) he is destitute. In short, every time he says he is the victim of bad luck, he plainly shows just how small-minded and petty he really is. One may see in such characteristics that avarice always accompanies the most miserable of men's circumstances, just as the she-wolf pairs off with the lowliest of wolves. (Papio, 101)

This inspired narrative moment in the *Esposizioni* reveals, I believe, the urgency of the *Commedia*'s message for Boccaccio's merchant audience, the expanded ranks of the *gente nuova* and those who, like the Cerchi, switched their status to that of *popolano* in the latter half of the fourteenth century. Within the flourishing of banking activity that sought to finance the Angevin papacy, or England, usury can be located at the ethical extremity of vice (as Boccaccio here mentions the progression *in malo* from avarice to usury: "diece o venti anni presterrà ad usura").[58]

Boccaccio's portrait of the miserable miser – miserable precisely because avarice, like the female wolf, he claims, seeks out the most miserable condition for living – can be read by extension as a condemnation of those figures who have succumbed to avarice in the First Day of the *Decameron*: Musciatto Franzesi and Cepparello (1.1), Ermino Avarizia (1.8), and the hypocritical clergy (1.2 and 1.6). In addition, Boccaccio here, by contrast, reveals the trap circumvented by such figures as Cangrande della Scala and the Abbot of Cluny (1.7). If Boccaccio, in the First Day in the *Decameron*, offers a spectrum of avarice composed of varying degrees of vice adopted by these characters, later in his life, during the composition of the *Esposizioni*, at the time in which the merchant class was becoming a majority in the Florentine population, he reveals the extreme of avarice that these characters either embrace or reject.[59]

This parallel between *Esposizioni* 1 and the *Decameron* First Day becomes more transparent as one reads Boccaccio's gloss further. For just as the virtue that remedies the vice of avarice in the First Day is *liberalità* (generosity, courtesy, magnanimity), so does Boccaccio once again identify this opposition in *Esposizioni* 1. Avarice, Boccaccio writes, can be found in evil and cowardly individuals, never in the virtuous or magnanimous (1.128, esp. all.). Likewise, in his elaboration of *avarizia* as the devil, Boccaccio posits that *liberalità* can be found at the opposite end of the spectrum from *avarizia* (1.153, esp. all.). The appearance of this opposition in the *Esposizioni*, while it follows the definition put forth by Aristotle in his *Ethics* and repeated by Boccaccio in *Esposizioni* 7, should not be taken for granted. Other commentators, such as Guido da Pisa (whose commentary was a source for the *Esposizioni*), gloss the *lupa* as *avarizia* but do not read the *veltro* as *liberalità*.

In the final pages of *Esposizioni* 1, where the author addresses the controversial issue of the *veltro*, the urgency of *liberalità* for Boccaccio and the originality of his reading become apparent. If the *lupa* is avarice, Boccaccio believes, then it logically follows that the *veltro* is not Christ (as Guido da Pisa argues in his commentary), but someone born under the "celestial affect" of generosity (1.159, esp. all.).[60] Dante metaphorically terms the effect of this impression upon man as the *veltro*,

The Ethical Framework of the *Decameron* 131

Boccaccio argues, because the hound is by nature the opposite of the wolf (hounds hunt wolves) (1.163, esp. all.). While Guido da Pisa opposes these two animals as well,[61] here the similarities with Guido's commentary end. Boccaccio is certain about the abstract identity of the *veltro*, but initially claims to find difficulty in explaining the following verse, that the *veltro* would be born "tra feltro e feltro" (1.164, esp. all.). Proceeding then to report the opinions of others on this subject, Boccaccio repeats the interpretation of the *veltro* as Christ (1.165, esp. all.), which was advanced by Graziolo and the Anonimo Selmiano but most forcefully argued by Guido da Pisa; but he then attempts to disprove this argument.[62] He gives two reasons: (1) Christ does not take inspiration from the movement of the stars, but rather the stars take inspiration from him, and (2) Christ will not be born again at the time of his second coming.

Boccaccio, contradicting his earlier claims, does have a specific opinion as to the proper gloss of this verse. Taking his cue from Jacopo della Lana,[63] he glosses "tra feltro e feltro" as an indication that the *veltro* would be born into poverty:

> Altri dicono, e al parer mio con più sentimento, dover potere avvenire, secondo la potenza conceduta alle stelle, che alcuno, poveramente e di parenti di bassa e infima condizione nato, il che paiono voler quelle parole 'tra feltro e feltro' in quanto questa spezie di panno è, oltre ad ogni altra, vilissima, potrebbe per virtù e laudevoli operazioni in tanta preeminenza venire e in tanta eccellenza di principato, che, dirizandosi tutte le sue operazioni a magnificenzia, senza avere in alcuno atto animo o appetito ad alcuno acquisto di reame o di tesoro, ed avendo in singulare abominazione il vizio dell'avarizia, e dando di sè ottimo esempio a tutti nelle cose apartenenti alla magnificenzia, e la costellazione del cielo essendogli a ciò favourevole, che egli potrebbe, o potrà, muovere gli animi de' subditi a seguire, faccendo il similiante, le sue vestige, e per conseguente cacciar questo vizio universalmente del mondo. (1.169–70, esp. all.)

Others say, in my opinion more convincingly, that, in conformity with the powers entrusted to the stars, someone will be born poor to parents of a low, indeed, the lowest station (which is what seems to be meant in the words "between felt and felt," inasmuch as this type of fabric is of the poorest quality). Through his virtue and praiseworthy acts, this man could come to such pre-eminence and in such an excellent kingdom that, by directing all his deeds towards magnificence without the least desire for or inclination to acquiring power or wealth, by considering the vice of avarice to be particularly abominable, by making himself the paramount model in all things related to magnificence, and enjoying the favour of the heavens' constellation, he would – or will – be able to stir the minds of his subjects to follow his example, and his footsteps, consequently eliminating this vice from the face of the earth. (Papio, 107)

According to Boccaccio the *veltro* is not Christ; he would be an individual who would not crave power or riches, but his hatred of avarice and his generosity would serve as an example for others to follow in changing their "operazioni" from avarice to *magnificenzia*. This person recalls a figure such as Guiglielmo Borsiere, whose suggestion of a visual depiction of *cortesia* inspires Ermino Avarizia to amend his ways. Indeed, Borsiere's accomplishment fits Boccaccio's words above perfectly ("che egli potrebbe [...] muovere gli animi de' subditi a seguire, faccendo il similiante, le sue vestige").

Here in the *Esposizioni* Boccaccio does not propose a specific person who would possess these qualities. He refutes yet another interpretation of "tra feltro e feltro," that the *veltro* will be a Tartar emperor who would be buried, according to custom, in a humble dress of felt, because the premise of this interpretation is that the wealth of the emperor will satisfy his desire to accumulate wealth.[64] No treasure exists, Boccaccio claims, which could ever sate the hunger of an avaricious person ("quanto tesoro fu mai sotto luna, o sarà, non avrebbe forza di saziare la fame di un solo avaro, non che d'infiniti, che sempre sopra la terra ne sono," 1.176, esp. all.). This is the danger of avarice for Boccaccio, and the ways of society will change to the better only when God decides they will, he concludes, with a tone of resignation (1.177, esp. all.). It is not hard to discern Boccaccio's frustration in these concluding remarks, which could be attributed either to the difficulty in explaining the *veltro* or to his exasperation with society, which must change its ways, and whose individuals must convert their "appetiti da avarizia in liberalità" (1.172, esp. all.; "desires from avarice to liberality"). Did Boccaccio revisit these same feelings of frustration with the plague of avarice in Florence when he had to return to the Tartars yet again in *Esposizioni* 17 in the final words of the commentary ("Sono i Tartari ...," "The Tartars are ...")? After having to explain the invective of the "gente nuova" from *Inferno* 16 to his Florentine audience, was the mere presence of the Tartars in *Inferno* 17 with their connection to the *veltro* of *Inferno* 1 too much for an infirm Boccaccio to tolerate? Did Boccaccio cease writing the commentary for this reason as well?

Though this provocative question is impossible to answer, a more concrete connection exists between Boccaccio's evocation of the Tartar emperors here in *Esposizioni* 1 and *Decameron* 10.3, the *novella* of Mithridanes and Nathan, thus indicating the importance of such an interpretation of *Inferno* 1 for Boccaccio.[65] A *novella* dealing with one of the most extreme illustrations of generosity, that of Nathan's willingness to offer his own life to satisfy Mithridanes's envy, this story has geographic coordinates that tie it to Cathay, the "imperio di mezzo," as Boccaccio incorrectly calls Tartary in *Esposizioni* 1.[66] His characterization of Nathan, a noble whose wealth was beyond comparison, evokes the wealth of Tartar emperors, according to *Esposizioni* 1 (1.172, esp. all.). Nathan, though not born into poverty, as Boccaccio believes the *veltro* would be, sets an outstanding example for others by means of his generous acts (10.3.5), including his incredible hospitality in one of the most beautiful palaces ever constructed. There he established a laudable custom of receiving and honouring noblemen, and his customary hospitality won him fame throughout the world (10.3.6). His reputation for generosity reached Mithridanes and incited Mithridanes's extreme envy.

The *novella* of Mithridanes and Nathan can be said to be the performance of a living *exemplum*, insofar as Mithridanes' envy, which comes from observing Nathan, precipitates his scheme to assume Nathan's identity and then to assassinate him. These actions constitute a fictional manifestation of the "essemplo" ("example") referred to in *Esposizioni* 1. If other commentators on *Inferno* 1 believe that the changing of the world's ways is already occurring in the "imperio di mezzo" ("Middle Kingdom") (1.172, esp. all.), then Nathan's example and Mithridanes's goal in life to be the most generous man of all would cause its transformation, as Nathan states (10.3.20). In this way, we can view *Decameron* 10.3 as a dramatic enactment of the issues raised by *Inferno* 1, which Boccaccio reveals later in the *Esposizioni*.

Before considering how these social concerns, Dantean in origin, inform several *novelle* in the first and last days of the *Decameron*, I will turn to a small but significant detail from the beginning of 10.3. For Boccaccio claims to have heard the story of Nathan from certain Genoese merchants (though the content of the story has been linked to Marco Polo's tales of Kublai Khan);[67] as he writes, "se fede si può dare alle parole d'alcuni genovesi e d'altri uomini che in quelle contrade stati sono" (10.3.4; "if the word of various Genoese and of others who have been to those parts may be trusted," McWilliam, 712). Representatives of the merchant class (whether through the tales of

Marco Polo or by word of mouth) learned of the reputation of Nathan and Mithridanes first-hand, Boccaccio claims, and they later brought back this information to Boccaccio. The navigations of merchants, as we have seen, are one focus of Boccaccio's long treatment of avarice in *Esposizioni* 7, where Boccaccio disapproves of their restlessness. But without their desire to travel the world, to wander through Nathan's kingdom and harvest this tale for Boccaccio's purposes, it is implied that perhaps 10.3, this fundamental *novella* of Day Ten, would not exist.

From Finance to Fowling: The Case of the Gianfigliazzi Family

There is yet another possible response to the question of why Boccaccio ceased lecturing on the *Inferno* at canto 17 (if one interprets the material lectures as congruous with the delivered lectures themselves). Was Boccaccio hesitant to address the accusation of usury lodged by Dante in *Inferno* 17 against two prominent Florentine families, the Gianfigliazzi and Obriachi, as his audience might have counted some of their relatives among its number? The Gianfigliazzi family, bankers who worked in the Peruzzi company but also practiced in their own right internationally, are placed by Dante in the circle of the usurers, *Inferno* 17.59–60: "in una borsa gialla vidi azzurro/che d'un leone avea faccia e contegno." The pilgrim observes the coat of arms for the Gianfigliazzi family – an azure lion against a gold field – on the purse of one of the usurers but never specifies which member of the Gianfigliazzi resides there. Their long-standing position in Florentine society and politics dates back to 1201, when one of their ancestors, Giovanni di Azzo, is listed amidst those consuls of the commune engaged in peace deliberatitons with Siena. As D'Addario notes, Cacciaguida in *Paradiso* 16 does not list the Gianfigliazzi among the noble families of Florence's past, though they certainly qualified as such. They do not compare with, for instance, the Donati, one of the oldest families of the knighted consular aristocracy (whose Florentine origins date to the eleventh century), they were not as "nuova" as the Spini, whose Florentine ancestry dates to the second half of the thirteenth century.[68] Designated as a magnate family by the Ordinances of Justice in 1293, the Gianfigliazzi are thought to have aligned themselves with the Guelph cause from the thirteenth century onwards, participating as well in the removal of Walter of Brienne in 1343.[69] The Gianfigliazzi had a prosperous firm based in Florence but also operating in Orange, France.[70]

Boccaccio personally knew various members of the Gianfigliazzi family (such as Alianora and Luigi), and features or addresses them in the *Decameron* and other works: Currado in *Decameron* 6.4, Alianora as Adiona in the *Comedia delle ninfe fiorentine* and again in the *Amorosa visione*, and Luigi in the *Esposizioni* and in his poem to Zanobi da Strada.[71] Currado Gianfigliazzi appears in a favourable light in *Dec.* 6.4, presented in terms of his generosity and other virtues that would have been known by the *brigata* ("Currado Gianfigliazzi, sì come ciascuna di voi e udito e veduto puote avere, sempre della nostra città è stato notabile cittadino, liberale e magnifico, e vita cavalleresca tenendo continuamente in cani e in uccelli s'è dilettato, le sue opere maggiori al presente lasciando stare," 6.4.4; "As all of you will have heard and seen for yourselves, Currado Gianfigliazzi has always played a notable part in the affairs of our city. Generous and hospitable, he lived the life of a true gentleman, and, to say nothing for the moment of his more important activities, he took a constant delight in hunting and hawking," McWilliam, 454). Currado appears in this story as the indignant master of Chichibio, who tries to hide the fact that he had served Brunetta, his love interest, one of the legs of the crane that Currado had hunted. By means of a *pronta risposta*, Chichibio escapes from the anger of Currado ("tutto ancor gonfiato") by claiming that cranes only have one leg, as they appear when they are sleeping, unless you frighten them by yelling ("ma voi non gridaste 'ho, ho!' a quella d'iersera; ché se cosí gridato aveste ella avrebbe cosí l'altra coscia e l'altro piè fuor mandata, come hanno fatto questa," 6.4.18; "'They do indeed, sir,' he said, 'but you never shouted "Oho!" to the one you had last night, otherwise it would have shoved its second leg out, like these others,'" McWilliam, 456). Currado's anger disappears and turns into joyous laughter.

Neifile draws attention to the fact that she does not give a full portrait of Currado's "opere maggiori." Branca proposes that this lacuna is an oblique reference to Currado's mercantile activity and role in civic politics.[72] Indeed, it is his biography that is most suggestive for an understanding of how Boccaccio viewed the members of the larger banking families within the ethical history of *cortesia* and avarice. Currado Gianfigliazzi was born either in Florence or in Avignon, where his father practised banking, in the last quarter of the thirteenth century, serving such figures as Charles II of Anjou and James II of Aragon.[73] He came into knighthood like many members of his family, which precluded him from taking a dominant role in civic politics because of the Ordinances of Justice. What is compelling about Currado's biography, though, is that he ceased working for the family's banking house when his father passed away in 1314.[74] In fact, unlike many of the new knights of Florence, who regarded their title as nothing more than honorific, Arringhi notes that he engaged in military activity as truly befitting a *nobiles miles*, such as at Montecatini against Uguccione Della Faggiuola (1314) and against Castruccio Castracani (1325). As the civic military went into decline and the commune began hiring mercenaries, Currado retired to a life in the country, much as we see him in *Decameron* 6.4.

While Currado was not a Corso Donati, an aristocrat from one of the oldest and knighted consular families, his abandonment of the commercial life distinguishes him from Geri Spini, an elite member of a banking family that was once one of the *gente nuova*. His espousal of the chivalric lifestyle as a military calling and not an empty status marks him as one of the few remaining figures of a culture of *cortesia* that would be replaced by mercenaries. He passed away shortly after 1353, and it is easy to read Boccaccio's portrait of him in the *Decameron* as nostalgic, just as Boccaccio was for the days of *cortesia* in Dante's times, as discussed vis-á-vis *Decameron* 6.9. Here, the fondness Boccaccio displays for Currado distinguishes him from the usurers that the pilgrim encounters in *Inferno* 17. Perhaps this is how Boccaccio wanted the Gianfigliazzi to be remembered after the plague: as one of the last families of *cortesia*, not as a banking family. The eventual public lecture on *Inferno* 17 would have forced Boccaccio to reconcile these two aspects of their family history. Here, Neifile can simply leave Currado's professional and political lives to the side ("le sue opere maggiori al presente lasciando stare").

If Currado Gianfigliazzi represents a crucial element in Boccaccio's different histories of the families of Florence, then yet another Gianfigliazzi – Luigi, a jurist – will be cited by Boccaccio in the *Esposizioni* as a source for the German history of the Guelphs and the Ghibellines ("E questi due nomi [Guelfi e Ghibellini], secondo che recitava il venerabile uomo messer Luigi Gianfigliazzi, il quale affermava averlo avuto da Carlo quarto imperadore, vennero della Magna, là dove dice nacquero in questa forma," *Esp.* 10.43; "These two names, according to what the venerable messer Luigi Gianfigliazzi used to say (and he claimed to have got it from Emperor Charles IV), came from Germany, where, he says, they were born in the following way," Papio, 444). This is the history – the earlier history of the Ghibellines – that, as I discuss in the next chapter, Boccaccio believes holds the promise for the future of *cortesia*.

Conclusion

This chapter has traced the continuity of the theme of avarice, as a vice both of the church and of the merchant class, in certain *novelle* from the *Decameron* that bear a Dantean pedigree, and their relation to Boccaccio's elaboration on that vice in the *Esposizioni*. These are tales that are historically centred on the coordinates of Dante's world: his first host in exile, Cangrande della Scala (1.7), the pope who sent Dante into exile, Pope Boniface VIII, and his accomplice Musciatto Franzesi (10.2, 6.2, 1.1). Boccaccio does not spare church prelates in these *novelle* or in related passages from the *Esposizioni*, instead betraying sympathy towards secular leaders that stand for empire (Cangrande della Scala) and papal reform (Ghino di Tacco). In his elaboration of the vice of avarice in the *Esposizioni*, Boccaccio's attention to merchants resembles an admonition more than an invective.

One cannot speak of the vices and virtues featured in Day One and Day Ten of the *Decameron* without acknowledging Boccaccio's large debt to Dante in this thematic development.[75] The *brigata* of the *cornice* reflects upon the vice of avarice by means of Dante's life and poem, and does so both upon their retreat from Florence and society and again before their return. The social and moral imperative of generosity resounds in these tales, so much so that it would be remiss for us as readers not to see this intention of the *Decameron* alongside the social and moral imperative of the *Commedia*.[76] Dante's imprint on the *novelle* of avarice and generosity in the First Day (1.1, 1.6, 1.7, and 1.8) and on their associated tales in Day Ten (10.2 and 10.3) has been rendered visible by means of the *Esposizioni*, and Boccaccio's later commentary appears remarkably harmonious with these issues in the earlier *Decameron*.

What, then, is the relationship between the culture of *cortesia* and the political history of the Ghibellines, the party that has been defunct in Florence since the late thirteenth century but that is seen as the original party of *cortesia*? In the next chapter, I return to the Dantean discourse of the lost customs of Florence (6.2, 6.9, 9.8) as it is embedded within Boccaccio's larger ethical discourse of *cortesia* and liberality. As in the case of his treatment of avarice, Boccaccio draws on Dante's times and poem for the figures that embody *cortesia* and *magnificenza* in the *Decameron*, such as Dante's other host in exile, the Malaspina family, in 2.6, and the families in the Romagna in 5.4 and 5.8. His history of the Guelphs and the Ghibellines, both in the *Esposizioni* (10) and in the *Decameron* (10.6, 10.7), marks the intersection between political affiliation, eros, and *cortesia* in his vision of the past. Did *cortesia* perish with the Malaspina, Lizio da Valbona, and others heralded by Dante in his nostalgic lament? Or, for Boccaccio, is there a way for *cortesia* to remain alive in the progeny of those families whose ancestors were Ghibellines?

4 Constructing a Future for *cortesia* in the Past: Virility, Nobility, and the History of the Guelphs and the Ghibellines

The conflict between the Guelphs and the Ghibellines would mark most of Florentine history for the thirteenth century, beginning with the Buondelmonti murder of 1216, as Dante (*Inf.* 28.106–8; *Par.* 16.66), Compagni (1.2), and Villani (1.7.38) recount.[1] The Ghibelline party in Florence would variously gain and lose power over the course of several decades during that century. Its varying fortunes spanned the rise to power of Frederick II, who assumed the title of *podestà* from 1238 to 1246; the exile of the Guelphs by the Ghibelline party in 1248; the death of Frederick II in 1250; the exile of the Ghibellines by the Guelphs in 1258; the defeat of the Florentine Guelphs at the hands of the Sienese Ghibellines at Montaperti in 1266; and finally, the defeat of Manfred by Charles of Anjou at Benevento in 1266. The Florentine Ghibelline party would meet its definitive end in 1267, when the Guelph party took control of the city.[2] The "peace" that was negotiated by papal legate Cardinal Latino (1280), who attempted to create a balance of power between the Guelphs and those Ghibellines whom he summoned back to the city, would also be undone by the Guelphs (Compagni, *Cronica* 1.4).[3] Thus, in the years following 1267, Florentine Ghibellines would gradually move into extinction, as arguably would aristocratic culture, leaving behind a Parte Guelfa composed of only the older elite families as well as the newer merchant families.

In this sense, by the time that Boccaccio was composing the *Decameron*, Ghibellinism was allegedly extinct in Florence. Furthermore, at that time, and more so by the time he was lecturing on the *Inferno*, the identification of someone as Ghibelline called forth a witch-hunt, the Parte Guelfa's practice of excluding political adversaries from office, which was called *ammonizione*, and which began in the middle to late 1340s. Elite families in the Parte sought to discredit new members of the *gente nuova* by accusing them of being foreigners and Ghibellines. This antipathy assumed legal form in 1346, in a law requiring the identification of recent immigrants from the *contado* who were unable to prove that they were first-, second-, or third-generation Florentines; those individuals were deprived of the right to hold office.[4] This ban was revived after the plague in 1358, and became an indiscriminate practice of *vendetta* and retaliation, with even Guelph individuals standing accused of Ghibelline proclivities.[5]

It is curious indeed, then, that Boccaccio looks to the past, including those Guelphs and Ghibellines who defeated each other in these pivotal events, in articulating the future promise of *cortesia*. The *Decameron* turns to those named by the *Commedia* as part of the extinct world of *cortesia* evoked in *Purgatorio* 7, 8, 14 and 16, and *Paradiso* 16: Currado Malaspina (*Dec.* 2.6), Frederick II (*Dec.* 1.7, 2.6), Charles I of Anjou (10.6), Peter III of Aragon (10.7), Lizio da Valbona and the Mainardi family (5.4), the Traversari and Anastagi families (5.8), and the Alberighi family (5.9). Though Dante may claim that *cortesia* lived and died with these lords and rulers in the Romagna and Lombardy, Boccaccio resists the demise of this practice by featuring these figures in narratives that deal with eros, virility, and procreation. If Boccaccio can promise regeneration and progeny for these figures, then *cortesia* will survive within the afterlife that the *Commedia* enjoys in the *Decameron* – yet the increase in anti-Ghibellinism would inflect his portrayal of the Ghibellines from the *Decameron* to the *Esposizioni*. Boccaccio would like to favour the most ancient families of the historical world of the *Commedia* in promising the future of *cortesia*, but the shadow of his present times looms large over such historical reconstructions.

Decameron 6.6 addresses with irony the intersection of nobility and antiquity for Boccaccio. Here Michele Scalza argues that the Baronci are the most ancient and noble family in the entire world because they are the products of God's first creations, when, as the text reads, he was still learning the rudiments of his craft, the disproportionate faces and facial features of the Baronci a testament to their antiquity. The irony of this *novella* can also be located in its political subtext, speaking to Boccaccio's interpretation of Ghibelline families: the Baronci family, a new elite family that aligned with the Guelphs (within a similar category as the Spini), contrast poorly with the Uberti or Lamberti families named in this *novella*, two of the most ancient and Ghibelline families who left Florence for other Ghibelline strongholds, such as Siena and Pisa.

Boccaccio's nostalgia for the days of *cortesia* informs his reading of the Guelph and Ghibelline past, which, unlike his historicization of the

Florentine civic conflict at the turn of the century, is more attuned to differences in political party affiliation. In the *Decameron* he revives the lost world of *cortesia* for Guelphs and Ghibelline families articulated in the *Commedia*. He does so in ways that do not necessarily support the Ghibelline cause, of course, but that reveal a conflicted view of these historical protagonists, naturally due to the anti-Ghibelline sentiment of his own times, one that increases in vigour over the second half of the fourteenth century. This revision of the lost world of *cortesia* includes those *novelle*, namely 1.7 and 2.6, that fall under the rubric of Frederick II and Manfred and the Hohenstaufen line. Not coincidentally, these are stories that focus on Dante's hosts in exile, which can be read as a commentary on Dante's own pro-imperial thought, to the degree to which it was harmonious with the Ghibelline cause.

His revision of Dante's lament for the disappearance of *cortesia* in these moments from the *Commedia* involves two main differences. First, it hinges upon his differing view of *cortesia*'s location (as discussed in chapter 1). Whereas Dante defines *cortesia* as an exclusive practice of former courts in the *Convivio* (2.10.7–8), in *Esposizioni* 16.53 Boccaccio views it as civil acts, "atti civili, cioè nel vivere insieme liberalmente e lietamente" that are not limited to the court. The tale of Currado Malaspina and Madonna Beritola (*Dec.* 2.6) charts the journey of *cortesia* with its protagonists, thereby enacting the diffusion of Malaspina's reputation, from *Purgatorio* 8, for his *cortesia*. Boccaccio abandons certain geographical and ideological constraints of Dante's vision, paving the way for *cortesia* to be practiced outside of the court.

Second, if nobility, as Dante sustains in *Purgatorio* 7, is not inherited, then Boccaccio focuses on how the *Commedia* only features aristocratic families with a Ghibelline heritage as the principal inheritors of *cortesia*. He thus teases out certain differences while blurring others in the relationship between nobility and aristocracy and the future of *cortesia*. For example, Currado Malaspina, whose family Dante presents as the exception to the nobility that is not inherited in *Purgatorio* 8, must negotiate the difference between Giusfredi's apparent lack of noble status and the desire to find his daughter Spina a spouse. But once he learns that Giusfredi, in fact, does possess noble blood, he is quick to have him marry Spina, for that implies the promise of a continued Malaspina line in the name of *cortesia*. *Cortesia* – once, according to Dante, the practice of the court – now finds its future in the house of the Malaspina, the "familial" court.

Negotiating the survival of *cortesia* and considerations of marriage, such as that of Currado regarding his daughter or, in other examples here discussed, the sublimation of erotic desire, are what Boccaccio highlights in his revival of Dante's vision of the past. The stories examined in this chapter suggest that it is generally those aligned with the Guelph cause who are the harbingers of sexual desire, while Ghibellines more often suppress their own or others' sexual desire. In one instance, two other figures from *Purgatorio* 7, Peter III and Charles I, are depicted in terms of their virility, which must be sublimated for effective, magnanimous rule in *Dec.* 10.6 and 10.7. However, it is the younger generation of Ghibelline men, such as Giusfredi and Ricciardo Mainardi, whose virility helps ensure the future of *cortesia*. While Giusfredi's youthful virility is couched within the promise of marriage, and thus of *cortesia*'s future, the virility of the older generation, that of the Guelph Charles I of Anjou, must be sublimated in the name of *cortesia*, reminiscent of the conventions of courtly love. Yet it is a Ghibelline, Peter III of Aragon, who has no difficulty in remaining passive in response to a young girl's love for him. The sexual potency of the Guelphs is also highlighted in Boccaccio's original interpretation of the origins of the Guelph and Ghibelline conflict. Deviating vastly from Giovanni Villani's *Nuova cronica*, Boccaccio invents a tale of castration and revenge between Guelph and Ghibelline that culminates in the inconsummate marriage between Guelph and Countess Matilda. *Cortesia* becomes represented by Boccaccio as the power of the Ghibellines to sublimate erotic impulses. *Cortesia*, in these moments, reads as the repression of male desire, and specifically of the desire of male rulers (such as Marco Lombardo describes in terms of the curbs needed for the appetites of the will in *Purg.* 16.94–6).

The situation is quite different in Boccaccio's rewriting of the female protagonists of the Romagna from *Purgatorio* 14. Guido del Duca bemoans the lack of "courteous" progeny in the houses of the Calboli, the Traversari, and the Anastagi. Yet Boccaccio features members from these families in two *novelle* from Day Five, 5.4 and 5.8, that promise future inheritors of a tradition of *cortesia*. Strikingly, in one case the fulfilment of a young woman's sexual desire renders this promise concrete: Caterina, the daughter of a Guelph, Lizio da Valbona, consummates her love with a Ghibelline nobleman, Ricciardo Mainardi, thus presenting a portrait of harmony between opposing political parties. Caterina's agency in the hunt for his nightingale, however, contrasts sharply with the destructive "caccia infernale" ("infernal hunt") of 5.8, where female desire is manipulated and determined by male desire. It is precisely the violence of this *novella*, in which Nastagio degli Onesti is at first powerless against the absolute will of the daughter of Paolo Traversari, that reverses *cortesia*'s fate in the Romagna in *Purgatorio* 14. Boccaccio also reverses the fortune for one Florentine family, the Alberighi, lamented by Cacciaguida as being lost to time in *Paradiso* 16, in the tale of *Decameron* 5.9. This tale likewise highlights the power of women to negotiate marriage alliances that will ensure the future of nobility.

The Familial Court of *cortesia*:
The Civil Acts of the Malaspina Family

Since Boccaccio employs Dante's host in exile, Cangrande della Scala, in 1.7, in order to forge a larger discourse on avarice in the church, readers of the *Decameron* should not be surprised to find Currado Malaspina (2.6), a relative of Dante's host in Lunigiana, Franceschino Malaspina, in a *novella* that belongs to Boccaccio's genealogy of *cortesia* in the *Decameron* and the history at large of the Guelphs and the Ghibellines he puts forth in the *Decameron* and *Esposizioni*. Dante's hosts in exile comprise the protagonists of a lost *cortesia* that Boccaccio figures as living members in his revision of the past. In this *novella*, which is set immediately after the defeat of King Manfred of Sicily and the Ghibellines at Benevento in 1266, Emilia recounts the vicissitudes of a certain Madonna Beritola, whose husband, the Ghibelline Arrighetto Capece, is imprisoned for his support of Manfred.[6] Boccaccio designates Arrighetto Capece as the leader of the island of Sicily when Charles I defeats Manfred. Ignorant of her husband's imprisonment, his pregnant wife Madonna Beritola flees to Lipari with her eight-year-old son Giusfredi, where she gives birth to another son, whom she names "Scacciato" (The Outcast). Beritola sets out to return to Naples with her two sons, but strong winds send their ship to the island of Ponza, where she engages in a daily ritual of mourning her absent husband. During one of these rituals a pirate ship arrives at Ponza and takes the ship's crew and her children by stealth. Bereft of her children, Madonna Beritola enters into despair but finds solace with a doe and two baby roebucks, thereby undergoing a transformation from nobility into an animal-like existence ("la gentil donna divenuta fiera," 2.6.17). Her change of status at the beginning of the story allows the rest of the *novella* to question the essence of nobility as defined by Dante in *Purgatorio* 7 and 8: is it inherited or performed? The vicissitudes of Madonna Beritola, her son, and Currado Malaspina perform Boccaccio's nuanced engagement with Dante's treatment of this concept.

After Madonna Beritola's transformation from "gentil donna" to "fiera," the Ghibelline Currado Malaspina happens to appear on the island of Ponza, himself a "gentile uomo" exalted by Dante for his family pedigree of *cortesia* in *Purgatorio* 8. In this desolate landscape, Boccaccio tests how both nobility and *cortesia* can be performed outside of the court. Currado and his wife disembark on the island of Ponza *en route* to Lunigiana after making a pilgrimage to Puglia, and Currado's dogs, while chasing the roebucks that have kept Beritola company, lead their owner and his wife to the cave where Beritola is hiding. After listening to her series of misfortunes, Currado and his wife, who knew Arrighetto Capece, finally succeed in getting Beritola to return with them to Lunigiana (she insists on going somewhere where she will not be recognized). There she leads a solitary life as Currado's wife's maid of honour, and is known by everyone as "Cavriuola" because of her doe and two roebucks. At this point the *novella* of Madonna Beritola shifts its attention to the fate of her two sons and their nurse, who have since arrived at Genoa.

Tracing the relations between this *novella* and the content and style of *Purgatorio* 8 reveals how Boccaccio engages with Dante's text on both thematic and stylistic levels. Currado II Malaspina, the Marquis of Villafranca, belonged to an illustrious line of wealthy noblemen who supported the Ghibelline cause, and thus naturally would have wanted to assist another Ghibelline family (such as that of Arrighetto Capece). As a Ghibelline, according to the *Commedia*'s history of *cortesia*, Currado would find himself within the company of those – Cangrande della Scala, Frederick II, and others – who have inherited the noble capacity to practice it. Currado, who temporarily dwells in the Valley of the Princes in Antepurgatory, introduces himself to the pilgrim in terms of this ancestry in *Purgatorio* 8:

> "Se la lucerna che ti mena in alto
>   truova nel tuo arbitrio tanta cera
>   quant'è mestiere infino al sommo smalto,"
> cominciò ella, "se novella vera
>   di Val di Magra o di parte vicina
>   sai, dillo a me, che già grande là era.
> Fui chiamato Currado Malaspina;
>   non son l'antico, ma di lui discesi;
>   a' miei portai l'amor che qui raffina."
>   (*Purg.* 8.112–20)

("So may the lantern leading you above/have ample wax in the candle of your will/to bring you to the enameled summit,"/he said, "if you have true news of Valdimagra/or of the parts around, please tell me,/for there I once was great./I was called Currado Malaspina,/not the old Currado but descended from him./To my own I bore the love that here is purified.")

Currado II was the son of Frederick I, grandson of Currado I, or Currado il Vecchio ("non son l'antico, ma di lui discesi"), and great-grandson of Emperor Frederick II (whose daughter Costanza was the wife of Currado I). He begins his conversation with Dante by offering words of encouragement for the pilgrim's journey up Mount Purgatory ("infino al sommo smalto"), adopting a gracious rhetoric reminiscent of a courtly or chivalric environment. The pilgrim honours the Malaspina family for its *cortesia*, famed throughout Europe, in his response:

"Oh!," diss'io lui, "per li vostri paesi
   già mai non fui; ma dove si dimora
   per tutta Europa ch'ei non sien palesi?
La fama che la vostra casa onora,
   grida i segnori e grida la contrada,
   sì che ne sa chi non vi fu ancora;
e io vi giuro, s'io di sopra vada,
   che vostra gente onrata non si sfregia
   del pregio de la borsa e de la spada.
Uso e natura sì la privilegia,
   che, perchè il capo reo il mondo torca,
   sola va dritta e 'l mal cammin dispregia" (*Purg.* 8.121–32)

("Oh," I said to him, "never have I been there,/in your country. But where do men dwell,/anywhere in Europe, that it is not renowned?/The fame that crowns your house with honor/proclaims alike its lords and lands –/even those who have not been there know them,/and, as I hope to go above, I swear to you/your honored race does not disgrace/the glory of its purse and of its sword./No matter how a wicked chief may warp the world,/privileged both by nature and by custom,/your race alone goes straight and scorns the evil path.")

Known for their *liberalità* ("la borsa") and military prowess ("la spada"), the Malaspina line is here exalted for its "pregio," a cognate of the

Provençal *pretz*, a term used to signify worth and prestige. The pilgrim states that the "uso e natura" of the Malaspina line do not have any counterpart in modern times, as the world has been misled by a corrupt guiding principle (the "capo reo" was interpreted alternatively by early commentators as Rome, the pope, or the devil). As the *cortesia* of the Malaspina line is famed throughout Europe (emphasized by the repetition of "grida" in *"grida* i segnori e *grida* la contrada"), Currado's voyage in *Decameron* 2.6 figuratively enacts the diffusion of this reputation for generosity on a smaller geographic scale, as Currado and his wife travel from Puglia to Ponza, and then to Lunigiana.

Currado concludes their dialogue by noting that Dante will experience first hand the generosity of his family before seven years have passed, a prophecy intended to indicate that Dante will be the guest of Currado's cousin Franceschino Malaspina in Lunigiana in 1306:[7]

> Ed elli: "Or va; che 'l sol non si ricorca
>   sette volte nel letto che 'l Montone
>   con tutti e quattro i piè cuopre e inforca,
> che cotesta cortese oppinione
>   ti fia chiavata in mezzo de la testa
>   con maggior chiovi che d'altrui sermone,
> se corso di giudicio non s'arresta." (*Purg.* 8.133–9)

> (Then he said: "Enough. Not seven times/shall the sun return to rest in the bed/the Ram covers and bestrides with all four feet/before this courteous opinion/shall be nailed within our brain/by stronger nails than the words of others,/if the course of Judgment is not stayed.")

Currado's description of Dante's rendering of honour to his family line as "courteous" ("cotesta *cortese* opinione") belongs as well to the language of courtly values, the "cortesia e valore" associated with Guiglielmo Borsiere in *Inferno* 16 (also, Borsiere's name recalls the "pregio de la borsa" of the Malaspina family). While alluding to Dante's personal experience of the *cortesia* of the Malaspina family in exile, these verses nostalgically recall an age in which these values were more widespread, as Dante would have us believe.

As these verses from *Purgatorio* 8 rhetorically evoke Dante's imagined, historical world of *cortesia* (and an act of generosity, namely the Malaspina patronage of Dante in exile), Boccaccio has Currado and his wife perform *cortesia* in the *novella* of Madonna Beritola. If Cangrande della Scala first appears a miser in 1.7 but then is afforded the opportunity by the narrative to display his famed generosity, at the beginning and at the end of 2.6, Currado and his wife enact *cortesia*, which for Boccaccio, in addition to building upon the practice of *liberalità*, also seems to include the concept of *compassione*. Emilia emphasizes the tears they shed from "compassione" at the fate of Arrighetto Capece and Madonna Beritola and the efforts they made to persuade the proud Madonna Beritola to accept their assistance:

> Il che udendo Currado, che molto bene Arrighetto Capece conosciuto avea, *di compassion pianse* e *con parole assai* s'ingegnò di rimuoverla da proponimento sì fiero, offerendole di rimenarla a casa sua o di seco tenerla in quello onore che sua sorella, e stesse tanto che Idio più lieta fortuna le mandasse innanzi. (2.6.22–4, emphasis added)

> On hearing this, Currado, who had been very well acquainted with Arrighetto Capece, wept with compassion, and attempted to talk her out of her proud decision, offering to take her back to her home, or alternatively, to honour her as a sister and keep her in his own family, where she could stay until such time as God granted her a kindlier fate. (McWilliam, 114)

The compassion shown by Currado and his wife, which recalls the opening words of the *Decameron*'s Proem ("Umana cosa è aver compassion degli afflitti"), is transformed into the numerous generous acts that Madonna Beritola does not readily accept. Madonna Beritola's obstinance serves the narrative function of emphasizing the active, energetic generosity of Currado and his wife, the latter of whom is described as having to exert "la maggior fatica del mondo" ("the greatest difficulty in the world") in persuading Beritola just to eat.

Purgatorio 8 claims a rhetorical moment of *cortesia*, where courtly language is the means by which the *pregio* of the Malaspina line is described, the means by which Dante pays honour to Currado and his family, and the medium for discussing a "future" act of generosity on behalf of Franceschino Malaspina. *Decameron* 2.6 enacts *cortesia*, representing Boccaccio's definition of *cortesia* as consisting of "atti civili." This contrast illustrates the subtle difference in how Dante and Boccaccio define *cortesia* in two other texts, the *Convivio* and *Esposizioni* 16, respectively. In his gloss of the verses "Mira quant'ell'è pietosa e

148 Courtesy Lost

umile,/saggia e cortese ne la sua grandezza" from "Voi che 'ntendendo il terzo ciel movete," Dante offers a definition of *cortesia* as a term that specifically belongs to the court:

> E non siano li miseri volgari anche di questo vocabulo ingannati, che credono che cortesia non sia altro che larghezza; e larghezza è una speziale, e non generale, cortesia! Cortesia e onestade è tutt'uno: e però che nelle corti anticamente le vertudi e li belli costumi s'usavano, sì come oggi s'usa lo contrario, si tolse quello vocabulo dalle corti, e fu tanto a dire cortesia quanto uso di corte. Lo qual vocabulo se oggi si togliesse dalle corti, massimamente d'Italia, non sarebbe altro a dire che turpezza. (2.10.7–8)

> And the wretches of the common herd should not be deceived as well by this word, thinking courtesy nothing other than liberality; for liberality is a special, not a general, kind of courtesy! Courtesy and dignity are one and the same; and because in the courts in times past virtue and fine manners were practiced, just as the contrary is now the case, this word was derived from courts and "courtesy" was as much as to say "the custom of the court." If this word were derived from the courts of the present day, especially those of Italy, it would mean nothing but rudeness. (Lansing, 64)

Cortesia is not just *larghezza*, or *liberalità*, Dante states, but rather a larger term that encompasses different virtues and practices that distinguished the courts of the past ("nelle corti anticamente le vertudi e li belli costumi s'usavano"), during a time in which *cortesia* was interchangeable with the phrase "uso di corte." Though *cortesia* still exists in Dante's time, it cannot be found in the court, as the decadence of Italy's courts has banished it from its place of origin ("sì come oggi s'usa lo contrario, si tolse quello vocabulo dalle corti"). Therefore "cortesia" is synonymous with "onestade," what De Robertis defines as "un comportamento altamente decoroso, degno di particolare onore e capace di allietare la mente per i valori morali e spirituali che lascia intravedere."[8] *Cortesia* does not designate any one particular virtue or practice, but rather encompasses honourable *costumi* and virtues that can stem from *onestade*.

Boccaccio's explicit definition of *cortesia* can be located precisely in *Esposizioni* 16 (as discussed in chapter 1), in his explication of Iacopo Rusticucci's question of whether or not courtesy and valour continue to exist in Florence: "cortesia e valor dì se dimora/ne la nostra città sì come suole,/o se del tutto se n'è gita fora" (*Inf.* 16.67–9; "tell us if valor and courtesy still live/there in our city, as once they used to do,/or have they utterly forsaken her?"). Iacopo's concern over whether *cortesia* still can be found in Florence occurs in a canto dealing with the disappearance of these *costume*, an evocation of the chivalric mentality of *cortesia* among the members of the Florentine elite, and thus with the advent of civic political strife. The language of Boccaccio's definition of *cortesia* refers to the world outside of the court:

> Cortesia e valor: cortesia par che consista negli *atti civili, cioè nel vivere insieme liberalmente e lietamente*, e fare onore a tutti secondo la possibilità. (16.53, emphasis added)

> "Courtesy and valour." "Courtesy" pertains to civil comportment, that is, to living both generously and contentedly, doing honour to everyone according to one's means. (Papio, 581)

Boccaccio does not locate *cortesia* in the court, as Dante does in the second book of the *Convivio*, but instead defines it as a practice of civil acts ("atti civili") characteristic of a condition of living together generously and happily, a practice linked with his nostalgic view of the *brigate*. A harmonious existence in the spirit of generosity and mutual respect evokes the many customs of the court to which Dante alludes, customs involving generosity but that comprise many aspects of a style of social comportment, as implied by the plural "atti civili" in this passage from the *Esposizioni*. Thus we find in the *novelle* of Guiglielmo Borsiere in 1.8 and Madonna Beritola in 2.6 – when *cortesia* is practiced *outside* of Florence – that *cortesia* can be a movable feast, so to speak, as Borsiere brings *cortesia* from his home in Florence to Genoa and Currado Malaspina and his wife carry it with them from their court in Lunigiana to the island of Ponza.

The relation between the *novella* of Madonna Beritola and *Purgatorio* 8 does not only consist of abstract and concrete manifestations of *cortesia*. As both *Purgatorio* 7 and 8 deal with the dilemma of whether or not nobility ("probitate") can be inherited, so Currado Malaspina confronts considerations of genealogy and nobility in the marriage of his daughter to one of Beritola's sons. After Beritola travels back to Lunigiana with the Malaspina family, Emilia recounts the fate of Beritola's sons and their nurse, who are taken to Genoa where they are sent to work for Guasparrino d'Oria. In order to protect the two boys from being attacked because of their family's political alliance (Genoa was sympathetic to the Angevins), the nurse decides to conceal their identities by changing the name of the older son from Giusfredi to Giannotto di Procida. Giusfredi, though, is not content with a servant's existence, being more ambitious than that ("avendo più animo che a servo non s'apparteneva"), and leaves Guasparino's service to become a seaman. His wanderings lead him, by coincidence, to Lunigiana and to the house of Currado Malaspina, where he is hired, but he and his mother Beritola never recognize each other because of the amount of time that had elapsed since their parting.

Giusfredi falls in love with Spina, one of Currado's daughters, a sixteen-year-old widow who returns Giusfredi's affection. Giusfredi and Spina consummate their love and continue to engage in amorous relations for months without anyone's knowledge, until one day they are caught *in flagrante* by Currado and her mother. As Tancredi is incensed to find his daughter Ghismonda with Guiscardo in 4.1, Currado is enraged to find the two young lovers ("doloroso oltre modo," 2.6.38; "excessively grieved"). No longer the sympathetic, generous Currado, Spina's father wishes to have them killed: "d'ira e di cruccio fremendo [...] disposto di fargli vituperosamente morire" (2.6.38; "seething with distress and anger, and intent on having them ignominiously put to death," McWilliam, 117). Currado's wife succeeds in convincing him not to have them killed but instead to hold them indefinitely in one of his prisons.

Giusfredi and Spina have passed about one year in that prison when the Sicilian Vespers take place, a historical event that marks a turning point in the plot:[9]

> [A]vvenne che il re Piero da Raona per trattato di messer Gian di Procida l'isola di Cicilia ribellò e tolse al re Carlo; di che Currado, come ghibellino, fece gran festa. (2.6.41)

> [I]t came about that King Peter of Aragon, with the aid of a subversive movement led by Messer Gian di Procida, stirred up a rebellion in Sicily and wrested the island from King Charles. Currado, being a Ghibelline, was overjoyed at the news. (McWilliam, 117–18)

After the Sicilian Vespers on 13 March 1282, the rebellion of the Ghibellines against Charles I of Anjou in which Giovanni da Procida was one of the main protagonists, Peter III of Aragon became king of the island. Boccaccio demonstrates how a historical event such as this

Ghibelline victory affects the personal lives of a few individuals via his quick transition from the mention of Peter of Aragon to the happiness of Currado Malaspina.[10] History, for Boccaccio, is best understood in terms of its impact upon the personal fortunes of his characters.[11] Historical events are first described and then interpreted in personal terms, as discussed earlier regarding the *Decameron* and the *Esposizioni*.

In the case of this victory for the Ghibelline cause, though, the impact is not only personal but familial, since Giusfredi will finally be able to disclose his identity to the Malaspina without fear of harm. Knowledge of his identity as a member of a noble Ghibelline family will allow Currado to approve of his union with Spina. The connection between the political success of the Ghibellines and Giusfredi and Spina's own fulfilment seems far-fetched to the prison guard, but Giusfredi knows that the affairs of kings concern him:

"E come?" disse il prigioniere *"che monta a te quello che i grandissimi re si facciano*? Che avevi tu a fare in Cicilia?" (2.42–3, emphasis added)

"What are you talking about?" said the gaoler. "Surely the affairs of mighty monarchs are no concern of yours? What was your business in Sicily?" (McWilliam, 118)

The business and vicissitudes of kings are of the utmost importance to Giusfredi; they decide his fate as a prisoner or as the happily wedded husband of Spina. Not coincidentally, this event and its ramifications for Giusfredi's life comprise the second half of the *novella*'s rubric: "Cicilia ribellata al re Carlo e il figliuolo riconosciuto dalla madre, sposa la figliuola del suo signore e il suo fratel ritrova e in grande stato ritornano" (2.6.1; "After the Sicilian rebellion against King Charles, the son is recognized by his mother, he marries his master's daughter, he is reunited with his brother, and they are all restored to positions of great honour," McWilliam, 111). This moment illustrates Boccaccio's vision of history as culminating in the domestic and personal sphere rather than on the international stage.

When Giannotto's true identity as Giusfredi, Arrighetto Capece's son, is revealed to Currado and to his mother, Madonna Beritola, this disclosure triggers a dramatic consideration of genealogy and nobility, issues at stake in *Purgatorio* 7 and 8. When Currado is told of the prisoner Giusfredi's true identity, he first attempts to ascertain if Madonna Beritola had a son who would be Giusfredi's age. Becoming convinced that Giusfredi is her son, Currado realizes that he could restore his honour and the honour of his daughter by offering Spina's hand in marriage to Giusfredi, thereby transforming a "dishonest" friendship into an "honest" marriage:

> Ora, poi che così è come tu mi di' *che tu figliuol se' di gentile uomo e di gentil donna*, io voglio alle tue angosce, quando tu medesimo vogli, porre fine e trarti della miseria e della captività nella qual tu dimori, e a una ora il tuo onore e 'l mio nel suo debito luogo riducere. (2.6.50, emphasis added)

> Now, since what you say is true, and you are a man of gentle birth, I desire with your consent to put an end to your suffering and release you from your wretched, captive existence, at the same time restoring both your own reputation and mine. (McWilliam, 119)

The noble origins of Giusfredi's ancestry change Currado's mind. It is that noble ancestry, and not Giusfredi's unwavering love for Spina, that ultimately pleases Currado – as one who perhaps believes only in the inheritance of nobility, as per *Purgatorio* 8.

Giusfredi corrects Currado's insinuation that his love for Spina is superficial, claiming that he never loved Spina in order to gain money or rank, but because he believed her to be worthy of his love. His disagreement with Currado can be read as both Dante's disagreement with Currado's investment in nobility as well as Boccaccio's belief in the nobility and strength of purpose of young lovers, as exemplified in several *novelle* of the Fourth Day. Though Giusfredi's body was weak from the time spent in prison, his noble spirit, which he reveals in his declaration of love for Spina, remained undiminished. Upon hearing Giusfredi's words, Currado is struck by the young man's "grande animo" (2.6.57) and has Spina immediately sent to them, where Currado performs the marriage ceremony without further ado. The *novella* then unwinds its long *dénouement* that consists of a series of reunions: first Giusfredi with his mother, Madonna Beritola; then the marriage of Scacciato with Guasparrino's daughter and their return to the Malaspina family; and finally the return of Madonna Beritola, her sons, and their respective wives to Arrighetto Capece in Sicily.

Critics have noted that the line from this *novella* that describes the happy reunion of Madonna Beritola and her oldest son ("poi che l'accoglienze oneste e liete furo iterate tre e quarto volte," 2.6.69; "when the chaste and joyful greetings had been repeated three or four times," McWilliam, 122) precisely recalls the first verses of *Purgatorio* 7, and the warm greetings of Sordello and Vergil ("Poscia che l'accoglienze oneste e liete/furo iterate tre e quattro volte," 1–2).[12] I suggest that Boccaccio echoes the incipit of *Purgatorio* 7 to signal his engagement with the larger issues of this canto; the inheritance of nobility at stake in the dialogue between Currado and Giusfredi clearly engages with Dante's treatment of this same concern at the end of *Purgatorio* 7. As Sordello indicates the souls in the Valley of the Princes, which include the reconciled protagonists of the Sicilian Vespers, Peter III of Aragon and his enemy Charles I of Anjou ("quel che par sì membruto e che s'accorda,/cantando, con colui dal maschio naso,/d'ogne valor portò cinta la corda," 112–14; "He who looks so tall and sturdy and who sings/in time with him who bears a manly nose/was girt with the cord of every virtue"),[13] he pauses to comment upon the inheritance of virtue: "Rade volte risurge per li rami/l'umana probitate; e questo vole/quei che la dà, perchè da lui si chiami" (121–3; "Rarely does human worth rise through the branches./And this He wills who gives it,/so that it shall be sought from Him"). Sons do not necessarily inherit virtue from their fathers, but should seek such virtue from its source in God.[14] Furthermore, some sons, such as Peter III of Aragon, can be more virtuous than their fathers, evidence that "probitate" does not always rise up the (medieval) family tree from fathers to their descendents (127–9).

The plot of 2.6 hinges upon the actions of Peter III of Aragon and his participation in the Sicilian Vespers, evoking these verses from *Purgatorio* 7 and the implication of his individual "probitate." Thus Boccaccio purposefully draws a connection between Peter III, a Ghibelline, and Giusfredi, whose nobility is under examination in this *novella*. Peter III's rise to the throne, and the victory of the Ghibelline cause, coincides with Giusfredi's liberation from prison and the revelation of his noble origins. But Giusfredi, despite his origins, always possessed an inner nobility, reflected by the other significance of "dalla sua origine" in Emilia's words: "il generoso animo dalla sua origine tratto non aveva ella in cosa alcuna diminuito" (2.6.54; "the innate nobility of his spirit was in no way impaired," McWilliam, 119). Giusfredi's response to Currado's sudden offer of his daughter in marriage seems to imply that he was noble *before* and *despite* Currado's newfound knowledge of his family line. His statement echoes that of Peter III of Aragon and Sordello about "umana probitate"; though Giusfredi does have a noble father, his virtue is his own.

Boccaccio's Currado is not being malicious or ignorant in not being able to discern Giusfredi's nobility until the prison guard informs him. In this sense, his Currado is consistent with Dante's Currado in *Purgatorio* 8. For the "pregio" of the Malaspina line stands in sharp contrast to the decadence of royalty at the end of *Purgatorio* 7. Dante highlights the exception of the Malaspina line in *Purgatorio* 8 in his treatment of nobility and genealogy. If Boccaccio's Currado only views Giusfredi favourably once he learns of his noble pedigree, then it is because Dante's Currado is singularly focused on preserving the nobility of his own family line, a nobility that is rare, as the pilgrim indicates ("sola va dritta e 'l mal cammin dispregia," 132).[15] Boccaccio elaborates upon his characterization of Currado and this concern from *Purgatorio* 8. At the same time, the dialogue between Currado and Giusfredi is Boccaccio's affirmation of the lesson of *Purgatorio* 7 that nobility is not inherited. This moment in the *novella* of Madonna Beritola can be interpreted as Boccaccio's attempt to gloss the message of Dante's poem for a character in Dante's poem. Through the dialogue between Giusfredi and Currado, Boccaccio applies the lesson of *Purgatorio* 7 (nobility is not hereditary) to the end of *Purgatorio* 8 (nobility is hereditary for the Malaspina family, an exception to the rule), attempting to reconcile the apparent contradictions of two consecutive *canti*.

At the same time, the *novella* of Currado Malaspina conveys the hope of *cortesia*'s survival, that the Malaspina family line would not become extinct because of the promise of offspring from Giusfredi and Spina. This hope is first kindled by the nobility of Giusfredi, who acts upon his desire for Spina in ways that can lead to a family line of their own. The virility of a young Ghibelline thus promises the future of *cortesia* for the Malaspina. This revision of Dante's lament for the golden age of *cortesia* can also be located in Boccaccio's treatment of the figure of a much older Ghibelline, Frederick II, the last Holy Roman Emperor, who is mentioned at the beginning of 2.6 and at the beginning of 1.7, the *novella* of Cangrande della Scala.[16] In *Purgatorio* 16 Dante specifies that the historical moment when "valore e cortesia" disappeared from Lombardy is the moment when the last Holy Roman Emperor, Frederick II, encountered conflict:

> In sul paese ch'Adice e Po riga,
>   solea valore e cortesia trovarsi,
>   prima che Federigo avesse briga. (*Purg.* 16.115–17)

(In the land watered by both the Adige and the Po/valour and courtesy could once be found/before Frederick encountered opposition.)

Marco Lombardo refers to the larger conflict between Frederick II and the papacy, and claims that no virtuous men can any longer be found in this region. In *Decameron* 1.7, Boccaccio points out the geographical limitations of Marco Lombardo's words in the larger context of the *Commedia* and Dante's life: if *cortesia* could no longer be found in Lombardy after Frederick II's strife, then what about Cangrande della Scala, Dante's host? Dante himself in *Paradiso* 17 claims to have experienced the *cortesia* of Cangrande and his family in Verona. By locating Cangrande in a genealogy of *cortesia* that includes Frederick II (1.7.5), Boccaccio identifies Dante's contradiction of these verses from *Purgatorio* 16, and thus promotes a view of *cortesia* as a virtue that has endured in Lombardy for longer than the Florentine poet would have us believe. Simply put, Boccaccio imagines a younger generation of non-Florentine Ghibellines who will be the new standard-bearers of *cortesia*. What would be the "passato remoto" ("absolute past tense") of Dante's world becomes the "passato prossimo" ("present perfect") of Boccaccio's world, which in turn transforms itself into a hopeful present and future for the "afterlife" of the *Decameron*.

Dante's "passato remoto" is evoked obliquely at the very beginning of this *novella*, where Frederick II and his relationship to the younger generation, his son Manfred, are referenced. A factual error exists in Emilia's early allusion to the coronation of Manfred at the death of Frederick II; while Emilia claims that Manfred was crowned after his father's death in 1250, Manfred was actually made king in 1258 ("appresso la morte di Federigo secondo imperadore fu re di Cicilia coronato Manfredi," 2.6.5; "Manfred, who was crowned King of Sicily after the death of the Emperor Frederick II," McWilliam, 111). This error reveals Boccaccio's desire to draw attention to the relationship between Frederick and his son Manfred at the expense of historical accuracy. We know that this relationship held greater significance for Boccaccio because of the content of *Esposizioni* 10, where Boccaccio, after discussing Frederick's battles with the church, describes him as a father. Boccaccio repeats Villani's anecdote that the emperor had been suffocated by his son Manfred, Prince of Taranto:

> Ebbe di diverse femine più figliuoli, de' quali così de' non legittimi, come de' legittimi, fece da cinque o vero sei re [...] Poi, avvenendo che egli infermò in Puglia, da Manfredi, allora prenze di Taranto, suo figliuolo naturale, e da altri suoi baroni ne fu così infermo portato in una terra in Puglia, la quale ha nome Fiorenza [...] Poi, come che la 'nfermità l'agravasse forte,

vogliono alcuni che, l'ultima notte che fece in terra, che 'l prenze Manfredi per disidèro d'avere il mobile suo gli ponesse un pimaccio in su la bocca e facessel morire. E così scomunicato e in contumacia di santa Chiesa finì in Fiorenza i giorni suoi. (10.100–1)

He had a number of children with different women and he made kings of about five or six of his sons, legitimate and illegitimate alike. [...] Later it so happened that he fell ill in Apulia. He was taken by his illegitimate son Manfred, then Prince of Tarentum, and other barons of his, as sick as he was, to a little town in Apulia that was called Florence. [...] Some say that, on the last night Frederick spent upon this earth, Prince Manfred was so eager to take possession of his fortunes that, although Frederick was already gravely afflicted by his illness, he put a pillow over Frederick's face and suffocated him. (Papio, 453)

This passage, which Boccaccio must have adapted from Villani's *Nuova cronica*, conveys the brutality and ruthlessness of political rulers, even among those of the same blood.[17] Boccaccio's tale of patricide, where Frederick's biological son killed him in order to appropriate his dominion, brings a different valence to the brief allusion to Frederick's death and Manfred's coronation at the beginning of 2.6, namely that the civility for which this Ghibelline ruler is famed stands in sharp contrast to the violence and lack of compassion practised within his own home.

Boccaccio's story in *Esposizioni* 10 relates to the opening of 2.6 and Currado Malaspina's investment in genealogy and the inheritance of virtue. To read the opening of 2.6 against Boccaccio's related context in *Esposizioni* 10 reveals the author's scepticism regarding Currado's belief in the sanctity of lineage, as well as, perhaps, a lack of interest in continuing to feature the future for various Ghibelline figures, as he did in the *Decameron*. This implicit scepticism is magnified by Boccaccio's allusion to a patricide committed by Currado's own ancestors, since Currado was the great-grandson of Frederick II. In keeping with the exception presented by Dante in *Purgatorio* 8, Boccaccio shows how the Malaspina family were and continue to be an exception insofar as nobility is hereditary. Yet it is important to remember that Giusfredi is not Currado's son, but his son-in-law. With the insertion of Giusfredi into the Malaspina line, a non-blood relative, Boccaccio indicates that *cortesia* can continue into the Malaspina future by the marriage of Spina to a man who is equally noble in spirit. Fathers who belonged to this courtly past must seek future sons outside of their own house to ensure *cortesia*'s future. They must construct the future of their families.

The complex relationship between fathers and sons in this *novella* (Giusfredi/Currado, Frederick II/Manfred) indicates not only the generational conflicts Boccaccio must reconcile in translating Dante's lament for *cortesia* into a hopeful future; it also points to the central location of relationships between men in the future of *cortesia*. A closer reading of *Decameron* 2.6 and *Esposizioni* 10, which features castration at the origins of the Guelph/Ghibelline conflict, reveals that Boccaccio was invested in illustrating the place of virility and erotic sublimation in these discussions of genealogy and inheritance. The power of men to repress their own sexuality as well as their capacity to repress the virility of others becomes central to his writing of the history of the Guelphs and the Ghibellines, and particularly of two landmark figures in this political arena: Peter III of Aragon and Charles of Anjou. Whereas in the case of Giusfredi, history allowed for the expression of his erotic desire, these two leaders must successfully repress theirs in order for history to follow a course favourable to their political agendas.

Cortesia Was Chaste: The Virility of the Guelphs and the Ghibellines

Purgatorio 7 features the protagonists of the Sicilian Vespers, Peter III of Aragon and his adversary Charles I of Anjou, dwelling together harmoniously (112–14). What is striking about this description of Peter III and Charles I is how Dante discusses these two historical personages in figurative language that foregrounds their virility (Peter is "membruto," manly, while Charles has a "maschio naso," a manly nose). Dante's decision to discuss these figures in gendered terms is mirrored in the content of Boccaccio's consecutive *novelle* that feature Peter III of Aragon (2.6 and 10.7) and Charles I of Anjou (10.6). This was already observed in 2.6, where Giusfredi's nobility is linked to his youthful virility; whereas the former quality is proven through his verbal declaration of love for Spina, the latter is affirmed by the sexual act between the two young lovers. Boccaccio focuses even more on the virility of Peter III and Charles I in 10.6 and 10.7, which respectively feature these two important Guelph and Ghibelline rulers in terms of sublimated sexual desire. But whereas the youthful virility of Giusfredi complemented his nobility and ensured the future of the courteous Malaspina line, in the case of Peter and Charles virility must be repressed for the survival of *cortesia*.

The tale of the Guelph leader Charles of Anjou, which like 2.6 shares the common history of the Sicilian Vespers and whose location as the sixth tale of the tenth day further supports its relation to 2.6, relates to Dante's allusion to the leader's virility in *Purgatorio* 7.[18] This *novella* takes place immediately after Charles's victory in Benevento (1266) over King Manfred and the Ghibellines: "Ciascuna di voi molte volte può avere udito ricordare il re Carlo vecchio o ver primo, per la cui magnifica impresa e poi per la gloriosa vittoria avuta del re Manfredi furon di Firenze i ghibellin cacciati e ritornaronvi i guelfi" (10.6.5; "Now, all of you will frequently have heard mention of King Charles the Old, or in other words Charles the First, by whose magnificent enterprise, as well as by the glorious victory he later achieved against King Manfred, the Ghibellines were expelled from Florence and the Guelphs returned to the city," McWilliam, 731–2). In addition to King Charles, there appears the historically undocumented figure of Neri degli Uberti, an unknown member of the prominent Ghibelline family that dominated twelfth- and thirteenth-century Florentine politics, who strangely decides that he wants to live near King Charles in Castellammare di Stabia. Once there, he buys a mansion and dedicates all of his time to the construction of a beautiful garden with a fish pond. The unlikely premise of this story is that not only a Ghibelline, but also a member of the Uberti family (who suffered at the hands of King Charles: Farinata degli Uberti's children were ordered to be imprisoned and put to death), would want to live near the Guelph king. Indeed, Boccaccio's manoeuvre appears to reconcile a Guelph and a Ghibelline in the magnanimous spirit of Day Ten and in the spirit of *Purgatorio* 7. But I believe that Boccaccio also intends to draw a comparison in this *novella* (as well as in 10.7) between the Guelphs and the Ghibellines in gendered terms that can also be found in his history of the two parties in *Esposizioni* 10.

First let us turn to the plot of *Decameron* 10.6. King Charles happens to go to Castellammare one summer to relax, and learns of Messer Neri's beautiful garden. However, sensitive to Messer Neri's political opposition to his party, King Charles sends word to Neri that he will attend incognito, or informally ("E avendo udito di cui era, pensò che, per ciò che di parte avversa alla sua era il cavaliere, più familiarmente con lui si volesse fare," 10.6.7; "But knowing to whom it belonged, he decided that since the knight was a political adversary of his, he would make his visit informal," McWilliam, 732). Neri prepares a lavish meal for the king, during which the king falls in love with Neri's two young daughters Ginevra and Isotta, who are approximately fifteen years old. Ginevra and Isotta, whose names unmistakably refer to the romantic tradition, are dressed in tight-fitting dresses made of white linen, and perform a scene with strong sexual overtones; the girls enter into the pool to catch fish, which they then toss to a servant standing at the side of the pool with a frying pan. They also toss some of these fish onto the table in front of the King, who throws them back to the girls, and the sight of the young girls fills the king with excitement and desire (10.6.15, 10.6.18). The king's passion grows as he continues to think about them (10.6.19). The phallic connotation of the fish and consequential erotic allusion of fishing cast this part of the *novella* in a strongly erotic light.[19]

King Charles ends up falling so hopelessly in love with Neri's daughters that he sees no other possibility than to abduct them both, since Neri claims that he cannot bestow them in marriage (10.6.20). He reveals these plans to Count Guy de Monfort, who has never before seen the king so overwhelmed by passion (10.6.27). Such designs would be unwise, the count advises him, so soon after his victory and especially among a people who might deceive him ("voi ancora siete con l'arme indosso nel regno nuovamente acquistato, tra nazion non conosciuta e piena d'inganni e di tradimenti," 10.6.28; "you are still on a warlike footing in a kingdom newly acquired, among an alien people, full of deceits and treachery," McWilliam, 735–6). Nor would it be appropriate to entertain erotic desire, the count argues, referring to the king's plans of abducting the young girls as the scheme of a young man taken over by love, not the designs of a magnanimous king ("Questo non è atto di re magnanimo anzi d'un pusillanimo giovinetto," 10.6.28–9; "This is not the action of a magnanimous king, but rather of a weak-willed youth," McWilliam, 736).[20] The reference to a "giovinetto" recalls the love of Giusfredi for Spina in 2.6, who partly justifies his desire as a symptom of his age. Giusfredi can understandably act on such desire because of his youth, whereas King Charles should resist because of his age as well as his royal status.[21]

As if these arguments were not sufficient to dissuade the king, Guy finally resorts to comparing the Guelph leader's blind passion with the sexual exploits of his Ghibelline adversary at Benevento, King Manfred: "Ora èvvi così tosto della memoria caduto le violenze fatte alle donne da Manfredi avervi l'entrata aperta in questo regno?" (10.6.30, "Can you have so soon forgotten that it was Manfred's abuse of his subjects' womenfolk that opened the gates of this realm to you?" McWilliam, 736).[22] Guy argues that Manfred's alleged inability to control his sexual passion led to King Charles's victory in the region. Not only does Guy suggest that for Charles to fulfil his erotic desires could be politically dangerous, but Guy's explicit comparison with a Ghibelline leader must have been intended to inspire the king's sense of rivalry: if Manfred could not control his desires, then King Charles must prove that he can. Guy argues that the king can garner far greater glory than from any of his political conquests by overcoming his sexual desires:

> "Voi forse estimate che sufficiente scusa fosse il dire: 'Io il feci per ciò che egli è ghibellino.' [...] Io vi ricordo, re, che grandissima gloria v'è aver vinto Manfredi, ma molto maggiore è se medesimo vincere; e per ciò voi, che avete gli altri a correggere, vincete voi medesimo e questo appetito raffrenate, nè vogliate con così fatta macchia ciò che gloriosamente acquistato avete guastare." (10.6.30–32)

> "Perhaps you think it would be a sufficient excuse to say: 'I did it because he is a Ghibelline.' [...] Let me remind you, my lord, that you covered yourself with glory by conquering Manfred and defeating Conradin. But it is far more glorious to conquer oneself. And therefore, as you have to govern others, conquer these feelings of yours, curb this wanton desire, and do not allow the splendour of your achievements to be dimmed by any such deed as this." (McWilliam, 736)

King Charles could plausibly abduct Neri's daughters out of sheer political partisanship, and could explain his actions as such. But the count implies that a political motive would not be the true cause, that the true impetus behind such an action would be the king's inability to govern himself as he is supposed to govern others. That Guy is correct in this surmise is confirmed by the strong effect his admonishment has on the king (10.6.33). Thus King Charles takes action to conquer his desires ("a me medesimo soprastare," 10.6.33; "to conquer myself"), endowing the two daughters in marriage to noble knights and returning to Naples, where he sublimates his ardent desire.[23]

Guy appeals to the king on two different levels, the personal (in terms of his individual will) and the political. Boccaccio communicates contradictory points in Guy's words and in the conclusion to this *novella*. For just as Guy argues that King Charles's personal ability to conquer himself is more important than any political conquest, the explicit and pointed comparisons with Manfred cannot be dismissed. The *novella* of 10.6 concludes with a Guelph leader who has violently sublimated his sexual longings, contrary to what his Ghibelline adversary had allegedly done. Though King Charles may be a more virtuous leader at the end of the story, he also appears as a man whose sexual desires must be brutally subdued, as conveyed in the vivid language that describes how he mortifies his desire ("con dolore inestimabile in Puglia se n'andò, e *con fatiche continue tanto e sì macerò il suo fiero appetito*, che, spezzate e rotte l'amorose catene, per quanto viver dovea libero rimase da tal passione" 10.6.35, emphasis added; "he retired in agonies of despair to Apulia, where by dint of constant effort he mortified his ardent longings to such good and purposeful effect that the chains of Love were shattered, and for as long as he lived he was never a slave to his kind of passion again," McWilliam, 737). Members of political parties are identified by the terms of sexual self-repression in these moments, not by ideology.

Boccaccio sustains this contrast between the Guelphs and the Ghibellines by following the *novella* of Charles of Anjou with the tale of Peter III of Aragon (10.7) ("una cosa [...] fatta da un suo avversario," 10.7.3; something performed by one of his adversaries). At the beginning of this story Boccaccio refers to the displeasure of a female member of the *brigata* with the Sixth Tale of the Tenth Day due to her political stance as a Ghibelline ("commendata era stata molto *la virile magnificenzia del re Carlo*, quantunque alcuna, che quivi era ghibellina, commendar nol volesse," 10.7.2, emphasis added; "fulsome praise had been accorded to the manly munificence of King Charles, though one of the ladies present, who was a Ghibelline, did not want to praise it," McWilliam, 737–8).[24] This *novella*, which recounts the story of a young woman's love for King Peter, clearly intends to oppose Charles's "manly munificence" with the *cortesia* and lack of sexual desire of King Peter. While Manfred appears as a Ghibelline who could not curb his sexual appetite in 10.6, 10.7 features a Ghibelline leader, none other than the man who conquered King Charles during the Sicilian Vespers, as the object of a poor woman's love. The Sicilian Vespers occur during the fictional "time" that lapses between the backgrounds of these two *novelle*: 10.6 takes place after Benevento in 1266; 10.7 occurs "nel tempo che i franceschi di Cicilia furon cacciati" ("at the time when the French were driven from Sicily," McWilliam, 738), after the Sicilian Vespers in 1282. This *novella* marks a turn from the aggressive sexual desire of Manfred and King Charles in 10.6 to the lack of sexual desire of King Peter, who, though the passive recipient of a woman's desire, is now lord of the island of Sicily (10.7.5).

Lisa, the daughter of the Florentine Bernardo Puccini, falls in love while watching King Peter of Aragon during a celebration of his victory in Palermo. Lisa broods over her love for the king, but knows that she could never have a future with him because of the difference in social class. This grieves her deeply, and as a result she falls into a deep melancholy and then becomes physically ill. She decides that before dying she wishes to make her love known to King Peter, and chooses to entrust her secret with the musician Minuccio, who works in Peter's court. Minuccio composes a *ballata* expressing a woman's love that he then plays to the king, and afterwards reveals Lisa's secret to Peter in private. The king, a generous and kind man ("il re, il quale liberale e benigno signore era," 10.7.30), has compassion for Lisa and decides to go and comfort her in person (10.7.27). In an interesting inversion of the preceding *novella*, in which a king decides how to react to his amorous desires for two young girls whom he meets in a garden, King Peter then goes to the garden of Bernardo's house, where he attempts to comfort a young girl who has fallen ill from an impossible love for him.

During his visit to comfort Lisa, King Peter develops respect for the young Lisa and pities her lack of noble birth (10.7.35). But the king is the recipient of her greater love, which Peter kindly reciprocates with acts of compassion, or *cortesia* (10.7.36). Indeed, the king's ultimate compensation for Lisa's love is to bestow her in marriage to a noble but to always remain her "knight," asking for nothing but a kiss in exchange ("intendendo sempre, non obstante questo, vostro cavaliere appelarci senza più di tanto amor voler da voi che un sol bascio," 10.7.37; "it being none the less our intention always to style ourselves your loyal knight, and of all your love we require no more than a single kiss," McWilliam, 743–4). As opposed to Charles's plans of abducting Messer Neri's two daughters, Peter steals nothing but a kiss on the forehead. This, Pampinea concludes, is the correct way to rule, as opposed to the current cruelty and tyranny of leaders ("Così adunque operando si pigliano gli animi de' subgetti, dassi altrui material di bene operare e le fame eterne s'acquistano: alla qual cosa oggi pochi o niuno ha l'arco teso dello 'ntelletto, essendo li più de' signori divenuti crudeli e tiranni," 10.7.49; "By deeds such as these, then, does a sovereign conquer the hearts of his subjects, furnish the occasion to others for similar deeds, and acquire eternal renown. But among the rulers of today, there are few if any who train the bowstrings of their minds upon any such objective, most of them having been changed into pitiless tyrants," McWilliam, 745). Pampinea's tale of the "umanità" of King Peter pleases everyone in the *brigata*, and the Ghibelline member most of all (10.8.2). Thus the Ghibelline leader's sublimation of sexual desire concludes this diptych of King Charles and King Peter of Aragon.[25]

Constructing a Future for *cortesia* 163

Boccaccio's romantic diptych of the two leaders in Day Ten might have been inspired by Dante's description of the virility of the protagonists of the Sicilian Vespers in *Purgatorio* 7. Dante's treatment in *Purgatorio* 20 and *Paradiso* 8 of the early victories of King Charles over the imperial cause and, more generally, of French rule is much more severe. King Charles, as the protector of Guelph interests in Italy (he was the vicar of Tuscany and *podestà* of Florence from 1267 until 1280), descended into Italy to take the kingdom of Naples from Manfred in Benevento in 1266 (alluded to in *Purg.* 3). He then defeated Conradin, who attempted to gain back Manfred's kingdom, at Tagliacozzo in 1268. Dante condemns this action with the ironic use of "per ammenda" in Hugh Capet's long condemnation of the house of France, where he mentions Charles I's rendering Conradin a "victim" and alludes to the rumour that he had Thomas of Aquinas poisoned (*Purg.* 20.64–9). But it is Charles Martel's discussion of the "bad rule" of his grandfather Charles I in *Paradiso* 8 that strongly resonates with Boccaccio's discussion of how Charles must "govern" his desires in *Decameron* 10.6:

> E la bella Trinacria, che caliga
>   tra Pachino e Peloro, sopra 'l golfo
>   che riceve da Euro maggior briga,
> non per Tifeo ma per nascente solfo,
>   attesi avrebbe li suoi regi ancora,
>   nati per me di Carlo e di Ridolfo,
> se *mala segnoria*, che sempra accora
>   li popoli suggetti, non avesse
>   mosso Palermo a gridar: "Mora, mora!"   (*Par.* 8.67–75, emphasis added)

(And fair Trinacria, overcast and murky/between Pachynus and Pelorus,/above the bay most vexed by the Sirocco,/darkened not by Typhon but by rising sulphur –/would still have waited for its kings,/born through me of Charles and Rudolph,/had not bad governance, which ever grieves the hearts/of subject peoples, impelled Parlermo/to cry out, "Kill them, kill!")

The "mala segnoria," as Charles Martel calls the rule of Charles I, led to the Sicilian Vespers ("mosso Palermo a gridar: 'Mora, mora!'"). While Dante does not convey that this bad government was the result of Charles's sexual desires, Boccaccio implies that the Sicilian Vespers had occurred as the result of his desire to act on his passion. The emotional texture of Boccaccio's writing of history also informs his composite treatment of the White and Black Guelphs in the *Decameron* and the *Esposizioni*, as observed earlier.

Another, more suggestive connection exists between Boccaccio's treatment of the virility of King Charles and King Peter and his particular history in *Esposizioni* 10 of the origins of the Guelph/Ghibelline conflict in Germany with regard to Countess Matilda. After the pilgrim reveals the identity of his ancestors to Farinata in *Inferno* 10, Farinata responds by noting that they were his adversaries (*Inf.* 10.46–7). Boccaccio glosses this verse with a long digression on the history of the German origins of the conflict between the Guelphs and the Ghibellines. The wealthy Italian countess Matilda, whom Boccaccio identifies with the Matilda who appears in the Earthly Paradise on Mount Purgatory, wanted to give birth to an heir but could not find a suitable mate in her own country.[26] She decided instead to go to Germany, where she encountered and chose to marry a certain duke named Guelph, a wealthy nobleman (10.44).

Unfortunately, however, a man named Ghibelline, who was a relative of Guelph, learned of Matilda's large dowry, according to Boccaccio. Envious of Guelph's good fortune, Ghibelline plotted to have Guelph rendered impotent:

> La qual cosa sentendo un parente di questo Gulfo, il cui nome fu Ghibellino, e udendo la maravigliosa dota che a costui dovea da questa donna esser data, divenne invidioso della sua buona fortuna e occultamente cominciò a cercar vie per le quali questo potesse sturbare; e ultimamente s'avvenne ad alcuna persona ammaestrata in ciò, il quale adoperò, con sue malie e con sue malvage operazioni, cose per le quali questo Gulfo fu del tutto privato del potere con alcuna femina giacere. (10.45)

> When a relative of this Welf [Guelph], whose name was Ghibelline, found out about the arrangement and heard what a marvellous dowry was going to be given by this lady to Welf, he became envious of Welf's good fortune and secretly began to look for ways in which he could spoil the arrangement. At last, he came upon a person skilled in these things who used magic powers and evil deeds in such a way that this Welf was completely deprived of the ability to lie with any woman. (Papio, 444)

Guelph travelled to Italy to consummate his marriage with Matilda (Boccaccio implies that Guelph was unaware of his newfound impotency) but was unable to perform. As a result, Matilda did not want to marry Guelph and sent him home, where Guelph suspected Ghibelline's role in his bad fortune and had him poisoned (10.46). As one would suspect, word spread immediately once Ghibelline was poisoned. Those who supported Guelph and those who supported the deceased Ghibelline formed opposite camps, taking on the "soprannomi" of the two individuals. This conflict did not limit itself to Germany, but spread down into Italy, where Countess Matilda supported those who fought in the name of Guelph, because she knew that he was innocent: "contessa Matelda, e conoscendo la inocenzia di Gulfo e la iniquità di Ghibellino, in aiuto di quegli che vendicar voleano la morte di Gulfo mandò grandissima subsidio" (10.48; "Once Matilda became aware of it (and because she knew both that Welf was innocent and that Ghibelline was a criminal), she sent significant assistance to those who wished to take revenge for Welf's murder," Papio, 444). Boccaccio continues in the *Esposizioni* to discuss how this curse first afflicted Florence in the assassination of Buondelmonte.

Boccaccio claims that this version of the tale of Matilda, Guelph, and Ghibelline was told by Luigi Gianfigliazzi, who in turn allegedly learned it from Charles IV (10.43). He thus identifies an oral tradition that, to my knowledge, does not have textual documentation except here in Boccaccio's *Esposizioni*. But Boccaccio either invented or chose this version of the Guelph/Ghibelline history as opposed to the one that can be found in Villani's chronicle, the alleged historical source for other moments in the *Esposizioni*, as in the case of Boccaccio's version of the Blacks and the Whites. Villani's account of the failed marriage of Matilda and Guelph differs vastly from Boccaccio's account, in that there is no one named Ghibelline who plays a role in Guelph's impotence:

> E alla perfine morto il padre e la madre della contessa Mattelda, e ella rimase ereda, si diliberò di maritare, e inteso la fama e la persona e l'altre cose d'uno nato di Soavia che avea nome Gulfo [...] Ma tosto la trestizia succedette e quella allegrezza, quando il contratto matrimonio non annodato si manifestò per lo mancamento dello ingenerare, il quale spezialmente è detto d'essere la volontà del matrimonio; perocchè Gulfo la moglie carnalmente non poteva conoscere nè altra femmina per frigidità naturale, o per altro impedimento perpetuo impedito; ma impertanto volendo ricoprire la sua vergogna, diceva alla moglie che questo gli avveniva per malie che fatte gli erano per alcuno che invidiava gli suoi felici avvenimenti. (*Nuova cronica*, 4.21)

166   Courtesy Lost

> In the end, when the Countess Matilda's father and mother were dead, and she was their heir, she thought to marry. Having heard of the fame and the person and the other qualities of a native of Swabia, whose name was Guelf [...] But soon did sadness follow gladness in that the marriage bond was not consummated, by failure of conception, which is expressly declared to be the purpose of marriage. [Translation to this point is from Selfe, 93–4.] Guelph could not know neither his wife nor any other woman either because of an inborn frigidity or because he was impeded by another constant obstacle. But wishing to hide his shame, he told his wife that this occurred because of offenses that had been done to him by someone who envied his felicitous developments in life. [Translation of last two sentences is mine.]

According to Villani, Guelph tried to hide the shame of his impotence by accusing an envious third party of committing "malie" (the same word found in *Esp.* 10) that deprived him of the ability to consummate the marriage. Villani never mentions Ghibelline, nor does he affirm, by providing a name or an account, that Guelph's impotence was caused by another person. Indeed, he claims that Matilda did not believe Guelph was the victim of a third party. When she confronts him on his inability to consumate the marriage, he "confesses himself":

> Ma la contessa Mattelda piena di fede dinanzi a Dio e dinanzi dagli uomini magnanimi, di questi maleficii nulla intendendo, schernita se per lo marito tenendo, la camera sua e tutti gli ornamenti e letti e vestimenta e tutte cose comandò che si votassero, e la mensa nuda fece apparecchiare, e chiamato Gulfo suo marito tutta spogliata di vestimenti, e' crini del capo diligentemente scrinati, questa disse: niune malie esser possono, vieni e usa il nostro congiungimento; e quegli non potendo, allora gli disse la contessa: alle nostre grandezze tu presumesti di fare inganno; per lo nostro onore a te perdonanza concediamo, ma comandiamti sanza dimoranza che ti debbi partire, e alle tue proprie case ritornare; la qual cosa se di fare ti starai, sanza pericolo di morte non puoi scampare; ed egli spaventato di paura, confessata la verità, avacciò il suo ritorno in Soavia. (4.21)

> But the Countess Matilda, full of faith in God and magnanimous men, having kept herself away from her husband, commanded that his room and all of his beds, clothes and ornaments be emptied. Entirely bereft of clothes and with her hair hanging down, she called her husband, Guelph, and said, "There could not have been any injuries done to you. Come and use our wedding bed." And as he was unable, the Countess said to him,

"You tried to make attempts upon my wealth. Because of my honor I will pardon you, but I command that you must leave and return to your home without delay. If you delay in doing this, you will not be able to escape the danger of death." Overwhelmed with fear, he confessed the truth and made his return to Swabia.

Villani would have us believe that Matilda revealed her doubts about Guelph's allegations. When he could not consummate the marriage, she accused him of designs on her wealth and commanded him to leave and return home. Unlike *Esposizioni* 10, this passage from Villani does not implicate a man named Ghibelline, whose malicious interference in the marriage between the countess and Guelph would lead to decades of political strife.

Bocccaccio's history of the original conflict between the Guelphs and Ghibellines might be symptomatic of the larger anti-Ghibelline sentiment of the mid-fourteenth century. Certainly it speaks again to how Boccaccio's historical vision reduces the motivations of its major protagonists to the personal and, in these moments, the sexual, attending to the relationship of the conventions of eros and of courtly culture to the political arenas of *cortesia*. His account of this political conflict attends as well to another aspect of expressions of virility: the ability to procreate. With Boccaccio's version of the competition between Ghibelline and Guelph for Matilda's hand in marriage seen in this light, then, the political rivalry between Neri degli Uberti and King Charles I in 10.6 is based on Charles's sublimation of his own sexual potency. King Peter's virility, on the other hand, is characterized by his powers of attraction, or his "manliness," recalling Dante's description of him in *Purgatorio* 7 as "membruto." Boccaccio's language of virility for these figures, which addresses both their manliness and their sexual potency, is more explicit than what we find in *Purgatorio* 7. While virility is the description of physical manliness for Dante, as in the "maschio naso" of King Charles and the "membruto" King Peter in *Purgatorio* 7, for Boccaccio virility consists of the expression or sublimation of sexual potency, and the wisdom to discern when erotic desire should be fulfilled (in the case of procreation) or thwarted (when the sexual act will not bear offspring).

Boccaccio seems to have teased out the association in the *Commedia* between virility and genealogy by casting these figures in *novelle* of a highly erotic, or romantic, nature. As Dante locates the figure of Currado Malaspina in a complex discourse on the inheritance of virtue (and, consequently, on the survival of *cortesia*), in 2.6 Boccaccio complements *Purgatorio* 8 by featuring the act of procreation itself, the act without which a family line would not survive, in the context of the romance of Giusfredi and Spina.[27] Both authors display a belief in the central role of the male in the act of procreation that was common cultural currency in the Middle Ages. In Vern Bullough's treatment of masculinity in the Middle Ages, he traces the medieval belief in the "overwhelming importance of the male principle in reproduction" back to Aristotle, who held that male semen was the active element in conception.[28] Medieval thinkers ranging from Avicenna to Albert the Great and Thomas Aquinas modified Aristotle's theory but agreed that the male contribution was the chief factor in the success of reproduction. Evidence of this theory of reproduction in Dante's works can be most clearly observed in *Purgatorio* 25, where Statius charts the course of "sangue perfetto" (perfect blood) as it becomes sperm that acts as a generative catalyst in the passive uterus ("scende ov'è più bello/tacer che dire; e quindi poscia geme/sovr' altrui sangue in natural vasello," 43–5; "it descends where silence/is more fit than speech and from there later/drops into the natural vessel on another's blood").[29]

Whether or not this philosophical background explains the focus on virility in *Purgatorio* 7 and 8, Boccaccio locates Dante's descriptions of physical virility in terms of the culture of romance that strongly characterized the construction of courtly love. We can observe this in 10.6 and 10.7, which both employ the protagonists and poetic language of courtly love: Neri degli Uberti's daughters are named Ginevra and Isotta, who sing a *ballata* entitled *Là ov'io son giunto, Amore*; Lisa's *amor de lonh* for King Peter inspires her to have a *ballata* composed by a troubadour.[30] Not coincidentally, Dante defines the world of *cortesia* in these terms of romance in *Purgatorio* 14 – "le donne e' cavalier, li affanni e li agi/che ne 'nvogliava amore e cortesia/là dove i cuor son fatti sì malvagi" (109–111; "the ladies and the knights, the toils and sport/that love and courtesy inspired,/where now is found a waste of evil hearts") – a canto that strongly influenced two other *novelle* from the *Decameron*, 5.4 and 5.8. In these *novelle* Boccaccio invents tales that attempt to define the role of women in this discourse on genealogy and procreation. He questions how courtly love, in which women are idealized and desirous men are chaste in practice, translates into the promise of progeny.

Virility as Nobility: *Cortesia* in Romagna

Boccaccio further demonstrates his understanding of the interstices among eros, genealogy, and social decadence in his interpretation in *novelle* 5.4 and 5.8 of *Purgatorio* 14, which features figures from the Romagna. In Dante's poem Guido del Duca, a Ghibelline from Bretinoro, laments the disapperance of virtue in the latest generations of current families from the Romagna:

> "Questi è Rinier; questi è 'l pregio e l'onore
>   de la casa da Calboli, ove nullo
>   fatto s'è reda poi del suo valore.
> E non pur lo suo sangue è fatto brullo,
>   tra 'l Po e 'l monte e la marina e 'l Reno,
>   del ben richiesto al vero e al trastullo;
> chè dentro a questi termini è ripieno
>   di venenosi sterpi, sì che tardi
>   per coltivare omai verrebber meno.
> Ov'è 'l buon Lizio e Arrigo Mainardi?
>   Pier Traversaro e Guido di Carpigna?
>   Oh Romagnuoli tornati in bastardi!
> Quando in Bologna un Fabbro si ralligna?
>   Quando in Faenza un Bernardin di Fosco,
>   verga gentil di picciola gramigna?
> Non ti maravigliar s'io piango, Tosco,
>   quando rimembro, con Guido da Prata,
>   Ugolin d'Azzo che vivette nosco,
> Federigo Tignoso e sua brigata,
>   la casa Traversara e li Anastagi
>   (e l'una gente e l'altra è diretata),
> le donne e' cavalier, li affanni e li agi
>   che ne 'nvogliava amore e cortesia
>   là dove i cuor son fatti sì malvagi."
>   (*Purg.* 14.88–111)

("This man is Rinieri, this is the pride and honor/of the house of Calboli, where no one since/has made himself an heir to his true worth./And not his blood alone – between Po and the mountains,/between Reno and the sea – is stripped of virtues/consonant with deeper thought and courtly pastime./For the land within these boundaries/is grown so dense with poisonous shoots/that even proper tillage now would come too late./Where is good Lizio, where Arrigo Mainardi,/Pier Traversaro and Guido di Carpigna?/O people of Romagna, how you've turned to bastards!/When, in Bologna, will another Fabbro grow?/When, in Faenza, a Bernardin di Fosco,/noble branch sprung from a lowly weed?/Do not marvel, Tuscan, if I weep/when, along with Guido da Prata, I recall/Ugolin d'Azzo, who lived among us,/Federico Tignoso and his companions,/ the house of Traversaro and of Anastagi –/both families now spent, without an heir –/the ladies and the knights, the toils and the sport/that love and courtesy inspired,/where now is found a waste of evil hearts.")

Similar to Sordello's "rimpianto" of the "probitate" that did not descend to current generations of European princes in *Purgatorio* 7, here Guido del Duca bemoans that the kin of various families – the houses of Calboli, Traversari, and Anastagi, for example – have not inherited the "valore" of previous generations (89–90). Nor is Romagna a land that could be cultivated again to produce such heirs, as it is too late. As Guido notes, some of these families, the Traversari and the Anastagi, do not have any progeny anyhow ("la casa Traversara e li Anastagi/(e l'una gente e l'altra è diretata)," 107–8). These families belonged to the courtly world where actions were inspired by "amore e cortesia" and not by malicious intentions.

Two *novelle* from Day Five feature some of the historical figures from these verses; Lizio da Valbona, together with an invented relative of Arrigo Mainardi, a certain Ricciardo Mainardi, appear in 5.4 ("Ov'è 'l buon Lizio e Arrigo Mainardi?" 97), and the Traversari and Anastagi families belong to the narrative of 5.8. Boccaccio directly responds to Guido del Duca's concern over the survival of these families by discussing Lizio da Valbona and the Traversari and Anastagi families in terms of their offspring, and more specifically in terms of the relationship of female desire to male desire within the paradigm of *cortesia*'s survival. In 5.4, Filostrato recounts the story of the historical figure Lizio da Valbona, "un cavaliere assai da bene e costumato" (5.4.4), a Guelph who assisted Guido Novello in Florence (around 1260) and who had a reputation for generosity and virtue. In his old age, Lizio and his wife had a daughter who was unparalleled in their *contrada* for her beauty and charm ("oltre a ogni della contrada crescendo divenne bella e piacevole," 5.4.5). Since she was their only child, Lizio and his wife were very protective of her and intent on finding her a nobleman as her husband. This is one similarity between 5.4 and the *novella* of Currado Malaspina, as Currado's daughter Spina was also his only daughter whom he fiercely protected, and perhaps serves as a reminder of the fragility of *cortesia*'s survival in families with few children.[31]

In contrast to 2.6, however, where Spina falls in love with Giusfredi before the disclosure of his noble ancestry, in 5.4 Lizio's daughter

Caterina returns the affections of a Ghibelline nobleman, Ricciardo Mainardi, who frequently pays friendly visits to her father. Caterina and Ricciardo plan to meet on the balcony near her father's garden. In order to fulfil their plan, Caterina complains to her mother that she suffered from the heat on the previous night and needs to sleep on the balcony where it would be cooler and she could hear the song of the nightingale. When her mother claims that it was not at all hot the night before, Caterina responds that younger women, of course, feel the heat much more than older women (5.4.17). After her mother confers with her father, supporting Caterina's claim that younger women enjoy the song of the nightingale, Lizio agrees to allow his daughter to sleep on the balcony and to listen to the nightingale's song to her heart's content.

The figurative language of the conversations between Caterina and her mother and between her mother and Lizio can be easily read as alluding to the desire of young women for men (and of youth in general, reminiscent of Giusfredi's words in 2.6). This meaning is conveyed by the description of their night together as having made the nightingale sing many times ("molte volte faccendo cantar l'usignolo," 5.4.29), and of her parents' discovery of the two of them together in bed the next morning, with Caterina holding the "nightingale" (5.4.36). Though her mother pretends, at first, to be angry with Caterina, Lizio reminds her that Ricciardo is a nobleman and that they should seize this opportunity to have them married ("Ricciardo è gentile uomo e ricco giovane; noi non possiamo aver di lui altro che buon parentado," 5.4.38; "Ricciardo is a rich young man, and comes of noble stock. We could do a lot worse than have him as our son-in-law," McWilliam, 397). When Lizio at first confronts Ricciardo, the surprised lover becomes afraid for his life (indeed, his reaction is more cowardly than that of Giusfredi in 2.6) and agrees to marry Caterina. The *novella* happily concludes with an allusion to the future sexual vitality of their marriage (5.4.49).[32]

The *novella* of Caterina and Ricciardo responds in manifold ways to *Purgatorio* 14. First, as in *Purgatorio* 14, whose *ubi sunt* topos pairs Guelphs and Ghibellines (the Ghibelline Guido del Duca and the Guelph Rinieri da Calboli; the Guelph Lizio da Valbona and the Ghibelline Arrigo Mainardi; the Ghibelline Pier Traversaro and the Guelph Guido Carpigna), in 5.4 the friendship and then familial relationship by marriage between Lizio da Valbona and Ricciardo Mainardi creates a sense of harmony between Guelph and Ghibelline noblemen. In response to *Purgatorio* 14's discussion of the lost *cortesia* in current generations in

Romagna, Boccaccio dramatizes the need for Lizio Valbona to have virtuous offspring by creating the fictional tale of Caterina and her marriage. Boccaccio creates the conditions for Lizio's family to keep *cortesia* alive by having his daughter Caterina marry a member of the Mainardi family, a pairing suggested by their proximity in the verse from *Purg.* 14: "Ov'è 'l buon Lizio e Arrigo Mainardi?" (97).

But the tale of Caterina and Ricciardo also implies that the survival of *cortesia* is dependent upon female desire (here, the desire of a Guelph woman) and her intelligence in creating the conditions to consummate that desire. Despite the rubric of this *novella*, which only names the male protagonists of this tale ("Ricciardo Manardi è trovato da messer Lizio da Valbona con la figliuola, la quale egli sposa e col padre di lei rimane in buona pace," 5.4.1; "Ricciardo Manardi is discovered by Messer Lizio da Valbona with his daughter, whom he marries, and remains on good terms with her father," McWilliam, 393), Caterina's words and actions ultimately result in the marriage that should bear heirs for Lizio's family. In other words, Caterina's susceptibility to the "heat" and her power of argumentation with her mother make possible her union with Ricciardo. Though Filostrato portrays the love of Caterina and Ricciardo as being reciprocal, Caterina's ability to convince her mother leads to the fulfilment of their tryst on the balcony. Furthermore, the image of Caterina who has "caught her nightingale," so to speak, casts the young woman in an active role. It is as if Caterina has taken the issue of her family's reputation for virtue into her own hands by choosing a rich, young nobleman like Ricciardo as the object of her sexual desire. Caterina's initiation of the plot, which culminates in the discovery of Ricciardo and herself by her parents, leads to the marriage that seems to promise a reversal of the gloomy fate of Romagna decried by Guido del Duca. In addition, Caterina's sexual conquest by means of literalizing her own metaphor renders her a powerful woman within the gendered economy of *parole* and *fatti* in the *Decameron* as articulated by Barolini.[33]

Boccaccio embellishes upon Dante's rhetoric of a lost age of *cortesia* by incorporating these important historical figures into tales of an erotic nature, which foreground both virility and female desire in different modes of power. As 10.6 and *Esposizioni* 10 express political rivalry through the sublimation of male desire or even castration, 5.4's harmonious coupling of Caterina and Ricciardo exists in a woman's "possession" of the male member. Dante does not explicitly address the power of sexual desire and relations in these *canti* concerned with issues of genealogy (or maintains the belief that it is better to be silent about the male organ than to name it: "ov'è più bello/tacer che dire," *Purg.* 25.43–4). By contrast, Boccaccio does not hesitate to illustrate the central nature of sexual desire in history by gesturing towards "quella cosa che voi tra gli uomini più vi vergognate di nominare" in his storytelling (5.4.30; "that part of his person which in mixed company you ladies are too embarrassed to mention," McWilliam, 396). This complementary nature of the *Decameron* is yet another way to read Boccaccio's *novelle* as a *galeotto* to Dante's poem, a true *mezzano* of romance.[34]

But in 5.4 and 5.8, Boccaccio lends prominence to the role of women in the survival of *cortesia*. Caterina holds her "nightingale" by dint of her own skills at negotiating with her parents. And 5.8, precisely because of its violence against women, communicates that women are meant to be ready and willing harbingers of sexual desire, if *cortesia* is to survive. If the Traversari daughter in 5.8, as I will now discuss, is terrorized into making a certain decision, the resignation of her will, and the cultivation of her desire, are necessary if Nastagio is to become a father.

If 5.4 is the happy tale of how hope for *cortesia* in Romagna can be renewed by a young woman, then 5.8 tragically depicts the violent oppression of women whose desires are not harmonious with male desire or authority. Here we find relatives from two other families listed as belonging to the lost world of *cortesia* in Romagna in *Purgatorio* 14, the Traversari and the Anastagi. Guido del Duca names the Traversari twice in his lament; first he asks where Pier Traversaro has gone ("Pier Traversaro? Guido di Carpigna?" 98). A few verses later, Guido recalls the lost houses of the Traversari and the Anastagi, neither of which have heirs ("la casa Traversara e li Anastagi/(e l'una gente e l'altra è diretata)," 106–7). If *Purgatorio* 14 bemoans the lack of heirs for these families, then I believe that Boccaccio indicates in 5.8 that the cause of this situation is the "cruelty" of a young woman from the Traversari family and the "cold-heartedness" of the beloved lady of a young man from the Anastagi family. Filomena's tale comprises two narratives. The first one describes the affections of a young wealthy nobleman named Nastagio degli Onesti for the daughter of Paolo Traversari, who was of an even nobler ancestry than his; the second, embedded story recounts the otherworldly scene of an infernal hunt involving Guido degli Anastagi and the woman who scorned his affections during his lifetime.

Nastagio degli Onesti, a young man susceptible to the power of love, tries in vain to win the affections of a daugher of Paolo Traversari. Her pride was perhaps due to her exceptional beauty or to her illustrious ancestry ("forse per la sua singular bellezza o per la sua nobiltà sì altiera e disdegnosa divenuta," 5.8.6; "on account possibly of her singular beauty, or perhaps because of her exalted rank, she became so haughty and contemptuous of him," McWilliam, 419–20). Whatever the cause of her haughty attitude towards Nastagio (the words that characterize her, "altiera e disdegnosa" and "crudel," recall the distant lady of Dante's *rime petrose*, as Branca notes),[35] Nastagio is consequently driven to thoughts of suicide, ceasing to give up the hope of wooing her. When Nastagio's friends notice the toll of his despair, they advise him to leave Ravenna. He embarks on a trip to Classe, where he decides to reside for some length of time. While in Classe, on a Friday morning, Nastagio wanders out into the forest and falls witness to a scene of a naked young woman being chased by large dogs and a knight on horseback carrying a rapier and intending to kill her.

The scene of the "caccia infernale" engenders fear and compassion in Nastagio for the woman he sees, and so he attempts to defend her life. The knight stops Nastagio, introduces himself as Guido degli Anastagi and explains the origins of this scene. Guido recounts how he fell in love with this woman when Nastagio was still very young (he adds that his love is much deeper than Nastagio's [5.8.21]); however, her "fierezza e crudeltà" drove him to suicide using the same rapier he now brandishes during the ritual of the infernal hunt. She was happy for his death but died shortly afterwards. Since her cruelty was a sin she was also condemned to hell. Together they received a special punishment that involved him pursuing her as if she were his enemy, killing her with the rapier and then feeding her heart and organs to his dogs, again and again.

Nastagio is at first horrified by Guido's words and this scene of violence, but then decides that he can use it in order to terrorize the daughter of Paolo Traversari into loving him. He invites Paolo Traversari and his wife and daughter to come to Classe for a feast the following Friday and has the tables arranged so that all of his guests can witness "lo strazio della crudel donna" (5.8.36). The effect of this scene upon those present is exactly what Nastagio wishes: the women weep (some of them were related to the woman or the knight), but the Traversari daughter is particularly terrified. She understands that this scene was intended for her because of her cruelty (5.8.40). Since she does not want a similar fate to befall her, she converts her hate into love ("avendo l'odio in amor tramutato," 5.8.41) and agrees to Nastagio's offer of marriage. The *novella* concludes with their marriage and the other "bene" (good) result of this terror: from that day onwards the other ladies of Ravenna always surrendered themselves to the desires of men ("che sempre poi troppo più arrendevoli a' piaceri degli uomini furono che prima state non erano," 5.8.44; "from that day forth the ladies of Ravenna in general were so frightened by it that they became much more tractable to men's pleasures than they had ever been in the past," McWilliam, 425).

The eighth tale of the Fifth Day bears a rich and varied pedigree of borrowings from the *Commedia* and from Dante's life.[36] Filomena's tale begins in Ravenna, another city that hosted Dante during his exile and that was the place of his death. An allusion to Nastagio's place of retreat, Classe, appears in the verses that describe the forest in the Earthly Paradise ("tal qual di ramo in ramo si raccoglie/per la pineta in su 'l lito di Chiassi," *Purg.* 28.19–20; "as builds from branch to branch/throughout the pine wood at the shore of Classe"). The "caccia infernale" recalls the brutality witnessed by Dante in the Wood of the Suicides in *Inferno* 13, a connection reinforced by Guido's taking of his own life; the presence of the spendthrifts in *Inferno* 13 resonates with Guido's own such status. Read in the context of Boccaccio's response to Dante's history of *cortesia* in *Purgatorio* 14, this *novella* reveals the role of women in the perseverence of *cortesia* and in the extinction of renowned families: the conformity to male desire. Boccaccio's *novella* appears to argue that the Anastagi family would still have prospered if not for the "crueltà" of Guido's beloved, whereas now they are doomed to re-enact their unsuccessful courtship for eternity. The Traversari daughter is forced to evade this fate for her family, and I believe that the presence of her parents in Classe suggests the consequences of her decision for the survival of her family line. Therefore, it is not coincidental that her parents are happy to hear that she will marry Nastagio.

The *novella* of Nastagio degli Onesti and the "caccia infernale" turns upon this generic inheritance of topographical and contextual themes from the *Commedia* and moments in Dante's life, as well as a parody of the ideals of courtly love, as put forth by Andreas Capellanus, as Mazzotta has argued.[37] It shows, as Michael Sherberg has observed, the power of textual interpretation. If, as Sherberg indicates, "Nastagio has exploited narrative to achieve his purpose,"[38] then this *novella* similarly reveals how Boccaccio's exploitation of Dante's texts allows him the power of revising history's course. The outcome of 5.8 also reveals the place of violence in the survival of *cortesia*, namely that *cortesia* can continue to exist if a woman's will is shaped by fear of violence. Hence it shares a portrayal of the ways of *cortesia* with *Decameron* 6.9, the *novella* of Guido Cavalcanti, where *cortesia* depends upon a culture of violence and intimidation, the manifestations of a chivalric mentality that dominated the former era of elite families. The violence of 5.8 also speaks to the context in which Boccaccio finds himself, caught in the moment in which accusations of Ghibelline *ancestry*, not necessarily Ghibelline affiliation, were largely the basis of *ammonizione*. Boccaccio, in refashioning Dante's chivalric world for the Malaspina line and the houses of the Traversari and Mainardi, composes *novelle* that recount marriage alliances and imply the promise of future progeny for them; he is concerned with the very issue of Ghibelline genealogy itself, imagining future generations that would arguably be his contemporaries. In the lighthearted tale of 5.4, this promise takes the shape of a combined alliance between Guelph and Ghibelline in the marriage between Caterina, daughter of Lizio, with the noble Ricciardo. Does the easily resolution of this tale here imply the benefits of political alliances between the Guelph and Ghibellines? Or does it point to the dangers of a purely Ghibelline line for a family *not* associated with Dante's experience in exile? Certainly Caterina's amorous hunt for Ricciardo's nightingale contrasts sharply with the destructive "caccia infernale" of 5.8, where women are forced to comply with male desire – and where, it should be added, there is no such political alliance across party lines. It is, ironically, the violence of this *novella*, in which Nastagio degli Onesti is at first powerless but ultimately breaks the will of the daughter of Paolo Traversari (Ghibelline) via the infernal hunt rehearsed daily by Guido degli Anastagi (Ghibelline), that avoids *cortesia*'s fate of extinction in the Romagna in *Purgatorio* 14.

Nobility's Inheritance: The Case of Federigo degli Alberighi

The families of the Romagna that find their Dantean pedigree in *Purgatorio* 14 are not the only families of the golden age of *cortesia* that can be found in both the *Commedia* and the *Decameron*. Boccaccio also promises a future for *cortesia* in Florence itself, and it is again a victory orchestrated by a woman, although on different terms than those just examined. Boccaccio's reversal of the *Commedia*'s lament for a Florentine golden age takes shape in the eventual good fortune of one of the *Decameron*'s tragicomic male youths, Federigo degli Alberighi, featured in *Decameron* 5.9, whose nobility of spirit succeeds in earning him the hand of his beloved in marriage and a considerable sum of money.[39] By creating the fictional character of Federigo, whose tale he claims to have heard from Coppo di Domenico Borghesi, Boccaccio delves deep into the annals of history for a tale whose oral tradition by the mid-fourteenth century would have been unlikely at best.[40] As in the case of the Mainardi, Traversari, and Anastagi families, the disappearance of the Alberighi family presents Boccaccio with the opportunity to reverse their decline in a tale whose conclusion promises a secure financial future for Federigo, and therefore reverses the "fall" of his family described in *Paradiso* 16. The brute fact of their disappearance – of the Alberighi well as the families of 5.4 and 5.8 – becomes the occasion for fiction to rewrite the future.

In *Paradiso* 16, Cacciaguida lists the Alberichi [Alberighi] amongst those great families from Florence's past, families whose fame had been erased by time: "Io vidi li Ughi e vidi i Catellini,/Filippi, Greci, Ormani e Alberichi,/già nel calare, illustri cittadini" ("I saw the Ughi, I saw the Catellini,/Filippi, Greci, Ormanni and Alberichi,/illustrious citizens already in decline," 88–90). Villani writes that the Alberighi, already in decline by the first half of the twelfth century, were extinct by the fourteenth century:[41]

> Nel quartiere di porta san Piero erano i Bisdomini che, come di sopra è detto, e' sono padroni del vescovado, e gli Alberighi, che fu loro la chiesa di santa Maria Alberighi da casa i Donati, e oggi non n'è nullo. (*Nuova cronica*, 4.11)

> In the quarter of Porta San Piero were the Bisdomini, which, as aforesaid, were the patrons of the bishopric, and the Alberighi, and theirs was the church of Santa Maria Alberighi towards the house of the Donati, and now, nought remains of them. (Selfe, 80)

That the Alberighi once dwelled in the same neighbourhood as the Donati invites comparison between the fictional character of Federigo degli Alberighi in *Decameron* 5.9 and Corso Donati, a long-standing member of the knighted, consular aristocracy of Florence. Like Corso, Federigo evokes the figure of the impoverished aristocrat, yet his family, faced with extinction early in Florentine history, belongs to an even more distant past than the leader of the Black Guelphs, one without a specified political affiliation. Though they did not live in the same neighbourhood, a comparison could also be drawn between Federigo and Currado Gianfigliazzi, another notable knight from Florence ("notabile cittadino, liberale e magnifico," 6.4.4; a noteworthy citizen, generous and hospitable), who also leaves the city in order to pursue the delights of the countryside, where birds of the hunt loom large in the landscape and in the narrative. Currado's decision to abandon a life of mercantile and political activity, however, is quite different from that of Federigo, who is likewise a generous knight ("in opera d'arme e in cortesia pregiato sopra ogni altro donzel di Toscana," 5.9.6; "who for his deeds of chivalry and courtly manners was more highly spoken of than any other squire in Tuscany," McWilliam, 426) but who has left the city and moved to his small farm ("poderetto") out of financial necessity. Whereas Currado leaves his life as a knight and merchant to enjoy the lighter pleasures of the "vita cavalleresca," Federigo must depart Florence after indulging in the spendthrift ways of youthful *brigate* (such as those discussed in the context of *Decameron* 6.9).

Federigo is thus reminiscent of the squanderers featured in *Inferno* 13 and the *brigata spendereccia* named in *Inferno* 29. As well, he evokes the protagonist of the preceding tale, Nastagio degli Onesti (*Dec.* 5.8), insofar as both men spend excessive sums of money in attempting to attract their love interests. Federigo falls in love with Monna Giovanna of Florence and dissipates his fortune in his efforts to "acquire" her love:

> E acciò che egli l'amor di lei acquistar potesse, giostrava, armeggiava, faceva feste e donava, e il suo senza alcun ritegno spendeva [...] Spendendo adunque Federigo oltre a ogni suo potere molto e niente acquistando, sì come di leggiere adiviene, le ricchezze mancarono e esso rimase povero, senza altra cosa che un suo poderetto piccolo essergli rimasa, delle rendite del quale strettissimamente viveva, e oltre a questo un suo falcone de' miglio del mondo. (5.9.6–8)

> And with the object of winning her love, he rode at the ring, tilted, gave sumptuous banquets, and distributed a large number of gifts, spending money without any restraint whatsoever. [...] In this way, spending far more than he could afford and deriving no profit in return, Federigo lost his entire fortune (as can easily happen) and reduced himself to poverty, being left with nothing other than a tiny little farm, which produced an income just sufficient for him to live very frugally, and one falcon of the finest breed in the whole world. (McWilliam, 426)

Federigo's profligacy in attempting to earn Giovanna's love is, Fiammetta reminds us, often indulged in by knights ("sì come di leggiere adiviene," 5.9.6); Nastagio degli Onesti's exemplum from the preceding *novella* is a case in point. Federigo leaves the city and goes to the countryside, Campi, a town listed by Cacciaguida as one of the origins of the city's now mixed population ("Ma la cittadinanza, ch'è or mista,/di Campi," *Par.* 16.49–50). Albeit in a different geographical direction, Federigo's emigration is thus akin to the process of immigration lamented by Cacciaguida, since he moves away from the site where he might have the opportunity to increase his wealth by means of mercantile activity, as Bruni has indicated.[42] In this, Federigo appears more like a Corso Donati than a Vieri de' Cerchi, belonging much more to the aristocratic way of life than to that of the new financial upstarts.

Yet, unlike Corso, who humbly manages to entertain his guests with a modest meal (9.8), or Currado, who becomes indignant at the prospect of improperly feeding his guests (6.4), Federigo suffers a disconnect with reality, especially insofar as he is unwilling to seek assistance in his state: "senza alcuna persona richiedere, pazientemente la sua povertà comportava," 5.9.8; "without seeking assistance from anyone, he patiently resigned himself to a life of poverty" McWilliam 426). He passes his time hunting with his falcon, a symbol of the aristocratic lifestyle he can no longer sustain. It is only when Giovanna arrives at his home for a meal that he realizes the extent of his poverty, for he cannot entertain her as would be fitting:

> Egli, con tutto che la sua povertà fosse strema, non s'era ancor tanto avveduto quanto bisogno gli facea che egli avesse fuor d'ordine spese le sue ricchezze; ma questa mattina niuna cosa trovandosi di che potere onorar la donna, per amor della quale egli già infiniti uomini onorati avea, il fé ravedere. E oltre modo angoscioso, seco stesso maledicendo la sua fortuna, come uomo che fuor di sé fosse or qua e or là trascorrendo, né denari né pegno trovandosi. (5.9.25)

> Though his poverty was acute, the extent to which he had squandered his wealth had not yet been fully borne home to Federigo; but on this particular morning, finding that he had nothing to set before the lady for whose love he had entertained so lavishly in the past, his eyes were well and truly opened to the fact. Distressed beyond all measure, he silently cursed his bad luck and rushed all over the house like one possessed, but could find no trace of either money or valuables. (McWilliam, 428–9)

Though he has an opportunity to entertain the woman in whose pursuit he has squandered his wealth, he is now penniless and unable to do so. The tragic irony of this moment invites a reading of this story that is not exclusively focused on Federigo's suffering *qua* courtly lover. The crisis of this *novella*, I would argue, is the inability of an aristocrat to manage his wealth, or, to put it differently, how the ways of *cortesia* undermine the courtly lover.

The focus on the financial is transparent from the very rubric of the *novella*:

> Federigo ama e non è amato, e *in cortesia spendendo si consuma* e rimangli un sol falcone, il quale, non avendo altro, dà da mangiare alla sua donna venutagli a casa; la qual, ciò sappiendo, mutata d'animo, il prende per marito e *fallo ricco*. (5.9.1, emphasis added)

> In courting a lady who does not return his love, Federigo degli Alberighi spends the whole of his substance, being left with nothing but a falcon, which, since his larder is bare, he offers to his lady to eat when she calls to see him at his house. On discovering the truth of the matter, she has a change of heart, accepts him as her husband, and makes a rich man of him. (McWilliam, 425)

Federigo "loves and is not loved"; he squanders himself in acts of *cortesia*, the rubric states, but by the end of this love story he will be rich. *Decameron* 5.9 might initially appear to be a story of love first unrequited but then reciprocated; however, the good fortune of the protagonist hinges upon Giovanna's ability to make him solvent again.

The circumstances that lead to reacquiring wealth – to "enriching" his nobility, so to speak – are outlined by Fiammetta immediately after the description of Federigo's difficult situation, towards the beginning of the *novella*. Consequently, the reader is meant to anticipate that Giovanna's wealth, as much as her love, will solve Federigo's problems.[43] Giovanna's husband passes away, leaving his considerable wealth to their son, with Giovanna as beneficiary should the son perish without issue. The story thus proceeds not only with Federigo's decline evoking the historical disappearance of his own family, but with the fate of Giovanna's family veiled in uncertainty: will the son survive his illness and become a patriarch in his own right, or will Giovanna inherit the money and find a suitable spouse in order to keep the inheritance in her family? Put another way, and returning to the relationship between this *novella* and Dante's poem, the decadence of the Alberighi must depend upon a lack of heirs in Giovanna's family.

The tale unfolds with its sentimental highs and lows: Federigo kills his precious falcon and serves it as a meal to Giovanna without her knowledge, and Giovanna's son dies without ever obtaining the falcon so dear to him. Giovanna goes through a period of mourning, after which her brothers pressure her to remarry for practical reasons; she is young, and has recently inherited her fortune. Giovanna would have preferred to have remained a widow ("la quale, come che voluto non avesse, pur veggendosi infestare," 5.9.39; though she would have preferred not to remarry, she was tormented). Her desire to marry Federigo is thus partly a compromise with her brothers. She also wishes to marry Federigo because she would rather marry a man without riches than riches without a man ("io voglio avanti uomo che abbia bisogno di ricchezza che ricchezza che abbia bisogno d'uomo," 5.9.42). Yet at the end of the story Federigo has become rich as a result of her alliance with him. Perhaps the greatest transformation wrought by their marriage is conveyed in the last line of the story, when we learn that Federigo not only marries the woman he desires, but also learns how to better administer his finances ("oltre a ciò ricchissimo, in letizia con lei, *miglior massaio* fatto, terminò gli anni suoi," 5.9.43, emphasis added).

To return to the rubric of this tale, the story of Federigo degli Alberighi conveys the message that women must administer their gifts themselves, or Fortune will decide such matters for them, often indiscriminately ("senza lasciarne sempre esser la fortuna guidatrice, la qual non discretamente ma, come s'aviene, smoderatamente il piú delle volte dona," 5.9.3; "instead of always leaving these matters to be decided for you by Fortune, who, as it happens, nearly always scatters her gifts with more abundance than discretion," McWilliam, 425). When women take up Fiammetta's advice, they avoid the whims of Fortune lamented by Cacciaguida for Florentine families like the Alberighi:

> Le vostre cose tutte hanno lor morte,
> sì come voi; ma celasi in alcuna
> che dura molto; e le vite son corte.
> E come 'l volger del ciel della luna
> cuopre e discoupre i liti sanza posa,
> così fa di Fiorenza la Fortuna. (*Par.* 16.79–84)

("All your concerns are mortal, even as are you,/but in some things that are more lasting/this lies hidden, because all lives are brief./And, as the turning of the lunar sphere covers/and endlessly uncovers the edges of the shore,/thus does fortune deal with Florence.")

In order for *cortesia* to survive, then, it must abandon the profligate and destructive ways of itself – the extreme, *smoderate*, ways of this lifestyle – and embrace the pragmatism of a woman like Giovanna – or a Griselda (10.10), as I will discuss below.[44] Boccaccio will reverse the mortality for Dante's families of the golden age of the past, including the extinct Alberighi ("le cose vostre tutte han lor morte/sì come voi"). In this way, not all of them will meet their death.

Conclusion

Does Boccaccio truly wish for the "golden age" of *cortesia*, born at the expense of suffering and pathos, to survive? Is Boccaccio illustrating the violence of the act of nostalgia – especially the nostalgia for a past that lives only in works of literature? Or is he showing, once again, the impossibility of reviving an era of aristocratic ideals that have become extinct? The tension between Boccaccio's endorsement of the civic ethos of *cortesia*, understood as an elaboration upon the concept of *liberalità*, and the brutality of the chivalric age mirrors the tension between Boccaccio's republican belief and his devotion to an older, aristocratic Florence and Italy, which is, by extension, his devotion to Florence's poet, Dante. It depicts Boccaccio torn between his affection for a historical and literary imagination and the civic ideals necessary for the Republic. Where one might be inclined to read sarcasm or parody, as in the case of *Decameron* 6.9 or 5.8, is instead, I believe, the *lapsus* between these two affinities for the author. The ideological and historical contradictions that have been explored in these pages – Boccaccio's affection for Corso Donati alongside his distrust for the greed of the newer merchant families in the *Esposizioni*, the *Decameron*'s tendency to criticize greed while promoting liberality, and the revival of a younger generation of Ghibelline standard bearers for *cortesia* – attest to the wide reaches of the incongruous and multi-valenced history of *cortesia* for this author in envisioning the past and his present, both within and beyond Dante's influence.

Nowhere is this dramatic tension more clear than in the last *novella* of the *Decameron* (10.10). As Houston and Wallace have noted, the tyrannical Gualtieri evokes the other, despotic Walter, the Duke of Athens who served as *signore* in Florence between 1342 and 1343, while Griselda represents the *popolo* of Florence, manipulated and abused beyond measure by her selfish husband – and the man upbraided by the spirit of Dante in the ninth book of the *De casibus* for his tyranny and wicked acts.⁴⁵ In addition, he is the Marquis of Saluzzo – one of the ancient marquisates (founded in 1125) that could be imagined as among those that cultivated a chivalric culture for *cortesia* in the twelfth century. The obedient, self-effacing Griselda embodies the original Ciceronian model of fortitude and magnanimity, as Scaglione argues.⁴⁶ At the same time, the Marquis of Saluzzo incarnates the chivalric ethos of *cortesia*, a far cry from the civic ethic described by Cicero. If there is no extreme victory by the end of the *novella*, then, likewise, it is not clear which aspect of *cortesia* will be dominant in the conclusion of the *Decameron* ("e savissimo reputaron Gualtieri, come che troppo reputassero agre e intollerabili l'esperienze prese della sua donna, e sopra tutti savissima tenner Griselda," 10.10.66; "Gualtieri was acknowledged to be very wise, though the trials to which he had subjected his lady were regarded as harsh and intolerable, whilst Griselda was accounted the wisest of all," McWilliam, 794). Will the civic ethic of *cortesia* triumph in the post-plague landscape, or will incivility, violence and tyranny continue instead? The answer that Boccaccio gives us, in 10.10, is that only Griselda could have suffered a Gualtieri – only someone who incarnates the Roman civic virtues could have endured the tortures of Gualtieri with such stoicism. It is that ethic, perhaps one that will herald the thought of civic humanism for a new age, which marks a narrow victory at the end of the *Decameron*. *Cortesia* might not be lost with the establishment of more *signorie* in the fourteenth and fifteenth centuries, but the civic ethic that Griselda embodies must stand alongside of it.

I have illustrated some ways in which Boccaccio writes about posterity in the shadow of his present times. From revising Dante's history of Corso Donati's life according to his views on the *gente nuova*, to his views on avarice and merchants and clerics, to rewriting Dante's history of a chivalric world populated by Ghibellines and Guelphs in ways that would be consonant with and different from Dante's thought, Boccaccio can be observed in a tension between the political thought of the *Commedia* and that of his own times. One way to theorize this difference is to turn, yet again, to their different definitions of *cortesia* itself. While in the *Convivio* Dante will identify *cortesia* as a practice of the courts ("uso di corte"), Boccaccio in *Esposizioni* 16.53 – in glossing the words of the *Commedia* itself – will define *cortesia* as the practice of "atti civili," civil acts, "nel vivere insieme liberalmente e lietamente, e fare onore a tutti secondo la possibilità." By taking *cortesia* out of the court, be it the imperial court of the Hohenstaufen line or the princely courts of Italy, Boccaccio at the end of his life defined this concept in a way that would anticipate the fourteenth-century precursors of civic humanism as analysed by Marvin Becker.[47] As Cristoforo Landino writes in his commentary on *Inferno* 16, *cortesia*, together with "valore," maintains harmony in the Republic ("*cortesia et valore*: liberalità et forteza overo magnanimità, le quali due virtù nella rep. mantengon la concordia").[48] Boccaccio's conflation of the ethical with the sociological definitions of *cortesia* speaks to the contradictions at the heart of the fourteenth-century precursors to civic humanism, where noble status and true nobility did not go hand in hand with each other, where the "incivility" of a sociological brand of *cortesia*, so to speak, was a jarring reminder of the lapse between this ideology and the interests of the wealthy elite. Boccaccio, in showing us the convergences and divergences between his imagined political realities of Florence and Italy and the idea of the common good, in looking to Dante's historic past while attending to his present, points us exactly in this future direction.

Notes

Introduction

1 Victoria Kirkham surveys the visual iconography (i.e., Giotto's Arena Chapel) and literary traditions of personifications (i.e., Prudentius's *Psychomachia*) that would have been available to Boccaccio. These include the opposition of Largitas and Avaritia, Charity versus Avarice, and Charity against Envy, but never Courtesy against Avarice. She argues that the personification of Courtesy come from "a *contaminatio* of ancient and medieval sources, fusions characteristic of Boccaccio's pervasive, rigorous eclecticism," and also discusses the visual rendering of Courtesy in some illuminated fifteenth-century manuscripts of the *Decameron* made in Paris. See Kirkham, "The Tale of Guiglielmo Borsiere (I.8)," in *The* Decameron *First Day in Perspective*, ed. Elissa Weaver (Toronto: University of Toronto Press, 2004), 182–3, 189–90.
2 Like Najemy, I use the term "elite" to refer to families that were not a part of the *popolo*. They are also often called the "aristocracy" in these pages. To call them all "magnates" would be false, as some elite families were designated as magnates in the Ordinances of Justice (1293) while others were not (John M. Najemy, *A History of Florence 1200–1575* [Malden, MA: Blackwell, 2006], 5–6).
3 Ronald G. Witt, "The Early Communal Historians, Forerunners of the Italian Humanists," in *The Renaissance in the Streets, Schools, and Studies: Essays in Honour of Paul F. Grendler*, ed. Konrad Eisenbichler, Paul F. Grendler, and Nicholas Terpstra (Toronto: Centre for Reformation and Renaissance Studies, 2008), 106.
4 Norbert Elias writes, "*Courtoisie, civilité* and *civilisation* mark three stages of a social development. They indicate which society is speaking

and being addressed at a given time." See Elias, *The Civilizing Process: Sociogenetic and Psychogenetic Investigations* (Oxford: Blackwell, 2000), 88.
5   Giuseppe Sansone, *La nozione di cortesia nei testi didattici di lingua d'oc* (Rome: Editrice ELIA, 1975), 5.
6   C.S. Jaeger, *The Origins of Courtliness: Civilizing Trends and the Formation of Courtly Ideals, 939–1210* (Philadelphia: University of Pennsylvania Press, 1985), 256.
7   Elias writes, "Even during the Middle Ages the meaning of the word clearly lost much of its original social restriction to the 'court,' coming into use in bourgeois circles as well" (*The Civilizing Process*, 87).
8   Aldo D. Scaglione, *Knights at Court: Courtliness, Chivalry & Courtesy from Ottonian Germany to the Italian Renaissance* (Berkeley: University of California Press, 1991), 7.
9   J.D. Burnley, *Courtliness and Literature in Medieval England* (London: Longman, 1998), 3.
10 C.S. Lewis, *The Allegory of Love: A Study in Medieval Tradition* (Oxford: Clarendon, 1936), 2.
11 Burnley, *Courtliness and Literature*, 23.
12 Elias, *The Civilizing Effect*, 54, 87, 252–3.
13 Elias, *The Civilizing Effect*, 187.
14 Elias, *The Civilizing Effect*, 54–5.
15 Elias, *The Civilizing Effect*, 87.
16 Jaeger, *The Origins of Courtliness*, 9.
17 Jaeger, *The Origins of Courtliness*, 4. The coronation of Otto I forms the historical backdrop to *Dec.* 2.8, the *novella* of the Count of Antwerp, Walter, who is described as the ideal "uomo di corte" – but not, of course, a member of Otto's court: "del corpo bellissimo e d'età forse di quaranta anni, e tanto piacevole e costumato quanto alcuno altro gentile uomo il piú esser potesse; e, oltre a tutto questo, era il piú leggiadro e il piú dilicato cavaliere che a quegli tempi si conoscesse e quegli che piú della persona andava ornato" (2.8.6; "This Walter was about forty years old, physically very handsome, and as agreeable and courteous a nobleman as you could ever imagine. Moreover, apart from being the most elegantly dressed, he was more refined and graceful in bearing than any other knight of his times," McWilliam, 149).
18 Jaeger, *The Origins of Courtliness*, 12–13.
19 Burnley, *Courtliness and Literature*, 26.
20 Burnley, *Courtliness and Literature*, 26–7.
21 Scaglione, *Knight at Court*, 47, 49–50.
22 Scaglione, *Knight at Court*, 50; Jaeger, *The Origins of Courtliness*, 50.

23 Scaglione, *Knight at Court*, 53. See Marcus Tullius Cicero, *De officiis*, trans. Walter Miller (New York: Macmillan, 1913), book 1 (esp. 1.27 and 1.93–116).
24 Scaglione, *Knight at Court*, 50–2.
25 Giuseppe Mazzotta, *The World at Play in Boccaccio's* Decameron (Princeton: Princeton University Press, 1986), 86–9.
26 Stanley L. Galpin, *Cortois and Vilain: A Study of the Distinctions Made between Them by the French and Provençal Poets of the 12th, 13th and 14th Centuries* (New Haven, CT: Ryder's, 1905), 6.
27 Galpin, *Cortois and Vilain*, 6.
28 Galpin, *Cortois and Vilain*, 98.
29 Ivos Margoni, *Fin'amors, mezura e cortezia: Saggio sulla lirica provenzale del XII secolo* (Milan: Istituto Editoriale Cisalpino, 1965), 10.
30 Burnley, *Courtliness and Literature*, 3–5.
31 Burnley, *Courtliness and Literature*, 8.
32 Scaglione, *Knights at Court*, 91.
33 Burnley, *Courtliness and Literature*, 20.
34 Scaglione, *Knights at Court*, 93.
35 Text and translation are from Frederick Goldin, *Lyrics of the Troubadours and Trouvères: An Anthology and a History* (Garden City, NY: Anchor, 1973), 196–7.
36 Scaglione, *Knights at Court*, 189–90.
37 See E.M.K. Brett's dissertation, "Avarice and Largesse: A Study of the Theme in Moral-Satirical Poetry in Provençal, Latin and Old French, 1100–1300," Cambridge University, 1986, for an examination of the diverse poetic ethics of *largesse* and *avarice*.
38 Margoni, *Fin'amors*, 26.
39 Margoni, *Fin'amors*, 41.
40 Scaglione, *Knights at Court*, 99.
41 Brett, "Avarice and Largesse," 176–7.
42 Scaglione, *Knights at Court*, 97.
43 Scaglione, *Knights at Court*, 33–41, 170.
44 Witt, "Early Communal Historians," 106.
45 Scaglione, *Knights at Court*, 174–5; Elias, *Civilizing Process*, 53; Jaeger, *Origins of Courtliness*, 266.
46 Scaglione, *Knights at Court*, 183; Elias, *Civilizing Process*, 53, 73, 121–2, 127–8.
47 Christopher Kleinhenz, "Dante as Reader and Critic of Courtly Literature," in *Courtly Literature: Culture and Context: Selected Papers from the 5th Triennial Congress of the International Courtly Literature Society*, ed.

Keith Busby and Erik Kooper (Amsterdam/Philadelphia: John Benjamins, 1990), 379.
48 Kleinhenz, "Dante as Reader," 379.
49 For text, see *Le rime della scuola siciliana*, ed. Bruno Panvini (Florence: Olschki, 1962).
50 "Cortesia cortesia cortesia chiamo/e da nessuna parte mi risponde,/e chi la dèe mostrar, sì la nasconde,/e perciò a cui bisogna vive gramo./ Avarizia le genti ha preso all'amo,/ed ogni grazia distrugge e confonde;/ però se eo mi doglio, eo so ben onde:/di voi, possenti, a Dio me ne richiamo./Ché la mia madre cortesia avete/messa sì sotto il piè che non si leva;/l'aver ci sta, voi non ci rimanete!/Tutti siem nati di Adamo e di Eva;/potendo, non donate e non spendete:/mal ha natura chi tai figli alleva." Text from Michelangelo Picone's *Il giuoco della vita bella: Folgore da San Gimignano, Studi e testi* (San Gimignano: Città di San Gimignano, 1988).
51 Kleinhenz, "Dante as Reader," 379.
52 Scaglione, *Knights at Court*, 181–3. Scaglione notes that these virtues are originally based on Cicero's four cardinal virtues that are the basis of a civic education in the *De officiis*.
53 Najemy, *A History of Florence*, 50.
54 See Brunetto Latini, *Tesoretto (The Little Treasure)*, edited and translated by Julia Bolton Holloway (New York: Garland, 1981), 80–1.
55 Cortesia also appears in Petrarch's *Trionfo della castità* (v. 86).
56 Teodolinda Barolini, "Aristotle's *Mezzo*, Courtly *Misura*, and Dante's Canzone *Le dolci rime*: Humanism, Ethics, and Social Anxiety," in *Dante and the Greeks*, ed. Jan M. Ziolkowski (Washington, DC: Dumbarton Oaks, 2014), 163–79.
57 See *Il Novellino*, ed. Salvatore Nigro (Bari: Laterza, 1975).
58 Najemy, *A History of Florence*, 31–2.
59 Kleinhenz, "Dante as Reader," 382–3.
60 Dispenza Crimi writes, "Dante, infatti, nelle opere techniche *De vulgari eloquentia* e *Convivio*, sarà il primo a codificarne l'uso, recuperandone i contenuti sostanziali ed imprimendovi anzi una connotazione politica, che ne aggiornerà l'esercizio." See Erminia Maria Dispenza Crimi, *"Cortesia" e "valore" dalla tradizione a Dante* (Cosenza: Marra Editore, 1993), 11.
61 Joan Ferrante, "*Cortes'Amor* in Medieval Texts," *Speculum* 55 (1980): 695.
62 Kleinhenz, "Dante as Reader," 380–2.
63 Scaglione, *Knights at Court*, 194.
64 Scaglione, *Knights at Court*, 190. Scaglione argues to the contrary, stating that this moment symbolizes Dante's distance from the feudal court – and

therefore of the Occitanian interest in this value – and his interest in the imperial court.
65 For the full texts of these lyric poems, see *Rime giovanili e della Vita nuova*, ed. Teodolinda Barolini (Milan: BUR Rizzoli, 2009).
66 See Ferrante, who writes: "For Dante, as for Jean de Meun's Reson, the source of all *cortesia* is God, who holds court in heaven. But God in the *Comedy* is Love. The sacrifice he makes to redeem man, he makes out of *cortesia* and *amore*: 'con l'atto sol del suo etterno amore' (*Pr.* 7.33) and 'che Dio solo per sua cortesia/dimesso avesse' (*Pr.* 7.91–2). It would seem that in God, *cortesia* and *amore* are one. Like everything else Dante values in his past, he does not reject the limited love and courtliness of the early poetry; he subsumes it within the higher love and courtesy of God" ("Cortes'Amor," 695).
67 *I Fioretti di San Francesco*, ed. Giovanni Getto (Milan: A. Martello, 1946), 119. Ugolino Bonforte of Sanarno was first proposed by Luigi Tassi as the author of the *Fioretti*. See *Disquisizione istorica intorno all'autore dei Fioretti di S. Francesco* (Fabriano: Tipografia Gentile, 1883), 7.
68 For the intersection of avarice with courtly love in the texts of "Doglia mi reca" and *Convivio* 3.15, see Barolini, *Dante and the Origins of Italian Literary Culture* (New York: Fordham University Press, 2006), 58–9.
69 See, for example, Aldo Vallone's *La "cortesia" dai provenzali a Dante* (Palermo: Palumbo, 1950).
70 The contexts for this term in *Purgatorio* and *Paradiso* are analysed in chapter 4.
71 For the influence of Cicero upon Boccaccio, see Michaela Paasche Grudin and Robert Grudin, *Boccaccio's* Decameron *and the Ciceronian Renaissance* (New York: Palgrave Macmillan, 2012), and Attilio Hortis, *M.T. Cicerone nelle opere del Petrarca e del Boccaccio: Ricerche intorno alla storia della erudizione classica nel medio evo* (Trieste: Herrmanstorer, 1878).
72 Vittore Branca, *Giovanni Boccaccio: Profilo biografico* (Florence: G.C. Sansoni, 1977), 7–8, 27.
73 Branca, *Giovanni Boccaccio*, 23.
74 Branca, *Giovanni Boccaccio*, 25, locates these moments in the following texts by Boccaccio: *Amorosa visione*, 49; *Filocolo* 1.1.14; *Fiammetta* 2.6.21; *Comedia delle ninfe fiorentine*, 35.31; *Epistola* XIII.
75 Robert's avarice is also noted by Villani in his *Nuova cronica*, 11.138. Branca calls this avarice a *"leitmotiv della pubblicistica politica fiorentina di quel periodo"* (*Giovanni Boccaccio*, 65).
76 Branca, *Giovanni Boccaccio*, 34–8.

77 Branca, *Giovanni Boccaccio,* 74–5.
78 Branca, *Giovanni Boccaccio,* 23.
79 Unless otherwise indicated, all translations of Boccaccio's *Trattatello in laude di Dante* are taken from Vincenzo Zin Bollettino's *The Life of Dante* (Trattatello in laude di Dante) (New York: Garland, 1990).
80 See, among others, Justin Steinberg, *Accounting for Dante: Urban Readers and Writers in Late Medieval Italy* (Notre Dame: University of Notre Dame Press, 2007); George Dameron, *Florence and Its Church in the Age of Dante* (Philadelphia: University of Pennsylvania Press, 2005); Teodolinda Barolini, "Dante and Francesca da Rimini: Realpolitik, Romance and Gender," *Speculum* 75 (2000): 1–28; John A. Scott, *Dante's Political Purgatory* (Philadelphia: University of Pennsylvania Press, 1996); George Holmes, *Florence, Rome and the Origins of the Renaissance* (Oxford: Clarendon, 1986); Joan M. Ferrante, *The Political Vision of the* Divine Comedy (Princeton: Princeton University Press, 1984); Charles Till Davis, *Dante's Italy, and Other Essays* (Philadelphia: University of Pennsylvania Press, 1984); Jeffrey Schnapp, *The Transfiguration of History at the Center of Dante's* Paradise (Princeton: Princeton University Press, 1982); Jeremy Catto, "Florence, Tuscany, and the World of Dante," in *The World of Dante*, ed. Cecil Grayson (Oxford: Clarendon, 1980); Giuseppe Mazzotta, *Dante, Poet of the Desert: History and Allegory in the* Divine Comedy (Princeton: Princeton University Press, 1979); Susan Noakes, "Dino Compagni and the Vow in San Giovanni: *Inferno* XIX, 16–21," *Dante Studies* 86 (1968): 41–63; A.P. d'Entrèves, *Dante as a Political Thinker* (Oxford: Clarendon, 1952).
81 Most notably, see Vittore Branca, *Boccaccio medievale* (Florence: Sansoni, 1998); Joan M. Ferrante, "Politics, Finance and Feminism in *Decameron*, II, 7," *Studi sul Boccaccio* (1993) 21: 151–74; Aldo S. Bernardo, "The Plague as Key to Meaning in Boccaccio's *Decameron*," in *The Black Death: The Impact of the Fourteenth-Century Plague*, ed. Daniel Williman (Binghamton: Center for Medieval & Early Renaissance Studies, 1982), 39–64; Brian Richardson, "The 'Ghibelline' Narrator in the *Decameron*," *Italian Studies* (1978) 33: 20–8.
82 See Vittorio Russo, *Con le Muse in Parnaso: Tre studi sul Boccaccio* (Naples: Bibliopolis, 1983), and Francesco Bruni, *Boccaccio: L'invenzione della letteratura mezzana* (Bologna: Il Mulino, 1990).
83 Russo, *Con le Muse,* 109–66.
84 Bruni, *Boccaccio,* 297. In a later essay, Bruni reiterates this conclusion while surveying Boccaccio's interpretation of the conflicts between the Black and White Guelphs: "Nei criteri che presiedono all'invenzione del Decameron (e delle opere precedenti), Boccaccio si tiene lontano, come dai massimi problemi della religione e della teologia (cruciali invece per

capire i fondamenti della *Commedia*), così dalle questioni della politica" ("La proiezione dell'attualità politica sul passato: Note su cronisti, narratori, commentatori della *Commedia* nel XIV secolo," *Modern Philology* 101.2 [November 2003]: 207).

85 Franco Fido, "Dante personaggio mancato del *Decameron*," in *Le metamorfosi del centauro* (Rome: Bulzoni, 1977), 77–90.

86 Giorgio Padoan, *L'ultima opera di Giovanni Boccaccio: Le Esposizioni sopra il Dante* (Padua: CEDAM, 1959), chaps. 1, 3.

87 See Michael Papio's introduction to his translation of the *Esposizioni* in *Boccaccio's Expositions on Dante's Comedy* (Toronto: University of Toronto Press, 2009), 3–37.

88 Carlo Delcorno, "Note sui dantismi nell'*Elegia di Madonna Fiammetta*," *Studi sul Boccaccio* 11 (1979): 251–94; *Diana's Hunt/Caccia di Diana*, trans. and ed. Anthony K. Cassell and Victoria Kirkham (Philadelphia: University of Pennsylvania Press, 1991), 12–13; Robert Hollander, *Boccaccio's Last Fiction: Il "Corbaccio"* (Philadelphia: University of Pennsylvania Press, 1998), appendix 1: "Texts in the *Corbaccio* Reflecting Passages in Dante," 59–71. Important earlier contributions to studies of Boccaccio *dantista* include those by Francesco Maggini, "Il Boccaccio dantista," *Miscellanea storica della Valdelsa* 29 (1921): 116–22; Giuseppe Billanovich, "La leggenda dantesca del Boccaccio," *Studi danteschi* 28 (1949): 45–144; and Branca, *Boccaccio medievale*. See also Vittore Branca and Ennio Sandal, *Dante e Boccaccio: Lectura Dantis Scaligera, 2004–2005, in Memoria di Vittore Branca* (Rome/Padua: Antenore, 2006).

89 Attilio Bettinzoli, "Per una definizione delle presenze dantesche nel 'Decameron,'" *Studi sul Boccaccio* 13 (1981–82): 267–326 and *Studi sul Boccaccio* 14 (1983–84): 209–40; Robert Hollander, "Boccaccio's Dante: Imitative Distance," *Studi sul Boccaccio* 13 (1981–82): 169–98; Victoria Kirkham, "Painters at Play on the Judgment Day (*Decameron* VIII 9)," *Studi sul Boccaccio* 14 (1983–84): 256–77.

90 Robert Hollander, *Boccaccio's Dante and the Shaping Force of Satire* (Ann Arbor: University of Michigan Press, 1997).

91 Jason M. Houston, *Building a Monument to Dante: Boccaccio as* Dantista (Toronto: University of Toronto Press, 2010).

92 De Robertis contrasts this definition of *cortesia* with the one offered in the *De vulgari eloquentia* (1.18.4) where the notion of the court ("curialitas") does not seem to be completely harmonious with the notion of *cortesia*. Concerning the passage from the *Convivio*, on the other hand, De Robertis writes, "Si deve, piuttoso, notare che, in questo passo, Dante espone tutti i temi che confluiscono nella sua concezione della cortesia, si tratti della

formazione storica di questa idea, della nostalgia per un'età di più alta rettitudine o della condanna per la decadenza dei costumi 'curiali.'" See De Robertis's note in Dante, *Convivio*, 2 vols., ed. Cesare Vasoli and Domenico De Robertis (Milan: Ricciardi, 1995), 196.

93 See Marvin B. Becker, "A Study in Political Failure: The Florentine Magnates 1280–1343," *Mediaeval Studies* 27 (1965): 249. Carol Lansing debates this idea, citing a discrepancy with the political realities of patronage and political offices in Florence during the fourteenth and fifteenth centuries; see Lansing, *The Florentine Magnates: Lineage and Faction in a Medieval Commune* (Princeton: Princeton University Press, 1991), 237.

94 Najemy discusses how Dante's voice itself vacillates between support and criticism of the *popolo*; see his chapter "Dante and Florence" in *The Cambridge Companion to Dante*, ed. Rachel Jacoff (Cambridge: Cambridge University Press, 1993), 91–4.

95 Najemy, *A History of Florence,* 25. Najemy writes that the fighting amongst the elite aimed to "neutralize the *popolo* by recruiting them into their factions" (27).

96 Dameron, "Revisiting the Italian Magnates," *Viator* 23 (1992): 282; Lansing, *Florentine Magnates*, 184–91.

97 I will discuss *Dec.* 5.8 and the Dantean pedigree of the Traversari family in chapter 4.

98 Klapisch-Zuber notes that while the magnates were disempowered by the Ordinances of Justice, they were not entirely disenfranchised from political life: "The Commune sent those reputed to be sufficiently loyal to command important strategic posts of the *contado* or to administer justice in its name in the localities of its territory. It counted as well upon their imposing bearing when sending them abroad on diplomatic missions or assigning them to prestigious appointments in foreign cities. The magnates are, therefore, belittled as citizens, but they were not entirely excluded from political life." See Christiane Klapisch-Zuber, "Nobles or Pariahs? The Exclusion of Florentine Magnates from the Thirteenth to the Fifteenth Centuries," in *Comparative Studies in Society and History* 39.2 (April 1997): 218.

Chapter One

1 Scaglione writes, "the courts acted as centers of social education by developing a continuous ethos of curial/courtly values" (*Knights at Court*, 47). For a discussion of the difference between systems of education in Tuscany and elsewhere in Europe, see Robert Black, *Education and Society in Florentine Tuscany* (Leiden: Brill, 2007), esp. pp. 175–85.

2 See Najemy, "Dante and Florence," for an analysis of these moments. See also Ferrante, *Political Vision*, esp. chap. 3.
3 Dameron, "Revisiting the Italian Magnates," 174. As Dameron notes, not all nobles were magnates, but all magnates were considered nobility. See also G. Masi, "La struttura sociale delle fazioni politiche fiorentine ai tempi di Dante," *Giornale dantesco* 31 (1930): 3–28.
4 David Wallace, *Boccaccio:* Decameron (Cambridge: Cambridge University Press, 1991), 11. He also writes that "the *Decameron* occupies, or shares, a crucial transitional moment in this historiographical tradition, this sequence of attempts to explain the meaning of history in Italian prose for an audience of Florentines" (11). I would argue that the *Esposizioni* occupy this role as well.
5 Witt, "Early Communal Historians," 103.
6 Witt, "Early Communal Historians," 106.
7 Witt, "Early Communal Historians," 106. Also see P.J. Jones, *The Italian City-State: From Commune to Signoria* (Oxford: Oxford University Press, 1997), 499–506.
8 Witt, "Early Communal Historians," 106–7.
9 As Witt writes, "While skill at arms was an attribute of lay courtliness, it was not a defining one. From the twelfth century, however, the emphasis in courtliness appears to shift toward the military character of the noble. Enshrined in the new courtly literature was the aesthetic and moral model of the knight, dedicated to loyal service whether to his lady, his God, his king, or all three." See Witt, *In the Footsteps of the Ancients: The Origins of Humanism from Lovato to Bruni* (Leiden: Brill, 2000), 46n30.
10 Najemy, *A History of Florence*, 12, 28. See also Lansing, *Florentine Magnates*, 154–61.
11 Lansing, *Florentine Magnates*, 155.
12 Witt, *In the Footsteps of the Ancients*, 55.
13 Najemy, *A History of Florence*, 13.
14 Najemy, *A History of Florence*, 13–16.
15 *Cronica fiorentina*, in *Testi fiorentini del Dugento e dei primi del Trecento*, ed. Alfredo Schiaffini (Florence: Sansoni, 1954), 118 (see 117–19 for the account of the event). The translation is mine.
16 Lansing writes, "The episode most obviously shows the volatility of the nobles, and how rapidly the chronicler believed a small insult could blow up into a major feud and ultimately into civil war" (*Florentine Magnates*, 167).
17 Witt, *In the Footsteps of the Ancients*, 60–2. Also see James Powell's *Albertanus da Brescia: The Pursuit of Happiness in the Early Thirteenth Century* (Philadelphia: University of Pennsylvania Press, 1992), especially chap. 4.

18 Witt, *In the Footsteps of the Ancients*, 64–5. He writes, "The urban ethical model, whether in republican or monarchical dress, struggled against the chivalric one for domination of Italian society throughout the Renaissance. The humanists never mentioned their rival's name: adherence to ancient models of diction meant it was literally impossible to discuss *cortesia* in their Latin. Nonetheless, the hold of the courtly ideal on the conscience of Italians and other Latin Christians remained strong down through the centuries. One might say that the battle ended only with the victory of the humanists' model in the aftermath of the French Revolution." See Scaglione, *Knights at Court*, chap. 11, for a survey of courtesy in France, England, and Germany after 1600.
19 Najemy, *A History of Florence*, 12.
20 Najemy, *A History of Florence*, 11–12. Charles Davis raises the question of whether or not Dante's recourse to Cacciaguida's memory betrayed his own class-based anxiety over the legitimacy of nobility. He writes, "Perhaps also the devotion with which he clings to the memory of his ancestor Cacciaguida, a crusader knighted by the Emperor, shows the insecurity of the minor aristocrat." See Davis, *Dante's Italy, and Other Essays* (Philadelphia: University of Pennsylvania Press, 1984), 64.
21 Davis, *Dante's Italy*, 64.
22 Pier Massimo Forni, *Adventures in Speech: Rhetoric and Narration in Boccaccio's* Decameron (Philadelphia: University of Pennsylvania Press, 1996), 3. See also his treatment of *Decameron* 6.9, pp. 76–9.
23 See Maurizio Vitale and Vittore Branca, *Il capolavoro di Boccaccio e due diverse redazioni* (Venice: Istituto Veneto di Scienze, Lettere ed Arti, 2002) for a comparison of the variants and a linguistic analysis of the two authorial redactions, Hamilton 90 and Ms. Ital. 482.
24 Text from the *Commedia* is set in italics, as can be found in this edition of the *Esposizioni*.
25 Dante is the historian of record for Guiglielmo Borsiere, as no other biographical information for this figure exists. What little we can deduce from Dante's text leads us to date Borsiere's birth before 1300, a date implied in Rusticucci's statement that Borsiere visited them recently, or in other words, shortly before the pilgrim's visit ("il quale si duole/con noi per poco," *Inf.* 16.70–1). As Vincenzo Presta confirms in his entry on Borsiere in the *Enciclopedia dantesca*, by dating Borsiere's death prior to 1300 we are led to the assumption that he was quite old when he died, since his companions from the realm of the living, Rusticucci, Aldobrandi, and Guerra, all died before 1272. See *Enciclopedia dantesca*, ed. Umberto Bosco (Rome: Istituto dell'Enciclopedia Dantesca, 1970), 1:78.

26 Guido da Pisa claims that Borsiere was a jester, not a courtier, and committed the same sin, sodomy, as his companions Rusticucci and Aldobrandi. Therefore, Guido interprets "per poco" as meaning that Borsiere stayed with them "for a little while," instead of "da poco" (that he visited them recently). According to him, then, Rusticucci was speaking ironically when he said that Borsiere spent only a small amount of time with the sodomites: "Iste Guillielmus fuit quidam florentinus optimus ioculator sive hystrio, qui multum fuit isto vitio maculatus. Ideo Iacobus Rusticuccii, loquens de eo, yronice dicit autori: 'lo qual si duol con noi per poco,' idest pro multo." See Guido da Pisa's *Expositiones et glose super 'Comediam' Dantis; or, Commentary on Dante's* Inferno, ed. Vincenzo Cioffari (Albany, NY: SUNY Press, 1974), 300.
27 Victoria Kirkham, "A Pedigree for Courtesy: 'Purser' Cured a Miser (*Decameron* 1.8)," *Studi sul Boccaccio* 25 (1997): 213–38, and especially pp. 216–17.
28 "Cortese" also appears in the *Commedia* (as "kind" or "courteous"), not coincidentally, towards the beginning of *Inferno* 16, when Vergil instructs the pilgrim to be "cortese" with Aldobrandi, Rusticucci, and Guerra ("a costor si vuole esser cortese" 15).
29 Steven Epstein, *Genoa and the Genoese, 958–1528* (Chapel Hill: University of North Carolina Press, 1996), 214–15.
30 Kirkham, "A Pedigree," 215–16. According to Vittore Branca, the Grimaldi, "furono fra le più antiche e potenti famiglie patrizie genovesi, e fino alla metà del Trecento mirarono alla supremazia nella Repubblica. Furono in rapporto coi fiorentini in varie azioni contro i pisani." See Branca's note in Boccaccio, *Decameron*, 109n4.
31 Branca, *Giovanni Boccaccio*, 148–50.
32 Branca, *Giovanni Boccaccio*, 146.
33 Kirkham notes that the provenance of Ermino Avarizia is also abstracted with the attribution of his new "soprannome." See "A Pedigree," 213–38.
34 Mario Baratto, *Realtà e stile nel* Decameron (Vicenza: Ponza, 1970), 23–4. Baratto argues for two chronological sources of inspiration for the *Decameron*: "la memoria di un mondo, soprattutto cavalleresco, che appare al tramonto; dall'altra l'osservazione di una realtà contemporanea, che è soprattutto cittadina" (23). Baratto compares the *Decameron*'s sense of a "presente" that responds to a "passato" with the lack of such a distinction in the *Novellino*. However, the *Decameron*'s past, Baratto elegantly states, does not involve a "passato remoto," just a "passato prossimo": "Le stesse novelle cavalleresche, avventurose e cortesi, del *Decameron* si raccolgono in un periodo di tempo più vicino allo scrittore: il passato remoto tende

a diventare, nel *Decameron*, passato prossimo, dal Duecento agli inizi del Trecento" (24).

35 The most pertinent example of such a *novella*, one that returns to the discourse of avarice and civility and once again demonstrates the relationship of this opposition to Boccaccio's familiarity with Dante, immediately precedes 1.8: the curing of Can Grande's momentary affliction of avarice by way of a story told by Bergamino (treated in chap. 3).

36 This assessment resonates with the importance of "circumstance and specificity" that Teodolinda Barolini has noted in Boccaccio's biography of Francesca da Rimini. See her "Dante and Francesca da Rimini: Realpolitik, Romance and Gender," *Speculum* 75 (2000): 1–28, especially pp. 12–13.

37 Baratto, *Realtà e stile nel* Decameron, 23–4.

38 See Hayden White, *The Content of the Form: Narrative Discourse and Historical Representation* (Baltimore: Johns Hopkins University Press, 1987), 93.

39 The following is a selection from the extensive bibliography for 6.9. See E.G. Parodi, "La miscredenza di Guido Cavalcanti e una fonte del Boccaccio," *Bulletino della società dantesca* 22 (1915): 37–47; Robert Durling, "Boccaccio on Interpretation: Guido's Escape (*Decameron* VI.9)," in *Dante, Petrarch, Boccaccio: Studies in the Italian Trecento in Honor of Charles S. Singleton*, ed. Aldo S. Bernardo and Anthony L. Pellegrini (Binghamton, NY: Medieval and Renaissance Texts and Studies, 1983); Paul Watson, "On Seeing Guido Cavalcanti and the Houses of the Dead," *Studi sul Boccaccio* 18 (1989): 301–18; Italo Calvino's chapter "Leggerezza" in *Lezioni americane: Sei proposte per il prossimo millennio* (Milan: Garzanti, 1988); Guiglielmo Gorni, "Invenzione e scrittura nel Boccaccio: Il caso di Guido Cavalcanti," *Letteratura italiana antica* 3 (2002): 359–74; Giuseppe Velli, "Seneca nel *Decameron*," *Giornale storico della letteratura italiana* 168 (1991): 321–34; Zygmunt Baranski, "'Alquanto tenea della oppinione degli Epicuri': The *auctoritas* of Boccaccio's Cavalcanti (and Dante)," in *Mittelalterliche Novellistik im europäischen Kontext: Kulturwissenschaftliche Perspektive*, ed. Mark Chinca (Berlin: Schmidt, 2006), 280–325; Forni, *Adventures in Speech*, 76–9.

40 Teodolinda Barolini, "Sociology of the *Brigata*: Gendered Groups in Dante, Forese, Folgore, Boccaccio – From 'Guido, i'vorrei' to Griselda," *Italian Studies* 67 (2012): 7–9. Barolini's essay highlights the exceptional nature of the frame *brigata* of the *Decameron* in terms of the non-normative mixture of both men and women. Michelangelo Picone addresses the subtext of *Inferno* 10 to this *novella*, reading the encounter between the money-seeking Brunelleschi and a self-absorbed Cavalcanti as competing visions of Epicureanism. See Picone, "La brigata di Folgore fra Dante e Boccaccio,"

in *Il Giuoco della vita bella: Folgore da San Gimignano: Studi e testi* (San Gimignano: Città di San Gimignano, 1988), 35–7.
41 Lansing, *Florentine Magnates*, 188.
42 Franco Cardini, *L'acciar de' cavalieri: Studi sulla cavalleria nel mondo toscano e italico (sec. XII–XV)* (Florence: Le lettere, 1997), 94–5.
43 Cardini also attends to this historical context. See *L'acciar de' cavalieri*, 95.
44 See Franco Cardini's entry on Brunelleschi in the *Dizionario biografico degli italiani*, vol. 14 (Rome: Istituto della Enciclopedia Italiana, 1987).
45 "[N]ella missione a Poggibonsi, in teoria come paciere, in pratica per intimidire quella terra che troppo spesso dava prova di voler tener testa a Firenze" (Cardini, "Brunelleschi," in *Dizionario biografico*, 532).
46 Cardini, "Brunelleschi," in *Dizionario biografico*, 534.
47 See Nicola Ottokar, *Il Comune di Firenze alla fine del Dugento* (Turin: Einaudi, 1962), 100n3, and Cardini, "Brunelleschi," in *Dizionario biografico*, 532–4. Ottokar writes, "Sui risultati di questa ambasciata messer Corso Donati fece una relazione il 18 aprile 1292 in un 'consilium Capitudinum 12 maiorum Artium et aliorum sapientium popularium civitatis Florentie.'" The *Consulte* date this embassy between 1290 and 1291, and the text reads: "exposita ambaxiata et relata per d. Cursum de Donatis, quam ipse et dominus Brunectus de Brunelleschis, ambaxiatores Comunis Florentie transmissi ad civitatem Ianue, occasione discordie orte inter quosdam Florentinos et quosdam Ianuenses in civitate Nemausii, fecerunt, ac etiam responsione facta" (*Le Consulte della repubblica fiorentina dell'anno MCCLXXX al MCCXCVIII*, ed. A. Gherardi [Florence: Sansoni, 1896–1898], vol. 2, 122).
48 Genoa and Florence, Najemy writes, began to mint gold florins (also known as the *genovino* in Genoa) almost simultaneously in 1252 (*A History of Florence*, 70). See also Richard Goldthwaite, *The Economy of Renaissance Florence* (Baltimore: Johns Hopkins University Press, 2009), 48–57.
49 See Martin G. Eisner, *Boccaccio and the Invention of Italian Literature: Dante, Petrarch, Cavalcanti, and the Authority of the Vernacular* (Cambridge: Cambridge University Press, 2013), chap. 4; Houston, *Building a Monument*, 21; Jonathan Usher, "Boccaccio, Cavalcanti's Canzone 'Donna me prega' and Dino's Glosses," *Heliotropia* 2.1 (2004); and Maria Luisa Ardizzone, *Guido Cavalcanti: The Other Middle Ages* (Toronto: University of Toronto Press, 2002), 66–7.
50 "Se mia laude scusasse te sovente/Dove se' negligente,/Amico, assai ti lodo, un poco vagli;/Come sei saggio, dico, intra la gente,/Visto, pro' e valente,/E come sai di varchi e di schermagli;/E come assai scrittura sai a mente/Sofisticosamente,/E come corri e salti e ti travagli./Ciò, ch'io dico,

ver te non provo niente/Appo ben conoscente,/Che non beltade ed arti insieme agguagli./E grande nobilità non t'ha mestiere,/Né gran masnada avere,/Che cortesia mantien leggera corte./Se' uomo di gran corte:/Ahi com' saresti stato uom mercantiere!/Se Dio recasse ogni uomo in dritta sorte,/Drizzando ciò che tort'è,/Daria cortesia cui è mestiere;/E te faria ovriere,/Pur guadagnando e ridonando forte." In *Poesie italiane inedite di Dugento autori dall'origine della lingua infino al secolo decimosettimo*, ed. Francesco Trucchi (Prato: Guasti, 1846), 262–5 (discussed by Najemy, *A History of Florence*, 30–1).

51 See Parodi, "La miscredenza di Guido Cavalcanti," for the origin of this *pronta risposta* in Psalm 48:12, "sepulchra eorum domus illorum in eternum," which, as he notes, was also interpreted by Salimbene de Adam, the possible source for *Dec.* 6.9. See also Olson, "'Concivus meus': Petrarch's *Rerum memorandarum libri* 2.60, Boccaccio's *Decameron* 6.9, and the Specter of Dino del Garbo," *Annali d'italianistica* 22 (2004): 375–80, for a reading of *Dec.* 6.9 in light of its Petrarchan analogue, the story of "Dinus florentinus" (Dino del Garbo?) from the *Rerum memorandarum libri* (2.60).

52 See Cardini, "Brunelleschi," *Dizionario biografico*, 533–4.

53 See Durling, "Boccaccio on Interpretation," 276–7.

54 Boccaccio refers to his gloss in *Esposizioni* 6 of Ciacco's prophecy in *Inferno* 6.65 ("la parte selvaggia"): "E la parte selvaggia, cioè la Bianca, la quale chiama 'selvaggia,' per ciò che messer Vieri de' Cerchi, il quale era, come detto è, capo della parte Bianca, e' suoi consorti erano tutti ricchi e agiati uomini, e per questo erano non solamente superbi e altieri, ma egli erano salvatichetti intorno a' costumi cittadineschi, per ciò che non erano acostanti all'usanze degli uomini, né gli careggiavano, come per avventura faceva la parte avversa, la quale era più povera" (6.34).

55 Padoan defines "salvatichetti" as "un po' ritrosi." See *Esposizioni*, 877n42.

56 Compagni, *Cronica*, 1.6.

57 Compagni, *Cronica*, 1.22.

58 Compagni, *Cronica*, 1.20.

59 Najemy, *A History of Florence*, 17.

60 Najemy, *A History of Florence*, 25–6.

61 Lansing, *Florentine Magnates*, 145–8; Najemy, *A History of Florence*, 82–6; Gaetano Salvemini, *Magnati e popolani in Firenze dal 1280 al 1295* (Milan: Feltrinelli, 1966), 384–423.

62 Lansing, *Florentine Magnates*, 147. Salvemini is responsible for the reconstruction of this definition from 1286; see Salvemini, *Magnati e popolani*, 118.

63 Lansing, *Florentine Magnates*, 163.

64 Najemy, *A History of Florence*, 147.
65 Gene A. Brucker, *Florentine Politics and Society, 1343–1378* (Princeton: Princeton University Press, 1962), 62.
66 Cardini writes: "Pare che in effetti i costumi cavallereschi abbiano attraversato una fase di declino dopo la cacciata del duca d'Atene, e giostre e tornei abbiano visto allora diminuire la loro importanza. Può darsi che il lungo periodo d'austerità fra quella data e la fine dell'ottavo decennio del secolo sia stato determinate da una serie di concause, che vanno dall'ascesa politica della "gente nova" portatrice d'una sensibilità e d'un costume meno inclino alla cortesia fino alla serie di rovesci economici e sociali in genere (basti pensare alle carestie e alle epidemie), che certo non creavano in città un'atmosfera propizia a fantasie equestri" (*L'acciar dei cavalieri*, 88).

Chapter Two

1 The sale of the castle of Montemurlo to Florence, which had belonged to the counts Guidi from the eleventh century, led to the urbanization of the Guidi (Bosco and Reggio, *La Divina Commedia*, 266n64).
2 As Branca writes, the earlier generations of the Boccaccio family abandoned their primarily agricultural trade to embark upon mercantile professions, becoming leading economic powers between Paris and Florence, but then met their downfall at the middle of the century (Branca, *Giovanni Boccaccio*, 5).
3 Boccaccio names Villani's *Nuova cronica* as a source for the history of the Florentine civil crisis in *Esposizioni* 6.41 (litterale): "Nondimeno chi questa istoria vuole pienamente sapere legga la *Cronica* di Giovanni Villani, per ciò che in essa distesamente si pone." For a comparison of sample passages from the *Esposizioni* and Villani's *Nuova cronica*, see Bruni, "La proiezione dell'attualità politica," 222–6.
4 It should be noted that this view of violence as developing along family lines is contested by some historians, including Carol Lansing. She argues that patrilineal culture created conflict and competition, which could exist within as well as between families, since she sees them as developing as neighbourhood rivalries (as in the case of the Cerchi and the Donati). See Lansing, *Florentine Magnates*, 164–91. Jacques Heers, by contrast, sees factionalism as originating between lineages; see *Parties and Political Life in the Medieval West* (Amsterdam: North-Holland, 1977).
5 For treatments of Villani and historiography, see Alberto del Monte, "La storiografia fiorentina dei secoli xii e xiii," *Bulletino dell'Istituto storico*

italiano per il Medio Evo 62 (1950): 175–282; Giuseppe Porta, "Giovanni Villani storico e scrittore," in *I racconti di Clio: Tecniche narrative della storiografia* (Pisa: Nistri-Lischi, 1989), 147–56; and Porta, "La costruzione della storia in Giovanni Villani," in *Il senso della storia nella cultura medievale italiana (1100–1350)* (Pistoia: Centro italiano di studi di storia e d'arte, 1995), 125–38.

6 Villani, *Nuova cronica*, 9.2.
7 Villani, *Nuova cronica*, 9.100.
8 Villani, *Nuova cronica*, 9.88. For a discussion of the decline of the Bardi and Peruzzi banking houses, see Armando Sapori, *La crisi delle compagnie mercantile dei Bardi e dei Peruzzi* (Florence: Olschki, 1926), 105–7.
9 Branca, *Giovanni Boccaccio*, 17–19; 66–7.
10 Branca, *Giovanni Boccaccio*, 14.
11 Branca, *Giovanni Boccaccio*, 15–19.
12 Branca, *Giovanni Boccaccio*, 4.
13 Branca, *Giovanni Boccaccio*, 4–5.
14 Branca, *Giovanni Boccaccio*, 5.
15 Jason Houston analyses how Boccaccio "brings Dante back from the afterworld to condemn the malfeasance of the magnates who installed Walter and the disastrous factionalism that permitted his short tyranny," thereby figuring Dante as the "poet of rectitude," a designation that originates in the *De vulgari eloquentia* (*Building a Monument*, 70). See also Becker, "Gualtieri di Brienne e l'uso delle dispense giudiziarie," *Archivo storico italiano* 113 (1955): 245–51, and Cardini, *Le cento novelle contro la morte: Giovanni Boccaccio e la rifondazione cavalleresca del mondo* (Rome: Salerno Editrice, 2007), 70.
16 Brucker, *Florentine Politics and Society*, 6.
17 King Robert, criticized by Boccaccio and others for his perceived avarice in failing to support the Florentine companies, would be portrayed as a King Midas in the *Comedia delle ninfe fiorentine* (35.32) and in the *Amorosa visione* (14.26). See Branca, *Giovanni Boccaccio*, 65–6.
18 Brucker, *Florentine Politics and Society*, 7; Sapori, *La crisi*, 141–5.
19 Najemy, *A History of Florence*, 135–8.
20 Villani, *Nuova cronica*, 12.12.
21 See Houston, *Building a Monument*, 69–73; Warren Ginsberg, *Chaucer's Italian Tradition* (Ann Arbor: University of Michigan Press, 2002), 208–25.
22 Najemy, *A History of Florence*, 145.
23 Brucker, *Florentine Politics and Society*, 21.
24 Brucker, *Florentine Politics and Society*, 23n93.
25 Brucker, *Florentine Politics and Society*, 25; Davidsohn, *Storia di Firenze*, 4.2.

26 Brucker, *Florentine Politics and Society*, 50.
27 Brucker, *Florentine Politics and Society*, 51–3.
28 Najemy, *A History of Florence*, 6.
29 Brucker, *Florentine Politics and Society*, 35. See also Marchionne di Coppo Stefani, *Cronica fiorentina di Marchionne di Coppo Stefani*, ed. Niccolò Rodolico (Città di Castello: S. Lapi, 1903), 592.
30 Brucker, *Florentine Politics and Society*, 113.
31 Philip Jones, "Florentine Families and Florentine Diaries in the Fourteenth Century," *Papers of the British School at Rome* 24 (1954): 184.
32 Najemy, *A History of Florence*, 138.
33 Najemy, *A History of Florence*, 12–13, 138.
34 Branca, *Giovanni Boccaccio*, 73–4.
35 Francesco Corazzini, *Le lettere edite e inedite di Giovanni Boccaccio* (Florence: Sansoni, 1877), 73–4.
36 Najemy, "Dante and Florence," 91–3.
37 The only article exclusively dedicated to *Decameron* 9.8 is Rosario Ferreri's "Ciacco, Biondello e Martellino," in *Studi sul Boccaccio* 24 (1996): 231–49. Ferreri's comparison of this *novella* with *Inferno* 21 and 22 is provocative. Franco Fido is interested in how Boccaccio creates "il nesso tematico: gola + classe politica + violenza" in this *novella* ("Dante personaggio," 85). See also Bruni (*Boccaccio*, 295–8), who asserts, "Non è solo questione del ritorno su questo mondo di personaggi dell'aldilà: nel *sollazzo* cui s'ispira il novellare sono assenti anche la politica, e con essa la grande storia, e non solo la filosofia e la teologia; o al massimo politica e cronaca forniscono uno sfondo piuttosto generico, ancorano il racconto a un insieme di determinazioni ... ma non costituiscono il centro di gravità della narrazione" (297).
38 Branca notes the similarity between this phrase and Dante's words concerning Filippo in *Inferno* 8: "In sé medesmo si volvea co' denti" (*Inferno* 8.63); see Branca's note in Boccaccio, *Decameron*, 1089n5.
39 Simone Marchesi addresses the meaning of Ciacco's name vis-à-vis Isidore's *Etymologiae* and Epicureanism in his essay "'Epicuri de grege porcus': Ciacco, Epicurus and Isidore of Seville," *Dante Studies, with the Annual Report of the Dante Society* 117 (1999): 117–31.
40 See *Guida da Pisa's Expositiones et Glose super Comediam Dantis or Commentary on Dante's Inferno*, ed. Vincenzo Cioffari (Albany: State University of New York Press, 1974), 128–30; and *L'ultima forma dell'Ottimo commento: Chiose sopra la Comedia di Dante Alleghieri fiorentino tracte da diversi ghiosatori: Inferno*, ed. Claudia Di Fonzo (Ravenna: Longo Editore, 2008), 97.

41 Branca notes this similarity "così il B. ampliando il primo periodo di questa novella, ma ripetendone alla lettera alcune espressioni" (Boccaccio, *Decameron*, 1084–5n4).
42 The almost verbatim parallels of these two passages are striking. It inspires the vision of Boccaccio, with his manuscript of the *Decameron* (composed around 1350) on his desk, composing the lectures of the *Esposizioni* (from 1373 to 1374, more than twenty years later). See Vittore Branca and Maurizio Vitale, *Il capolavoro del Boccaccio e due diverse redazioni*, for a comparison of the two manuscripts of the *Decameron*. From what I could deduce from their lists of variants, there were no substantial changes made to any of the *novelle* treated in these chapters.
43 Modern historians consider the split of the Guelph party into the Whites and the Blacks mystifying, since, as John Najemy writes, there were families with the same social and economic characteristics on both sides (see Najemy, "Dante and Florence," 81. See also Susan Noakes, "Virility, Nobility, and Banking: The Crossing of Discourses in the Tenzione with Forese," in *Dante for the New Millennium*, ed. Teodolinda Barolini and H. Wayne Storey (New York: Fordham University Press, 2003), 241–58. As Noakes states, "The changes in the structure of Florentine society at this time cannot be adequately described with merely two stark labels: 'Black' and 'White' ... These now-familiar labels simplify a historical, legal, and anthropological process of great complexity, still not entirely understood" (247–8). For a study of this period of political tension in terms of rivalry between magnates, see Lansing, *Florentine Magnates*, and also Salvemini, *Magnati e popolani*.
44 For a survey of the critical literature regarding the influence of the *fabliaux* on the *Decameron*, see Luciano Rossi, "In luogo di sollazzo: I *fabliaux* del Decameron," in *Leggiadre donne: Novella e racconto breve in Italia*, ed. Francesco Bruni (Venice: Marsilio, 2000). Timothy Kircher contrasts mendicant *exempla* with the First Day of the *Decameron* in "The Modality of Moral Communication in the *Decameron*'s First Day, in Contrast to the Mirror of the *Exemplum*," *Renaissance Quarterly*, 54.4 (Winter 2001): 1035–73.
45 Teodolinda Barolini, in "Dante and Francesca da Rimini," 1–28, observes how Boccaccio's penchant for detail in storytelling results in Francesca's exculpation in *Esposizioni* 5.
46 For a discussion of Corso Donati's prominent role in the resurgence of the elite class against the *popolo*, see Najemy, *A History of Florence*, 88–95. Najemy interprets Corso Donati's death as the end of an era of factionalism within the elite class. After Corso's death, Najemy writes, "Nor, for the next century, would any Florentine dominate the political stage as

thoroughly as did Corso Donati: not until Cosimo de' Medici did so with very different means in a transformed political world" (95).
47 For a comparison of the *novi homines* with the *gente nuova* of Dante's times, see Isidoro Del Lungo's *La gente nuova in Firenze ai tempi di Dante* (Florence: Uffizio della Rassegna Nazionale, 1882), 4–9.
48 See Patricia J. Osmond, "Catiline in Florence and Fiesole: The Medieval and Renaissance After-life of a Roman Conspirator," *International Journal of the Classical Tradition* 7 (2000–2001), 31–3. Davidsohn also notes that Corso Donati was "un Catilina su misura toscana"; Ernesto Sestan, s.v. "Donati, Corso," *Enciclopedia dantesca*, vol. 2 (1970), 560.
49 Dante, *Convivio* (4.5.19): "E non puose Iddio le mani quando uno nuovo cittadino di picciola condizione, cioè Tulio, contra tanto cittadino quanto era Catellina la romana libertate difese?"
50 See Antonio La Penna, "Il ritratto 'paradossale' da Silla a Petronio," *Rivista di filologia e d'istruzione classica* 3.104 (1976): 270–93.
51 For a consideration of Villani's interpretation of the *Commedia*, see Rala Isobel Diakité, "Writing Political Realities in Fourteenth-Century Italy: Giovanni Villani's 'Nuova Cronica' and Dante's 'Commedia,'" PhD diss., Brown University, 2003. See also Ferdinando Neri, "Dante e il primo Villani," *Giornale dantesco* 20 (1912): 1–31; Giovanni Aquilecchia, "Dante and the Florentine Chroniclers," *Bulletin of the John Rylands Library* 48 (1965–6): 48–51; and Louis Green, *Chronicle into History: An Essay on the Interpretation of History in Florentine Fourteenth-Century Chronicles* (Cambridge: Cambridge University Press, 1972), 9–43.
52 In the midst of Boccaccio's account of the mission of Charles of Valois to Florence later in *Esposizioni* 6 (which will be given particular attention in this chapter), he writes, "Nondimeno chi questa istoria vuole pienamente sapere legga la *Cronica* di Giovanni Villani, per ciò che in essa distesamente si pone" (6.41).
53 Giorgio Padoan indicates the references to Villani's *Nuova cronica* (book 8) in his notes to *Esposizioni* 6.
54 Compagni writes that the Cardinal clearly wanted to reduce the power of the Cerchi family and restore power to the Donati family (*Cronica*, 1.21).
55 Mazzotta, *The World at Play in Boccaccio's Decameron*, 80.
56 Dameron, *Florence and Its Church*, 80–1.
57 See Najemy, *A History of Florence*, 108. See also Giovanni Spani, "Il vino di Boccaccio: Usi e abusi in alcune novelle del *Decameron*," *Heliotropia* 8–9 (2011–12): 79–98.
58 See Najemy, *A History of Florence*, 43–4, for a discussion of the proliferation of the minor guilds. Cisti would have feasibly belonged to Arte de' Fornai.

See also *Statuti delle arti dei fornai e dei vinattieri di Firenze (1337–1339)*, ed. Francesca Morandini (Florence: Olschki, 1956).

59 See G. Masi, "I banchieri fiorentini nella vita politica della città sulla fine del Dugento," *Archivo giuridico* 9 (1931): 57–89; Masi, "La struttura sociale delle fazioni fiorentine politiche ai tempi di Dante," *Giornale dantesco* 31 (1928): 1–28.

60 See Branca's note in Boccaccio, *Decameron*, 722n4.

61 Najemy questions why the Donati family, a non-mercantile elite family, would allow a mercantile family to lead their faction (*A History of Florence*, 90).

62 See Bornstein's clarification regarding this distinction, p. 82n36.

63 See Dameron's terminology regarding these social groupings in "Revisiting the Italian Magnates," 177–8.

64 Messer Geri also appears much less shrewd in these matters than his wife, Madonna Oretta, the protagonist of the preceding *novella*, *Decameron* 6.1.

65 Najemy, *A History of Florence*, 25–7.

66 Najemy, *A History of Florence*, 92.

67 See Branca's note in Boccaccio, *Decameron*, 721n5.

68 Ferrante, *Political Vision*, writes, "Filippo Argenti … was a political enemy of Dante's, a Black and a member of the family which received Dante's confiscated goods after his exile" (145–6).

69 The exile of Petrarch's family also had a lasting impact upon Boccaccio's reception and negotiation of the other *corone*. Petrarch's father was sent into exile (1311) in the same year as Dante. Boccaccio exploits this coincidence in order to implore Petrarch to return to Florence and assume a political role. This appears in various works, from the *Vita Petracchi* to "Ytalie iam certus honos" (*Carmina* V), as well as in their correspondence (*Familiares* X). See Houston, *Building a Monument*, 57–8 and 95–100.

70 Boccaccio's exploitation of the *novella* genre for fiction and chronicle might be more indicative of his times than his particular trademark. See John Ahern's "Dioneo's Repertory: Performance and Writing in Boccaccio's *Decameron*," in *Performing Medieval Narrative*, ed. Evelyn Birge Vitz, Nancy Freeman Regalado, and Marilyn Lawrence (Rochester, NY: Cambridge Press, 2005), 41–58. In referring to Hugh of Reggio's mixing of stories into his sermons, Ahern states, "This was a culture that organized and preserved collective and personal experience in *novelle* … *Novelle* served many purposes: winning arguments, silencing opponents, obtaining favors, getting out of difficult situations, entertaining peers, instructing the young, affirming group values, memorializing important family and local events" (44).

Chapter Three

1 See Ferrante, *Political Vision*, especially chap. 2, for the relationship between church and state in the *Commedia*. See also George Holmes, "Dante and the Popes," in *The World of Dante*, ed. Cecil Grayson (Oxford: Clarendon, 1980), 18–43.
2 Cormac Ó Cuilleanáin, *Religion and the Clergy in Boccaccio's* Decameron (Rome: Edizioni di Storia e Letteratura, 1984), 96, 96n21.
3 Brucker, *Florentine Politics*, 138–9.
4 Brucker, *Florentine Politics*, 140.
5 George Dameron discusses how Florentine merchant bankers were "managers of papal finances," overseeing the management of income and subsidies, and even serving as papal creditors (*Florence and Its Church*, 110).
6 Dameron, *Florence and Its Church*, 110.
7 Barolini illustrates how Dante himself notes the hypocrisy of the "non-noble nobles" when they mistake prodigality for liberality in "Poscia ch'Amor." For this observation, and for Dante's interpretation of the Aristotelian template of avarice, liberality, and prodigality, see Barolini's "Aristotle's *Mezzo*, Courtly *Misura*, and Dante's Canzone *Le dolci rime*: Humanism, Ethics, and Social Anxiety," in *Dante and the Greeks*, ed. Jan Ziolkowski (Dumbarton Oaks, forthcoming).
8 See Thomas Aquinas, *Summa Theologiae*, II, II q. 77, a. 4, 1: "Lucrum tamen, quod est negotiationis finis, etsi in sui ratione non importet aliquid honestum vel necessarium, nihil tamen importat in sui ratione vitiosum vel virtuti contrarium. Unde nihil prohibet lucrum ordinari ad aliquem finem necessarium, vel etiam honestum. Et sic negotatio licita reddetur. Sicut cum aliquis lucrum moderatum, quod negotiando quaerit, ordinat ad domus suae sustentationem, vel etiam honestum. Et sic negotiatio licita reddetur. Sicut cum aliquis lucrum moderatum, quod negotiando quaerit, ordinat ad domus suae sustentationem, vel etiamo ad subveniendum indigentibus, vel etiamo cum aliquis negotiationi intendit propter publicam utilitatem, ne scilicet res necessariae ad vitam patriae desint, et lucrum expetit non quasi finem, sed quasi stipendium laboris." Also see the discussion of this quotation in Juliann Vitullo and Diane Wolfthal, "Trading Values: Negotiating Masculinity in Late Medieval and Early Modern Europe," in *Money, Morality, and Culture in Late Medieval and Early Modern Europe*, ed. Vitullo and Wolfthal (Burlington, VT: Ashgate, 2010), 155–7.
9 See Nicholas Havely, *Dante and the Franciscans: Poverty and the Papacy in the* Commedia (Cambridge: Cambridge University Press, 2004).

10 Ferrante writes, "For Italy's merchant-bankers, the whole civilized world was a potential or actual market, an imperfect foreshadowing of the united world Dante would like to see for all men. Like religion, commerce linked northern Italy with the rest of Europe and made the Italian cities sensitive to all the vagaries of international politics" (*Political Vision*, 314).

11 One of Petrarch's anecdotes from the *Rerum memorandarum libri* about Cangrande is discussed below; the other can be found in *RML* 3.97.

12 See Girolamo Arnaldi, "L'immagine di Cangrande e le profezie del canto XVII del *Paradiso*," in *Cangrande della Scala: La morte e il corredo di un principe nel medioevo europeo* (Venice: Marsilio, 2004), 6.

13 See Ferrante, *Political Vision*, 284–6.

14 See Arnaldi, "L'immagine di Cangrande," 5.

15 See, for example, Guido da Pisa, who writes in his commentary on *Inferno* 23: "Fredericus imperator homines sceleratos per istum modum aliquando puniebat: Ponebatur enim homo nudus in caldaria erea, et super eum una capa plumbea ponebatur, dictum hominem undique circumdantem. Et de subter caldariam fiebat ignis, qui plumbum liquefaciens, hominem comburebat" (*Guido da Pisa's Expositiones*, 441).

16 See David Abulafia's *Frederick II: A Medieval Emperor* (Oxford: Oxford University Press, 1988), 168–70, for Frederick II's condemnations of the greed of the papacy. For Dante's positive and negative views of Frederick II, see Ferrante, *Political Vision*, chap. 2, and especially pp.123–4. Villani calls Frederick II an enemy of the church in his *Nuova cronica* (6.1).

17 *Purgatorio* 16 and its history of *cortesia* in Lombardy are examined in the following chapter.

18 Dante refers to him in this capacity in *Epistola XIII*, the dedicatory letter to the *Paradiso*: "Magnifico atque victorioso domino domino Cani Grandi de la Scala sacratissimi Cesarei Principatus in urbe Verona et civitate Vicentie Vicario generali, devotissimus suus Dantes Alagherii florentinus natione non moribus, vitam orat per tempora diuturna felicem et gloriosi nominis perpetuum incrementum" (XIII, i). For a recent overview on the authenticity of the Epistle see John A. Scott, *Understanding Dante* (Notre Dame: University of Notre Dame Press, 2004), 345–7, 409. Also see, amongst others, Robert Hollander's *Dante's Epistle to Cangrande* (Ann Arbor: University of Michigan Press, 1993); and John Ahern's "Can the *Epistle to Cangrande* Be Read as a Forgery?" and Albert Ascoli's "Access to Authority: Dante in the *Epistle to Cangrande*," both in *Seminario dantesco internazionale: International Dante Seminar I*, ed. Z.G. Baranski (Florence: Le Lettere, 1997), 279–307; 309–52.

19 Boccaccio puts forth in the *Trattatello* his belief that Dante composed the first seven *canti* of *Inferno* before he was sent into exile ("Dico che, mentre che egli era più attento al glorioso lavoro, e già della prima parte di quello, la quale intitola *Inferno*, aveva composti sette canti […] sopravenne il gravoso accidente della sua cacciata, o fuga che chiamar si convegna, per lo quale egli e quella e ogni altra cosa abandonata"; 1.179).
20 All citations are from the first redaction of the *Trattatello in laude di Dante* edited by Pier Giorgio Ricci (Milan: Mondadori, 2002).
21 See Ricci's notes to this passage, *Trattatello*.
22 Ferrante also notes that Cangrande would have been most receptive to the political message of Dante's poem. See Ferrante, *Political Vision*, 284–6.
23 See Kristina M. Olson, "'Concivis meus': Petrarch's *Rerum memorandarum libri* 2.60, Boccaccio's *Decameron* 6.9, and the Specter of Dino del Garbo," *Annali d'italianistica* 22 (2004): 375–80. Picone notes this analogy to the *RML*, though he does not integrate an analysis of Petrarch's text. See Michelangelo Picone, "The Tale of Bergamino," in *The* Decameron *First Day in Perspective: Volume One of the Lecturae Boccaccii*, ed. Elissa B. Weaver (Toronto: University of Toronto Press, 2004), 168. Other interesting treatments of this *novella* include Luigi Russo, *Lettere critiche del 'Decameron'* (Bari: Laterza, 1956), 112–26, and Baratto, *Realtà e stile*, 214–17. I hope that the substance of my arguments in these chapters disproves Russo's statement that Boccaccio's use of satire in the First Day is simply artistic fantasy and nothing more ("In Boccaccio, la satira è stata ammazzata come satira, nel suo scopo vendicativo o correttivo dei costumi, ed essa è diventata mero contenuto, uno spasso della fantasia dell'artista," 119).
24 I thank Carolin Hahnemann for her translation of this text.
25 Though he interprets the presence of these religious figures in the *Decameron* in a different light, Cormac Ó Cuilleanáin also notes that "the Papacy figures in the first and last tales of the *Decameron* as the remote cause of certain events which are then presented at close quarters" (*Religion and the Clergy*, 96).
26 In this way, as Timothy Kircher notes, "Filostrato emphasizes the degree to which the social elites, especially the clergy, fail to achieve their prescribed ideals. But these ideals, in this case, are more secular than spiritual" (*The Poet's Wisdom: The Humanists, the Church, and the Formation of Philosophy in the Early Renaissance*, Brill's Studies in Intellectual History 133 [Leiden: Brill, 2006], 127). See his discussion of *Dec.* 1.7 in 123–8.
27 See Branca's note in Boccaccio, *Decameron*, 1120n3.
28 See Branca's note in Boccaccio, *Decameron*, 1120n3. Interestingly, later commentators who cite the *Decameron* in their writing tend to discuss Ghino

in terms of his "liberalità," perhaps because of his juxtaposition to the abbot's avarice in the *Decameron*. For example, Cristoforo Landino (1481) writes, "Dicono che Ghino fu grande di statura. Membruto, et robustissimo, et molto liberale, et exercitava el latrocinio, non per avaritia, ma per poter usar liberalità." Alessandro Velutello (1544) writes, "Ghino, dicono essere stato liberalissimo, e che per altro non rubava, che per poter usar liberalità." Both commentaries can be accessed on the Dartmouth Dante Project (http://dante.dartmouth.edu/; last accessed 12 March 2014).

29 Branca notes that the baths of San Casciano and Rapolano were not far from Radicofani. See his note in Boccaccio, *Decameron*, 1121n4.
30 See Ó Cuilleanáin, *Religion and the Clergy*, 98.
31 See George Holmes's essay "Dante and the Popes" (18–43), which illustrates how Boniface's papacy was condemned by many Florentines, not just by Dante. Holmes sees Dante's condemnations of the papacy as a "conversion to a fanatical belief that the contemporary Papacy had been degraded" (40). On the other hand, Ferrante believes that "Boniface's role in Italian, particularly Florentine, politics and in Dante's own exile, along with his extreme position on papal supremacy, would be enough to explain Dante's animosity towards him" (*Political Vision*, 77–8).
32 For the diffusion of this account in the chronicle and commentary traditions, see Padoan's "Colui che fece per viltà il gran rifiuto," *Studi danteschi* 38 (1961): 90–3.
33 Boccaccio attempts to clear Dante of appearing to damn a saint by stating that Piero del Morrone was canonized much later, during the time of Pope John XXII, around 1328. This is an error that he derived from Villani's *Nuova cronica*; see Padoan's note in Boccaccio, *Esposizioni*, 814.
34 As Ó Cuilleanáin writes, "Boniface's aura of bland liberality still comes oddly from such a devoted Dantist as Boccaccio" (*Religion and the Clergy*, 96).
35 See Branca's note in Boccaccio, *Decameron*, 1126n10.
36 In this way, Boniface is one of two historical personages (the other is Saladin) that appear in the first and last days of the *Decameron*.
37 Goldthwaite, *Economy of Renaissance Florence*, 145–7, discusses how "Avignon became a major node in the Florentine network." Also see Goldthwaite, 245–55, for a review of the banking crises and the relationship between the papacy and Florentine and non-Florentine banking houses.
38 Najemy, *A History of Florence*, 112–17. Goldthwaite notes how these Florentine merchants, such as the Bardi, the Altoviti, the Valori, and the Gianfigliazzi, in addition to the major firms of the Peruzzi and the Spini,

were located in Marseilles by the end of the thirteenth century (*Economy of Renaissance Florence*, 144–5).
39 Najemy, *A History of Florence*, 111.
40 Goldthwaite, *Economy of Renaissance Florence*, 238.
41 The Franzesi, after serving both the Duke of Brabant and the Philip the Fair, were knighted in France, eventually to return to great power in Tuscany. They failed, however, when the Gran Tavola of the Bonsignori of Siena went bankrupt in 1303. Musciatto ("Mouche") was condemned to death by the Florentine government in 1305. See Goldthwaite, *Economy of Renaissance Florence*, 238–9, and Ferrante, *Political Vision*, 314n6. Musciatto's fall from grace stands as an interesting counterpoint to the legendary sainthood of Ser Ciappelletto in *Dec.* 1.1.
42 In his survey of the critical history of 1.1, Franco Fido notes that the "historical background evolved with great precision" in this *novella*. See his *lectura Boccaccii*, "The Tale of Ser Ciappelletto (I.1)" in *The* Decameron *First Day in Perspective*, ed. Elissa Weaver (Toronto: University of Toronto Press, 2004), 65.
43 See, for example, Villani's *Nuova cronica*: "Nel detto anno, la notte di calen di maggio, il re Filippo il Bello di Francia, per consiglio di Biccio e Musciatto Franzesi, fece prendere tutti gl'Italiani ch'erano in suo reame, sotto protesto di prendere i prestatori; ma così fece prendere e rimedire i buoni mercatanti come i prestatori; onde molto fu ripreso e in grande abbominazione, e d'allora innanzi il reame di Francia sempre andò abassando e peggiorando. E nota che tra la perdita d'Acri e questa presura di Francia i mercatanti di Firenze ricevettono grande danno e ruina di loro avere" (8.49).
44 Branca writes, "Il crescendo di fredda, calcolata empietà di Ciappelletto grandeggia su quel tessuto di spregiudicatezza e di spietezza mercantile che regola, secondo usi e necessità ben storicamente documentate, l'agire di Musciatto Franzesi e dei fratelli usurai" (*Boccaccio medievale*, 159).
45 See Branca, *Boccaccio medievale*, 135.
46 Branca writes, "il Boccaccio proprio sulle soglie del suo *Decameron* ha posto l'episodio dove il dominio della 'ragion di mercatura' è più assoluto e spietato, fino al disumano" (*Boccaccio medievale*, 156).
47 Branca, *Boccaccio medievale*, 159.
48 See Susanna Barsella's "I marginalia di Boccaccio all'*Etica Nicomachea* (Ms Milano, Ambrosiana, A 204 inf.)," in *Boccaccio in America: Proceedings of the 2010 International Boccaccio Conference at the University of Massachusetts Amherst*, ed. Elsa Filosa and Michael Papio (Ravenna: Longo, 2012), 143–55, for an analysis of Boccaccio's scribal activity as regards the *Ethics*

and Aquinas's commentary, and for an assessment of how, as she writes, "il *Decameron* non è solo un'opera con esplicito intento morale, ma anche intrinsicamente etica, e di un'etica – ed un'estetica – non più medievale e non più aristotelica o tomista in senso stretto" (144).

49 See Tobias Foster Gittes, *Boccaccio's Naked Muse: Eros, Culture and the Mythopoeic Imagination* (Toronto: University of Toronto Press, 2008), chap. 1, for an analysis of the Golden Age motif in Boccaccio's works.

50 Boccaccio, in glossing Cerberus's three heads as the three different types of avarice, proposes three categories of the avaricious: "e così per Cerbero sarà da intendere l'avaro, al quale perciò sono tre teste discritte, a dinotare tre spezie d'avari: per ciò che alcuni sono li quali si ardentemente disiderano l'oro, che essi cupidamente in ogni disonesto guadagno, per averne, si lascian correre, acciò che quello che acquistato avranno, pazamente spendano, donino e gittin via [...] La seconda spezie è quella di coloro li quali con grandissimo suo pericolo e fatica ragunano d'ogni parte e in qualunque maniera, acciò che tengano e servino e guardino, e nè a sè nè ad altrui dell'acquistato fanno pro o utile alcuno. La terza specie è quella di coloro li quali non per alcuna sua opera o ingegno o fatica, ma per opera de' suoi passati, ricchi divengono e di queste ricchezze sono sì vigilanti e studiosi guardiani che essi, non altrimenti che se da altrui loro fossero state diposte, le servano, nè alcuno ardire hanno di toccarle: questi cotali sono da dire tristissimi e miseri guardiani di Dite" (7.23–6, esp. all.).

51 The similarities between Boccaccio's analysis of the desire for travel and the desire for material gain and Dante's anatomy of desire, as articulated by Teodolinda Barolini in her work on *Convivio* (4.12) and on the figure of Ulysses in the *Commedia*, merit further examination. See Barolini, *The Undivine Comedy: Detheologizing Dante* (Princeton: Princeton University Press, 1992), chap. 5.

52 I do not, therefore, see how Padoan could view this particular passage as a celebration of the merchant class, as Boccaccio is explicitly condemning the consequence of their activities. He writes, "traspare ancora una certa ammirazione per quell'epopea mercantile, che egli aveva esaltato nel *Decameron*" (Boccaccio, *Esposizioni*, 899). Branca, though he examines Boccaccio's critique of the merchant class in the *Decameron*, does not investigate Boccaccio's articulation of this criticism in the *Esposizioni*.

53 For an analysis of *cupiditas* in Guittone and Dante that resonates with Boccaccio's elaborate discourse on avarice, see Teodolinda Barolini, "Guittone's *Ora parrà*, Dante's *Doglia mi reca*, and the *Commedia*'s Anatomy of Desire," from the *Seminario Dantesco internazionale*: International dante Seminar 1, ed. Z. Baranski (Florence: Le Lettere, 1997), 3–23.

54 At the beginning of his invective, Tedaldo states, "Furon già i frati santissimi e valenti uomini, ma quegli che oggi frati si chiamano e così vogliono esser tenuti, niuna altra cosa hanno di frate se non la cappa" (3.7.34). This is to identify but two cases of anti-clerical sentiment in the *Decameron*, a text pervaded by such moments.
55 Kircher, *Poet's Wisdom*, 5.
56 Boccaccio interprets the *lonza* as *lussuria*, the other vice associated with *cupiditas*. Jacopo Alighieri, Jacopo della Lana, and the Anonimo Selmiano all gloss the *lupa* as avarice.
57 Giorgio Padoan notes the extraordinary nature of this narrative: "Il B. delinea con vivacità questo ritratto dell'avaro: proprio nei passi in cui il certaldese descrive i vizi, i loro dannosi effetti e le debolezze dei peccatori, egli pare ritrovare lo stile di un tempo, nonostante che, per l'argomento stesso, non sappia liberarsi da un tono che troppo concede alla letterarietà" (Boccaccio, *Esposizioni*, 795–6).
58 For a historical exploration of usury as one of the "labor pains of capitalism," see Jacques Le Goff, *Your Money or Your Life: Economy and Religion in the Middle Ages* (New York: Zone Books, 1990).
59 Vittore Branca, in the chapter "L'epopea dei mercatanti," notes the "sinister" nature of the First Day precisely due to Boccaccio's preoccupation with avarice in these *novelle*: "Nell'amara riprensione dei vizi, che fornisce il tema alla prima giornata, la spietata avidità dei Franzesi, la calcolata empietà di Ciappelletto, la gretta avarizia di Ermino Grimaldi approfondiscono di luci livide e di ombre sinistre la rappresentazione aspramente polemica dei 'grandi' del secolo" (Branca, *Boccaccio medievale*, 149).
60 None of the early commentators interpret the *veltro* as Cangrande della Scala, and likewise they do not try to geographically locate the place "tra feltro e feltro" on earth. See Leonardo Olschki, *The Myth of Felt* (Berkeley: University of California Press, 1949), 5.
61 "Circa primum nota quod iste venturus dominus dicitur canis leporarius propter quasdam laudabiles conditiones quas habet canis leporarius," writes Guido da Pisa (*Guido da Pisa*, 32–3).
62 In the conclusion of his gloss on these verses, Guido da Pisa states, "Vel aliter anagogice exponendo: Per istum leporarium accipere possumus Christum, qui venturus est ad iudicium, cuius natio, idest apparitio, erit inter feltrum et feltrum, hoc est inter bonos et reprobos, ibique avaritia" (*Guido da Pisa*, 33). Padoan writes, "Che il veltro fosse 'ipse verus Deus' (o, in subordine, almeno un imperatore o un pontefice), era ipotesi avanzata da Graziolo, mentre già l'anonimo Selmiano accenna a Cristo [...]: ma qui il B. pensa particolarmente a Guido da Pisa, che tale interpretazione

aveva sottolineato con forza" (Boccaccio, *Esposizioni*, 798). Pietro Alighieri identifies the *veltro* as an emperor who will rule over the world (the DXV). See Pietro Alighieri, *Comentum super poema Comedia Dantis*, ed. Massimiliano Chiamenti (Tempe, AZ: Arizona Center for Medieval and Renaissance Studies, 2002), 101–2. The Ottimo claims that the *veltro* will be an unusual lord (see *L'ultima forma dell'Ottimo Commento*, 63–4). See also Charles T. Davis's entry on the *veltro* in *Enciclopedia dantesca* (Rome: Istituto della Enciclopedia italiana, 1970) 5:909, and Ferrante, *Political Vision*, 115–19.

63 Jacopo della Lana writes, "Questo si può intendere in due modi: tra feltro e feltro, ciò vuol dire per constellazione. L'altro modo tra feltro e feltro, cioè che nascerà di assai vile nazione, chè feltro è vile panno." See *Commedia di Dante degli Allagherii col commento di Jacopo di Giovanni della Lana bolognese*, ed. L. Scarabelli, 3 vols. (Milan: Civelli, 1864–1865).

64 See Olschki, *Myth of Felt*, 7–10. According to Olschki, Boccaccio's source for this anecdote (in fact, it does not appear in any of the other early commentaries) must have been a merchant, perhaps a Genoese one.

65 Numerous critics have dismissed the *novella* of Mithridanes and Nathan, as Franco Fido notes ("nessuno, a lettura finita, ricorda più Mitridane e Nathan o Tito e Gisippo"). See Fido, *Le metamorfosi del centauro: Studi e letture da Boccaccio a Pirandello* (Rome: Bulzoni, 1977), 31.

66 Tartary and the Middle Kingdom ("imperio di mezzo") are not the same thing, as Olschki indicates, the latter representing Cathay instead. Olschki writes, "The allusion to the unbelievable wealth of the Tartar emperors corresponds with the descriptions given of it by Marco Polo in dealing with Kublai Khan's China. That country is designated by Boccaccio as an 'imperio di mezzo' and thus properly distinguished from Tartary, then a province of the Yüan empire. Nowhere else in Western medieval sources is China mentioned by its proper name as the 'Country, or Kingdom, of the Middle' [...] It is under that name that China is mentioned also in the *Decameron*" (*Myth of Felt*, 9–10).

67 See Branca's note in Boccaccio, *Decameron*, 1128n1.

68 See Arnaldo D'Addario's entry on the Gianfigliazzi family in the *Enciclopedia dantesca* (Rome: Istituto della Enciclopedia italiana, 1970), 3:153, and Renato Piattoli's entry on the Donati family, *Enciclopedia dantesca*, 2:555.

69 See D'Addario's entry on the Gianfigliazzi family in the *Enciclopedia dantesca*, 3:153.

70 See Goldthwaite, *Economy of Renaissance Florence*, 144; Sapori, *I libri della ragione bancaria dei Gianfigliazzi* (Milan: Garzanti, 1946).

71 See Branca in his notes to the *Decameron*, 730–31n5. Alianora, the daughter of Niccolò and wife of Pacino Peruzzi, appears as Adiona in the *Comedia delle ninfe fiesolane*, and also in the *Amorosa visione* (14.7).
72 See Branca in his notes to the *Decameron*, 731n2.
73 See Vanna Arringhi's entry on Currado Gianfigliazzi in the *Dizionario biografico degli italiani*, vol. 54 (2000).
74 See Arringhi, *Dizionario biografico*.
75 I agree with Barolini's assessment that the *Decameron* obeys a wheel-like structure rather than a linear progression from vice to virtue, the latter of which was first proposed by Neri. See Barolini, "The Wheel of the *Decameron*," *Romance Philology* 36 (1983): 521–38, esp. 521; and Ferdinando Neri, "Il disegno ideale del *Decameron*," in *Storia e poesia* (Turin: Chiantore, 1944), 73–82. Evidence of this in the *novelle* examined here can be seen in the lack of an explicit conversion for the Abbot of Cluny and Boniface in 10.2. See also Janet Smarr, "Symmetry and Balance in the *Decameron*," *Medievalia* 2 (1976): 159–87. Smarr argues for a Dantean narrative system in the *Decameron*'s "nine plus one pattern" (160).
76 Ferrante writes, "We find here an ethical code of social responsibility and personal virtue, and its informing principle is love." See Joan Ferrante, "The Frame Characters in the *Decameron*: A Progression of Virtues," *Romance Philology* 19 (1965): 212–26, esp. 226.

Chapter Four

1 Compagni dates this murder to 1215, but Najemy dates it to 1216 (*A History of Florence*, 21).
2 See Sergio Raveggi et al., *Ghibellini, guelfi e popolo grasso: I detentori del potere politico a Firenze nella seconda metà del Dugento* (Florence: La nuova Italia, 1978), chap. 1 ("Il regime ghibellino"), and especially pp. 63–8 for this history.
3 For this history, see Bornstein, *Dino Compagni's Cronicle of Florence*, xvi–xviii; Compagni 1.3–4; *Cronica fiorentina* (in *Testi fiorentini*, ed. Schiaffini), 148; Najemy, *A History of Florence*, 20–2, 58.
4 Brucker, *Florentine Politics*, 159–63; Najemy, *A History of Florence*, 144–5. As a result, Najemy estimates that 426 individuals were stripped of the right to hold office. See Najemy, *Corporatism and Consensus in Florentine Electoral Politics, 1280–1400* (Chapel Hill: University of North Carolina Press, 1982), 153–7.
5 Najemy notes how Matteo Villani stood such persecution, perhaps because of his anti-Parte sentiment in the chronicle (*A History of Florence*,

147). See also Brucker, *Renaissance Florence*, 29–36; David Wallace, *Chaucerian Polity: Absolutist Lineages and Associational Forms in England and Italy* (Stanford: Stanford University Press, 1997), 16.

6 No exclusive study of 2.6 exists. Branca notes that there is a record of a Ghibelline Capece who rebelled against the Angevins and was imprisoned and tortured (*Boccaccio medievale*, 178–9).

7 Dante wrote Epistle IV to Moruello Malaspina along with a copy of the canzone "Amor, da che convien pur ch'io mi doglia" between 1307 and 1308. In his letter he recalls the hospitality of the Malaspina family ("Ne lateant dominum vincula servi sui, quam affectus gratuitas dominantis"). Branca examines how Boccaccio imitated this letter in the epistle "Mavortis miles extrenue" (*Boccaccio medievale*, 219).

8 De Robertis contrasts this definition of *cortesia* with the one offered in the *De vulgari eloquentia* (1.18.4) where the notion of the court ("curialitas") does not seem to be completely harmonious with the notion of *cortesia*. Concerning the passage from the *Convivio*, on the other hand, De Robertis writes, "Si deve, piuttosto, notare che, in questo passo, Dante espone tutti i temi che confluiscono nella sua concezione della *cortesia*, si tratti della formazione storica di questa idea, della nostalgia per un'età di più alta rettitudine o della condanna per la decadenza dei costumi 'curiali'" (see De Robertis's note in Dante, *Convivio*, 196).

9 The preceding *novella* of Andreuccio (2.5) also contains a reference to the long history of struggle between the Aragonese and the Angevins for control of Sicily, though it is told from the Guelph perspective of Andreuccio's "sister" (who supposedly flees Sicily to escape King Frederick II, son of Peter III and Constance).

10 Concerning the function of history in this *novella*, Branca writes, "sono proprio le precise dimensioni storiche in cui è ambientato che gli danno questa concretezza fantastica e questo significato centrale" (*Boccaccio medievale*, 178).

11 Jason Houston comes to a similar conclusion in analysing the actions of Phillip IV in the ninth book of the *De casibus*: "This passage also reflects Boccaccio's insistence on the interaction between personal and civic history" (*Building a Monument*, 68–9).

12 See Branca's footnote in Boccaccio, *Decameron*, 219n2.

13 Could the tale of the nobility of the Baronci (*Dec.* 6.6) also parody the idea that "masculine noses" are such an indicator ("tale v'è col naso molto lungo e tale l'ha corto," 6.6.14)?

14 Charles Martel also discusses this theme in *Paradiso* 8, which is addressed below. In the Fourth Book of the *Convivio*, where Dante glosses his poem

"Le dolci rime," he writes that God infuses individuals, and not clans or families, with nobility ("ché 'l divino seme non cade in ischiatta, cioè in istirpe, ma cade nelle singulari persone; e, sì come di sotto si proverà, la stirpe non fa le singulari persone nobili, ma le singulari persone fanno nobile la stirpe," 4.20.4–5). *Paradiso* 8 is examined in the context of the Angevins in the following section.

15   Could Currado's sudden desire to marry Spina to Giusfredi in this tale stem from Boccaccio's understanding that Currado did not have any male heirs? Benvenuto da Imola, in his commentary on *Purg.* 8, writes that Currado died without producing any sons: "quod veniens ad mortem sine prole." Or is Benvenuto elaborating on *Decameron* 2.6's fictional biography of Currado?

16   Ferrante explores Dante's ambivalence towards Frederick II, pointing out that Frederick's treatment of "heresy as a crime against the state, as treason" might have bothered Dante (*Political Vision*, 123–4). Dante exalts Frederick elsewhere in the *Convivio* (4.3.6) and with his son Manfred in the *De vulgari eloquentia* (1.12.3).

17   Villani writes, "Nel detto anno 1250, essendo Federigo imperadore in Puglia nella città di Firenzuola all'uscita d'Abruzzi, si ammalò forte, e già del suo agurio non si seppe guardare, che trovava che dovea morire in Firenze, nè in Faenza; ma male seppe interpretrare [sic] la parola mendace del demonio, che gli disse si guardasse che morrebbe in Firenze, è egli non si guardò di Firenzuola. Avvenne che aggravando della detta malattia, essendo con lui uno suo figliuolo bastardo ch'avea nome Manfredi, disiderando d'avere il tesoro di Federigo suo padre, e la signoria del Regno e di Cicilia, e temendo che Federigo di quella malattia non iscampasse o facesse testamento, concordandosi col suo segreto ciamberlano, promettendoli molti doni e signoria, con uno primaccio che a Federigo puose il detto Manfredi in sulla bocca, sì l'affogò, e per lo detto modo morì il detto Federigo disposto dello 'mperio e scomunicato da santa Chiesa, sanza penitenzia, o nullo sagramento di santa Chiesa" (6.41). Villani's choice of the word "bastardo" for Manfred offers an interesting contrast to Boccaccio's use of the term "figliuolo naturale."

18   The *Novellino* (LX) features Charles in a tale of romance, as implied by its rubric: "Carlo nobile re di Cicilia e di Gerusalem, quando era conte d'Angiò sì amò per amore la bella contessa di Ceti."

19   Gittes relates this "erotic foreplay" to the fishing scene in the *Valle delle donne* in Day Six. See Tobias Foster Gittes, "Boccaccio's 'Valley of Women': Fetishized Foreplay in Decameron VI," *Italica* 76.2 (1999): 147–74, esp. 159–162. Gittes also observes King Charles's state of impotence, which he

believes is the consequence of the king's inability to choose between the two daughters (161).

20 Branca makes the provocative observation that Boccaccio might be attempting to predict the Sicilian Vespers in the words of Count Guy de Monfort. The centaur indicates the soul of Guy de Monfort amongst the violent in *Inferno* 12 ("Colui fesse in grembo a Dio/lo cor che 'n su Tamici ancor si cola," 119–20), where Dante locates his soul because he committed murder (Guy avenged his father's death by killing Henry III of England).

21 The passion of King Charles also belongs to the larger thematic of older men and erotic desire in Boccaccio's works, from Maestro Alberto (1.10) to the scholar Rinieri (8.7) to the older lover in the *Corbaccio*.

22 Branca, citing a passage from the *Filocolo*, believes that this anecdote must have been widespread: "Doveva essere accusa diffusa, se anche nel *Filocolo*, parlando della conquista del Regno e dell'impresa di Carlo, narra che per favorirla Aletto, 'gli animi de' più possenti impregnò di volontà iniqua contra 'l principale signore [Manfredi], mostrando loro come venereamente le loro matrimoniali letta avea violate' (1.1.2)" (see his note in Boccaccio, *Decameron*, 1164n5). Villani describes the "lussuria" of Manfredi in his *Cronica* (6.46).

23 Similarities between these *novelle* and with the language of *Inf.* 5 deserve further examination.

24 Richardson believes that the "ghibellina" is Emilia, since she tells 2.6 (which is a tale of Ghibelline victories in both political and personal ways) and three anti-clerical stories (1.6, 3.7, and 8.4). See Brian Richardson, "The 'Ghibelline' Narrator in the *Decameron*," *Italian Studies* 33 (1978): 20–8, esp. 21–22.

25 Boccaccio features Gianni di Procida, the alleged hero of the Ghibelline cause during the Sicilian Vespers in 5.6, in another *novella* that treats the romantic exploits of a political figure. Regarding his instrumental role in upholding the Ghibelline claim to Sicily, Villani writes in his *Nuova cronica*, "Questi per suo senno e industria si pensò di recare la forza del re Carlo in basso stato, e in parte gli venne fatto" (8.7). In an interesting parallel to 10.6, King Frederick III abducts Gianni of Procida's lover, and his advisor admonishes him in the end for such a politically unwise move. This stealth action on behalf of King Frederick supports Dante's claim in *Purgatorio* 20 that the descendants of Peter of Aragon did not inherit Peter's "probitate."

26 Other early commentators, such as Jacopo della Lana, also identified Countess Matilda with the Matilda in the Earthly Paradise. In his gloss of

Purgatorio 28.37–40, Jacopo writes: "Questa fu la contessa Matelda, proba, savia e virtudiosa, la quale elli pone per la vita attiva."
27 The "sacra rappresentazione" in *Purg.* 8 that precedes Currado's monologue, that of the snake sent into flight by three angels, recalls the act of original sin in Eden, and perhaps the sexual act. The snake is likened to the one from whom Eve received the forbidden fruit: "Da quella parte onde non ha riparo/la picciola vallea, era una biscia,/forse qual diede ad Eva il cibo amaro" (*Purg.* 8.97–9). Currado, interestingly, does not watch this scene, but is completely engrossed with the pilgrim ("per tutto quello assalto/punto non fu da me guardare sciolta," 110–11). Does Boccaccio "open" Currado's eyes to the sexual act in 2.6 by having him encounter Giannotto and Spina *in flagrante*?
28 See Vern Bullough, "On Being a Male in the Middle Ages," in *Medieval Masculinities: Regarding Men in the Middle Ages*, ed. Claire Lees (Minneapolis: University of Minnesota Press, 1994), 31–45. Bullough refers to Aristotle's *De generatione animalium* (729 A, 25–34), Avicenna's *Canon of Medicine* (I, 196), Albert the Great's *De animalibus libri XXVI*, and Thomas Aquinas's *Summa theologica* (pt.3, q.2, "Die conceptione Christia quod activum principium") (*Medieval Masculinities*, 31–2). For a feminist approach to medieval thought regarding the roles of both sexes in reproduction, see Joan Cadden, *The Meanings of Sex Difference in the Middle Ages: Medicine, Science, and Culture* (Cambridge: Cambridge University Press, 1993). See also Heather Webb's parsing of the "engendering heart" in *The Medieval Heart* (New Haven: Yale University Press, 2010), 107–22.
29 Dante's main source for this theory of reproduction has been deeply disputed, as some critics believe that Dante's generation of the soul is exclusively Thomistic (Giovanni Busnelli) while others view different influences (Bruno Nardi); see a summary of this debate in Manuele Gragnolati's "From Plurality to (Near) Unicity of Forms: Embryology in *Purgatorio* 25," in *Dante for the New Millennium*, ed. Teodolinda Barolini and H. Wayne Storey (New York: Fordham University Press, 2003), 192–210, esp. 193. Gragnolati treats the variety of philosophical and theological issues surrounding the embryological doctrine of *Purgatorio* 25.
30 Bruni offers the provocative interpretation of this *novella* as being stylized as a Provençal *razo* (*Boccaccio*, 329).
31 The other *novella* that features an only daughter zealously protected by her parents is 4.1, the tale of Tancredi and Ghismonda. According to Fiammetta, Tancredi "in tutto lo spazio della sua vita non ebbe che una figliuola" (4.1.4).

32 Forni views 5.4 as a positive version of the tragic story of 4.1 (*Adventures in Speech*, 35–9).
33 See Teodolinda Barolini, "'Le parole son femmine e i fatti sono maschi': Toward a Sexual Poetics of the Decameron (*Dec.* 2.9, 2.10, 5.10)," *Studi sul Boccaccio* 21 (1993): 175–97, esp. 192. For a detailed comparison with Marie de France's *lai*, *Laustic*, see Bruni, *Boccaccio*, 364–7. For a discussion of the "literalized metaphor" trope in Boccaccio, see Forni, *Adventures in Speech*, 66. For a treatment of "literalizing metaphors" in the context of the contingencies of language and selfhood, see Richard Rorty, *Contingency, Irony and Solidarity* (Cambridge: Cambridge University Press, 1989).
34 This reading of "quella cosa che voi tra gli uomini più vi vergognate di nominare" supports Migiel's definition of this phrase as signifying something more complex than just "penis," but instead many different dynamics in this *novella*: "the puissance of the legitimate husband/father; the virility of the male rival who threatens the husband/father; and the woman who is the object of their desires." See Marilyn Migiel, *A Rhetoric of the* Decameron (Toronto: University of Toronto Press, 2003), 137. Migiel does not see the young lovers Caterina and Ricciardo as possessing that much freedom; rather, the "expression of their desires" is simply compatible with "the dominant ideology of their immediate family and community" (129).
35 See Branca's note in Boccaccio, *Decameron*, 672n2.
36 Hollander, *Boccaccio's Dante*, 4.
37 Mazzotta, *The World at Play in Boccaccio's* Decameron, 86–9. See also Houston, who likens the public spectacle of the infernal hunt to Boccaccio's public lectures of the *Esposizioni* (*Building a Monument*, 168). Also see Kamber, "Antitesi e sintesi in 'Nastagio degli Onesti,'" *Italica* 44 (1967): 61–8; Migiel, *A Rhetoric of the* Decameron, 156–7; Cesare Segre, "La novella di Nastagio degli Onesti (*Dec.* V, 8): I due tempi della visione," in *In ricordo di Cesare Angelini* (Pavia: Saggiatore, 1980), 65–74.
38 Michael Sherberg, *The Governance of Friendship: Law and Gender in the* Decameron (Columbus: Ohio State University Press, 2011), 48–9.
39 Migiel calls Federigo a "flawed comic hero" in a tale that "overturns Filostrato's trajectory toward tragedy." Such a trajectory comprises, in addition to his actions as king of the Fourth Day, his tale of *Decameron* 4.9 (*A Rhetoric of the* Decameron, 54).
40 Coppo di Domenico Borghesi is also Boccaccio's acknowledged source for the tale of Filippo Argenti in *Decameron* 9.8, and is cited in the *Esposizioni*. See Bruni, "La proiezione dell'attualità politica," 210–12.

41 See Arnaldo D'Addario's entry on the Alberighi family in the *Enciclopedia dantesca* (Rome: Istituto della Enciclopedia italiana, 1970), 1:146. Villani lists the Ughi and Catellini families (as well as the Lamberti) as residents of the Porta San Brancazio neighbourhood (*Nuova cronica*, 4.12); he lists the Greci and Uberti as residents of Porta Santa Maria (4.13).
42 Bruni writes, "Impoverito per le folli spese sostenute, inutilmente, per amore di monna Giovanna, Federigo si ritira a vivere nella piccola proprietà di Campi. Egli muove dalla città al contado; al contrario, alle origini dell'espansione di Firenze si era prodotta la spinta inversa dell'inurbamento, che aveva garantito la crescita della città e aveva promosso quello che a Cacciaguida appariva un negativo rimescolamento sociale" ("La proiezione dell'attualità politica," 211).
43 As Sherberg writes, "While the *novella* draws attention to Federigo, plot developments hinge significantly on Monna Giovanna's position as wife, mother, and sister" (*Governance of Friendship*, 140).
44 Sherberg observes that "Federigo behaves as *smoderatamente* as fortune itself, making a public spectacle of his love" (*Governance of Friendship*, 140).
45 Houston, *Building a Monument*, 69–75; Wallace, *Chaucerian Polity*, 281–2.
46 See Scaglione, *Knights at Court*, 215 and 215n85, for his identification of Griselda as the Ciceronian heroine of fortitude (vis-à-vis Aristotle): "considerata periculorum susceptio et laborum perpessio" nourished on "magnificentia, fidentia, patientia, perseverantia" from Cicero, *De inventione* 2.54.163.
47 This is the thesis of Marvin Becker's *Florence in Transition* (Baltimore: Johns Hopkins Press, 1967), esp. chap. 1, "The Communal Paideia and the Emerging Humanism of the Early *Trecento*."
48 For a comprehensive study of the reception of Dante's poem in the fourteenth and fifteenth centuries, and particularly the commentary of Cristoforo Landino, see Simon Gilson, *Dante and Renaissance Florence* (Cambridge: Cambridge University Press, 2005), 163–92, and Deborah Parker, *Commentary and Ideology: Dante in the Renaissance* (Durham: Duke University Press, 1993).

Bibliography

Abulafia, David. *Frederick II: A Medieval Emperor*. Oxford: Oxford University Press, 1988.
Ahern, John. "Can the *Epistle to Cangrande* Be Read as a Forgery?" In *Seminario dantesco internazionale: International Dante Seminar I*, ed. Z.G. Baranski, 279–307. Florence: Le Lettere, 1997.
– "Dioneo's Repertory: Performance and Writing in Boccaccio's *Decameron*." In *Performing Medieval Narrative*, ed. Evelyn Birge Vitz, Nancy Freeman Regalado, and Marilyn Lawrence, 41–58. Rochester, NY: D.S. Brewer, 2005.
Alfie, Fabian. "Poetics Enacted: A Comparison of the Novellas of Guido Cavalcanti and Cecco Angiulieri in Boccaccio's *Decameron*." *Studi sul Boccaccio* 23 (1995): 171–96.
Alighieri, Dante. *La Commedia secondo l'antica vulgata*. Edited by Giorgio Petrocchi. Milan: Mondadori, 1966–7.
– *Convivio*. Edited by Cesare Vasoli and Domenico de Robertis. Milan: Ricciardi, 1995.
– *De vulgari eloquentia; Monarchia*. Edited by Pier Vincenzo Mengaldo. Milan: Ricciardi, 1996.
– *La Divina Commedia*. Edited by Umberto Bosco and Giovanni Reggio. Florence: Le Monnier, 1979.
– *Inferno*. Translated by Robert Hollander and Jean Hollander. New York: Doubleday, 2000.
– *Paradiso*. Translated by Robert Hollander and Jean Hollander. New York: Doubleday, 2007.
– *Purgatorio*. Translated by Robert Hollander and Jean Hollander. New York: Doubleday, 2003.
– *Rime giovanili e della Vita nuova*. Edited by Teodolinda Barolini. Milan: BUR Rizzoli, 2009.

Alighieri, Pietro. *Comentum super poema Comedia Dantis.* Ed. Massimiliano Chiamenti. Tempe, AZ: Arizona Center for Medieval and Renaissance Studies, 2002.

Aquilecchia, Giovanni. "Dante and the Florentine Chroniclers." *Bulletin of the John Rylands Library* 48 (1965–6): 48–51.

Aquinas, Thomas, Saint. *Summa Theologiae.* 60 vols. Edited and translated by Thomas Gilby et al. London: Blackfriars, 1964–76.

Ardizzone, Maria Luisa. *Guido Cavalcanti: The Other Middle Ages.* Toronto: University of Toronto Press, 2002.

Armstrong, Nancy, and Leonard Tennenhouse. *The Ideology of Conduct: Essays on Literature and the History of Sexuality.* New York: Methuen, 1987.

Arnaldi, Girolamo. "L'immagine di Cangrande e le profezie del canto XVII del *Paradiso.*" In *Cangrande della Scala: La morte e il corredo di un principe nel medioevo europeo,* 3–10. Venice: Marsilio, 2004.

Ascoli, Albert Russell. "Access to Authority: Dante in the *Epistle to Cangrande.*" In *Seminario dantesco internazionale: International Dante Seminar I,* ed. Z.G. Baranski, 309–52. Florence: Le Lettere, 1997.

– "Boccaccio's Auerbach: Holding the Mirror Up to Mimesis." *Studi sul Boccaccio* 20 (1991): 377–97.

– *Dante and the Making of a Modern Author.* Cambridge: Cambridge University Press, 2008.

Ashley, Kathleen M., and Robert L.A. Clark, eds. *Medieval Conduct.* Minneapolis: University of Minnesota Press, 2001.

Auerbach, Erich. *Mimesis: The Representation of Reality in Western Literature.* Trans. Willard R. Trask. Princeton: Princeton University Press, 1953.

Baranski, Zygmunt G. "'Alquanto tenea della oppinione degli Epicuri': The *auctoritas* of Boccaccio's Cavalcanti (and Dante)." In *Mittelalterliche Novellistik im europäischen Kontext: Kulturwissenschaftliche Perspektive,* ed. Mark Chinca, 280–325. Berlin: Schmidt, 2006.

– ed. *Seminario dantesco internazionale: International Dante Seminar I.* Florence: Le Lettere, 1997.

Baranski, Zygmunt G., and M.L. McLaughlin, eds. *Italy's Three Crowns: Reading Dante, Petrarch and Boccaccio.* Oxford: Bodleian Library, 2007.

Baratto, Mario. *Realtà e stile nel* Decameron. Vicenza: Ponza, 1970.

Bàrberi-Squarotti, Giorgio. *Il potere della parola: Studi sul 'Decameron.'* Naples: Federico & Ardia, 1989.

Barolini, Teodolinda. "Aristotle's *Mezzo,* Courtly *Misura,* and Dante's Canzone *Le dolci rime*: Humanism, Ethics, and Social Anxiety." In *Dante and the Greeks,* ed. Jan M. Ziolkowski, 163–79. Washington, DC: Dumbarton Oaks, 2014.

- "Dante and Francesca da Rimini: Realpolitik, Romance and Gender." *Speculum* 75 (2000): 1–28.
- *Dante and the Origins of Italian Literary Culture*. New York: Fordham University Press, 2006.
- "Guittone's *Ora parrà*, Dante's *Doglia mi reca*, and the *Commedia*'s Anatomy of Desire." In *Seminario dantesco internazionale*: International Dante Seminar 1, ed. Z. Baranski, 3–23. Florence: Le Lettere, 1997.
- "'Le parole son femmine e i fatti sono maschi': Toward a Sexual Poetics of the Decameron (*Dec.* 2.9, 2.10, 5.10)." *Studi sul Boccaccio* 21 (1993): 175–97.
- "Sociology of the *Brigata*: Gendered Groups in Dante, Forese, Folgore, Boccaccio – From 'Guido, i' vorrei' to Griselda." *Italian Studies* 67 (2012): 4–22.
- *The Undivine Comedy: Detheologizing Dante*. Princeton: Princeton University Press, 1992.
- "The Wheel of the Decameron." *Romance Philology* 36 (1983): 521–38.

Baron, Hans. *The Crisis of the Early Italian Renaissance: Civic Humanism and Republican Liberty in an Age of Classicism and Tyranny*. Princeton: Princeton University Press, 1966.

Barsella, Susanna. "I marginalia di Boccaccio all'*Etica Nicomachea* (Ms Milano, Ambrosiana, A 204 inf.)." In *Boccaccio in America: Proceedings of the 2010 International Boccaccio Conference at the University of Massachusetts Amherst*, ed. Elsa Filosa and Michael Papio, 143–55. Ravenna: Longo, 2012.

Bausi, Francesco. "Gli spiriti magni: Filigrane aristoteliche e tomistiche nella decima giornata del 'Decameron.'" *Studi sul Boccaccio* 27 (1999): 205–53.

Becker, Marvin. *Florence in Transition*. 2 vols. Baltimore: Johns Hopkins University Press, 1967.
- "Gualtieri di Brienne e l'uso delle dispense giudiziarie." *Archivo storico italiano* 113 (1955): 245–51.
- "A Study in Political Failure: The Florentine Magnates 1280–1343." *Mediaeval Studies* 27 (1965): 246–308.

Bernardo, Aldo S. "The Plague as Key to Meaning in Boccaccio's *Decameron*." In *The Black Death: The Impact of the Fourteenth-Century Plague*, ed. Daniel Williman, 39–64. Binghamton, NY: Center for Medieval & Early Renaissance Studies, 1982.

Bettinzoli, Attilio. "Per una definizione delle presenze dantesche nel 'Decameron.'" *Studi sul Boccaccio* 13 (1981–2): 267–326.
- "Per una definizione delle presenze dantesche nel 'Decameron.'" *Studi sul Boccaccio* 14 (1983–4): 209–40.

Billanovich, Giuseppe. "La leggenda dantesca del Boccaccio." *Studi danteschi* 28 (1949): 45–144.

- *Restauri boccacceschi*. Rome: Edizioni di Storia e letteratura, 1947.
Bird, Otto. "The Canzone d'Amore of Cavalcanti According to the Commentary of Dino del Garbo." *Mediaeval Studies* 2 (1940): 150–203.
Black, Robert. *Education and Society in Florentine Tuscany: Teachers, Pupils and Schools*. Vol. 1. Leiden: Brill, 2007.
Bloom, Harold. *The Anxiety of Influence: A Theory of Poetry*. New York: Oxford University Press, 1973.
Boccaccio, Giovanni. *Decameron*. Edited by Vittore Branca. Turin: Einaudi, 1992.
- *Diana's Hunt/Caccia di Diana*. Translated and edited by Anthony K. Cassell and Victoria Kirkham. Philadelphia: University of Pennsylvania Press, 1991.
- *Le Esposizioni sopra la Comedia*. Edited by Giorgio Padoan. Milan: Mondadori, 1965.
- *Trattatello in laude di Dante*. Edited by Pier Giorgio Ricci. Milan: Mondadori, 2002.
- *Tutte le opere di Giovanni Boccaccio*. 10 vols. Edited by Vittore Branca. Milan: Mondadori, 1964–68.
- *Vite di Dante*. Edited by Pier G. Ricci. Milan: Mondadori, 2002.
- *Boccaccio's* Expositions on Dante's Comedy. Translated with an introduction by Michael Papio. Toronto: University of Toronto Press, 2009.
- *The Decameron*. Translated with an introduction by G.H. McWilliam. 2nd ed. New York: Penguin Books, 1995.
- *The Life of Dante (Trattatello in laude di Dante)*. Translated by Vincenzo Zin Bollettino. New York: Garland, 1990.
Boli, Todd. "Boccaccio's *Trattatello in laude di Dante*, Or Dante Resartus." *Renaissance Quarterly* 41.3 (1988): 389–412.
Bornstein, Diane. *The Lady in the Tower: Medieval Courtesy Literature for Women*. Hamden, CT: Archon, 1983.
Bragantini, Renzo, and Pier M. Forni. *Lessico critico decameroniano*. Turin: Bollati Boringhieri, 1995.
Branca, Vittore. *Boccaccio medievale*. 2nd ed. Florence: Sansoni, 1996.
- *Giovanni Boccaccio: Profilo biografico*. Florence: Sansoni, 1977.
Branca, Vittore, and Ennio Sandal. *Dante e Boccaccio: Lectura Dantis Scaligera, 2004–2005, in Memoria di Vittore Branca*. Rome/Padua: Antenore, 2006.
Branca, Vittore, and Maurizio Vitale. *Il capolavoro del Boccaccio e due diverse redazioni*. Venice: Istituto veneto di scienze, lettere ed arti, 2002.
Brett, E.M.K. "Avarice and Largesse: A Study of the Theme in Moral-Satirical Poetry in Provençal, Latin and Old French, 1100–1300." PhD diss., Cambridge University, 1986.
Brucker, Gene A. *Florentine Politics and Society, 1343–1378*. Princeton: Princeton University Press, 1962.

Bruni, Francesco. *Boccaccio: L'invenzione della letteratura mezzana.* Bologna: Il Mulino, 1990.
- *La città divisa: Parti e bene comune da Dante al Guicciardini.* Bologna: Il Mulino, 2003.
- "La proiezione dell'attualità politica sul passato: Note su cronisti, narratori, commentatori della *Commedia* nel XIV secolo." *Modern Philology* 101.2 (November 2003): 204–34.
Bullough, Vern L. "On Being a Male in the Middle Ages." In *Medieval Masculinities: Regarding Men in the Middle Ages,* ed. Claire Lees, 31–45. Minneapolis: University of Minnesota Press, 1994.
Bumke, Joachim. *Courtly Culture: Literature and Society in the High Middle Ages.* Berkeley: University of California Press, 1991.
Burnley, J. David. *Courtliness and Literature in Medieval England.* London: Longman, 1998.
Busby, Keith, and Erik Kooper, eds. *Courtly Literature: Culture and Context.* Amsterdam: J. Benjamins, 1990.
Cadden, Joan. *The Meanings of Sex Difference in the Middle Ages: Medicine, Science, and Culture.* Cambridge: Cambridge University Press, 1993.
Calvino, Italo. *Lezioni americane: Sei proposte per il prossimo millennio.* Milan: Garzanti, 1988.
Cardini, Franco. *L'acciar de' cavalieri: Studi sulla cavalleria nel mondo toscano e italico (sec. XII–XV).* Florence: Le Lettere, 1997.
- *Le cento novelle contro la morte: Giovanni Boccaccio e la rifondazione cavalleresca del mondo.* Rome: Salerno Editrice, 2007.
Catto, Jeremy. "Florence, Tuscany and the World of Dante." In *The World of Dante,* ed. Cecil Grayson, 1–17. Oxford: Clarendon, 1980.
Cervigni, Dino S. *From Divine to Human: Dante's Circle vs. Boccaccio's Parodic Centers.* Binghamton, NY: Center for Medieval & Renaissance Studies, 2009.
Cestaro, Gary. *Dante and the Grammar of the Nursing Body.* Notre Dame: Notre Dame University Press, 2003.
Cicero, Marcus Tullius. *De inventione; De optimo genere oratorum; Topica.* Edited by H.M. Hubbell. London: Heinemann, 1949.
- *De officiis.* Translated by Walter Miller. New York: Macmillan, 1913.
Cioffari, Vincenzo, ed. *Guido da Pisa's* Expositiones et glose super Comediam Dantis *or Commentary on Dante's Inferno.* Albany, NY: State University of New York Press, 1974.
Compagni, Dino. *Cronica.* Edited by Gino Luzzatto. Turin: Einaudi, 1978.
- *Dino Compagni's Chronicle of Florence.* Translated with an introduction and notes by Daniel E. Bornstein. Philadelphia: University of Pennsylvania Press, 1986.

Corazzini, Francesco. *Le lettere edite e inedite di Giovanni Boccaccio*. Florence: Sansoni, 1877.
Cornish, Alison. *Vernacular Translation in Dante's Italy: Illiterate Literature*. New York: Cambridge University Press, 2011.
Cottino-Jones, Marga. *Order from Chaos: Social and Aesthetic Harmonies in Boccaccio's* Decameron. Washington: University Press of America, 1982.
Crane, Susan. *Gender and Romance in Chaucer's* Canterbury Tales. Princeton: Princeton University Press, 1994.
Curtius, Ernst Robert. *European Literature and the Latin Middle Ages*. New York: Pantheon, 1953.
Dale, Sharon, Alison W. Lewin, and Duane J. Osheim, eds. *Chronicling History: Chroniclers and Historians in Medieval and Renaissance Italy*. University Park: Pennsylvania State University Press, 2007.
Dameron, George. *Florence and Its Church in the Age of Dante*. Philadelphia: University of Pennsylvania Press, 2005.
– "Revisiting the Italian Magnates." *Viator* 23 (1992): 259–82.
Davetian, Benet. *Civility: A Cultural History*. Toronto: University of Toronto Press, 2009.
Davidsohn, Robert. *Storia di Firenze*. Florence: Sansoni, 1956.
Davis, Charles T. *Dante's Italy, and Other Essays*. Philadelphia: University of Pennsylvania Press, 1984.
Delcorno, Carlo. "Note sui dantismi nell' 'Elegia di Madonna Fiammetta.'" *Studi sul Boccaccio* 11 (1979): 251–94.
Del Lungo, Isidoro. *Dante ne' tempi di Dante*. Bologna: Zanichelli, 1888.
– *La gente nuova in Firenze ai tempi di Dante*. Florence: Uffizio della Rassegna Nazionale, 1882.
del Monte, Alberto. "La storiografia fiorentina dei secoli xii e xiii." *Bulletino dell'Istituto storico italiano per il Medio Evo* 62 (1950): 175–282.
d'Entrèves, A.P. *Dante as a Political Thinker*. Oxford: Clarendon, 1952.
Diakité, Raola Isobel. "Writing Political Realities in Fourteenth-Century Italy: Giovanni Villani's *Nuova Cronica* and Dante's *Commedia*." PhD diss., Brown University, 2003.
Dispenza Crimi, Erminia Maria. *"Cortesia" e "valore" dalla tradizione a Dante*. Cosenza: Marra Editore, 1993.
Duby, Georges. *The Chivalrous Society*. Berkeley: University of California Press, 1977.
Dupin, Henri. *La courtoisie au moyen age (d'apres les textes du XIIe et du XIIIe siecle)*. Paris: Slatkine Reprints, 1931.
Durling, Robert. "Boccaccio on Interpretation: Guido's Escape (*Decameron* VI.9)." In *Dante, Petrarch, Boccaccio: Studies in the Italian Trecento in Honor of*

Charles S. Singleton, ed. Aldo S. Bernardo and Anthony L. Pellegrini, 273–304. Binghamton, NY: Medieval and Renaissance Texts and Studies, 1983.

Eisner, Martin G. *Boccaccio and the Invention of Italian Literature: Dante, Petrarch, Cavalcanti, and the Authority of the Vernacular*. Cambridge: Cambridge University Press, 2013.

Elias, Norbert. *The Civilizing Process: Sociogenetic and Psychogenetic Investigations*. Oxford: Blackwell, 2000.

Epstein, Steven. *Genoa and the Genoese, 958–1528*. Chapel Hill: University of North Carolina Press, 1996.

Fassò, Andrea. *Gioie cavalleresche: Barbarie e civiltà fra epica e lirica medievale*. Rome: Carocci, 2005.

Ferrante, Joan. "*Cortes'Amor* in Medieval Texts." *Speculum* 55 (1980): 686–95.

– "The Frame Characters in the *Decameron*: A Progression of Virtues." *Romance Philology* 19 (1965): 212–26.

– "History is Myth, Myth is History." In *Dante, mito e poesia. Atti del secondo Seminario dantesco internazionale*, ed. Michelangelo Picone and Tatiana Crivelli, 317–33. Florence: Franco Cesati, 1999.

– "Narrative Patterns in the *Decameron*." *Romance Philology* 31 (1978): 585–604.

– *The Political Vision of the* Divine Comedy. Princeton: Princeton University Press, 1984.

– "Politics, Finance and Feminism in *Decameron* II, 7." *Studi sul Boccaccio* 21 (1993): 151–74.

Ferreri, Rosario. "Ciacco, Biondello e Martellino." *Studi sul Boccaccio* 24 (1996): 231–49.

Fido, Franco. "Dante personaggio mancato del *Decameron*." In *Le metamorfosi del centauro*, 77–90. Rome: Bulzoni, 1977.

– *Le metamorfosi del centauro: Studi e letture da Boccaccio a Pirandello*. Rome: Bulzoni, 1977.

– *Il regime delle simmetrie imperfette: Studi sul 'Decameron.'* Milan: Franco Angeli, 1988.

– "The Tale of Ser Ciappelletto (I.1)." In *The* Decameron *First Day in Perspective: Volume One of the Lecturae Boccaccii*, ed. Elissa Weaver, 59–76. Toronto: University of Toronto Press, 2004.

Filosa, Elsa, and Michael Papio, eds. *Boccaccio in America. Proceedings of the 2010 International Boccaccio Conference at the University of Massachusetts Amherst*. Ravenna: Longo, 2012.

Flasch, Kurt. *Poesia dopo la peste: Saggio su Boccaccio*. Rome: Laterza, 1995.

Fleckenstein, Josef. *Curialitas: Studien zu Grundfragen der höfisch-Ritterlichen Kultur*. Göttingen: Vandenhoeck & Ruprecht, 1990.

Forni, Pier Massimo. *Adventures in Speech: Rhetoric and Narration in Boccaccio's Decameron*. Philadelphia: University of Pennsylvania Press, 1996.
– *Choosing Civility: The Twenty-Five Rules of Considerate Conduct*. New York: St. Martin's, 2002.
Galpin, Stanley L. *Cortois and Vilain: A Study of the Distinctions Made between Them by the French and Provençal Poets of the 12th, 13th and 14th Centuries*. New Haven, CT: Ryder's, 1905.
Getto, Giovanni, ed. *I Fioretti di San Francesco*. Milan: A. Martello, 1946.
– *Vita di forme e forme di vita nel 'Decameron.'* Turin: Petrini, 1958.
Gherardi, A., ed. *Le Consulte della repubblica fiorentina dell'anno MCCLXXX al MCCXCVIII*. Vol. 2. Florence: Sansoni, 1896–8.
Gilson, Simon. *Dante and Renaissance Florence*. New York: Cambridge University Press, 2005.
Ginsberg, Warren. *Chaucer's Italian Tradition*. Ann Arbor: University of Michigan Press, 2002.
Gittes, Tobias F. *Boccaccio's Naked Muse: Eros, Culture, and the Mythopoeic Imagination*. Toronto: University of Toronto Press, 2008.
– "Boccaccio's 'Valley of Women': Fetishized Foreplay in *Decameron* VI." *Italica* 76.2 (1999): 147–74.
Goldin, Frederick. *Lyrics of the Troubadours and Trouvères: An Anthology and a History*. Garden City, NY: Anchor, 1973.
Goldthwaite, Richard A. *The Building of Renaissance Florence: An Economic and Social History*. Baltimore: Johns Hopkins University Press, 1980.
Gorni, Guglielmo. "Invenzione e scrittura nel Boccaccio: Il caso di Guido Cavalcanti." *Letteratura italiana antica* 3 (2002): 359–74.
Grabher, Carlo. "Il culto del Boccaccio per Dante e alcuni aspetti delle sue opere dantesche." *Annali della Facoltà di Lettere e Filosofia dell'Università di Perugia* 5 (1967–8): 285–308.
Gragnolati, Manuele. "From Plurality to (Near) Unicity of Forms: Embryology in *Purgatorio* 25." In *Dante for the New Millennium*, ed. Teodolinda Barolini and H. Wayne Storey, 192–210. New York: Fordham University Press, 2003.
Grayson, Cecil, ed. *The World of Dante: Essays on Dante and His Times*. New York: Oxford University Press, 1980.
Green, Louis. *Chronicle into History: An Essay on the Interpretation of History in Florentine Fourteenth-Century Chronicles*. Cambridge: Cambridge University Press, 1972.
Greene, Thomas. "Forms of Accommodation in the *Decameron*." *Italica* 45 (1968): 297–313.
Grudin, Michaela Paasche, and Robert Grudin. *Boccaccio's* Decameron *and the Ciceronian Renaissance*. New York: Palgrave Macmillan, 2012.

Guerri, Domenico. *Il Commento del Boccaccio a Dante: Limiti della sua autenticità e questioni critiche che n'emergono.* Bari: Laterza, 1926.
Guido da Pisa. *Guida da Pisa's* Expositiones et Flose super Comediam Dantis *or* Commentary on Dante's Inferno. Edited by Vincenzo Cioffari. Albany: State University of New York Press, 1974.
Hagedorn, Suzanne C. *Abandoned Women: Rewriting the Classics in Dante, Boccaccio, & Chaucer.* Ann Arbor: University of Michigan Press, 2007.
Havely, Nicholas R. *Dante and the Franciscans: Poverty and the Papacy in the* Commedia. Cambridge: Cambridge University Press, 2004.
Heers, Jacques. *Parties and Political Life in the Medieval West.* Amsterdam, New York: North-Holland, 1977.
Hollander, Robert. *Boccaccio's Dante and the Shaping Force of Satire.* Ann Arbor: University of Michigan Press, 1997.
– "Boccaccio's Dante: Imitative Distance." *Studi sul Boccaccio* 13 (1981–2): 169–98.
– *Boccaccio's Last Fiction: Il "Corbaccio."* Phildelphia: University of Philadelphia Press, 1988.
– *Boccaccio's Two Venuses.* New York: Columbia University Press, 1977.
– *Dante's Epistle to Cangrande.* Ann Arbor: University of Michigan Press, 1993.
Holmes, George. "Dante and the Popes." In *The World of Dante*, ed. Cecil Grayson, 18–43. Oxford: Clarendon, 1980.
– *Florence, Rome and the Origins of the Renaissance.* Oxford: Clarendon, 1986.
Hortis, Attilio. *M.T. Cicerone nelle opere del Petrarca e del Boccaccio: Ricerche intorno alla storia della erudizione classica nel medio evo.* Trieste: Herrmanstorer, 1878.
Houston, Jason M. *Building a Monument to Dante: Boccaccio as* Dantista. Toronto: University of Toronto Press, 2010.
Hyde, John K. *Society and Politics in Medieval Italy: The Evolution of the Civil Life, 1000–1350.* New York: St. Martin's Press, 1973.
Jaeger, C. Stephen. *The Origins of Courtliness: Civilizing Trends and the Formation of Courtly Ideals, 939–1210.* Philadelphia: University of Pennsylvania Press, 1985.
Jones, P.J. "Florentine Families and Florentine Diaries in the Fourteenth Century." *Papers of the British School at Rome* 24 (1954): 183–205.
– *The Italian City-State: From Commune to Signoria.* New York: Oxford University Press, 1997.
Kamber, G. "Antitesi e sintesi in 'Nastagio degli Onesti.'" *Italica* 44 (1967): 61–8.
Kircher, Timothy. "The Modality of Moral Communication in the *Decameron*'s First Day, in Contrast to the Mirror of the *Exemplum*." *Renaissance Quarterly* 54.4 (2001): 1035–73.

- *The Poet's Wisdom: The Humanists, the Church, and the Formation of Philosophy in the Early Renaissance*. Leiden: Brill, 2006.
Kirkham, Victoria. *Fabulous Vernacular: Boccaccio's* Filocolo *and the Art of Medieval Fiction*. Ann Arbor: University of Michigan Press, 2001.
- "Painters at Play on the Judgment Day (*Decameron* VIII 9)." *Studi sul Boccaccio* 14 (1983–4): 256–77.
- "A Pedigree for Courtesy: 'Purser' Cured a Miser (Decameron 1.8)." *Studi sul Boccaccio* 25 (1997): 213–38.
- *The Sign of Reason in Boccaccio's Fiction*. Florence: Olschki, 1993.
- "The Tale of Guiglielmo Borsiere (I.8)." in *The* Decameron *First Day in Perspective*, ed. Elissa Weaver, 179–206. Toronto: University of Toronto Press, 2004.
Klapisch-Zuber, Christiane. "Nobles or Pariahs? The Exclusion of Florentine Magnates from the Thirteenth to the Fifteenth Centuries." *Comparative Studies in Society and History* 39.2 (1997): 215–30.
Kleinhenz, Christopher. "Dante as Reader and Critic of Courtly Literature." In *Courtly Literature: Culture and Context: Selected Papers from the 5th Triennial Congress of the International Courtly Literature Society*, ed. Keith Busby and Erik Kooper, 379–92. Amsterdam/Philadelphia: John Benjamins, 1990.
- *Medieval Italy: An Encyclopedia*. New York: Routledge, 2004.
Lansing, Carol. *The Florentine Magnates: Lineage and Faction in a Medieval Commune*. Princeton: Princeton University Press, 1991.
Lansing, Richard H. *Dante's Afterlife: The Influence and Reception of the* Commedia. New York: Routledge, 2003.
La Penna, Antonio. "Il ritratto 'paradossale' da Silla a Petronio." *Rivista di filologia e d'istruzione classica* 3.104 (1976): 270–93.
Latini, Brunetto. *Il Tesoretto: The Little Treasure*. Translated by Julia B. Holloway. New York: Garland Pub, 1981.
Le Goff, Jacques. *Time, Work & Culture in the Middle Ages*. Chicago: University of Chicago Press, 1980.
- *Your Money or Your Life: Economy and Religion in the Middle Ages*. New York: Zone Books, 1990.
Lee, A. Collingwood. *The* Decameron: *Its Sources and Analogues*. New York: Haskell House, 1972.
Lewis, C.S. *The Allegory of Love: A Study in Medieval Tradition*. Oxford: Clarendon, 1936.
Lo Cascio, Renzo. "Le nozioni di cortesia e di nobilita dei siciliani a Dante." In *Atti del Convegno di Studi su Dante e la Magna Curia*, ed. the Centro di Studi filologici e linguistici siciliani, 113–84. Palermo: Centro di studi filologici e linguistici siciliani, 1967.

Maggini, Francesco. "Il Boccaccio dantista." *Miscellanea storica della Valdelsa* 29 (1921): 116–22.
Marchesi, Simone. "'Epicuri de grege porcus': Ciacco, Epicurus and Isidore of Seville." *Dante Studies* 117 (1999): 117–31.
– "Intertextuality and Interdiscoursivity in the *Decameron*." *Heliotropia* 7.1–2 (2010): 31–50.
– *Stratigrafie decameroniane*. Florence: L.S. Olschki, 2004.
Marcus, Millicent Joy. *An Allegory of Form: Literary Self-Consciousness in the Decameron*. Saratoga, CA: Anma Libri, 1979.
Margoni, Ivos. *Fin'amors, mezura e cortezia: Saggio sulla lirica provenzale del XII secolo*. Milan: Istituto Editoriale Cisalpino, 1965.
Martines, Lauro. *Violence and Civil Disorder in Italian Cities, 1200–1500*. Berkeley: University of California Press, 1972.
– *The World at Play in Boccaccio's Decameron*. Princeton: Princeton University Press, 1986.
Masi, G. "I banchieri fiorentini nella vita politica della città sulla fine del Dugento." *Archivo giuridico* 9 (1931): 57–89.
– "La struttura sociale delle fazioni fiorentine politiche ai tempi di Dante." *Giornale dantesco* 31 (1928): 1–28.
Mazzoni, Francesco. "Guido da Pisa interprete di Dante e la sua fortuna presso Boccaccio." *Studi danteschi* 35 (1958): 29–128.
Mazzotta, Giuseppe. *Dante, Poet of the Desert: History and Allegory in the* Divine Comedy. Princeton: Princeton University Press, 1979.
– *The World at Play in Boccaccio's* Decameron. Princeton: Princeton University Press, 1986.
Meier, Franziska F. "The *Novellino* or 'How to Do Things with Words': An Early Italian Reflection on a Specific Western Way of Using Language." *MLN* 125.1 (2010): 1–25.
Menocal, Maria Rosa. *Writing in Dante's Cult of Truth: From Borges to Boccaccio*. Durham: Duke University Press, 1991.
Migiel, Marilyn. *A Rhetoric of the* Decameron. Toronto: University of Toronto Press, 2003.
Morandini, Francesca, ed. *Statuti delle arti dei fornai e dei vinattieri di Firenze (1337–1339)*. Florence: Olschki, 1956.
Muscetta, Carlo. *Giovanni Boccaccio*. Bari: Laterza, 1972.
Najemy, John N. *Corporatism and Consensus in Florentine Electoral Politics, 1280–1400*. Chapel Hill: University of North Carolina Press, 1982.
– "Dante and Florence." In *The Cambridge Companion to Dante*, 80–99. Cambridge: Cambridge University Press, 1993.
– *A History of Florence 1200–1575*. Oxford: Blackwell, 2006.

Neri, Ferdinando. "Dante e il primo Villani." *Giornale dantesco* 20 (1912): 1–31.
- "Il disegno ideale del *Decameron*." In *Storia e poesia*, 51–60. Turin: Chiantore, 1944.
Nigro, Salvatore, ed. *Il Novellino*. Bari: Laterza, 1975.
Nissen, Christopher. *Ethics and Retribution in the* Decameron *and the Late Medieval Italian Novella: Beyond the Circle*. Lewiston, NY: Mellen University Press, 1993.
Noakes, Susan. "Dino Compagni and the Vow in San Giovanni: *Inferno* XIX, 16–21." *Dante Studies* 86 (1968): 41–61.
- "Virility, Nobility, and Banking: The Crossing of Discourses in the Tenzione with Forese." In *Dante for the New Millennium*, ed. Teodolinda Barolini and H. Wayne Storey, 241–58. New York: Fordham University Press, 2003.
Ó Cuilleanáin, Cormac. *Religion and the Clergy in Boccaccio's* Decameron. Rome: Edizioni di Storia e Letteratura, 1984.
Olschki, Leonardo. *The Myth of Felt*. Berkeley: University of California Press, 1949.
Olson, Kristina M. "'Concivis meus': Petrarch's *Rerum memorandarum libri* 2.60, Boccaccio's *Decameron* 6.9, and the Specter of Dino del Garbo." *Annali d'italianistica* 22 (2004): 375–80.
- "Resurrecting Dante's Florence: Figural Realism in the *Decameron* and the *Esposizioni*." *MLN* 124.1 (2009): 45–65.
Osmond, Patricia J. "Catiline in Florence and Fiesole: The Medieval and Renaissance After-life of a Roman Conspirator." *International Journal of the Classical Tradition* 7 (2000–1): 3–38.
[Ottimo] *L'ultima forma dell'Ottimo commento: Chiose sopra la Comedia di Dante Alleghieri fiorentino tracte da diversi ghiosatori: Inferno*. Edited by Claudia Di Fonzo. Ravenna: Longo Editore, 2008.
Ottokar, Nicola. *Il Comune di Firenze alla fine del Dugento*. Turin: Einaudi, 1962.
Padoan, Giorgio. *Il Boccaccio, le muse, il Parnaso e l'Arno*. Biblioteca di lettere italiane: Studi e testi 21. Florence: Olschki, 1978.
- "Colui che fece per viltà il gran rifiuto." *Studi danteschi* 38 (1961): 75–128.
- *L'ultima opera di Boccaccio: Le Esposizioni sopra il Dante*. Padua: CEDAM, 1959.
Panvini, Bruno. *Le rime della scuola siciliana*. Florence: Olschki, 1962.
Papio, Michael. *Keen and Violent Remedies: Social Satire and the Grotesque in Masuccio Salernitano's "Novellino."* New York: Peter Lang, 2000.
Parker, Deborah. *Commentary and Ideology: Dante and the Renaissance*. Durham: Duke University Press, 1993.
Parodi, Ernesto Giacomo. "La miscredenza di Guido Cavalcanti e una fonte del Boccaccio." *Bulletino della società dantesca* 22 (1915): 37–47.
Petrarca, Francesco. *Rerum memorandarum libri.* Edited by Giuseppe Billanovich. Florence: Sansoni, 1943.

Picone, Michelangelo. "La brigata di Folgore fra Dante e Boccaccio." In *Il Giuoco della vita bella: Folgore da San Gimignano: Studi e testi*, 25–40. San Gimignano: Città di San Gimignano, 1988.
- *Il giuoco della vita bella: Folgore da San Gimignano*. San Gimignano: Studi e testi San Gimignano, 1988.
- "The Tale of Bergamino" (I.7). In *The* Decameron *First Day in Perspective: Volume One of the Lecturae Boccaccii*, ed. Elissa B. Weaver, 160–78. Toronto: University of Toronto Press, 2004.

Porcelli, Bruno. *Dante maggiore e Boccaccio minore: Strutture e modelli*. Pisa: Giardini, 1987.

Porta, Giuseppe. "La costruzione della storia in Giovanni Villani." In *Il senso della storia nella cultura medievale italiana (1100–1350)*, 125–38. Pistoia: Centro italiano di studi di storia e d'arte, 1995.
- "Giovanni Villani storico e scrittore." In *I racconti di Clio: Tecniche narrative della storiografia*, 147–56. Pisa: Nistri-Lischi, 1989.

Potter, Joy Hambuechen. *Five Frames for the* Decameron*: Communication and Social Systems in the Cornice*. Princeton: Princeton University Press, 1982.

Powell, James M. *Albertanus of Brescia: The Pursuit of Happiness in the Early Thirteenth Century*. Philadelphia: University of Pennsylvania Press, 1992.

Quaglio, Antonio Enzo. "Prima fortuna della glossa garbiana a 'Donna me prega' del Cavalcanti." *Giornale storico della letteratura italiana* 141 (1964): 336–68.

Ramat, Raffaello. "Indicazioni per una lettura del 'Decameron.'" In *Scritti su Giovanni Boccaccio*, ed. Sergio Gensini, 7–19. Florence: Olschki, 1964.

Raveggi, Sergio, Massimo Tarassi, Daniela Medici, and Patrizia Parenti. *Ghibellini, guelfi e popolo grasso: I detentori del potere politico a Firenze nella seconda metà del Dugento*. Florence: La nuova Italia, 1978.

Richardson, Brian. "The 'Ghibelline' Narrator in the *Decameron*." *Italian Studies* 33 (1978): 20–8.

Roncaglia, Aurelio, and Anna Ferrari. *Le origini della lingua e della letteratura italiana*. Turin: UTET libreria, 2006.

Rorty, Richard. *Contingency, Irony, and Solidarity*. Cambridge: Cambridge University Press, 1989.

Rossi, Luciano. "In luogo di sollazzo: I *fabliaux* del *Decameron*." In *Leggiadre donne: Novella e racconto breve in Italia*, ed. Francesco Bruni, 13–27. Venice: Marsilio, 2000.

Rubinstein, Nicolai. "The Beginnings of Political Thought in Florence: A Study in Mediaeval Historiography." *Journal of the Warburg and Courtauld Institutes* 5 (1942): 198–227.

Ruggieri, Ruggero M. *L'umanesimo cavalleresco italiano da Dante al Pulci*. Rome: Edizioni dell'Ateneo, 1962.

Russo, Luigi. *Lettere critiche del 'Decameron.'* Bari: Laterza, 1956.
Russo, Vittorio. *Con le Muse in Parnaso: Tre studi sul Boccaccio.* Naples: Bibliopolis, 1983.
Salernitano, Masuccio. *Il Novellino.* Edited by Salvatore S. Nigro. Bari: Laterza, 1975.
Salvemini, Gaetano. *Magnati e popolani in Firenze dal 1280 al 1295.* Turin: Einaudi, 1960.
Sansone, Giuseppe. *La nozione di cortesia nei testi didattici di lingua d'oc.* Rome: Editrice ELIA, 1975.
Sapori, Armando. *La crisi delle compagnie mercantile dei Bardi e dei Peruzzi.* Florence: Olschki, 1926.
– *I libri della ragione bancaria dei Gianfigliazzi.* Milan: Garzanti, 1946.
Scaglione, Aldo. *Knights at Court: Courtliness, Chivalry, and Courtesy from Ottonian Germany to the Italian Renaissance.* Berkeley: University of California Press, 1991.
Scarabelli, L., ed. *Commedia di Dante degli Allagherii col commento di Iacopo di Giovanni della Lana Bolognese.* 3 vols. Milan: Civelli, 1864–5.
Schiaffini, Alfredo, ed. *Testi fiorentini del Dugento e dei primi del Trecento.* Florence: Sansoni, 1954.
Schnapp, Jeffrey. *The Transfiguration of History at the Center of Dante's Paradise.* Princeton: Princeton University Press, 1982.
Scott, John A. *Dante's Political Purgatory.* Philadelphia: University of Philadelphia Press, 1996.
– *Understanding Dante.* Notre Dame, IN: University of Notre Dame Press, 2004.
Segre, Cesare. "La novella di Nastagio degli Onesti (*Dec.* V, 8): I due tempi della visione." In *In ricordo di Cesare Angelini: Studi di letteratura e filologia*, ed. Franco Alessio and Angelo Stella, 65–74. Milan: Saggiatore, 1979.
Sherberg, Michael. *The Governance of Friendship: Law and Gender in the Decameron.* Columbus: Ohio State University Press, 2011.
Smarr, Janet Levarie. *Boccaccio and Fiammetta: The Narrator as Lover.* Urbana: University of Illinois Press, 1986.
– "Symmetry and Balance in the *Decameron*." *Medievalia* 2 (1976): 159–87.
Spani, Giovanni. "Il vino di Boccaccio: Usi e abusi in alcune novelle del *Decameron*." *Heliotropia* 8–9 (2011–12): 79–98.
Spiegel, Gabrielle M. *The Past as Text: The Theory and Practice of Medieval Historiography.* Baltimore: Johns Hopkins University Press, 1997.
Stefani, Marchionne di Coppo. *Cronica fiorentina di Marchionne di Coppo Stefani.* Edited by Niccolò Rodolico. Città di Castello: S. Lapi, 1903.
Steinberg, Justin. *Accounting for Dante: Urban Readers and Writers in Late Medieval Italy.* Notre Dame: University of Notre Dame Press, 2007.

Stewart, Pamela D. "La novella di madonna Oretta e le due parti del *Decameron*." *Yearbook of Italian Studies* (1973–5): 27–39.

Stone, Gregory B. *The Ethics of Nature in the Middle Ages: On Boccaccio's Poetaphysics*. New York: St. Martin's, 1998.

Tassi, Luigi. *Disquisizione istorica intorno all'autore dei Fioretti di S. Francesco*. Fabriano: Tipografia Gentile, 1883.

Trabalza, Ciro. *Esempi di analisi letteraria*. Turin: G.B. Paravia, 1925.

Trachtenberg, Marvin. "Founding the Palazzo Vecchio in 1299: The Corso Donati Paradox." *Renaissance Quarterly* 52 (1999): 966–93.

Trucchi, Francesco, ed. *Poesie italiane inedite di Dugento autori dall'origine della lingua infino al secolo decimosettimo*. Prato: Guasti, 1846.

Usher, Jonathan. "Boccaccio, Cavalcanti's Canzone 'Donna me prega' and Dino's Glosses." *Heliotropia* 2.1 (2004). http://www.brown.edu/Departments/Italian_Studies/heliotropia/02-01/usher.pdf (last accessed 12 March 2014).

– "Paolo and Francesca in the *Filocolo* and the *Esposizioni*." *Lectura Dantis* [*virginiana*] 10 (Spring 1992): 22–33.

Vallone, Aldo. *La 'cortesia' dai provenzali a Dante*. Palermo: Palumbo, 1950.

Vandelli, Giuseppe. *Giovanni Boccaccio: Editore di Dante*. Florence: Accademia della Crusca per la lingua d'Italia, 1923.

Veglia, Marco. *"La Vita Lieta": Una lettura del* Decameron. Ravenna: Longo, 2000.

Velli, Giuseppe. *Petrarca e Boccaccio: Tradizione-memoria-scrittura*. Padua: Antenore, 1979.

– "Seneca nel *Decameron*." *Giornale storico della letteratura italiana* 168 (1991): 321–34.

Villani, Giovanni. *Nuova cronica*. Edited by Giuseppe Porta. Parma: Guanda, 1990-91.

– *Villani's Chronicle: Being Selections from the First Nine Books of the* Croniche Fiorentine *of Giovanni Villani*. Translated by Rose E. Selfe. London: Archibald Constable & Co. Ltd, 1906.

Vitullo, Juliann, and Diane Wolfthal. "Trading Values: Negotiating Masculinity in Late Medieval and Early Modern Europe." In *Money, Morality, and Culture in Late Medieval and Early Modern Europe*, ed. Juliann Vitullo and Diane Wolfthal, 155–96. Burlington, VT: Ashgate, 2010.

Wallace, David. *Chaucerian Polity: Absolutist Lineages and Associational Forms in England and Italy*. Stanford: Stanford University Press, 1997.

– *Boccaccio*: Decameron. Cambridge: Cambridge University Press, 1991.

Watson, Paul. "On Seeing Guido Cavalcanti and the Houses of the Dead." *Studi sul Boccaccio* 18 (1989): 301–18.

Weaver, Elissa, ed. *The* Decameron *First Day in Perspective: Volume One of the Lecturae Boccaccii*. Toronto: University of Toronto Press, 2004.
Webb, Heather. *The Medieval Heart*. New Haven, CT: Yale University Press, 2010.
West, Constance B. *Courtoisie in Anglo-Norman Literature*. New York: Haskell House, 1966.
White, Hayden. *The Content of the Form: Narrative Discourse and Historical Representation*. Baltimore: Johns Hopkins University Press, 1987.
– *Figural Realism: Studies in the Mimesis Effect*. Baltimore: Johns Hopkins University Press, 1999.
Whitman, Jon. *Interpretation and Allegory: Antiquity to the Modern Period*. Leiden: Brill, 2000.
Wilkins, Ernest H. *Studies on Petrarch and Boccaccio.* Padua: Antenore, 1978.
Witt, Ronald. "The Early Communal Historians, Forerunners of the Italian Humanists." In *The Renaissance in the Streets, Schools, and Studies: Essays in Honour of Paul F. Grendler*, ed. Konrad Eisenbichler, Paul F. Grendler, and Nicholas Terpstra, 103–24. Toronto: Centre for Reformation and Renaissance Studies, 2008.
– *In the Footsteps of the Ancients: The Origins of Humanism from Lovato to Bruni*. Leiden: Brill, 2000.

Index

Acciaiuoli, Nicola, 11, 18–20
Acquasparta, Matteo, 82, 84, 86–7
Alberighi family (*Par.* 16), 140, 143, 177, 219n41
    Federigo degli Alberighi (*Dec.* 5.9), 176–81, 219n42, 219n44
Albert the Great, 168, 217n28
Alighieri, Dante
    anti-clerical sentiment of, 99–100, 105–6, 110, 112, 208n33
    on Boniface VIII, 115–16
    Cacciaguida and, 33, 56, 103–4, 194n20
    on Charles I, 157, 163
    Commedia, 22–5, 35, 45, 129; anti-clerical sentiment in, 99–100, 112, 116; *cortesia* and, 14, 17, 42, 141, 144, 155, 176, 183, 195n28; Dante's exile and, 96–7, 99–103, 109–10, 120–1, 137, 141, 175–6; *Inferno*, 67, 207n19; *Inferno* 1, 101, 115, 127, 129, 132–3; *Inferno* 6, 57–8, 67–73, 83, 96; *Inferno* 7, 85, 123; *Inferno* 8, 67, 95; *Inferno* 10, 164; *Inferno* 13, 175, 178; *Inferno* 15, 33–4, 68; *Inferno* 16, 17, 26, 33–9, 43–5, 55–6, 64, 132, 146, 148–9, 184; *Inferno* 17, 132, 134, 136; *Inferno* 19, 99; *Inferno* 23, 105–6; *Inferno* 29, 178; *Inferno* 33, 41–2; and nostalgia, 34, 40, 176; *Paradiso* 7, 16; *Paradiso* 8, 163; *Paradiso* 16, 32, 34, 56–7, 60, 64, 134, 139–40, 143, 177, 181; *Paradiso* 17, 17, 102–4, 110, 155; as political text, 3, 23, 57–8; *Purgatorio* 6, 64; *Purgatorio* 7, 140–3, 149, 151–4, 157–8, 163, 167, 170; *Purgatorio* 8, 140, 143–9, 151–2, 154, 167–8; *Purgatorio* 14, 17, 140, 142–3, 168–73, 175–6; *Purgatorio* 16, 17, 106, 140, 142, 154–5; *Purgatorio* 17, 33; *Purgatorio* 20, 121–2, 163; *Purgatorio* 24, 73–4, 76; *Purgatorio* 25, 168; read by Cangrande, 102, 106–8; realism, in contrast with *Decameron*, 44–5
    Convivio, 6, 10, 13–14, 16, 26, 33, 141, 147–9, 183
    on Corso Donati, 71, 73–4
    cortesia and, 3, 5–6, 13–17, 26, 32–4, 147–8, 168, 183–4, 189n66
    De vulgari eloquentia, 14, 191n92, 200n15

exile of, 4, 17, 20–2, 96–7, 101–3, 110, 121, 137, 143, 175
on Guelph-Ghibelline conflict, 139
influences on, 10, 13–14
Malaspina family and, 137, 146
"Morte villana, di pietà nemica," 16
negative view of Genoese, 41–2
on nobility, 151–4
nostalgia for lost *cortesia*, 6, 10, 53, 140–2, 154–5, 157
popolo and, 97, 192n94
relationship with Cangrande, 101–3, 107–10
view of history, 57–9
on virility, 157–8, 167–8
Vita nuova, 14–16
Anastagi family (*Purg.* 14), 22, 140, 142, 169, 170, 173, 175–7
Guido degli Anastagi (*Dec.* 5.8), 173–4
Andreuccio di Pietro (*Dec.* 2.5), 122, 214n9
Angevin court, 18–19, 22, 55, 59–60
Aquinas, Thomas, 101, 163, 168, 205n8, 209–10n48, 217n28
Argenti, Filippo (*Inf.* 8; *Dec.* 9.8), 58–9, 65–7, 94–6, 114, 204n68
Aristotle, 4, 101, 168, 205n7, 217n28, 218n40
definition of avarice, 122–3, 130
Arrighi, Oddo, 31
Ascoli, Albert Russell, 22
Auerback, Erich, 22
avarice (*avarizia*), 120–30, 137, 183
Aristotle's definition of, 122–3, 130
of Cangrande, 102, 104
of Cerchi family, 52, 84, 99, 115
of church figures, 99–101, 110–14, 123, 126, 137
contrasted with *cortesia*, 10–12, 17–18, 21–2, 57, 65, 97, 99–100, 120

of Ermino Grimaldi (*Dec.* 1.8), 40–1
of Florence, 35
of *gente nuova*, 53, 57, 64, 97
lupa as, 128–30
of merchant class, 22, 120–6, 128–30, 137
mythological origins of, 124
of Pope Boniface VIII, 17
remedied by *cortesia*, 132
remedied by liberality, 101, 130
usury and, 130
Avarizia, Ermino. *See* Grimaldi, Ermino de'
Avicenna, 168, 217n28

Baratto, Mario, 43, 45, 195n34, 196n37, 207n23
Barbarossa, Frederick, 30
Bardi family, 59–61
Bardi banking company, 18, 59–60, 120, 200n8, 208n38
Barolini, Teodolinda, 16, 22, 172, 189n68, 196n36, 196n40, 205n7, 210n51, 210n53, 213n75
Baronci family (*Dec.* 6.6), 140
Barsella, Susanna, 209n48
Bartolomeo della Scala (*Par.* 17), 33, 102
Battle of Campaldino (1289), 74
Becker, Marvin, 22, 26–7, 184, 192n93, 200n15, 219n47
Benincasa da Laterina (*Purg.* 6), 112
Bergamino (*Dec.* 1.7), 40, 103–8, 110–13, 116, 196n35, 207n23
Beritola, Madonna (*Dec.* 2.6), 141, 143–4, 147, 149–52, 154
Bernardino da Polenta, 19
Bertran de Born, 10
Bettinzoli, Attilo, 25, 191n89
Biondello (*Dec.* 9.8), 65–7, 72, 84–5, 93, 96, 114

Index 239

Black Death, 4, 30, 42, 57, 61, 86
Boccaccio, Giovanni
 affinity for Corso Donati, 58–9, 63–4, 71, 73, 74, 77, 84–6, 97, 182
 affinity for Grimaldi family, 43
 Amorosa visione, 18, 25, 135, 189n74, 200n17, 213n71
 anti-clerical views of, 105–6, 114–16, 127, 137
 Bardi banking company and, 59–60
 on Boniface VIII, 98, 99–100, 119
 Caccia di Diana, 18
 Comedia delle ninfe fiorentine, 189n74
 cortesia and, 3–6, 17–18, 25–7, 29–30, 43, 53, 94, 137–8, 147–9, 182–4
 courtly experiences of, 18–20, 59–60
 Dante's exile and, 17, 20, 96–7
 Decameron, 17, 22–4, 98 (*see also individual chapters*); anti-clerical sentiment in, 99–100; as history, 3, 23–4, 30, 71, 84–5, 151, 164, 193n4; merchant class in, 120, 122–3, 125–6
 Decameron 1.1, 101, 120–2, 130, 137
 Decameron 1.2, 130
 Decameron 1.6, 105–6, 130, 137
 Decameron 1.7, 100, 102–6, 108, 110–11, 116, 130, 137, 140–1, 154–5
 Decameron 1.8, 3, 6, 27–8, 34–5, 39–42, 49, 69, 92, 104, 130, 137, 149
 Decameron 2.4, 41
 Decameron 2.6, 137, 140–1, 143, 147, 149–59, 167, 170–1, 216n24
 Decameron 2.7, 42, 61
 Decameron 2.8, 186n17
 Decameron 3.7, 127
 Decameron 4.1, 150, 217n31
 Decameron 5.4, 137, 140, 142, 168–73, 176–7, 218n32

Decameron 5.8, 9, 137, 140, 142, 168–70, 173–7, 182
Decameron 5.9, 140, 143, 176–81
Decameron 6.2, 59, 86–7, 89–94
Decameron 6.4, 135–6, 177–9
Decameron 6.6, 140, 214n13
Decameron 6.9, 27, 34–9, 44–54, 57, 78, 86, 96, 136, 176, 182
Decameron 9.8, 58–9, 65–7, 69–72, 84–6, 94–6, 114, 179; motif of the Arno in, 66, 93, 114–15; source for, 218n40
Decameron 10.2, 110–19, 137
Decameron 10.3, 101, 133–4, 137
Decameron 10.6, 100, 137, 140, 142, 157–61, 163, 167–8, 172
Decameron 10.7, 137, 140, 142, 157–8, 161–2, 168
Decameron 10.10, 182–3
De casibus virorum illustrium, 3, 18, 60–1, 182, 214n11
distaste for *gente nuova*, 4, 55, 56–7, 62, 64, 71, 94, 183
Elegia di Madonna Fiammetta, 18, 20, 25, 189n74
Epistole, 18–19, 59, 189n74; *Consolatoria (Epistola a Pino de' Rossi)*, 64
Esposizioni sopra la Comedia di Dante, 22–5; avarice in, 130, 137; Cangrande and, 108; critique of merchant class in, 28, 58, 98, 100; as history, 3, 30, 71, 84–5, 136, 151, 164; merchant class in, 120, 125, 182; Villani as source for, 78, 80, 165, 199n3
Esposizioni 1, 115–16, 127–33
Esposizioni 3, 117, 119, 122
Esposizioni 6, 57–8, 69–70, 88, 94, 96; banquets in, 91–2; Boniface VIII

240   Index

in, 121; Cerchi family in, 72–3, 82; Corso Donati in, 77–9, 114; Florentine political struggle in, 82–4, 199n3
Esposizioni 7, 85, 101, 127; avarice in, 122, 127–8, 130, 134
Esposizioni 8, 59, 95–6
Esposizioni 10, 155–8, 172; Guelph-Ghibelline conflict in, 137, 164–7
Esposizioni 16, 26, 35–9, 56, 69, 78, 84, 141, 147–9, 183; Borsiere in, 69; *brigate* in, 36–8, 45–6
Esposizioni 17, 132
Filocolo, 18, 189n74
Filostrato, 18
on Frederick II, 154–5
gente nuova origins, 57, 60, 199n2
as historian, 65, 71, 84–5, 97–8
influence of Dante on, 4, 22–5, 28, 137, 163
on nobility, 152–3, 156
nostalgia for lost *cortesia*, 6, 26, 140–1
political preferences of, 25–6, 49, 55, 58–9, 80, 84–6
Teseida, 18
Trattatello in laude di Dante, 20, 22, 25, 30, 106–7
veltro and, 130–2
on vices of merchant class, 120–7, 129–30, 137
view of history, 57–9, 150–1, 163–4
Boccaccio, Vanni, 60
Boniface VIII (*Inf.* 19; *Dec.* 1.1, 6.2, 10.2), 17, 57–8, 82–3, 84, 86–7, 116–20, 123, 208n31, 208n34, 208n36, 213n75
avarice of, 110, 112
Boccaccio's view of, 98–100, 114–17, 119
Dante's exile and, 137

Dante's view of, 115–16
Guelph conflict and, 68, 115–16, 121
Bonvesin de la Riva, 12
Borghesi, Coppo di Domenico (*Dec.* 5.9, 9.8), 177, 218n40
Borsiere, Guiglielmo (*Inf.* 16; *Dec.* 1.8), 3–4, 6, 22, 27–8, 33–4, 37–40, 42–4, 47, 49, 67, 69–70, 92, 95, 132, 146, 149, 194n25, 195n26
contrasted with Ciacco, 69–70
diplomatic abilities of, 93
Branca, Vittore, 19, 24, 59–60, 122, 126, 135, 174, 189n75, 190n81, 191n88, 194n23, 195n30, 199n2, 201n38, 202n41, 202n42, 208n29, 209n44, 209n46, 210n52, 211n59, 214n6, 214n7, 214n10, 216n20, 216n22
Brescia, Albertano da, 30
brigate, 35–8, 45–7, 51–4, 135, 149, 178
Brucker, Gene A., 22, 54, 60–2, 100
Brunelleschi, Betto (*Dec.* 6.9), 27–8, 34–5, 45, 47–52, 57, 71, 86, 197n47
diplomatic abilities of, 93
as member of Guelph party, 76, 89
Brunelleschi family, 27, 51
Bruni, Francesco, 23–4, 179, 190n84, 201n37, 217n30, 219n42
Buondelmonte dei Buondelmonti, murder of, 31–2, 53, 139, 165, 213n1
Buondelmonti family, 56
Burnley, J. David, 7

Cacciaguida degli Elisei (*Par.* 15–17), 32–3, 56–7, 60–2, 102–3, 134, 143, 177, 179, 181, 194n20, 219n42
Calboli family, 142, 169–70
Rineri da Calboli (*Purg.* 14), 169–71
Calimala guild, 61
Cambi, Nero, 87–8

Cangrande della Scala (*Par.* 17; *Dec.* 1.7), 99–111, 116, 130, 143, 155
  relationship with Dante, 101–3, 107–10, 137
  reputation for liberality of, 100, 102–3, 111–12, 120
  temporary avarice of, 104, 147, 196n35
Capece, Arrighetto (*Dec.* 2.6), 143–4, 147, 151–2, 214n6
Capellanus, Andreas, 9, 175
  De amore libri, 9
Capet, Hugh, 121, 163
Cardenal, Piere, 10–1
Cardini, Franco, 22, 47, 49, 55, 197n43, 197n45, 199n66
Castracani, Castruccio, 136
castration, 142, 157, 172
Caterina da Valbona (*Dec.* 5.4), 142, 171–2, 176, 218n34
Catiline (Lucius Sergius Catilina), 75–6
Cavalcanti, Guido (*Dec.* 6.9), 27, 34–5, 37, 45, 47, 49–51, 57, 96, 108, 176, 196n40, 197n49
Cavalcanti, Mainardo, 19
Cavalcanti, Masino, 51
Cavalcanti family, 27, 50–1
Celestine V (*Inf.* 3), 117–18
Cerchi family (*Par.* 16), 45, 56–8, 62–3, 79–80, 84–5
  avarice of, 52, 84, 115
  conflict with Donati family, 17, 46–7, 53, 57, 62, 71–3, 75, 79–82, 97, 199n4
  conflict with Spini family, 87–8
  as *gente nuova*, 28, 34, 43, 52–3, 55, 56, 61–2, 94
  Guelph party conflict and, 45, 63
  as *popolani*, 86, 129–30
  Ricoverino de' Cerchi, 88

Vieri de' Cerchi (*Dec.* 9.8), 27, 53, 55, 57, 65, 71, 73, 79–80, 96–7, 99, 198n54; contrasted with Corso Donati, 8; contrasted with Federigo degli Alberighi, 179; as *gente nuova*, 57; Pope Boniface and, 83–4
  wealth of, 72–3, 79–80
Charles I. *See* Charles of Anjou
Charles II, 118, 135
Charles of Anjou (*Purg.* 7; *Dec.* 10.6), 139, 140, 143, 150–1, 153, 157–64
  sexual restraint of, 159–61, 216n21
  virility of, 142, 164, 167
Charles of Valois (*Purg.* 20; *Dec.* 1.1), 75, 83, 84, 90, 110, 119, 121–2
chivalric mentality, 3, 25, 29–34, 44, 149
  cortesia and, 34, 45, 176
  urban mentality and, 194n18
  violence and, 30–1
Ciacco (*Inf.* 6; *Dec.* 9.8), 22, 27, 58–9, 65–73, 78, 80, 83, 84–5, 94–6, 114, 198n54, 201n39
Cicero, Marcus Tullius, 4, 8, 15, 29–30, 47, 75, 183, 189n71, 219n46
  De officiis, 4, 8, 17, 188n52
Cisti the Baker (*Dec.* 6.2), 59, 86–7, 89–94, 119, 203n58
civilité, 7, 185n4
Clement V, 110, 119
Cluny, Abbot of (*Dec.* 1.7, 10.2), 100, 104–6, 110–16, 118–19, 130, 213n75
Commedia. *See under* Alighieri, Dante
Compagni, Dino, 23, 27, 31–2, 46–50, 87–9, 90–1, 93, 203n54
  on Corso Donati, 58–9, 71, 73–7
  Cronica, 47–8, 75, 77, 88, 90–1, 122
  on Guelph-Ghibelline conflict, 139
Conradin (*Purg.* 20; *Dec.* 10.6), 160, 163
cortesia, 3–22, 25–7, 140, 182–4

of aristocratic families, 57, 63, 71, 73, 86, 136, 140, 144–7, 173
Boccaccio and, 25–7, 94
of Cangrande, 102, 110, 155
of Cavalcanti, 50
chivalric mentality and, 176
chivalry as, 29–32, 34, 45
as civic ethic, 29–30, 34, 47, 141, 182–3
contrasted with avarice, 10–12, 17–18, 21–2, 57, 65, 97, 99–100, 120
of Corso Donati, 93, 99
courtesy books and, 11–12
courtliness and, 4–5
courtly love and, 11, 142, 180
in *Decameron* 1.8, 104
in *Decameron* 10.10, 183
differing definitions of, 4–5, 7, 147–9, 183–4, 191n92, 214n8
of Donati family, 66, 99
erotic connotations of, 12, 14–16
etymological origins of, 8–9
female desire and, 170, 172–3
future of, 140–2, 154, 156–7, 171–2, 176, 182–4
geographic location of, 12, 99, 141, 144, 148–9, 154–5, 183
Ghibelline party and, 137, 155, 182
God as source of, 189n66
in *Inferno* 16, 33–4, 184
in *Inferno* 33, 42
lacking in Genoese, 42–3
lacking in *gente nuova*, 43, 45, 53, 58
lacking in merchant class, 28, 86, 89
larghezza as, 13, 15
liberality and, 12–13, 22, 111–12, 148
of magnate families, 65–6
of Malaspina family, 144–7, 154
nobility gained through, 12

nostalgia for lost, 5–6, 10, 13, 18, 34, 135, 138, 140–1, 154–5
as *onestade*, 15
of Peter III, 161–2
in *Purgatorio* 8, 146–7
as remedy for avarice, 132
role of women in survival of, 173, 175
sexual desire and, 142, 157, 161, 167–8
superficial nature of, 92–3
theoretical origins of, 6–7
in Tuscan commune, 33
violence and, 27, 175–6
courtesy books, 5, 11–13
courtliness, 4–9, 193n9
courtly ethics, 5, 7
courtly love, 9, 168, 175
cortesia and, 11, 142, 180
courtois, 7–8
Cronica fiorentina compilata nel secolo XIII, 27, 31
curiae, 8, 29
curialis, 8, 14
curialitas, 8, 29, 191n92

Dameron, George, 22, 27, 30, 86, 89, 193n3, 204n63, 205n5
Dante. *See* Alighieri, Dante
Davis, Charles, 33, 194n20
Decameron. *See under* Boccaccio, Giovanni
De Robertis, Domenico, 148, 191n92
dispositio, 35
Donati, Corso (*Purg.* 24; *Dec.* 9.8), 25, 28, 46–50, 62–3, 71–84, 93, 113–14, 202n46, 203n98
Boccaccio's affinity for, 55, 58–9, 63–4, 71, 73, 74, 77–8, 84–6, 97, 182
Compagni on, 74–7
contrasted with Currado Gianfigliazzi, 134, 136

contrasted with Federigo degli
    Alberighi, 177, 179
contrasted with Vieri de Cerchi, 8, 71
cortesia of, 93, 99
death of, 47–8, 74–7, 120
in *Decameron* 9.8, 65–6, 71–2, 114
Geri Spini and, 88–9
Ghino di Tacco and, 114
Guelph party and, 93
Pope Boniface and, 83–4, 203n54
as representative of landed aristocracy, 57
Villani on, 77–8
violent deeds of, 27, 55
Donati, Forese (*Purg.* 24), 32, 73–4
Donati family, 79–80, 84–5, 134, 204n61, 212n61
    Boccaccio's affinity for, 63
    conflict with Cerchi family, 17, 46–7, 53, 57, 62, 71–3, 79–82, 120, 199n4
    contrasted with Spini family, 89
    cortesia of, 57, 63, 66, 71, 86
    envy felt by, 72–3, 79–80
    knighthood of, 32
    popolo and, 94
    poverty of, 81–2, 84
Donation of Constantine, 99
Doria, Branca (*Inf.* 33), 42
Duke of Athens. *See* Walter of Brienne
Durling, Robert, 51, 196n39

Edward III, 119, 126
Elias, Norbert, 5, 7, 185–6n4, 186n7
Elissa (frame character in *Decameron*), 35, 47, 51, 111, 112, 114, 119,
Emilia (frame character in *Decameron*), 105, 143, 147, 149, 153, 155, 216n24
Epstein, Steven, 42, 195n29
Esposizioni. *See under* Boccaccio, Giovanni

Farinata degli Uberti (*Inf.* 10), 102, 158, 164
Federigo degli Alberighi (*Dec.* 5.9), 176–81, 219n42, 219n44
Ferrante, Joan, 14, 16, 101, 189n66, 190n80, 190n81, 204n68, 205n1, 206n10, 206n16, 207n22, 208n31, 213n76, 215n16
Fiammetta (frame character in *Decameron*), 178, 180–1
Fido, Franco, 24, 201n37, 209n42, 212n65
Filomena (frame character in *Decameron*), 65, 173, 175
Filostrato (frame character in *Decameron*), 40, 102–3, 105, 108, 110, 170, 172, 219n39
fin'amors, 9, 14, 18
Fioretti di San Francesco, 16, 189n67
Florence, 59–63, 78–9
    Acquasparta's visit to, 87
    banking collapse in, 59–60
    Black Death in, 61
    brigate of, 35–8
    conflict with Pisa, 43
    contrasted with Naples, 20
    cortesia in, 149, 176
    Dante's exile from, 20–2
    Guelph-Ghibelline conflict in, 139–40, 158
    papal involvement in political affairs, 82–3, 87
    relations with papacy, 100
    vices of the city, 35, 71–2
    violence in, 94
Folgore da San Gimignano, 12–13, 46, 188n50
Folquet de Romans, 11
Forni, Pier Massimo, 22, 35, 218n32, 218n33

Franzesi, Musciatto (*Dec.* 1.1), 100–1, 119–23, 125, 130, 137, 209n43
Franzesi family, 120–1, 209n44, 211n59, 219n41
Frate Alberigo (*Inf.* 33), 42
Frederick II (*Inf.* 23, *Purg.* 16; *Dec.* 1.7, 2.6), 106–7, 139, 206n16, 215n16
  Boccaccio's treatment of, 154–5
  cortesia of, 140–1
  death of, 155–7
  poetry of, 12
Frederick III, 108, 216n25
Frederick of Aragon, 83

Genoa, 41–3
gente nuova, 33–4, 53, 56–7, 60–4
  accused of Ghibellism, 140
  as audience for *Esposizioni*, 129–30
  Boccaccio family as, 57, 60
  Boccaccio's distaste for, 4, 55, 62, 64, 71, 94, 183
  Cerchi family as, 55, 61–2, 94
  Dante's distaste for, 56
  Geri Spini as, 89, 91
  in *Inferno* 16, 132
  lacking in *cortesia*, 43, 45, 53, 97
  popolo as voice of, 85
  rise to power of, 61
  vices attributed to, 64
  See also merchant class
Ghibelline party, 139–40, 150–1
  Cangrande and, 107
  conflict with Guelf party, 4, 29, 32, 43, 53, 137, 139–40, 142–3, 157
  cooperation with Guelphs, 171, 176
  cortesia and, 137, 138, 155, 182
  Currado Malaspina and, 144
  expelled from Florence, 158
  Frederick II and, 156
  geneaology and, 176
  origins of Guelph-Ghibelline conflict, 164–7
  Peter III and, 153
  sexual desire and, 142, 158–62
Ghino di Tacco (*Purg.* 6; *Dec.* 10.6), 99–100, 112–19, 137
  liberality of, 207n28
Gianfigliazzi, Currado (*Dec.* 6.4), 135–6, 177–9, 215n15
Gianfigliazzi, Luigi, 136, 165
Gianfigliazzi family (*Inf.* 17), 120, 134–6, 208n38
Gianni di Procida (*Dec.* 2.6), 150, 216n25
Giannotto di Procida (*Dec.* 2.6). *See* Giusfredi
Ginsberg, Warren, 61
Giovanna, Monna (*Dec.* 5.9), 178–82, 219n43
Giovanni da Strada, 18
Gittes, Tobias Foster, 215n19
Giusfredi (Giannotto di Procida, *Dec.* 2.6), 141–2, 143, 150–4, 156–7, 159
Goldthwaite, Richard A., 120, 208n37, 208n38
Gragnolati, Manuele, 217n29
Graziolo, 131, 211n62
Grimaldi, Ermino de' (*Dec.* 1.8), 3–4, 28, 40–4, 49, 129–30, 132, 211n59
Grimaldi family, 27, 42–3, 53, 195n30
Griselda (*Dec.* 10.10), 182–3, 219n46
Gualteri, Marquis of Saluzzo (*Dec.* 10.10), 61, 182–3
Guelph party, 58–9, 80–1
  Boccaccio and, 25–6, 49, 55, 86
  Charles I and, 163
  clash between White and Black Guelphs, 22, 29, 47–9, 54, 62, 68, 80–1, 202n43
  conflict with Ghibelline party, 4, 29, 32, 43, 53, 137, 139–40, 142–3, 157

Index   245

conflict within Black Guelph party, 76, 88–9, 93
cooperation with Ghibellines, 171, 176
Gianfigliazzi family and, 134
greed of White Guelphs, 53
origins of Guelph-Ghibelline conflict, 164–7
role of church in conflict, 82–3, 93, 115–16, 121
sexual desire and, 142, 158–61
Guido da Pisa, 38, 67–8, 130–1, 195n26, 206n15, 211n61, 211n62
Guido degli Anastagi (*Dec.* 5.8), 173–4
Guido del Duca (*Purg.* 14), 142, 169–73
Guiraut de Bornelh, 10–1
Guy de Monfort (*Inf.* 12; *Dec.* 10.6), 159–60, 216n20

Henry VII, 14, 101, 103
Hohenstaufen family, 14, 141
Hollander, Robert, 25
Houston, Jason M., 25, 61, 182, 218n37

Il Fiore, 13
invidie, 79, 85, 94
Inferno. See under Alighieri, Dante
inventio, 35

Jacobo della Lana, 131, 211n56, 212n63, 216–17n26
Jaeger, Stephen, 5–8, 11
James II of Aragon, 135
Jones, P.J., 22, 56, 63, 85

Kircher, Timothy, 127, 202n44, 207n26
Kirkham, Victoria, 25, 40, 42, 185n1, 195n33

Klapisch-Zuber, Christiane, 192n98
Kleinhenz, Christopher, 12–13
knighthood, 9–10, 29, 31–2, 51
  liberality of knights, 11
  as marker of status, 86
  violence of knights, 54

Lamberti family, 140, 219n41
Landino, Cristoforo, 184, 207–8n28
Lansing, Carol, 22, 31, 46, 54, 192n93, 193n16, 199n4, 202n43
larghezza, 13, 15
Latini, Brunetto (*Inf.* 15), 13, 15, 31, 33, 68, 93, 102
  Tesoretto, 13–15, 93
laudatio temporis acti, 5
Lauretta (frame character in *Decameron*), 40–4, 65, 70
liberality, 4, 10–13, 182
  Aristotle on, 101
  avarice and, 123, 130
  of Cangrande, 100
  of church figures, 111
  cortesia and, 12–13, 111–12, 148
  lacking in church figures, 99
  of Malaspina family, 147
  of *veltro*, 101
Lizio da Valbona (*Purg.* 14; *Dec.* 5.4), 138, 140, 169–72
logomimesis, 22
Lombardo, Marco (*Purg.* 16), 142, 155
Lovato dei Lovati, 30
lupa, 127–30

magnate families, 50–1, 53–5, 61–3, 134, 185n2, 192n98, 193n3
  cortesia of, 65–6
  Spini family as, 86
Mainardi, Arrigo (*Purg.* 14), 169–72

Mainardi, Ricciardo (*Dec.* 5.4), 142, 170–2, 176, 218n34
Mainardi family (*Purg.* 14), 140, 176, 177
Malaspina, Currado (*Purg.* 8; *Dec.* 2.6), 140–1, 143–7, 149–54, 156–7, 167, 170
   cortesia of, 140–1
Malaspina, Franceschino (*Purg.* 8), 143
Malaspina, Spina (*Dec.* 2.6), 150–2, 154, 157, 159, 170
Malaspina family, 137–8, 141, 143, 145–7, 157, 176
   cortesia of, 154, 156
   nobility of, 156–7
Malespina, Moroello, 108, 214n7
Manfred (*Dec.* 2.6, 10.6), 57, 139, 141, 143, 155–61, 163, 215n16, 215n17, 216n22
Marcabru, 10
Marchesi, Simone, 201n39
Margoni, Ivos, 11
Martel, Charles (*Par.* 8), 163, 214n14
Matilda, Countess, 142, 164–7, 216n26
Mazzotta, Giuseppe, 9, 84, 175
Mercanzia, 120
merchant class, 133–4, 182–3, 205n5, 206n10
   avarice of, 22, 101, 120–6, 128–30, 137
   critiqued in *Esposizioni*, 100
   lacking in *cortesia*, 28, 58, 86, 89
   usury of, 134
   See also *gente nuova*
mesura, 11
Migiel, Marilyn, 218n34, 218n39
milites, 31
Mithridanes (*Dec.* 10.3), 101, 133–4

Najemy, John N., 22, 27, 31, 53, 64, 90, 120, 185n2, 192n94, 192n95, 197n48, 202n43, 202n46, 204n61, 213n1, 213n4, 213n5
Naples, 17–20, 22, 55, 59–60, 143, 160
Nastagio degli Onesti (*Dec.* 5.8), 27, 142–3, 173–5, 178
Nathan (*Dec.* 10.3), 101, 133–4
Neifile (frame character in *Decameron*), 135–6
Nelli, Francesco, 19–20
Niccolò di Bartolo del Buono, 64
Noakes, Susan, 202n43
nostalgia, 5–6, 10, 13, 18, 34, 135, 138, 140–1
   for *brigate*, 36
   violence of, 182
Novellino, 13–14, 195n34, 215n18
Novello da Polenta, Guido, 21, 74, 170

Obriachi family (*Inf.* 17), 134
Ó Cuilleanáin, Cormac, 100, 113, 207n25, 208n34
Ordelaffi, Francesco, 18–19
Ordinances of Justice, 27, 32, 54, 62, 93–4
   abolishment of, 61
   effect of on magnate families, 185n2, 192n98
   Cavalcanti family and, 50
   Cerchi family and, 34, 62
   Donati family and, 62
   Gianfigliazzi family and, 134–5
   Spini family and, 86
Orsini, Cardinal, 48, 93
Ostagio da Polenta, 19
Ottimo Commento, 38, 68, 211–12n62

Ottokar, Nicola, 49
Otto the Great (*Dec.* 2.8), 7, 186n17

Padoan, Giorgio, 23, 25, 203n53, 208n32, 210n52, 211n57, 211n62
Palazzo dei Signori, 75
Pampinea (frame character in *Decameron*), 54, 86–7, 162,
Panfilo (frame character in *Decameron*), 121
Paradiso. See under Alighieri, Dante
Parodi, Ernesto, 198n51
Pazzino de' Pazzi, 76, 89
Peace of Constance, 3, 29–30
Peruzzi family, 59–61, 63, 120, 134, 200n8, 208n38
Peter III of Aragon (*Purg.* 7; *Dec.* 10.7), 150–1, 153, 157, 161–2
   cortesia of, 140
   virility of, 142, 164, 167
Petrarca, Francesco, 102, 108–10, 188n55, 204n69
   Rerum memorandarum libri, 108, 198n51, 206n11, 207n23
Piero del Morrone. *See* Celestine V
Pino de' Rossi, 62–4, 71
popolo, 29–32, 31, 63–4, 86, 90, 93–4
   Cerchi family as, 129–30
   Cisti as member of, 90
   conflicts with elite families, 61, 94, 192n95, 202n46
   as critics of papacy, 100
   Dante's favouring of, 97
   in *Dec.* 10.10, 182
   as voice of *gente nuova*, 85
popolo minuto, 85–6, 91, 94, 97
Primas (*Dec.* 1.7), 104, 105, 108, 111, 113–16
procreation, 140, 167–8
Provençal lyric poetry, 9–10, 16

Purgatorio. See under Alighieri, Dante

Re Enzo, 12
Ricciardi family, 119
Richardson, Brian, 216n24
Rineri da Calboli (*Purg.* 14), 169–71
Robert, King of Naples, 18–19, 22, 59–60, 189n75
Rosso della Tosa, 76, 89
Rufolo, Landolfo (*Dec.* 2.4), 41, 42, 122
Russo, Vittorio, 23, 207n23
Rusticucci, Iacopo (*Inf.* 16), 37, 148–9, 194n25

Sallust, 75–7
Saluzzo, Marquis of (*Dec.* 10.10), 61, 182–3
Santo Stefano in Badia, 25, 127, 129
Scaglione, Aldo, 5, 8, 10, 11, 183, 188n52, 188n64, 192n1, 219n46
Scalza, Michele (*Dec.* 6.6), 140
Ser Cepparello (San Ciappelletto, *Dec.* 1.1), 119, 122, 130, 209n41, 209n42, 211n59
Sherberg, Michael, 175, 219n43, 219n44
Sicilian Vespers, 150, 153, 157, 161, 163, 216n20, 216n25
Smarr, Janet Levarie, 75
solatz, 10
Sordello, 10, 153, 170
Spini, Geri (*Dec.* 6.2), 27, 48, 58–9, 86–94, 119
   contrasted with Currado Gianfigliazzi, 134, 136, 140
   Corso Donati and, 88–9
   as *gente nuova*, 89, 91
   Guelph party and, 76

Spini family, 61, 86, 100, 208n38
  contrasted with Donati family, 89

Tartars, 132–3, 212n66
Tedaldo degli Elisei (*Dec.* 3.7), 127, 211n54
Tesoretto, 13–15, 93
Thomasin Von Zirclaria (Tommasino dei Cerchiari), 11–12
  Der Wälsche Gast, 11–12
Tosinghi family, 85
Traversari, Paolo (*Dec.* 5.8), 143, 173–4
Traversari family (*Purg.* 14), 140, 142, 170, 173–7
Traversaro, Pier (*Purg.* 14), 169–71, 173
troubador lyric, 5, 8–11, 14, 31, 168
Tuscany, 12, 33, 48, 78, 92, 121, 163, 178, 192n1, 209n41

Uberti family, 32, 140, 219n41
  Farinata degli Uberti (*Inf.* 10), 102, 158, 164
  Neri degli Uberti (*Dec.* 10.6), 158, 167
Uguiccione della Faggiuola, 108
Urbanity (*urbanitas*), 8, 29–30, 32, 47, 194n18
usury, 100–1, 122, 125, 130, 134, 211n58

Valbona family, 140
  Caterina da Valbona (*Dec.* 5.4), 142, 171–2, 176, 218n34
  Lizio da Valbona (*Purg.* 14; *Dec.* 5.4), 138, 140, 169–72
veltro, 101, 130–3, 211n60, 211–12n62
vendette, 4, 13, 27, 31, 50–4, 57, 65, 94
  Guelph-Ghibelline conflict and, 140
Vergil, 95, 153, 195n28

Vieri de' Cerchi. *See under* Cerchi family
Villani, Giovanni, 23, 49, 59, 77–83, 177, 199n3
  on Corso Donati, 58, 71, 73–4, 77–8
  on Frederick II, 155
  on Guelph-Ghibelline conflict, 139, 165–7
  on Musciatto Franzesi, 122
  Nuova cronica, 49–50, 74, 78, 83, 165, 177, 189n75, 199n3, 203n53, 208n33, 216n25
  as source for *Esposizioni*, 78, 80, 165, 199n3
Villani, Matteo, 213n5
violence, 27, 53–5, 94, 199n4
  of Black Guelphs, 45
  brigate and, 46–7
  chivalric morality and, 30–1
  of Corso Donati, 58
  cortesia and, 29–32, 175–6
  Dante's exile and, 96
  in *Dec.* 5.8, 174–6
  of magnate families, 62, 65
  of nostalgia, 182
  of *popolani*, 90
virility, 157–8, 163–4, 167–8, 172
  future of *cortesia* and, 142, 154, 157
Visconti family, 63

Wallace, David, 30, 182, 193n4
Walter of Brienne (Duke of Athens), 4, 19, 55, 58, 60–1, 62–3, 85, 182, 186n17
  Gianfigliazzi family and, 134
White, Hayden, 22, 45
Witt, Ronald, 3, 22, 30, 32, 44, 193n9, 194n18

Zanche, Michele (*Inf.* 33), 42
zuffe, 54–5, 88, 94

www.ingramcontent.com/pod-product-compliance
Lightning Source LLC
Chambersburg PA
CBHW030312080526
44584CB00012B/543